Movements, Borders, and Identities in Africa

Rochester Studies in
African History and the Diaspora

Toyin Falola, Senior Editor
The Frances Higginbotham Nalle Centennial Professor in History
University of Texas at Austin

(ISSN: 1092–5228)

A complete list of titles in the Rochester Studies in African History and the
Diaspora, in order of publication, may be found at the end of this book.

Movements, Borders, and Identities in Africa

Edited by
Toyin Falola and Aribidesi Usman

Ⓡ UNIVERSITY OF ROCHESTER PRESS

First published 2009

University of Rochester Press
668 Mt. Hope Avenue, Rochester, NY 14620, USA
www.urpress.com
and Boydell & Brewer Limited
PO Box 9, Woodbridge, Suffolk IP12 3DF, UK
www.boydellandbrewer.com

ISBN-13: 978-1-58046-296-9
ISSN: 1092-5228

Library of Congress Cataloging-in-Publication Data

Movements, borders, and identities in Africa / edited by Toyin Falola and
    Aribidesi Usman.
        p. cm. — (Rochester studies in African history and the diaspora,
ISSN 1092-5228 ; v. 40)
    Includes bibliographical references and index.
    ISBN-13: 978-1-58046-296-9 (hardcover : alk. paper)
    ISBN-10: 1-58046-296-0 (alk. paper)
    1. Africa—Emigration and immigration—History. 2. Africa—Boundaries.
3. Ethnicity—Africa. 4. Africa—Historical geography. I. Falola, Toyin. II. Usman,
Aribidesi Adisa.
    JV8790.M68   2009
    304.8096—dc22

                                                                2009001818

A catalogue record for this title is available from the British Library.

This publication is printed on acid-free paper.
Printed in the United States of America.

For Dr. Ted Gordon, for his contributions to diaspora studies

Contents

Preface

The story of Africa is the story of human movements. No phase of African history is complete or can be adequately understood without reference to migration, a central component in the evolution and growth of many African societies. The drafts of the chapters in this volume were originally presented at a conference held at the University of Texas at Austin (March 24–26, 2006), on the subject of "Movements, Migrations, and Displacements in Africa." This conference provided a forum for the exchange of ideas and experience on the phenomenon of movements, migrations, and displacements in Africa, and the understanding of its changing forms and dynamics. The origin of the volume shapes its outcome, especially in terms of its geographical coverage and interdisciplinary range, which offer an accessible scholarly analysis of population movement in the local, regional, and inter-regional setting.

The chapters are based on original research and recent thinking on migrations in Africa and their changing forms and dynamics since the pre-colonial period. The various topics addressed include the causes and consequences of migration, population movements, displacements, migration experiences, settlement patterns and strategies, labor mobility, immigrant societies, identity, and culture contact, as well as conceptual and methodological aspects of research on migration.

The contributors represent scholars from diverse fields with extensive teaching and research experience, making use of different sources—oral, archaeological, written, and ethnographic—and focusing on various issues and regions. Thus, the book provides a broad but insightful overview of the subject of migrations and the varying impact of slavery, commerce, gender, religion, colonialism, poverty, and development.

We want to thank all the contributors who, despite security and financial concerns, traveled long distances to be with us in Texas. Presenters and participants engaged in lively discussion throughout the three days of the conference. Such an undertaking entails copious debts. We are grateful to a host of graduate students (Roy Doron, Tyler Fleming, Matthew Heaton, Ann Genova, and Saheed Aderinto); the technical personnel (especially Sam Saverance); and many staff members of the University of Texas (especially Gail Davis, Laura Flack, and Martha Gail Moore). The organizations and departments that supported us financially include the Departments of History, Government, and English, the Center for African and African American Studies, the Office of the Vice President, College of Liberal Arts, the Office of the Dean of Students, the Texas Cowboys Fund, the Louann and Larry Temple Fund, the Frances Higgenbotham Nalle Fund, and Dedman College, Southern Methodist University, Dallas. We are also grateful to Dr. Vik Bahl of Green River Community College in Auburn, Ms. Ronke Obadina of Austin, and Dr. Segun Fayemi of New York for their commitment to the conference.

Toyin Falola, Austin, 2009
Aribidesi Usman, Tempe, 2009

Introduction

Migrations in African History: An Introduction

ARIBIDESI USMAN AND TOYIN FALOLA

Migration has become a continuous phenomenon in the history of human societies. Migration is synonymous with the history of Africa itself. The migration of individuals and groups over time is associated with the emergence of cultures and of civilizations throughout the world. This book establishes the centrality of migrations and movements of people in the historical evolution of African peoples and societies. By making use of different sources—oral, archaeological, and written—and focusing on various subjects and geographical areas, the book shows that migration was a multifaceted phenomenon, which varied in nature and character, over time and in different places. Using carefully selected case studies drawn from across the continent, the book provides a broad but insightful overview of the subject of migrations, and the varying impact of slavery, commerce, gender, religion, colonialism, poverty, and development on the movements of people and ideas, and on the development of states and societies on the continent, most especially in the last two centuries.

There are two forms of migration patterns in Africa. These are internal and international migrations. Internal migrations are migrations within countries, while international migrations are movements between countries. The most common form of international migration in the past was the forced migration of the slave trade, conducted by Arab and European traders. Internal migration consists of rural-urban mobility, rural-rural mobility, urban-rural mobility, and urban-urban mobility.[1] The poorly defined boundaries between nations, the complementary nature of the economies of neighboring countries, and the cultural relationship between ethnic groups in various countries obscure the differences between internal and international migration in Africa.[2]

There are a number of reasons why people in Africa migrate or leave their original homes for places sometimes dissimilar to their prior location. Such reasons have been discussed at length by various scholars.[3] They include wars, droughts, and floods; regional inequality of economic development and income; severe population pressure with low agricultural productivity; poverty and hunger in specific regions; the attraction of towns and cities as centers of education, higher incomes, and social amenities; the presence of affiliated ethnic groups and/or kinsmen; the presence of people from the same religious denomination; safety from persecution; and simply personal adventurism. It is not easy to determine the impact of any of these factors individually or as a whole. In most cases, they also depend on the existing political, economic, social, religious, and personal circumstances.

Migration has occurred on a substantial scale many times in the history of the people of the continent, and it goes back in time to the origin of human beings. Migration and population movement in Africa can best be understood within the context of the political and historical evolution of African societies.[4] This introductory chapter examines migration in the context of the precolonial, colonial, and postcolonial eras, and the effects of various forces—internal as well as external—on society and hence on migration.

The Precolonial Period

Africa has a long history of population movement aimed at lessening the effect of ecological problems and aiding in the search for food, shelter, and security. In the precolonial era, population movements similar to present-day international migration occurred over a wide area. These early movements were unsystematic, and entire groups or villages are known to have moved. Studies have shown that our earliest ancestors, the australopithecines, lived for several million years with the ability to walk upright before developing stone tools.[5] The earliest known stone tool assemblages date to roughly 2.6 million years ago. The Oldowan stone tools from Olduvai Gorge in Tanzania include "pebble tools," or "core-choppers," and small tools that have been lightly modified and may have been used as scrapers. The maker of the Oldowan tools is a hominid called *Homo habilis,* with a brain size of 630 cubic centimeters. The geographical range of *Homo habilis* is the grasslands of eastern and southern Africa, while the climate and microecology continued to change and affect the lives of hominids.[6]

About two million years ago, another hominid, *Homo erectus,* with a larger brain (between 800 and 1,200 cubic centimeters), emerged in eastern Africa. *Homo erectus* coexisted for a time with australopithecines and *Homo habilis,* and by one million years ago had become the only surviving hominid species.[7] *Homo erectus* was able to spread into new areas through colonization—a process by which "small groups left the home society to form equivalent communities in ecologically similar territories."[8] Fossil remains of *Homo erectus* have been found at Olduvai Gorge, at East and West Turkana, and at Swartkrans in South Africa, as well as at sites in Uganda, Ethiopia, and Eritrea. Related fossils have also been found far to the north in both Morocco and Algeria. About one and half million years ago in East Africa, a new stone technology, the Acheulian, or "hand axe" tool, was associated with Homo erectus. These hand axes or bifacial tools are well refined and more carefully made than the early pebble tools of the Oldowan. The Acheulian hand axes continued to be used for over a million years, until just over 100,000 years ago.[9]

An important indication of the successful adaptation of early hominids to a variety of environments is the expansion of *Homo erectus* out of Africa. It was the first hominid to move beyond the African continent. Evidence of this appears to have been found at the important site of Zhoukoudian in northern China, dating to about 500,000 to 240,000 years ago.[10] However, the Asian and European evidence is still controversial, particularly on the issue of chronology, and the excavated stone artifacts, which are more common than fossil remains. Nevertheless, this period saw an increasing capacity to adapt to a wide variety of environments, a capacity that enabled early humans to spread through most of Africa and the wider world. Another hominid species, *Homo sapiens,* whose brain is slightly larger than that of *Homo erectus,* emerged about 200,000 years ago. The evolutionary changes now became more social and were accompanied by increasing population size and the expansion of the geographical range of the hominid.[11] There was a substantial change in population distribution in the first hundred thousand years of human existence. During the last 60,000 years, African populations migrated from the savannas of eastern and southern Africa, the home of their hominid ancestors, to the east-west area between modern Sudan and Senegal. The four language groups that are identified on the African continent correspond to the distribution and movement of people over thousands of years.[12]

In the period from 15,000 BP to 5000 BP, agriculture revolution was witnessed in several regions of the world. It appears that the development of agriculture stimulated migration.[13] The popular theory is that Southwest Asia was the sole site of the invention of agriculture. Studies now indicate, however, that there were long preludes to the development of agriculture and that similar developments took place in several areas of the world, including Africa. Evidence of intensified food gathering, supplemented by intensive harvesting of certain plants as early as 15,000 years ago, has been reported in parts of Africa. In northeast Africa, linguistic evidence indicates that Nilo-Saharan speakers developed an association with cattle, while Afroasiatic speakers were associated with sheep and goats.[14] By about 9,000 years ago, the stone-using people of Napta Playa in the eastern Saharan were domesticating cattle and using pottery.[15] In West Africa, the people belonging to the Niger-Congo language group developed the practice of harvesting of tubers. It is suggested that the harvesting of wild grasses in West Africa probably led to the domestication of rice, and the harvesting of wild tubers led to the development of several types of yam.[16]

Agriculture spread to every part of Africa through colonization by farmers as well as by crop migration.[17] In Africa, paleoclimatic studies have demonstrated that significant climatic change occurred in the Sahara during the late Pleistocene and early Holocene periods. Arid conditions prevailed from 21,000 to 12,500 years BP, giving way to a moist period lasting until ca. 10,000 years BP.[18] The period roughly spanning 10,000–5,000 years BP was characterized by the expansion of rivers, marshes, and forests. It was during such moist periods that the spread of agriculture from the Nile Valley or the Mediterranean into the Sahara took place.[19] With the intensification of aridity (ca. 2000 BC) came the movement of populations out of the Sahara, some of them toward the south, taking with them their Middle Eastern wheat and barley. It is likely that the ideas of agriculture spread more rapidly and more thoroughly than farming communities could move. As Manning indicates, "small numbers of migrants, in discussion with those experienced in the lands where they settled, could learn together how to implement agricultural practice in each new era."[20]

The expansion of the Bantu-speaking peoples, beginning in distant times and continuing into the modern period, is one of the most challenging problems in migration studies. It is generally recognized that many people living in sub-Saharan Africa speak Bantu languages, over four hundred of these languages, all deriving from the same ancestral language, known as "proto-Bantu." These languages share the word *ntu*, meaning "person," while the prefix *ba* denotes the plural in most of these languages, so that *ba-ntu* means, literally, "people."[21] These similarities have been established on the basis of lexical, phonetic, morphological, and syntactic resemblances, which cannot be possible by mere chance or by borrowings.[22] The Bantu language expansion must have begun after agriculture had spread to the area of origin of the Bantu. Archaeology, linguistic studies, and studies of plant origins show that proto-Bantu probably had its foundation about 3,000 years ago near the Benue River in the western African savanna, where fairly large settlements headed by councils of elders were present.[23]

It is generally believed that it was population movement that disseminated the Bantu languages over the subcontinent. Two theories have been suggested to explain the Bantu expansion from the original homelands.[24] First, it is claimed that the abandonment of hunting–gathering subsistence economy in favor of an agricultural subsistence economy led to population growth, which consequently led to migrations of people seeking new land.

According to this theory, the migrations of the Bantu peoples from West Africa to central Africa are said to have involved agricultural communities, and the movement is said to have increased after banana and yam, introduced by the Indonesians, spread to the forest peoples of central Africa.[25] The second theory provides a link between the expansion of the Bantu and the beginnings of the Iron Age. The working of iron encouraged agricultural production by providing more effective tools that allowed the Bantu to dominate the peoples in the areas where they settled. It is suggested that the Bantu "were a dominant minority, specialized to hunting with the spear, constantly attracting new adherents . . . by their fabulous prestige as suppliers of meat, constantly throwing off new bands of migratory adventurers, until the whole southern sub-continent was iron-using and Bantu-speaking."[26] Other factors, such as famine—leading to the search for better living conditions in the form of good farming and grazing land—epidemics, wars and a sheer spirit of adventure could also have motivated the early Bantu movements.

The Bantu migration, unlike migrations in Africa in recent times, was carried out very slowly over very short distances and probably involved a movement of small numbers of people from one village to the next. This process was repeated over and over again until successive generations reached all parts of subequatorial Africa, perhaps over a thousand or more years.[27] After reaching the Congo, the Bantu groups spread to the Zambezi and on to southern Africa. They probably intermarried with or assimilated the Khoisan speakers and other populations they came across. The original inhabitants were foragers and fishermen, but the newcomers were farmers who domesticated goats, produced pottery, and may have practiced weaving. This advanced culture is clearly suggested by the proto-Bantu vocabulary relating to ceramics, goat, and to the cultivation of cereal and root crops."[28] A new social organization was also created under the influence of the newcomers. By a thousand years ago, most of central and southern Africa was populated by iron-smelting, Bantu-speaking village inhabitants, who had replaced most of the original hunting and gathering peoples.[29]

The mass migration of Africans to the Americas, the Middle East, and Europe through the transatlantic and other branches of the slave trade constitutes one of the major events of African history. This emigration, largely involuntary, lasted for centuries, resulting in wider distribution of African communities in various parts of the world, particularly Europe, the Middle East, and the Americas. Compared to those passing through the Atlantic slave trade system, the numbers of Africans transported per year to the Mediterranean world were relatively low, since the Mediterranean world did not practice plantation agriculture on an extensive scale. The migration of Africans into Asia and the Levantine was the oldest sector of the African diaspora, and this movement probably started before the beginning of the Christian era.[30] This trade is less well known than the Atlantic trade but is perhaps of equal demographic size. Composed of what is usually referred to as the trans-Saharan, this trade lasted more than a millennium—from the arrival of Islam in the southern Sahara and Sahel in the eighth and ninth centuries to the consolidation of European colonial control between the two world wars.

Most Africans entered the Middle East via the trans-Saharan slave routes but some migrated as free individuals, scholars, teachers, traders, and pilgrims, to the holy cities of Mecca and Medina.[31] Following the pilgrimage of Mansa Kanka Musa, the king of Mali in the fourteenth century, wealthy African pilgrims were "accompanied by a number of slaves, some of whom were sold as a kind of traveller's cheque—to pay the expenses of the journey."[32] The annual pilgrimage to Mecca therefore contributed to the involuntary and voluntary movement of Africans to the Middle East. Mecca emerged as the principal slave market in Arabian Peninsula, where Africans as well as Circassians, Malays, Indians, and central Asians were brought for resale to individual buyers throughout the Muslim world.[33] Some Africans remained in the holy cities of western Arabia for higher religious education, including studies in the Malikite School of law.[34] In the Middle East, especially in Arabia, African slaves were employed in various capacities as sailors, soldiers, administrators, shop assistants, agricultural laborers, water carriers, camel drivers, and shepherds.[35] Within the Ottoman Empire, large numbers of Africans were employed as soldiers and sailors, concubines, and administrators.[36] Africans accompanied the spread of Islam by land and sea into India and the Far East. As late as the 1520s and 1530s, some 5,000 African soldiers served under Sultan Bahadur of Gujarat, while Africans were also found in the armies and administration of the sultan of Delhi, as well as in Bengal and the Deccan.[37]

By the fifteenth century, African contact with Europe led to a relatively small-scale trade in African slaves, with substantial numbers of Africans found in Sicily, Cyprus, Crete, Malaga, Huelva, Cadiz, and Lisbon.[38] The African presence in Europe increased with direct maritime contact between Europe and Africa. By the late eighteenth century the black population, estimated at about 2,000 in France and 15,000 in England, created major concern in both countries that led to changes in attitudes toward blacks. For example, a royal decree in France in 1777 forbade interracial marriages, while in England the celebrated Mansfield Judgment in 1772 outlawed the enslavement of Africans in England.[39] It was in the Americas, however, that the African presence was most pronounced and African labor was most used. Africans and their descendants played a prominent part in the development of the New World, starting from the Europeans' arrival in the region in the late fifteenth century until modern times.

The fundamental cause of migration during the seventeenth century to about the end of the nineteenth century was the slave trade across the Atlantic Ocean. In the early eighteenth century, the changing world economy led to an expansion in the migration of Africans through the slave trade. Large numbers of Africans were forcefully removed from their homes every year and transported across the Atlantic to the New World. The export of Africans rose sharply to nearly one hundred thousand per year at the end of the eighteenth century, while thousands of additional captives were forcibly sent to other destinations, in Africa and the Middle East.[40] The Atlantic slave trade is certainly the form of historical migration most closely associated with the African continent. Often regarded as the largest forced migration in world history, it is estimated that nearly fifteen million people were exported from the coasts of Africa between the late fifteenth and late nineteenth centuries.

Africans helped clear and cultivate the vast wilderness in the New World. They accompanied the first European "explorers" of the New World, helped conquer the indigenous people and the complex societies of Mexico and Peru, helped build the cities and ports of the English settlers in the Americas, and participated in establishing the new communities that formed the foundation for the later heterogeneous societies.[41] The Africans performed various tasks and played different roles. They served as pioneers and conquistadors, pirates and buccaneers, *gauchos, llaneros, bandeirantes,* slave-owners, merchants, servants, and slaves, while being legally excluded from the highest statuses.[42] After the seventeenth century, Africans were the only legal slaves in the Americas; this burdening the African population in American societies with an enduring social stigma.[43]

The African migration to the Americas reached its apogee in the eighteenth century. Both the established plantation systems in the Americas and the slave trade that supplied their human labor reached their fullest maturity. It is suggested that between 1700 and 1810, more than half of all the Africans ever to come to the New World arrived there, a figure estimated at more than six million people.[44] The African population of the Americas in the early nineteenth century has been estimated at approximately 8.5 million. Of this number, more than two million lived in the United States, with the majority found in the so-called "slave states" along the Atlantic seaboard from Delaware to Florida, and small concentratrations in the northern cities east of the Mississippi River, especially New York, Boston, and Philadelphia.[45]

Slavery was associated with the growth of industrial production and European economic change through the expansion of plantation production of sugar, tobacco, indigo, and cotton. In the New World, it was common for slaves to be sold away, separated from each other and family members, and moved great distances with their masters. Before slavery was finally abolished in Brazil in 1888, most Africans in the Americas were slaves, performing tasks without which the colonies could not have been successful economically. The Africans' long association with the evolution of American societies allowed them to make a permanent impact on the languages, cultures, economies, and ethnic composition of most communities in the New World. The greatest evidence of this impact was in the plantation zones, among communities established along the Atlantic and Caribbean coastlands from the southeastern United States to northeastern Brazil, and along the Pacific coastlands of Colombia, Ecuador, and Peru.[46]

African oral traditions are full of stories recounting migrations for colonization or the settlement of new lands. Such movements are generally characterized as "traditional," "archaic," or "local," as forms of migration that mostly recreate the original society in a new setting.[47] The migrations of the Lobi may be used to examine this type of mobility. Lobi migration has been described as "the most important vestige of traditional 'movements of peoples' in West Africa."[48] The Lobi live in Burkina Faso, Ghana, and Côte d'Ivoire. The Lobi began migrating from areas in northern Ghana toward Burkina Faso in the second half of the eighteenth century, perhaps as a result of instability in the Dagomba and Gonja states.[49] About a century later, Lobi from Burkina Faso began to arrive in northern Côte d'Ivoire, and by the late 1960s, Lobi expanded to absorb Abron kingdom and the Bondoukou prefecture.[50] It has been observed that despite the precolonial beginnings of Lobi migration, the Lobi in Côte d'Ivoire did more than just reproduce their society in Burkina Faso. The new context produced variations in religion as well as social, political, and economic organization. In the religious sphere, for example, Lobi in Côte d'Ivoire did not try to recreate the religious shrines of their homeland. But the sacred sites in the lands of origin generated a "reverse flow" of migrants who returned to Burkina Faso for important religious ceremonies.[51] Some social practices also changed, with important implications for migration. For example, the custom during the "ceremony of the father's millet" of requesting "permission" from the male ancestors to migrate was less observed.[52] This change has been interpreted as a weakening of the influence of elders over migration.[53] The settlement patterns of the Lobi also changed. The Lobi villages in Burkina Faso in the 1960s continued to reproduce the traditional large aggregated, fortified settlements, while those in Côte d'Ivoire were more dispersed. It has been suggested that since the Lobi no longer needed warriors for defense, the new Lobi settlements in Côte d'Ivoire have populations only half as large as their Burkina counterparts.[54]

Warriors also migrated in the central Sahel. According to oral tradition, in the sixteenth century, warriors moved west and south from the Niger region, conquering local peoples and creating patron-client and marital relationships with their leaders.[55] These warriors established the Dagomba states in present-day Ghana and the Mossi kingdoms in Burkina Faso.[56] Other examples from the region include the migrations of Zarma warriors in the mid-nineteenth century from western Niger to Karaga in Dagomba, where they sold horses received in exchange for captives taken in wars with the Fulani jihadists.[57] From the mid-1860s, the Zarma warriors served as mercenaries under the ruler of Karaga, a subordinate entity who paid tribute in slaves to the Asante king. The Zarma raided the Gurunsi in Burkina, established bases in Gurunsi, built their own forces of Gurunsi slaves, and consequently invaded their former patrons—the Karaga and the Dagomba.[58]

Commercial migration has been an important feature of West African life for many centuries. Many traders in precolonial West Africa traveled frequently along established trade networks forged by ethnicity, religion, or both.[59] A number of these networks have survived into the colonial and postcolonial periods and demonstrate the ways in which this pattern of "traditional" mobility gave rise to contemporary migrations.[60] The most extensive of the commercial migrations in West Africa involved the Muslim commercial networks. Here, religion held the networks together through common ethical and cultural practices. These networks included that of the Juula in the western Sahel, with its origin among the Soninke from the ancient empire of Ghana.[61] Over time, Juula merchants became increasingly absorbed into local communities, creating subnetworks such as the Jahanke in the Senegambia and Futa Jallon, the Maraka among the Bambara, and the Yarse in the Mossi kingdoms of Burkina Faso.[62] The Soninke migrations, which gave rise to those of the Juula, have continued into the present time. A recent study of Soninke migration from the Mauritania and Senegal to other parts of Senegal, including Dakar, and France suggests that historical experience of migration makes it a more attractive economic strategy today.[63]

Another, similarly elaborate, set of Muslim diasporas integrated the central savanna and Sahel. According to Paul Lovejoy, the traders from the Bariba states refer to themselves as Wangarawa, which implied an earlier connection with Songhay and the gold trade of the Juula. It is claimed that Hausa merchants identified with their city of residence or place of origin or both. The term "Wangarawa" was a local adaptation of the term "Wangara" and was used to refer to immigrants from the west.[64]

These networks, mainly in northern Nigeria and Benin and southern Niger, connected areas as far as Ghana in the west and Sudan in the east, establishing trading communities near the forest, where imports were exchanged for local products such as kola nuts, an important stimulant in Hausaland.[65] The migration continued into and beyond the Sahara in the north, and by the late nineteenth century, Hausa became the second or third most spoken language in Tripoli.[66]

Principally for religious reasons, West Africans have embarked on long and difficult migrations to the east. Since the beginning of Islamic influence in West Africa during the eleventh century, Muslim pilgrims have made the long journey to Mecca.[67] There were increasing numbers of such trips from the time of Uthman Dan Fodio (the Muslim jihadist in northern Nigeria) in the early nineteenth century, and especially from the mid-nineteenth century. Two routes were utilized for this journey.[68] The first was the North African trade route via Tripoli, Benghazi, and Egypt. This route was also used by people traveling to the student quarters in Al-Azhar University in Cairo to learn more about Islam. The second route passed along the savanna belt that stretches from northern Nigeria through the Central Sudan to the Red Sea. The Tripoli route was taken by some pilgrims who had enough money to buy or hire a camel for the journey across the Sahara. The savanna belt route was initially used by pilgrims who could not afford the journey via North Africa. Later, by the early nineteenth century, the savanna belt route became the most popular route.[69]

In the nineteenth century, there was considerable immigration of West and central Africans into the Upper Nile Valley (modern Sudan), for which religious motives were in large part responsible. It was a belief among West Africans that the Mahdi would appear in the East (that is, in the Upper Nile region).[70] As early as 1837, a number of people had started to migrate from Hausaland to the Nile Valley in anticipation of meeting the "expected Mahdi." This created so much unrest and anxiety that the Sultan of Sokoto issued proclamations declaring that the time of the exodus had not yet come, "since there is still some good remaining among us."[71] However, the agitation and unrest continued for most of the nineteenth century, leading to the migration of a large number of people from the Sokoto Caliphate to Sudan and to Mecca.[72]

The actual appearance of the Mahdi in the Upper Nile region in 1881 created excitement among the Muslim inhabitants of West Africa.[73] Men, women, and children migrated from the Niger-Chad region to Sudan to seek the blessing of the Mahdi.[74] After the Mahdi appeared, for some time the pilgrimage to Mecca almost stopped, because a visit to him was now considered of greater reward than the pilgrimage to Mecca. After the Mahdi's death in 1885, his tomb became the most sacred and holy place in Sudan.[75]

The pilgrims traveled on foot, stopping along the way to earn money or beg for alms to enable them to continue the journey. There were many routes used by the pilgrims. According to Ayoub Balamoan, John Lewis Burckhardt, who traveled from the Nile Valley to the Hijaz in 1814, revealed that the pilgrims gathered together around Lake Chad and walked to a location in Darfur, then across to the White Nile and across the Gezirah to the Blue Nile, and then through the interior of Abyssinia to Massawa or through Shendi and across the Atbara River to Sawakin on the Red Sea.[76]

The Hausa community in Sudan is thought to be the largest Hausa diaspora community in the world.[77] One major factor leading to the establishment of permanent Hausa communities in Sudan was the pilgrimage, to which certain economic factors can be added. The journey to and from

Mecca might be completed only after many years; some pilgrims became lost on the way, and unable to proceed further, settled down permanently. This was described by R. C. Abraham in 1946:

> While en route to Eritrea via the Sudan, I was amazed to see a young girl selling bean-cakes and calling out waina! Waina! She told me that she was of Kano origin and that there were many hundreds of Hausa living in Wadi Medani like herself. These people of Wadi Medani and many other towns of the Sudan were Hausa pilgrims to Mecca who ran short of money on their return journey and were unable to make their way back to their home towns in Nigeria. They have retained [the] Hausa [language] and taught it to their children born in Sudan.[78]

Throughout its history, the Muslim pilgrimage or *hajj* has been well organized, with chiefs, supervisors, and heads of caravans, checkpoints, and resting stations (*zango* in the Hausa language) on the way.[79] Many *zango* in the larger towns across the Sudan eventually developed into permanent settlements. Among these are the Hausa quarters in Nyala, El Fashir, El Obeid, Wadi Medani, Gedarif, and Port Sudan.[80]

Hausa were also valued for their skills and their manpower, and this also sustained Hausa migration and settlement in the Sudan. It has been suggested that governments were aware of the qualities of the Hausa and in fact encouraged their settlement in the Sudan. For example, in the nineteenth century, a large number of "Fallata" (Hausa-Fulani) settled in eastern Sudan up to the Ethiopian border and were employed as laborers in the cotton-growing projects of Gash and Baraka, because Mumtaz Pasha (the Turkish governor) was not successful in recruiting the Beja (the local population) for this purpose.[81]

There were many other population movements in different parts of the African continent before the colonial period. These included the Fulani expansion in West Africa, the Luba-Lunda migration into Congo and Angola, the Indian migration to Zanzibar and coastal areas of East Africa from 1830 to 1890, the migration of the Ndebele from Zululand to Rhodesia in 1837, the movement of Sotho groups to Botswana and the western Transvaal, the internal migration in Madagascar following the formation of the Merina kingdom, and the migrations of the Fang in Cameroon and Gabon, which began in the latter half of the eighteenth century and lasted for about a hundred and fifty years.[82] These population movements affected large numbers of people and have undoubtedly influenced significantly the present distribution of population and ethnic groups. The movement of laborers and cash-crop farmers in West Africa is considered to have begun well before the partition of the continent, following the abolition of the slave trade and slavery in Europe and the Americas. For instance, the Akwapim farmers of Ghana were migrating by the middle of the nineteenth century to vacant lands where they could grow oil palms and subsistence crops.[83]

The Colonial Period

In the final decades of the nineteenth century, European powers annexed vast territories in Africa through conquest. The conquest of Africa by the Europeans was undertaken so as to control the continent's resources. In some instances, Europeans took over land by signing treaties with African rulers who sometimes did not understand the complexities of the treaties. For the Africans, the conquests led to resistance, assimilation, and expulsion. Forceful acquisition of land resulted in conflicts with Europeans, such as the military encounters with the Zulu kingdom in 1879–80, with Egypt in 1882, Madagascar in 1895–96, and the Sokoto Caliphate in 1898.[84]

These conflicts might lead to migrations. For example, the expansion of British rule into the Sokoto Caliphate, which required military force and was not completed until approximately 1903 to 1906, led to further migration toward Sudan.[85] The British forces encountered stiff resistance before they occupied Sokoto in 1903. The Sultan of Sokoto, Mohammed Al-Tahiru (the former Mai Wurno), fought the British forces. Although he was killed in the battle, his supporters increased in number as they moved toward the Nile.[86] The battle of Burmi (1903), regarded as the climax of the British occupation of Hausaland, forced a large number of Fulani, estimated at 25,000, to rally around their new leader, Al-Tahiru's son, the new Mai Wurno, and to migrate to the Blue Nile, an area that provided a new focus for Hausa-Fulani settlement.[87] Sultan Omar Al-Futi of Senegal followed Mai Wurno's supporters to the Nile Valley and established Dar El Salaam, near old Sennar, on the Blue Nile.[88] The settlement bearing Mai Wurno's name became "the nucleus of a large 'western colony' extending from Semnar to El-Roseiris."[89] The establishment of new settlements in this region continued long after 1900 and continues even to the present day. It is claimed that numerous men, women, and children entered every year to work and eventually settle in the Nile Valley. The settlement of West Africans was also encouraged by the land tenure policy of the colonial government of Sudan, which proved to be advantageous to the immigrants.[90]

Once the acquisition of territories in Africa had been achieved, small numbers of migrants from European countries came to settle in these territories and establish control of them. The European nations seized the most productive lands and used taxation and other tactics to force the inhabitants to work on the land or in whatever enterprises were set up. The French, for example, conquered the Upper Niger Valley of West Africa in 1883 and then utilized the slaves of the previous regime to produce grain for the use of the French army.[91] As Patrick Manning has pointed out, in the French and Portuguese colonies of western and eastern Africa, forced labor and the compulsory cultivation of certain crops were designed largely to obtain the labor force needed to grow export crops, such as cotton in Mozambique and Angola, and to consolidate the labor supply.

Later, forced labor gave way to the free migration of people in search of better employment and living conditions. Seasonal migration was greater in West Africa than elsewhere in tropical Africa. The migration was short term and male dominated and frequently took place during the long dry season when the demand for labor on the farms at home was low.[92] In southern Africa, the migrant labor system encouraged thousands of African males to leave their homes to work in the mines, farms, and factories of South Africa and Southern Rhodesia (now Zimbabwe). The common explanation for this migration is that it was economic, brought about by the general under-development, unemployment, low standard of living, and poverty of the migrants' homelands, in comparison with the booming economy, development, employment opportunities, and high standard of living of the countries of destination.[93] In places like Basutoland, Bechuanaland, Swaziland, Mozambique, and Angola, recruitment agents enticed local people with advance payments and goods and with glamorous advertisements of urban life in South Africa and Southern Rhodesia. The Portuguese in Mozambique even used force to recruit Africans for migrant labor, and facilitated this exploitation by signing the Mozambique Convention with South Africa in 1928 and the Tete Agreement with Southern Rhodesia in 1934.[94] Transit camps were built in the countries of origin, and in these camps the job seekers were housed, fed, interviewed, examined, and certified, before being led to the mines, farms, and factories. At the end of twelve to eighteen months of work, the migrant laborer was provided with transport services and sent back home. The economic rewards for the countries of origin of the migrant laborers came in the form of licensing, passport, and attestation fees, and in hut tax, all of which earned foreign currency.[95]

In central Africa, most of the colonies up to the time of independence were tied in with the international capitalist system, which was dominated by the European colonizers, with local people engaging in noncapitalist agriculture. The development of capitalist relations of production was very slow and unimportant except in the areas settled by Europeans, who confiscated the land and forced peasants to become temporary or permanent agricultural laborers.[96] Countries like Equatorial Guinea, São Tomé and Principe, Rwanda, and Burundi, with small territory and no mineral resources were victims of this economic exploitation. In São Tomé and Principe, plantations, dominated by Europeans with large estates, were worked by contractual laborers who came from Cape Verde, Angola, and Mozambique.[97] In Angola, the European agricultural sector grew substantially with an increased population of European settlers in the region after World War II. These Europeans, mostly from the lower classes, saw Angola as "a land of unhoped-for material success."[98] Unlike these predominantly agricultural economies, the Belgian Congo up to independence had an economy that concentrated on mining (for example, in the mining provinces of Kasai and

Katanga) and transport. The government of the colony participated actively in the economy through government companies, through the private sector, and through the authoritarian mobilization of manpower.[99]

The economic situation, as well as the general development of schools and government departments in the various colonies in Africa, led to crises. One of the major problems was migration to the towns, which also triggered the new crisis of urbanization. In the Belgian Congo, the number of town dwellers rose from 8.8 percent in 1938 to 14.8 percent in 1945 and 24 percent in 1955.[100] A working class developed, including a large number of exploited workers, a number that increased dramatically in the mid-1950s. In Angola, in 1960, one out of three Africans lived in a makeshift dwelling in a town.[101] Thus, from the beginning of the twentieth century—particularly from 1935 until the 1960s—the colonial system became the principal cause of migration. The strategy of dispossessing Africans of their land led to migration. The development of the foreign-dominated export economy, with emphasis on the urban economy to the detriment of the rural economy, set the stage for migration brought about by the demand for labor on plantations and in administrative departments.

An increasing number of Africans uprooted by economic and political factors migrated to European countries to seek protection or opportunities. Thousands of people moved to France and Belgium from the French North African and Belgian colonies. At the time of the Algerian War of Independence there were about 450,000 Algerians in France.[102] The need for higher education, an area neglected by most colonial powers, was another important push factor leading to migration. Thus the number of Africans going to Europe and the United States to attend schools increased greatly between 1935 and 1960, and a substantial number of them, as well as other migrants, did not come back home.

The Postcolonial Period

The postcolonial period saw a continuation of the developments that began in colonial times. After independence, the African governments continued with the colonial development approach by investing in industry, commerce, administration, social amenities, and postprimary education. The export-oriented economic development and the concentration of investment in a few cities were major causes of regional inequality and rural-urban migration, and rural-rural migration in regions where plantation economies predominated.[103] The expansion of mining and cocoa farming and the export-oriented economy created a considerable demand for labor, which could not be met locally. In the early to middle 1970s, Ghana and Côte d'Ivoire became the major destinations of migrants in West Africa. But by the late

1970s, Ghana was beset by economic problems that forced many of its own citizens to emigrate to Nigeria and Côte d'Ivoire.[104]

The primary push factors in rural areas of Africa have included low incomes, inadequate essential services, the unfavorable rural socioeconomic structure, low skills in peasant farming, the displacement of small farmers for large-scale farming, landlessness, and the concentration of available land in the hands of a small number of landlords. In Lesotho, for example, most labor migrants to South Africa have come from rural areas because of a decline in arable land and the landlessness of many rural households.[105] In most African countries, young men, both single and married, tend to migrate alone to the cities, to secure available urban jobs and save enough money to pay for the transport and maintenance of family members who might subsequently join them. As a result of continuous migration to urban centers, the great cities of Africa (for example, Cairo, Lagos, Abidjan, Johannesburg, and Nairobi) have recorded populations that range from five to fifteen million people. During the colonial era, educated persons tended to migrate to urban areas while uneducated persons moved toward rural areas. Nowadays, migrants to the cities generally tend to be young and educated, while rural-rural migrants are mostly unskilled middle-aged people.[106] Rural-rural movement may have been chosen as a way to avoid the uncertainties of urban centers, especially with issues such as employment, accommodation, transportation, cost of living, and others associated with living in the city.

The worsening economic conditions and the structural adjustment programs implemented by many African countries to satisfy foreign creditors have led to a brain drain. Unemployment, low salaries of professionals, salary cuts for those still holding jobs, and retrenchment in the public and private sectors are consequences of the harsh economic conditions. These have led to the exodus of both skilled and unskilled persons to various African countries, notably Botswana, Namibia, and South Africa, as well as to the United States, Europe, and Canada. Uganda accounted for the largest exodus of highly skilled persons in the early 1970s, closely followed by Ghana from 1970 to 1982.[107] The oil boom of the 1970s and the infrastructural development that accompanied it made Nigeria a preferred destination. But with the collapse of oil prices in the early 1980s that led to a wage freeze, inflation, unemployment, and the structural adjustment program employed by the government, Nigeria has joined the ranks of major labor exporting countries. The destination of international migration has been the countries with which people have historical and political links. For example, migrants from Francophone countries are more likely to go to France, those from Anglophone countries to the United Kingdom or United States, and others from Lusophone countries to Portugal. Belgium continues to receive migrants from Rwanda and Zaire, while Italy hosts a large number of Ethiopians and some Senegalese.[108] In addition, unstable governments, dictatorships, and civil wars in countries like Ethiopia, Uganda, Sudan, Mozambique, Angola, Liberia, and Sierra Leone have led to a loss of freedom of the press and expression, resulting in human rights abuses. Academics, students, workers, union leaders, and other groups have been harassed and intimidated. Many of Uganda's professional and technical experts and numerous Ugandan Asians immigrated to the United Kingdom during Idi Amin's regime, which was notorious for human rights violations.[109]

Refugees dominated international migratory movements in the 1980s and 1990s. Africa has experienced the most serious refugee problems in terms of both size and complexity. The continent is home to one out of every two or three of the world's refugees.[110] By 1990, the total number of refugees had reached 5.6 million, while the number of countries that received refugee populations had increased from eighteen to forty-two.[111] These refugees originate from and settle in countries that are the least developed in the world and are plagued with famine, civil war, drought, and political instability. One key example of the creation of "environmental" refugees occurred during recent famines in Ethiopia in 1984–85, when inadequate rainfall triggered a large-scale migration of population from rural areas.[112] This situation was also experienced in Sudan, where more than 100,000 people left their homes to avoid starvation.[113] Aside from the population displaced by the environmental factor such as poor rainfall, about 4.5 million Sudanese, mostly from the south, have been displaced by war.[114] The Rwanda crisis of 1994 forced more than 250,000 Rwandans to flee the country within a short period of time.[115] The war in Liberia, for example, prompted military intervention by Africans in an African refugee crisis. Ghana, Nigeria, and Senegal sent peacekeeping troops to Liberia.

African refugees are generally confined to the continent and are assisted by fellow Africans in similarly poor countries within the continent. For example, Sudan admitted 726,500 refugees in late 1990, mostly Ethiopians (700,000) and Chadians (20,000) and a few Ugandans and Zaireans.[116] The war in southern Sudan and Somalia produced an additional exodus of displaced populations fleeing to Ethiopia. Only one in ten thousand African refugees resettled in a third country outside the continent.[117] The United States, Canada, and Australia are the only countries with policies providing for an annual intake of African refugees, and they take them in only on an ad hoc basis. A report published on the U.S. Department of State Web site and reported by news organizations such as the Associated Press on October 17, 2006, claimed that the United States had offered to take in 10,000 refugees from Burundi over the following two years. Most African refugees within or outside the continent cannot return home. Some Burundian refugees have been living in camps in neighboring Tanzania ever since 1972, when they fled from the Tutsi-dominated government's ethnic killings of the Hutu. Some were born in the camps and know no other home. The only real option left to most African refugees is to settle in their host country.

Female Migration

Unlike the migration of men in Africa, the independent rural-urban migration of women has not been rigorously studied. Three categories of independent rural-urban migration of women are suggested by recent studies.[118] In the first category, young, unmarried women with little formal education move to town to work at first as domestic help. An example from the Serer region of Senegal shows that in the 1950s, unmarried girls between the ages of ten and twenty seasonally migrated to work as domestic servants in Dakar for at least six months at a time. These girls usually stayed with a male relation. After about seven years of seasonal migration they returned home permanently, usually to marry.[119] Similarly, among the Bamana communities in central Mali, unmarried girls between the ages of about fifteen and twenty go to Bamako to work as domestic servants and usually return to the village for the cultivation season.[120] In Ghana and Nigeria, many female domestics in households in cities are poor relatives from the villages, lured by the promises of educational and economic opportunities in the city.[121] The same pattern can be found in the context of the traditional practices of child fostering, which still occur in many parts of Africa.[122]

The second category of women includes those who have benefited from educational opportunities elsewhere and migrated to the cities in search of jobs.[123] Many postpone marriage or prefer to remain unmarried, while improving their standard of living with the contributions of male friends.[124] Divorced or separated women also move independently from the rural areas to the city. In Ethiopia, it is reported that men and women have equal land rights, but cultivation is almost entirely the domain of men. Hence, cultural, physical, and capital constraints prevent women from ox-plowing, the dominant mode of production in many areas.[125] Here, the divorce rates are high and, with limited rural employment opportunities, urban areas offer much better choices.[126] This is different from the situation in most of Africa, with traditional hoe cultivation and women playing a major role in agriculture. In Kampala, aside from the death of a husband or divorce, an unhappy marriage was the reason commonly given by women for moving to town alone.[127] In northern Nigeria, Hausa girls sometimes flee from their homes due to the fear of the possibility of a forced marriage and eventually become *karuwai* (courtesans) or independent women in the city.[128] Generally, the difficult life in the rural areas and the social relationship established during the period of residence in the city, with its greater attractions for trade and

economic independence, may have discouraged such women from returning to the rural areas.[129]

The death of a husband often leaves women no option but to migrate,
and such women represent the third category of independent female rural-
urban migrants. A younger woman who has lost her husband, a woman
whose village of origin and the village of her in-laws provide little or no refuge, and whose sons have moved to the city, may decide to leave the village
on her own.[130] Also, witchcraft, or the possibility of it, is prevalent in rural
Africa, with organized witch persecutions or "jungle justice" aimed at eradi-
cating it. Women, especially older women with no husband or son around to
protect them, are vulnerable to accusations for calamities that occur in the
family or in the community. In addition, some women come to the city to
stay with a married son and help with childcare. These older women, while
helping to rear their grandchildren, also receive proper care and access to
better health facilities that cannot be found in villages.[131]

In Burkina Faso, the common belief, which has been supported by several studies, is that most women have migrated for family reasons.[132] However, recent data suggest that important, though not enormous, numbers of
women have been making migration decisions that take into consideration
other factors besides domestic ones. A few women have been involved in
forced labor. But a significant number of women—particularly those who
have moved to urban centers—have mentioned economic factors such as
work transfers, wage labor, or schooling opportunity as reasons for migrating.[133] However, given the importance attached to family in Africa, it is possible that women citing economic reasons for migrating to the city have also
considered their domestic situations.

Burkinabe women have migrated while young. In the period 1900–31,
almost all the women who migrated from one rural zone to another, and
from rural to urban areas, were between fifteen and nineteen years of age.[134]
In most Burkinabe societies, a very large part of female mobility has been
associated with marriage and women have married young. Thus, according
to the data, women have migrated at younger ages than men, and the age at
which women migrated corresponds with the age women got married.[135]

International migration among Burkinabe women has not been considered as important as internal migration, and is often represented as
migration to Ghana and Côte d'Ivoire.[136] Like internal migration, female
international migration has largely been motivated by domestic or family
factors. However, some distinctive characteristics have been seen. From
1932–46, forced labor was the cause for the migration of about 5 percent
of women who went to international destinations; most of them probably
worked as cooks for male labor conscripts or military recruits.[137] Also, while
the proportion of women claiming families as the reason for migrating to
international destinations rose from 80 percent to 90 percent in the periods

1947–59 and 1960–73, a small but significant number of women said that they migrated to seek wage labor.[138]

Those Left Behind

Migrations in Africa have important consequences for those who remain behind. Those people who stay behind face both the social and the economic effects of the loss of a family member. The migrants are usually young able-bodied men and women, who would have played an important role in the local economy. The loss of many young people to migration may threaten the viability of the rural economy, as the maintenance of various crucial physical and social facilities can no longer be assured.[139] When young families migrate from villages, the care of the old may be put in danger. In addition, the people who stay behind deal with the expense of providing for the migrants so that their journey and adjustments may be less stressful. If the family is poor, loans may be obtained from family friends or neighbors with a promise to pay them back as soon as the migrant settles down and secures a job. How soon this loan is paid back depends on when the migrant secures a job and earns enough money, which can further complicate the situation of the family members at home. It has been suggested that circular labor migration is one way of tackling the problem of losing important family members as a result of migration. In circular migration, young men migrate during the season when little work is needed on the farm and return before the onset of the rains so that the agricultural cycle in their villages are not disrupted.[140] However, the immediate problem facing the people who stay behind is how to survive socially and economically before the migrant returns or is able to work long enough to send home remittances.

The survival of families left behind is predicated on continuous support from migrants. In fact, relations between migrants and their home areas have often been viewed solely in terms of remittances (that is, money and goods moved from the migrant to the family back home). The "sending of remittances by migrants is one of the strongest and most pervasive phenomena in Africa's migration systems."[141] Migration in Africa is principally a family affair and part of the survival strategy of the rural family.[142] However, structural adjustment, price increases, reductions in wages and employment in urban areas, and the dashed hopes of many African immigrants overseas have affected the social obligation of migrants to their families back home. In a way, migration is no longer a one-way obligation, in the form of remittances from the migrant to the family left behind. Rural links have been "vital safety-valves and welfare options for urban people who are very vulnerable to economic fluctuations."[143] Urban dwellers are increasingly becoming partly dependent on rural sources of food and/or income, causing a reverse flow of goods and perhaps even money from rural to urban areas.

Return Migration

Urban-rural migration, often equated with return migration, involves people living in towns who go back to their rural home after retirement. This "retirement migration," as it is sometimes called, has an economic base, because people can find an abode, retain or regain land rights, and support themselves by farming at home.[144] Parents who have reached retirement age, or become sick, or simply lost the ability to cope with the "ups and downs" of city life sometimes hand over their business ventures to their children and return home (to rural areas) to rest. The children continue to manage the investments and use part of the profits to cater for their parents. Younger urbanites that are not at retirement age are also moving to rural areas because of the lack of employment and income opportunities in towns.[145] Generally, the diminishing hope of "making it" in cities is increasingly forcing people to return to rural areas. Given the economic uncertainties and the unstable political conditions in Africa, most Africans prefer to return to their place of origin at or before retirement, rather than settling permanently and dying in the host location. A study of senior citizens in five localities in Nigeria, Sierra Leone, and Zimbabwe shows that small rural towns are preferred as places of retirement because they provide services like health clinics, hospitals, and sources of water that are less easily available in villages, and facilitate visits from retirees' children.[146] Retirees can make enough cash for their daily needs from petty trading or small-scale farming, or they may receive support from their children who are still living in the cities. Above all, former city dwellers who return to rural areas find the places less stressful and less expensive to live in. They are happy to be relieved of the daily worries in the cities over such things as housing, congestion, transportation, and pollution. There is also what demographers term the "risk" of return migration,[147] due to the possible impact of such migration in middle or old age. Urban-rural migration is still a new and emerging issue and cannot be covered extensively in this volume. However, it is an important issue that requires further study.

Conclusion

The impulse to migrate is inherent in human nature. It has been suggested that the separation of the human species into ethnic, cultural, linguistic, and racial groups was the consequence of migration.[148] Migration has been a strategy for human survival since time immemorial. This occurred in the earliest period of our existence as human, when foragers walked across Africa, into Eurasia, and then North and South America. It was also the case when early explorers, guided by rivers, oceans, and coastlines, voyaged to unknown lands, and when nations colonized new territories in search of power and wealth, uprooting and redistributing citizens, servants, and slaves around the world. It is therefore not an overstatement to say that population movement in Africa has been an integral part of human existence, one that is still continuing at the present day.

The patterns and dynamics of the process of migration have changed over time. These changes have been attributed to European colonization of the continent, accompanied by the modernization and monetization of the economy. The challenges that new institutions produced in the social system, consciousness, beliefs, and behaviors of African societies and peoples were different from those that obtained in precolonial period.[149] Precolonial population movements were less organized and often involved entire villages, ethnic groups, and families moving to escape the ravages of warfare or unfavorable agricultural and climatic conditions. During colonial rule, movement and migration became largely determined by the labor needs of plantations, mines, and industries and by the colonial administration. Colonial migration was usually short term and male dominated. Postcolonial migration has been essentially a continuation of colonial migration, that is, directed toward resource-rich areas and urban centers, although the present-day migratory trend is more closely connected to the globalization of the capitalist economy. An attempt has been made to distinguish between migration of people and labor migration.[150] This distinction also roughly corresponds to the distinction between the precolonial and colonial/postcolonial periods and the nature of migrations during these periods. For example, it is recognized that migrations of people lead to the establishment of societies that are often similar to those the migrants originally came from, though sometimes people indigenous to a conquered area are integrated into the migrants' society and acquire new culture. On the other hand, modern migrations are considered migrations of labor, not of peoples. Here, the migrants take their place in an organized and structured host society, and generally acquire an inferior status, such as that of wage earners or sharecroppers.[151]

Migration in Africa has exhibited both diversity and continuity in its causes, magnitude, and impact on society and the economy in Africa. Differing political, economic, social, cultural, demographic, and colonial experiences have influenced the patterns and motivations of migration. There are indications that migration in Africa is increasing, and patterns of mobility are also changing, with new forms emerging and old forms declining. Rural-urban migration is decreasing, and in some countries urban-rural migration (return migration) is increasing. Intercontinental migration, particularly to northwest Europe, has continued to grow in importance. The number of cross-border labor migrants in southern Africa has declined substantially as a result of the new political and economic policies of South Africa, while the number of people in Africa who can be labeled as "refugees" has increased. The migration of family, group, or community members can put a heavy strain on those left behind, both economically and socially. However, although rural-urban migration is on the decline, it is still part of the survival strategy of the rural family.

Overview of This Volume

This book brings together a range of recent research on migration in Africa. The various contributors to this book represent a wide range of focus and disciplinary background. The book provides a variety of information on movements, migrations, and displacements in Africa and their changing forms and dynamics, from the precolonial period through the colonial and post colonial periods to the present day. The book consists of an introduction and thirteen chapters, dealing with a wide range of topics relating to African migration, and covering the period from precolonial to colonial and postcolonial times. Some of the topics are concerned with the conceptual and methodological aspects of research on migration especially where no (or little) documentary evidence exist. Important issues address in the volume include causes and consequences of migration, population movement, displacements, migration experiences, settlement patterns and strategies, labor mobility, immigrant societies, and identity.

In chapter 1, Akinwumi Ogundiran challenges some of the assumptions of the "internal African frontier" model as presented by Igor Kopytoff. These assumptions include the conceptualization of frontier communities as more conservative than innovative; the view of the frontier as a mere off-shoot of larger societies with the ability to replicate events in the "home" society; and the emphasis placed by the model on metropolis-frontier migration. Using oral historical and archaeological evidence from Osogbo, in the Upper Osun area of southwestern Nigeria, Ogundiran suggests that the early Osogbo immigrants, who were merely fortune seekers, came essentially from small-scale frontier communities in central Yorubaland and not from a large metropolitan center. This is contrary to Kopytoff's internal frontier model, which sees large political centers as a determining factor in frontier migration. Ogundiran also claims that while the early settlement of Osogbo coincided with the expansion of the large polity of Ilesa into the Upper Osun area in the sixteenth century, the Ilesa polity did not play any role in the making of Osogbo. Rather, Osogbo was absorbed by the Ilesa kingdom for strategic reasons only later. Early Osogbo was a successful frontier trading and production center with commercial linkages that focused on the Atlantic coast.

In chapter 2, Olatunji Ojo examines the two scholarly views on the origin of pan-Yoruba ethnicity. The first is that of the age-old ethnic consciousness that placed Ile-Ife as the cradle of the Yoruba people, from which all political systems and linguistic affinities emanated. The second view sees Yoruba ethnic consciousness as arising out of the Atlantic slave trade, developing among enslaved Yoruba speakers in the diaspora. This implies that until the nineteenth century, Yorubaland was divided into several ethnic groups. One of the goals of Ojo's chapter is to modify and unite these two viewpoints, while emphasizing the nondiasporic factors that shaped the development of Yoruba ethnicity. According to Ojo, the diasporic and homeland Yoruba encountered related challenges such as warfare, enslavement, and population movement. The political unrest in Yorubaland in the nineteenth century created ethnic factionalization and slaving. Warfare led to population displacement and the conversion of freeborn people to slaves and refugees.

Using an archaeological approach, in chapter 3, Adisa Ogunfolakan argues for the utility of material evidence as an indicator of culture movement and cultural interaction. His research in the northeastern area of Osun State, Nigeria, has resulted in the discovery, at a number of centers, of potsherd pavements that are similar to the famous potsherd pavements at Ile-Ife. Ogunfolakan describes the research strategy/methods he employed in the collection of evidence and in the course of experimentation to explain how the potsherd pavements may have been constructed in the past. The potsherd pavement is an important aspect of ancient Yoruba culture, and its construction is evidence of advanced sociopolitcal institutions. It is widely claimed in Yorubaland that Yoruba dynasties trace their origins to Ife, whether as a primary or a secondary center. This is sometimes expressed in the oral tradition of various Yoruba groups as the movement of descendants of Oduduwa who came from Ife to establish settlements in Yorubaland. Ogunfolakan claims that the ceramic attributes and potsherd pavements found in the northeastern Osun region are an indication of Ife influence, which probably spread through the migration of people from the Ife area.

The need to capture some experiences of migration and to understand their various causes and effects is the concern of Aribidesi Usman in chapter 4. As seen above, the Yoruba people of Nigeria, like most other African groups, are believed to have migrated to their present places of residence. Usman's chapter provides a chronological analysis of regional migrations and abandonment of settlements. The chapter examines the regional migration of Yoruba, especially south-north migration. Important migration phases were identified with associated sociopolitical and material-cultural innovations in the periods discussed below. The Classical Period (AD 1000–1400) was characterized by stone carving, distinctive ceramic types, potsherd pavements, city walls, and copper-alloy sculptures. The Intermediate Period (AD 1400–1600) saw an increase in the general population, and migration to frontiers as a result of factional competitions and conflicts. The Old Oyo period (AD 1600–1800) witnessed large-scale migration to the northern part of Yorubaland. The Revolutionary Period (AD 1800–1900) was associated with the collapse of Old Oyo, regional internecine warfare, population displacements, and the emergence of new political formations. Usman also examines the challenges of identifying migration and social groups in the archaeological record through ceramic assemblages. Changes in ceramic design and the presence of many examples of certain decorative motifs may indicate not only the contribution of new ideas from new social groups but also the dominance of certain social groups over others.

Like other disciplines, architecture can provide significant information about African history, identities, and acculturation. This is the focus of Brigitte Oshineye in chapter 5. The author's focus is on the nineteenth- and twentieth-century "Afro-Brazilian" buildings in the Yoruba coastal city of Lagos. These buildings were constructed by ex-slave returnees to coastal West Africa who introduced the architectural styles of the lands where they were enslaved. Following the partition of Africa in the late nineteenth century, the Europeans brought their architectural styles to their colonies. However, only a few of the buildings in the West African coastal regions were constructed according to colonial architectural styles. As Oshineye indicates, the abolition of the slave trade probably influenced the structural landscape and cultural changes more than colonialism did. The different architectural patterns of the Afro-Brazilian style on the coast of West Africa are connected with people of different cultures and ethnicities who came to the coastal region as a result of the abolition of slavery. Drawing on physical evidence, genealogies, oral narratives, and written records, Oshineye suggests that studying the architecture produced as a consequence of international and interregional migration can help us to detect and understand the various attributes or characteristics that contributed to and strengthened Yoruba culture in the coastal region. It is unfortunate that tangible cultural relics such as Afro-Brazilian buildings and examples of other historical types of architecture in the West African coastal regions are fast disappearing, giving way to the new commercial edifices that now adorn our cities.

Illegal squatter settlements abound in large cities in Africa, particularly capital cities. This is a direct result of rural-urban migration, a phenomenon that still continues today, although, overall, it is in decline. In chapter 6, Gerald Steyn examines the impact of such migration on the form and function of an informal settlement, with a focus on the illegal shantytown of Mamelodi, South Africa. Informal settlements include squatter camps and slums. Mamelodi is part of Pretoria, an economic dynamo of sub-Saharan Africa and an attractive destination for migrants. The rapid urbanization in this region has been linked to migration from rural areas, illegal migration from other African countries, and natural population increase. As Steyn claims, for many young people, living in the city or surviving there for some time before returning home is considered a form of initiation into adulthood. Precolonial African urbanism with its strong rural characteristics probably served as a source of collective memories or forces shaping informal settlements. Thus, while squatters often face an insecure future, they still maintain a dignified existence, albeit a rather precarious one, because they have adopted the paradigm of that ancient guardian institution, the African village.

In chapter 7, Meshack Owino examines population displacement during the colonial conquest of Africa. Africans resisted colonial subjugation, but suffered immensely through loss of lives and displacement of population. The anticolonial resistance and migration among the Jo-Ugenya of western Kenya provides an example of the course of events in Africa in the nineteenth century preparatory to European colonization. The British exploited the old enmities between various groups by playing off one group against another to achieve their objectives. The Wanga were traditional enemies of the Jo-Ugenya, and by a strange twist of fate became allies of the British. This alliance helped the British to defeat the Jo-Ugenya. The chapter looks at the consequences of this and the story of how the conquered group arrived at new locations. The Jo-Ugenya were displaced by the war and came to occupy new lands, whose location was often determined by closeness to their homeland (since most hoped to return there at some point), kinship ties, and existing social and economic networks. Various appeals made to the British by the Jo-Ugenya to allow them to return to their homeland failed. As Owino indicates, one of the reasons for the British refusal of the Jo-Ugenya's request was that some of the vacated territories had already been occupied by the Wanga during the Jo-Ugenya resistance. Thus, like most African migration and population displacements, the scattering of the Jo-Ugenya during the late nineteenth century has turned out to be a permanent migration, with no hope of any return to their original homes.

Trading diasporas have often been regarded as a form of voluntary migration and therefore have not been well served by Africanist researchers, who have tended to concentrate on forced migrations, such as those involving slaves. In chapter 8, Edmund Abaka examines the Hausa diaspora in Ghana in terms of both voluntary and forced migration and in terms of migrants' experience in their host societies. The history of the Hausa has been characterized by spatial mobility. Abaka suggests that the Hausa role in the history of Ghana was essentially twofold, with Hausa functioning both as traders and as soldiers. In the Asante gold trade, the Hausa were an important link in the desert sector between the Sokoto Caliphate, Asante, and the Volta-Afram basin. In the early colonial period, the British created a Hausa constabulary and used it to consolidate their Gold Coast territory. Abaka also argues that during the period of the caliphate, Hausa slaves were supplied to the Atlantic trade network and also to Asante and the Volta basin where they performed various tasks.

Colonial administrations in Africa introduced a number of economic measures designed to obtain the labor they needed. Forced labor and the compulsory cultivation of certain crops were designed largely to obtain the desired export crops. In chapter 9, Pius Nyambara provides insights into the ways in which migration was brought about by the economic policies of colonial governments. The attraction of the cotton agriculture of the Gokwe region of northwestern Zimbabwe led to an upsurge in Madheruka migration. The development of cotton agriculture in the region in the early 1960s also played a major role in the construction of ethnic identities. In similar fashion to the French in their perception of the Senegalese and Dahomeyan workers in the Ivory Coast (Côte d'Ivoire) discussed in chapter 10 by Geloin, the colonial administration in Southern Rhodesia (Zimbabwe) perceived the Madheruka as more amenable to cotton cultivation than the indigenous people. As Nyambara clearly indicates, the Madheruka farmers dominated cotton farming because of their prior education about commercial farming in their original homes. The immigrants (Madheruka) themselves were very cognizant of this identity, and regarded the indigenous Shangwe as local and unenlightened. As Nyambara points out, while the construction of a Shangwe ethnic identity started in the early colonial period, it was in the early 1960s, with the arrival of the Madheruka and the introduction of cotton, that Shangwe identity became strengthened.

Ghislaine Geloin focuses essentially on the novel, *The Suns of Independence,* by Ahmadou Kourouma from the Ivory Coast (Côte d'Ivoire), published in 1968. The novel, as described by Geloin, depicts the disillusionment and the tragedy that colonization and independence brought to the Malinke of the Ivory Coast and Guinea. The artificial political borders within Africa were created at the Berlin Conference in 1885, when the European powers met to carve up African territories into colonial states. The consequences of the borders thus created for African rural society have included a series of other evils, including movements and displacements of populations. The artificial borders often divide the same people between two or more states. The Malinke, who constituted a powerful state in the past, lost their past glory and are scattered today among six West African nations. Under colonial administration, the development of the foreign export sector led to a mass exodus of people from rural areas to urban centers. Anticolonial protests also led to the arrest and exile of many African intellectuals. The French colonizers employed preferential treatment in their dealings with various ethnic groups. For example, Dahomeyans and Senegalese were brought to work in the Ivory Coast because they were considered more literate than the native inhabitants of the country. Large population movements occurred around the time of independence in 1960. The Ivory Coast needed a large supply of cheap migrant workers to replace forced labor and the Dahomeyans and Senegalese who had been sent away. The independence of the Ivory Coast and the policies of the new African government did not improve the labor situation or human rights, as the independent African government maintained close cooperation with the former colonial masters. Like the colonial government, the government of the independent Ivory Coast introduced various repressive measures and concocted allegations to quell critics and political competition from intellectuals and middle-class business people. As indicated by Geloin, the Malinke, who believe in divination and "fetishes," were easy prey for President Houphouët-Boigny's policies, and many disappeared following accusations that they had used fetishist practices against the president.

Africans who have migrated to foreign and unfamiliar lands, thousands of miles from their original homes, have often devised various means to make their stay in the new environment as comfortable as possible. This attitude is reflected in the familiar phrase, "home away from home." In chapter 11, Jean-Luc Martineau looks at local associations and identity building among Nigerian Yoruba communities in Dahomey/Republic of Benin. Hometown-based associations are considered in West Africa as the "natural" way for people to organize themselves abroad. They are the best and most efficient means of protection in an unknown environment. Besides providing the feeling of security that comes with existing within a larger whole, local associations also serve as a constant reminder of the home country. Martineau addresses two important questions: first, how these associations evolved and became rallying points for migrants; and second, how the associations have changed and how they have survived in the political and social environment of their host country, particularly in the second half of the twentieth century.

The issue of the identity of the Swahili culture in East African coast still remains unresolved, despite various studies on the subject. In chapter 12, Maurice Amutabi revisits this important issue of ethnicity and identity on the coast of Kenya, using the Swahili as a case study. Amutabi challenges the approach taken by early studies of ethnic identity in Kenya, which relied essentially on records of descendants of Arabs and Muslim archival and written sources, while neglecting the everyday experience of ordinary African people and their contribution to the historical process of identity creation. To better understand and analyze the coast of Kenya, Amutabi used a variety of sources, including the experience of his own family and himself, songs and poetry, works of art, oral interviews, and textual historical materials. Unlike the previous studies, which declared the dominant Swahili coastal culture to be fixed, static, and unchanging, Amutabi argues that a "great deal of hybridity and multiculturalism" is contained in the Swahili culture, acquired through the diffusion of mostly African ideas, a point that has often been neglected. The traumatic experiences of slavery at the coast of Kenya have produced oppositional identities. As Amutabi suggests, many coastal Africans (the Bantu) deny their "African-ness," which is considered as an indicator of slave descent, preferring the Arab "ancestry" that links them to their former slave masters. The chapter also touches on the privileging of Muslim and Arab agency in Swahili culture at the expense of the agency of Africans (mainly Bantu). Various forms of evidence—linguistic, ethnographic, and archaeological—are utilized in support of the early presence of the Bantu on the coast of Kenya. Amutabi calls for more attention to the history of the Mijikenda people as a way to understand the history of the coast of Kenya.

Isiakka Mande's study of migrant workers from Upper Volta (now Burkina Faso) in chapter 13 illustrates the paradoxical nature of European colonization and colonial policies in West Africa. The main issue is whether the colonial government was interested in the colony's growth and development or mainly in its exploitation and the strengthening of migratory flows. The forced labor system in the French colonies was designed to obtain the labor force needed to grow export crops and to consolidate the labor supply. Upper Volta, with a large population and a large expanse of land but few natural resources, was seen as a source to be tapped to meet the needs of neighboring colonies. In order to achieve the economic objectives set out by the French government, the administrators of Upper Volta relied on tax revenue. The people of Upper Volta were impoverished by this tax and forced to cross the border to sell their labor outside the colony. Money repatriated by the workers was used in most cases to pay the poll tax of their family members at home. People from Upper Volta were recruited by private operators outside the colony, for example, in Senegal and Côte d'Ivoire. All this led to the migration of largely unskilled laborers from Upper Volta to the cocoa farms of the Gold Coast (now Ghana), Senegal and Côte d'Ivoire.

Notes

1.   Tade Aina, "Internal Non-Metropolitan Migration and the Development Process in Africa," in *The Migration Experience in Africa*, ed. Jonathan Baker and Tade Aina, 41–53 (Uppsala, Sweden: Nordiska Afrikainstitutet, 1995).

2.   Aderanti Adepoju, "Binational Communities and Labor Circulation in Sub-Saharan Africa," in *The Unsettled Relationship: Labor Migration and Economic Development*, ed. D. G. Papademetriou and P. L. Martin, 45–64 (New York: Greenwood Press, 1991).

3.   William Hance, *Population, Migration, and Urbanization in Africa* (New York: Columbia University Press, 1970); R. K. Udo, *Migrant Tenant Farmers of Nigeria* (Lagos,

Nigeria: African University Press, 1975);J. I. Clarke and L.A. Kosinski, eds., *Redistribution of Population in Africa* (London: Heinemann, 1982); Aina, "Internal Non-Metropolitan Migration," 48.

4. Aderanti Adepoju, "Migration in Africa: An Overview," in Baker and Aina, *The Migration Experience in Africa*, 87–108.

5. Graham Connah, *Forgotten Africa: An Introduction to Its Archaeology* (London: Routledge, 2004), 2; Patrick Manning, *Migration in World History* (London: Routledge, 2005), 18.

6. Manning, *Migration*, 18.

7. Ibid.

8. Ibid.

9. Ibid.

10. Connah, *Forgotten Africa*, 11.

11. Manning, Migration, 19.

12. Ibid, 21.

13. Ibid., 59.

14. Ibid., 61.

15. Connah, *Forgotten Africa*, 40.

16. Manning, *Migration*, 61.

17. Ibid., 74

18. Ann Stahl, "A History and Critique of Investigations into Early African Agriculture," in *From Hunters to Farmers*, ed. J. Desmond Clark and Steven Brandt, 9–25 (Berkeley: University of California Press, 1984).

19. Ibid., 15.

20. Manning, *Migration*, 74.

21. Thomas O'Toole, "The Historical Context," in *Understanding Contemporary Africa*, 3rd ed., ed. April Gordon and Donald Gordon, 223–54 (London: Lynne Rienner, 2001); see also John Lamphear and Toyin Falola, "Aspects of Early African History," in *Africa*, 3rd ed., ed. Phyllis M. Martin and Patrick O'Meara, 73–96 (Bloomington: Indiana University Press, 1995).

22. S. Lwanga-Lunyiigo and J. Vansina, "The Bantu-Speaking peoples and Their Expansion," in Elfasi, *General History of Africa*, vol. 3, 140–62.

23. O'Toole, "Historical Context," 30.

24. S. Lwanga-Lunyiigo and Vansina, "Bantu-Speaking Peoples," 150.

25. Merrick Posnansky, "Bantu genesis," *Uganda Journal*, 25, 1 (1964): 86–92.

26. C. C. Wrigley, "Speculations on the Economic Prehistory of Africa," *Journal of African History* 1, no. 2 (1960): 189–204.

27. Lwanga-Lunyiigo and Vansina, "Bantu-Speaking Peoples," 151.

28. Jan Vansina, "The Roots of African Cultures," in *African History: From Earliest Times to Independence*, 2nd ed., ed. Philip Curtin, Steven Feierman, Leonard Thompson, and Jan Vansina, 1–28 (New York: Longman, 1995).

29. Lamphear and Falola, "Aspects of Early African History," 86–94

30. F. W. Knight, "The African Diaspora," in *General History of Africa*, vol. 6, ed. J. F. Ade Ajayi, 749–72 (Paris: UNESCO, 1989).

31. Ibid., 749.

32. B. Lewis, "Hadjdj," in *The Encyclopedia of Islam*, vol. 3, ed. B. Lewis, V. L. Menage, C. Pellat, and J. Schacht, 37–38 (Leiden, Netherlands: Brill, 1971).

33.   Christiaan Hurgronje, *Mekka in the Latter Part of the 19th Century: Daily Life, Customs and Learning of the Moslims of the East-Indian Archipelago* (Leiden, Netherlands: Brill, 1970), 14–15.

34.   Ibid., 182.

35.   Ibid., 11, 13

36.   Knight, "The African Diaspora," 749.

37.   Ibid., 750.

38.   Ibid., 751.

39.   Ibid.

40.   Manning, *Migration,* 132.

41.   Knight, "The African Diaspora," 751.

42.   Ibid., 751

43.   D. B. Davis, *The Problem of Slavery in Western Culture* (Ithaca, NY: Cornell University Press, 1966), 223–61.

44.   Knight, "The African Diaspora," 762.

45.   Ibid., 760.

46.   Ibid., 752.

47.   Igor Kopytoff, ed., *The African Frontier* (Bloomington: Indiana University Press, 1987); Samir Amin, "Introduction," in *Modern Migrations in Western Africa,* ed. Samir Amin, 53–54 (London: Oxford University Press, 1974).

48.   Ibid

49.   Dennis Cordell, Joel Gregory, and Victor Piche, *Hoe and Wage: A Social History of a Circular Migration System in West Africa* (Boulder, CO: Westview Press, 1996), 21.

50.   Michele Fieloux, "Les migrations Lobi en Côte d'Ivoire: Archaïsme ou création sociale," in *Les migrations africaines,* ed. Jean-Loup Amselle (Paris: François Maspero, 1976), 43–49.

51.   Cordell, Gregory, and Piche, *Hoe and Wage,* 22; Fieloux, "Les migrations," 60–61; Jean-Loup Amselle, ed., *Les migrations africaines: Réseau et processus migratoires* (Paris: François Maspero, 1976), 5.

52.   Cordell, Gregory, and Piche, *Hoe and Wage.*

53.   Fieloux, "Les migrations," 51–52, 61.

54.   Ibid, 54–56.

55.   Cordell, Gregory, and Piche, *Hoe and Wage,* 20.

56.   John Fage, "Reflections on the Early History of the Mossi-Dagomba Group of States," in *The Historian in Tropical Africa,* ed. J. Vansina, R. Mauny, and L. V. Thomas, 177–91 (London: International African Institute, 1964).

57.   Cordell, Gregory, and Piche, *Hoe and Wage,* 20–21; J. J. Holden, "The Zabarima Conquest of Northwest Ghana, Part 1," *Transactions of the Historical Society of Ghana* 8 (1965): 60–86; Thomas Painter, "From Warriors to Migrants: Critical Perspectives on Early Migrations among the Zarma of Niger," *Africa* 58 (1988): 87–100.

58.   Cordell, Gregory, and Piche, *Hoe and Wage,* 21.

59.   Ibid., 24; Phillip Curtin, *Cross-Cultural Trade in World History* (Cambridge: Cambridge University Press, 1984), 15–60; George Brooks, *Landlords and Strangers: Ecology, Society, and Trade in Western Africa,* 1000–1630 (Boulder, CO: Westview Press, 1993).

60.   Cordell, Gregory, and Piche, *Hoe and Wage,* 24.

61.   Ibid.

62. Paul Lovejoy, *Transformations in Slavery: A History of Slavery in Africa* (Cambridge: Cambridge University Press, 1973), 90–91.

63. Cordell, Gregory, and Piche, *Hoe and Wage*, 24.

64. Ibid., 25; Lovejoy, *Transformations*, 91.

65. Lovejoy, *Transformations*, 198

66. Dennis Cordell, "Eastern Libya, Wadai, and the Sanusiyya: A Tariqa and a Trade Route," *Journal of African History* 18 (1977): 21–36.

67. Ayoub Balamoan, *Peoples and Economics in the Sudan 1884 to 1956* (Cambridge, MA: Harvard University Center for Population Studies, 1976), 156.

68. Ibid.

69. Ibid.; see also Dixon Denham, *Narrative of travels and discoveries in Northern and Central Africa, in the years 1822, 1823, and 1824, by Major Denham, Captain Clapperton, and the late Dr. Oudney* (London: J. Murray, 1826), 456.

70. Saburi Biobaku and Mohammed Al-Hajj, "The Sudanese Mahdiyya and the Niger-Chad Region," in *Islam in Tropical Africa*, ed. I. M. Lewis, 425–41 (London: Oxford University Press, 1966).

71. Ibid.

72. Balamoan, *Peoples and Economics*, 157.

73. Ibid., 16

74. Ibid, 156.

75. Ibid.

76. Ibid., 157.

77. Al-Amin Abu-Manga, *Hausa in the Sudan* (Frankfurt: Rüdiger Köppe Verlag, 1999), 7.

78. R. C. Abraham, *Dictionary of the Hausa Language* (London: Hodder & Stoughton, 1946), iii,

79. Abu-Manga, *Hausa*, 10

80. Ibid.

81. Ibid.

82. Virginia Thompson and Richard Adloff, *The Emerging States of French Equatorial Africa* (Stanford, CA: Stanford University Press, 1960), 343; see also Hance, *Population, Migration, and Urbanization*, 130.

83. Ibid.

84. Manning, *Migration*, 152.

85. Balamoan, *Peoples and Economics*, 204.

86. Ibid., 205.

87. Biobaku and Al-Hajj, "The Sudanese Mahdiyya."

88. Ibid.; see also Isam Hassoun, "Western Migration and Settlement in the Gezira," *Sudan Notes and Records* 33 (1952): 60–114; H. C. Jackson, *Behind the Modern Sudan* (London: Macmillan, 1955), 1–5.

89. Balamoan, *Peoples and Economics*, 205.

90. Ibid., 170.

91. Manning, *Migration*, 152.

92. Mansell Prothero, "Migration in Tropical Africa," in *The Population of Tropical Africa*, ed. J. C. Caldwell and C. Okonjo, 250–63 (London: Longmans, 1968).

93. David Chanaiwa, "Southern Africa since 1945," in *General History of Africa*, vol. 8, ed. Ali A. Mazrui, 246–81 (Paris: UNESCO, 1993).

94. Ibid., 253.

95. Ibid.

96. Elikia M'bokolo, "Equatorial West Africa," in Mazrui, *General History of Africa,* vol. 8, 192–220.

97. Ibid., 198.

98. Ibid., 199.

99. Ibid., 200.

100. Ibid., 201,

101. Ibid.

102. Joseph Harris, "Africa and Its Diaspora since 1935," in Mazrui, *General History of Africa,* vol. 8, 705–23.

103. Aderanti Adepoju, "An Overview of Rural Migration and Agricultural Labor Force Structure in Africa," *African Population Studies* 1 (1988): 5–25.

104. Adepoju, "Migration in Africa," 91.

105. Timothy Thahane, "International Labor Migration in Southern Africa," in *The Unsettled Relationship,* 65–87.

106. Adepoju, "Migration in Africa," 92.

107. Ibid., 98; see also Aderanti Adepoju, ed., *The Impact of Structural Adjustment on the Population of Africa: The Implication for Education, Health and Employment* (London: James Currey, 1993), 1–6.

108. Adepoju, "The Impact of StructuralAdjustment," 6.

109. Adepoju, "Migration in Africa," 99.

110. Ibid., 101.

111. Jonathan Bascom, "The New Nomads," in Baker and Aina, *The Migration Experience in Africa,* 197–219.

112. Ibid., 201

113. Ibid.

114. Adepoju, "Migration in Africa," 102.

115. Bascom, "New Nomads," 214.

116. Adepoju, "Migration in Africa," 102.

117. Bascom, "New Nomads," 203.

118. Joseph Gugler and Gudrun Ludwar-Ene, "Gender and Migration in Africa South of the Sahara," in Baker and Aina, *The Migration Experience in Africa,* 257–68; Alice Hamer, "Diola Woman and Migration: A Case Study," in *The Uprooted of the Western Sahel,* ed. L. G. Colvin et al., 163–203 (New York: Praeger, 1981).

119. Gugler and Ludwar-Ene, "Gender and Migration," 262.

120. Ibid.

121. Richard Anker and Catherine Hein, "Introduction and Overview," in *Sex Inequalities in Urban Employment in the Third World,* ed. Richard Anker and Catherine Hein, 1–56 (New York: St. Martin's Press, 1986).

122. Esther Goody, "Parental Strategies: Calculation or Sentiment? Fostering Practices among West Africans," in *Interest and Emotion. Essays on the Study of Family and Kinship,* ed. Hans Medick and David Warren Sabean, 266–72 (Cambridge: Cambridge University Press, 1986); Nici Nelson, "Rural-Urban Child Fostering in Kenya: Migration, Kinship Ideology, and Class," in *Migrants, Workers, and the Social Order,* ASA Monograph 26, ed. Jeremy Eades, 181–98 (New York: Tavistock Publications, 1987); Hilary Page, "Childrearing versus Childbearing: Coresidence of Mother and Child in

Sub-Saharan Africa," in *Reproduction and Social Organization in Sub-Saharan Africa,* ed. Ron J. Lesthaeghe, 401–41 (Berkeley: University of California Press, 1989).

123. Marida Hollos, "Migration, Education, and the Status of Women in Southern Nigeria," *American Anthropologist* 93 (1991): 852–70; Niara Sudarkasa, "Women and Migration in Contemporary West Africa," *Signs* 3 (1977): 178–80.

124. Carmel Dinan, "Sugar Daddies and Gold-Diggers: The White-Collar Single Women in Accra," in *Female and Male in West Africa,* ed. Christine Oppong, 344–66 (London: George Allen & Unwin, 1983).

125. Jonathan Baker, "Small Urban Centers and Their Role in Rural Restructuring," in *Ethiopia in Change: Peasantry, Nationalism and Democracy,* ed. Abebe Zegeye and Siegfried Pausewang, 152–71 (London: British Academic Press. 1994).

126. Helen Pankhurst, *Gender, Development and Identity: An Ethiopian Study* (London: Zed Books, 1992), 114–23.

127. Christine Obbo, *African Women: Their Struggle for Economic Independence* (London: Zed Press, 1980), 76–77.

128. Gugler and Ludwar-Ene, "Gender and Migration," 263.

129. Renee Pittin, Renee, "Houses of Women: A Focus on Alternative Life-Styles in Katsina City," in Oppong, *Female and Male in West Africa,* 291–302.

130. Daniel Offiong, "The 1978–1979 Akpan Ekwong Antiwitchcraft Crusade in Nigeria," *Anthropologica* 24 (1982): 27–42.

131. Margaret Peil, Stephen Ekpenyong, and Olatunji Oyeneye, "Going Home: Migration Careers of Southern Nigerians," *International Migration Review* 22 (1988): 563–85.

132. Joel Gregory, "Underdevelopment, Dependency, and Migration in Upper Volta" PhD diss., Cornell University, 1974), 122; Sidiki Coulibay, *Les migrations voltaïques: Les origins, les motifs et les perceptions des politiques* (PhD diss., Département de Démographie, Université de Montréal: Collection de thèses et mémoires sur le Sahel, no. 7, 1978), 189–92.

133. Cordell, Gregory, and Piche, *Hoe and Wage,* 240.

134. Ibid., 243.

135. A. Quesnel and J. Vaugelade, *Les mouvements de population mossi: Démographie et migration* (Ouagadougou, Burkina Faso: Ministère du Travail et de la Fonction Publique, dossier 2, fascicule 1, 1975), 122.

136. Cordell, Gregory, and Piche, *Hoe and Wage,* 249.

137. Ibid., 250.

138. Ibid.

139. Han van Dijik, Dick Foeken, and Kiky van Til, "Population Mobility in Africa: An Overview," in *Mobile Africa,* ed. Mirjam de Bruijn, Rijk van Dijk, and Dick Foeken, 9–26 (Boston: Brill, 2001).

140. Ibid., 22.

141. Adepoju, "Migration in Africa," 100.

142. Van Dijik, Foeken, and van Til, "Population Mobility," 23.

143. David Potts, "Urban Lives: Adopting New Strategies and Adapting Rural Links," in *The Urban Challenge in Africa: Growth and Management of the Large Cities,* ed. C. Rakodi, 447–94 (New York: United Nations University Press, 1997).

144. Margaret Peil, "The Small Town as a Retirement Center," in Baker and Aina, *The Migration Experience in Africa,* 149–66; Alan Gilbert and Josef Gugler, *Cities, Poverty,*

and Development: Urbanization in the Third World, 2nd ed. (Oxford: Oxford University Press, 1992), 192–200.

145. Potts, "Urban Lives," 461.

146. Peil, "Small Town," 151.

147. Cordell, Gregory, and Piche, *Hoe and Wage,* 293.

148. Anthony Marsella and Erin Ring, "Human Migration and Immigration: An Overview," in *Migration,* ed. Leonore Loeb Adler and Uwe P. Gielen, 3–22 (London: Praeger, 2003).

149. Aina, "Internal Non-Metropolitan Migration," 41.

150. Samir Amin, "Migrations in Contemporary Africa: A Retrospective View," in Baker and Aina, *The Migration Experience in Africa,* 29–40.

151. Ibid., 29.

Part A

State Formation and Migration Crossroads

1

Frontier Migrations and Cultural Transformations in the Yoruba Hinterland, ca. 1575–1700

The Case of Upper Osun

Akinwumi Ogundiran

Introduction

This essay revisits the "internal African frontier" model proposed by Igor Kopytoff.[1] Archaeological data are applied to test some of the assumptions and propositions of the model, with a focus on an area in the Yoruba hinterland: Upper Osun. Osogbo was one of the frontier communities that evolved in this region between ca. 1575 and 1700 as a result of a combination of many factors: episodes of drought, the thrust of the new imperial age, and the economic opportunities and challenges from the Atlantic coast. Though sandwiched between two competing hegemonic interests—Oyo and Ilesa— the fledgling community of Osogbo followed distinct cultural and economic pathways. These pathways were the focus of the archaeological and historical investigations conducted in Osun Osogbo Grove in 2004. This chapter examines the implications of some of the results of the investigations for understanding a precolonial internal African frontier process.

The years covered in this chapter belong to what I have called the Atlantic period in Yoruba cultural history.[2] This was a period of Oyo imperial expansion, the consolidation of the hegemonic power of a few polities over the Yoruba and adjacent regions, and the integration of Yoruba hinterland areas into the Atlantic commerce. Diffuse regional interaction networks, developed through migration and the establishment of new towns and villages, also characterized the period. It was these migration and regional interaction processes that transformed the Upper Osun into an active frontier region in

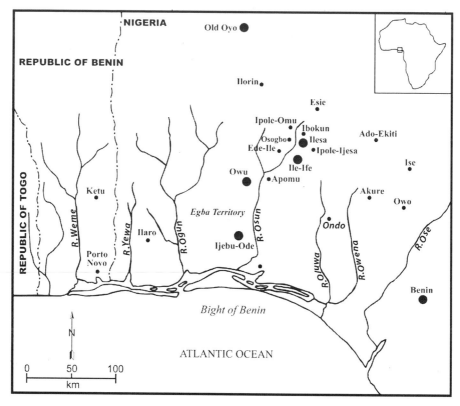

Figure 1.1. Yorubaland, showing Upper Osun. Credit: Akin Ogundiran.

central Yorubaland during the seventeenth century (see figure 1.1). Historical and archaeological evidence indicates that these frontier migrations and
the associated historical processes culminated in the foundation of Osogbo
settlement on the periphery of major political centers in Yorubaland.

A number of authors have noted the enormous importance of the frontier, as a geopolitical zone at the periphery of metropolises, for understanding the dynamics of regional cultural historical changes.[3] The concern with
frontier processes in anthropological and historical studies has been articulated primarily within the framework of core-periphery relations.[4] The
focus has been on how metropolises with advanced political organizations
and sociocultural infrastructures dominate and influence the cultural-
historical trajectories of their passive peripheries that have lower levels of
sociocultural infrastructure.[5] This conceptual framework is best articulated
for Africa in a seminal essay by Igor Kopytoff titled "The Internal African
Frontier," which focuses above all on (1) the historical processes by which
small-scale polities developed at the geopolitical periphery of one or more

metropolises, and on (2) the process by which new societies and new ethnicities grew out of the new sociopolitical formations created by the frontiersmen.[6] Kopytoff conceptualizes the frontier as "politically open areas nestling between organized societies," with no institutional or undeveloped structures of social organization. This, he argues, makes the frontier ideal as an area "that can offer little political resistance to [the] intrusion" of frontiersmen.[7] As an institutional vacuum, the frontier is conceived as the ultimate area in which the structures of the metropolis are replicated through political conquest, migration, and cultural expansion. This perspective sees the frontier as socially conservative and underdeveloped, and as primarily a recipient of innovations from the metropolis.

The grand design of Kopytoff's frontier process is to lay out a structural framework for the history of population movement in sub-Saharan Africa, based on the intuitive presumption that there is a "fundamental cultural unity" "over the past couple of millennia" in the continent, as a result of overlapping frontier migrations dating back to about 14,000 years ago, and associated with the advent of aqualithic subsistence, pastoralism, agriculture, metallurgy, state formation, and environmental crises.[8] There has been some ambivalence toward Kopytoff's frontier perspective, partly because of the supposed ambiguity of the evidential status of some of his generalizations.[9] The continental scale of the thesis indeed requires some generalizations; however, only diachronic and microscale analysis, like the one being attempted here, can fine-tune these for a better understanding of the historical processes of frontier migrations and social reproduction in Africa.

This essay responds to the following specific characteristics of Kopytoff's frontier thesis:

1. the conceptualization of frontier societies as essentially conservative rather than innovative;

2. the treatment of frontiers as appendages of metropolises, and the implication that local events in the frontier simply mirror the changes within the metropolis; and

3. the emphasis on metropolis-frontier migration, thus excluding the importance and perhaps far more common incidence of intra-frontier (frontier-frontier) migrations in precolonial Africa.

To what extent does the archaeological evidence in Upper Osun support these claims about the internal frontier in Africa? This is the central question that this essay sets out to answer.

Background Information

Three historical processes converged in Upper Osun during the late sixteenth and early seventeenth century. First, the drought episodes of the period created favorable conditions for population movements into Upper Osun, because the area is well watered by the River Osun and its tributaries, and were a haven for the concentration of wild game. Hunters, some of whom were displaced by the drought episodes, began to increase their activities in Upper Osun and eventually became the harbingers of new settlements in the area. Second, the thrust of the new imperial age and the hegemonic political ambitions of Old Oyo and Ilesa, among other states, increased the hegemonic activities in Upper Osun between 1575 and 1700. And third, the economic opportunities and challenges from the Atlantic coast reshuffled the regional routes and directions of commercial networks, favorably placing Upper Osun at the center of regional commerce. With all these parallel but interrelated developments, new frontier communities evolved, as four groups of people converged in the Upper Osun area between ca. 1575 and 1700: drought refugees, hunters, traders, and imperial agents. All of them were fortune seekers. Population and settlement units increased, and Upper Osun became perhaps the most important frontier zone in the Yoruba region during the seventeenth century. Various settlements developed in Upper Osun during the period as a result of these frontier migrations. The focus in this chapter is Osogbo, one of the most successful of all the new communities that developed at this crossroads of internal frontier migrations. I will use mainly archaeological data and secondarily historical ethnography to answer a set of interrelated questions that seek to assess the extent to which Early Osogbo supports Kopytoff's internal African frontier model: what kind of frontier was Osogbo in its seventeenth-century existence? Was Osogbo a cultural backwater depending on the nearby and faraway metropolises for cultural substance, or did it forge its own pathway of self-reproduction? Were its innovations internal to it, or were they due to significant regional influence?

Oral historical trails indicate that present-day Osogbo was not the early site of the town. This is not unusual in the settlement history of most Yoruba towns. The ability to transfer the location of a settlement, a community, a kingdom, or a town from one place to another is an important factor in the survival of most corporate entities and institutions, often spatially manifested as villages, towns, and kingdoms, in the history of Africa.[10] Local historians inform us that the present site of the Osun Sacred Grove was the location of the Early Osogbo settlement during the late sixteenth century and the seventeenth century. The settlement grew to become an important regional market town in the seventeenth century but was abandoned toward the end of that century, with its population resettling at the present-day site of Osogbo about a kilometer to the north. The old settlement site was then converted into a grove for the worship of Osun, goddess of the river that meanders through the grove and serves as patron deity of Osogbo.[11]

Early Osogbo: Archaeology, Settlement Chronology, and Oral Traditions

Archaeological investigations were conducted in 2003 and 2004, focusing on the Osun Grove (see figure 1.2) with a view to identifying the abandoned settlement(s), assessing their chronology with chronometric and artifactual data in relation to the oral traditions, and using the artifact profile to assess the frontier characteristics of Early Osogbo during the seventeenth century. The archaeological investigations involved survey and excavations. The survey shows that an abandoned settlement of about five hectares in size was associated with the grove. A 25m^2 excavation unit was opened at a midden located in the settlement. One of the animal bones collected from the foundation level of the midden (96 cm depth) has yielded a radiocarbon date of 200±70 BP (Beta-197305).[12] The intercept of the radiocarbon age with the calibration curve at 2-sigma (98 percent probability) provides wide ranges of calibrated ages between AD 1520–1590 and ca. AD 1620–1950. This single date range is not by itself useful for understanding the age of the lowermost deposits of the midden. We need to consider the C14 date with reference to the oral traditions, which place the foundation of Early Osogbo in the late sixteenth and early seventeenth centuries. With this information, we can more confidently date the foundation levels of the archaeological deposits, from which the dating sample originated, to somewhere between ca. 1590 and 1620. Apart from the midden, which was 102 cm deep, other occupation deposits of the settlement are shallow, only 20–30 cm deep for the most part. This shows that the occupation of the settlement was of short duration, lasting not more than two to three generations and with no significant demolition and rebuilding of structures at the site. The archaeological deposits broadly agree with the oral traditions that the grove settlement lasted about 150 years.

The chronostratigraphy of the midden offers an insight into the occupational history of the settlement. Remains of large animals, especially the skulls, mandibles, and teeth of wild bovids and wild pigs were found at the lowermost cultural level of the midden, 90–102 cm below the surface. The fact that these remains of exclusively wild fauna were on top of the sterile layer and at the very beginning of the cultural levels indicates that a section of the grove was originally used as a hunting camp where game was butchered and shared among hunters. The occurrence of wild animal remains at the foundation level of the midden agrees with the oral historical information that the grove settlement was founded by two hunters—Laaroye and

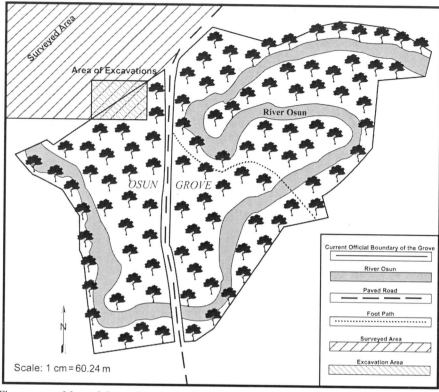

Figure 1.2. Map of Osun Grove. Credit: Akin Ogundiran.

Timehin. Traditions suggest different names for the original villages/towns from which these hunters originally came. Ipole-Omu, Ipole-Ijesa, and Ibokun, all in the Ijesa region of Yorubaland, have been mentioned as the original sources of the frontier immigrants (see figure 1.1). There is more agreement on Ipole-Omu in recent historical traditions. According to some of our sources,[13] Ipole-Omu itself was originally founded by a group of immigrants from Ibokun—a northern Ijesa town—during the sixteenth century. All the variants of the oral traditions agree that the frontiersmen who settled in Osogbo in the late sixteenth century belonged to the Ijesa subgroup of the Yoruba. The traditions also include the following:

1. Laaroye and Timehin were at the head of a party sent from their drought-stricken town to look for a new settlement with a dependable source of water.

2. The two hunters arrived in the present area of the grove in search of game and in search of a new settlement site. In the process of hunting

and trying to set up a new settlement, however, they destroyed the dye-pots of a female forest/river spirit and deity, Osun, who reprimanded the hunters for their carelessness.

3. After the hunters pleaded with the spirit and acknowledged her over-lordship of the area, Osun agreed to help the hunters establish a pros-perous settlement. A partnership was therefore developed between the hunters—the political leaders of the new settlement—and Osun, the goddess and protector of the new settlement.

The historicity of the above mytho-historical narratives can be summed up as follows. Some time in the late sixteenth century, a settlement was estab-lished in the Osun grove by new frontiersmen who themselves were coming from older frontier communities from within the neighboring Ijesa region of Yorubaland. The immigrants included hunters who possibly "discovered" the suitability of the site for both hunting and settlement as a result of the availability of large species of wild game and a dependable source of water. Given the prominence of these hunters in the narratives of origins, and the fact that an elaborate shrine dedicated to them is found in the present town of Osogbo, there are strong indications that the leadership of Early Osogbo was supplied from among these frontier hunter-immigrants. However, the land that the frontiersmen (and, most likely, women) were settling on dur-ing the seventeenth century was not devoid of human population. There was already at least one thriving settlement within the vicinity of the grove; or at the very least there was a hive of human activities, which included dye manufacture and cloth dyeing, on the banks of the Osun River. It is likely that the River Osun not only attracted hunters and new settlers during the seventeenth century, in an era of shortage of water, but that dyers and dye makers also camped on the banks of the river. Dye manufacture and cloth dyeing required an appreciable amount of water, and factors similar to those that encouraged hunters to camp on the banks of River Osun seem also to have attracted dyers to the area.

The traditions suggest that the dyers preceded the frontier-hunters. The clash between the dyers and the Timehin/Laaroye group was not so much due to the fact that the latter were hunters but to the fact that they were also settlers, whose forest-clearing activities and perhaps greater strength, in num-ber and coercive power, threatened the autonomy of the autochthonous dyers and their family members, both male and female. A pact was, however, estab-lished between the new "masculine" frontiersmen and the "feminine" autoch-thons—hunters and dyers respectively, as constructed in the oral traditions. The gender dimensions of the encounter between the two groups, so elabo-rately emphasized in the oral traditions, deserve further investigation.[14]

Different versions of oral traditions suggest that, following the truce between the frontier immigrants and the autochthons, Early Osogbo grew in population and it soon became a popular regional market center. Parts of the praise poem (*oriki*) of Osogbo inform us of the kinds of industries and commodities that Osogbo was famous for:

Osogbo . . . , a refuge town and land of kolanuts
Osogbo the town of dye, dark dyes indeed
A fearless woman who saves her children from great dangers.
The mother of Larooye who came from Ipole to build a house in Osogbo.
Osun because of ornamental brass, has a long neck
Because of ornamental brass, has long arms
She is the owner of *Ogidan* (leopard) who used brass mortar to make medicine
I like to visit Osogbo and Osun grove where they dye cloths
and use a brass mortar to pound.[15]

Kolanuts and dye production have frequently been referred to in the oral traditions as the two dominant commodities that Early Osogbo produced for the regional market. Brass also frequently appears in the oral traditions as the prestigious imported item for which Osogbo and its market were famous. Kolanuts are not generally preserved in archaeological deposits, but the archaeological evidence at the grove reveals indirect evidence of dyeing in Early Osogbo. The sediments that constituted the excavated midden were mainly of ash that most likely came from the intensive burning activities often associated with dye-making, iron-smelting, and glass bead-making activities. Given the paucity of iron manufacturing remains and the frequent mention of dye manufacture as a specialty of Osogbo (*Osogbo ilu aro;* Osogbo, the town of dyers), it is likely that the ash deposits that made up the midden's sediments derived from dye-making activities.

Other than hunting and dyeing, the artifacts that overlaid the earlier game-butchering/sharing camp reflected a more complex everyday life: a wide variety of domestic pottery, fauna remains, clay smoking pipes, iron artifacts, cowries, a brass bangle, and remains of glass beads. This artifact profile reveals that Early Osogbo was connected to wider interaction networks during the seventeenth century, in an era when the directions of regional interactions were undergoing intensive reshuffling and trade routes were also carrying a larger volume and variety of products across Yorubaland.

Early Osogbo in Its Regional Contexts

Ceramics are essential to the archaeological understanding of regional interactions and cultural historical relationships, a point already well illustrated in Yoruba archaeology and in other parts of the world.[16] The domestic pottery in Osogbo is no exception. In terms of forms, decorations (surface patterns), and style of finishing, the ceramic assemblage at Osogbo is distinct from the other known ceramic complexes in Yorubaland, especially the dominant ones—Ife, Oyo, and the coastal (e.g., Badagry) complexes.[17] Bowls, rather than jars, are the signature items distinguishing the ceramic complex at Osogbo from other known sites in Yorubaland (see figure 1.3, figure 1.4). Unlike the signature characteristics of the dominant Ife and Oyo ceramic spheres in the region, the Early Osogbo bowls have minimal decorations. The majority of the serving and cooking bowls are not decorated with patterns such as incisions, roulettes, and stamps, which are characteristic of other known sites in Yorubaland. Most Early Osogbo bowls were, however, highly burnished and covered with a bright red or reddish orange slip. Their durability and functionality were emphasized over the elegance of their surface decorations. The latter are useful for social display, which tends to characterize the bowls of Ile-Ife and Oyo-Ile. In the few instances in which Early Osogbo bowls are decorated, the decorations are mostly placed only on the neck or shoulder. The simplicity of the decoration, I would argue, privileges functionality over social display.

All the bowl forms in Early Osogbo are generically similar to those of the Ife ceramic complex, although these forms bear only very limited surface treatment/decoration patterns of the Ife style. It appears that the Osogbo ceramic assemblage was inspired by the same regional ceramic style that gave birth to the Classical Ife ceramic complex some time between the ninth and eleventh centuries. For this reason, I propose that the Osogbo assemblage was a subcategory of the larger, regional, central Yoruba ceramic sphere from which the Ife ceramic complex developed. In geo-cultural-historical terms, the Osogbo assemblage is not a reflection of the periphery of the Ife ceramic sphere. Rather, it is a close relative of the Ife complex and other complexes in the Ife ceramic sphere, such as those of Owo and Benin.[18] It is not surprising that this is the case: after all, the frontiersmen of Early Osogbo originated from one or more frontiers in the central Yoruba region in which Ile-Ife is located. This view has implications for our understanding of intergroup relations, migrations, and cultural origins in the Upper Osun region and Yorubaland in general.

Archaeological research confirms that hunters were among the founders of Early Osogbo. The material culture that overlay the hunting context was, however, complex. The artifacts reveal the changes taking place in everyday material life from the seventeenth century onward as a result of the connection of Upper Osun to the Atlantic trade. Rather than immersing itself in subsistence farming, Early Osogbo thrived on commerce, and soon became a frontier of traders, potters, bead makers, and dyers. Hunting and agricultural production continued, but these were oriented toward meeting the demands of the sectors of the population engaged in crafts and commerce.

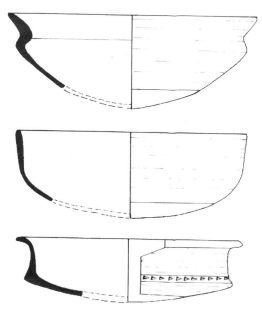

Figure 1.3. Pottery bowls. Credit: Akin Ogundiran.

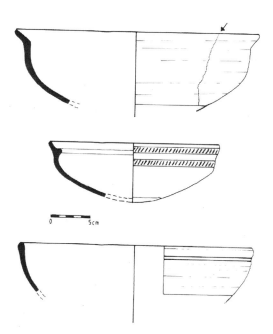

Figure 1.4. Pottery bowls. Credit: Akin Ogundiran.

Contrary to Kopytoff's internal frontier model, in which metropolises sent waves of ambitious and disgruntled immigrants into the frontiers, the Early Osogbo immigrants came mostly from small-scale frontier towns and villages in central Yorubaland. Early Osogbo seems to have been originally peopled by men and women seeking new opportunities in a microenvironment flush with water, game, and arable land. But commerce soon became an important aspect of economic life, attracting young men and women to the settlement with the desire to partake in the Atlantic Age pursuit of commercial wealth. The emergence of Early Osogbo also coincided with the foray of the Ilesa kingdom into Upper Osun in the second half of the sixteenth century. Marauders from Ilesa metropolis are said to have undertaken predatory activities in Upper Osun during this period, kidnapping and selling their victims to Ijebu traders, who in turn delivered their captives to the European slaving factories on the coast. Of course, the victims of these marauding activities were the small communities such as Awo, where the narratives of Ilesa's marauding activities are most elaborate.[19] The political expansion of Ilesa merged with the nascent expansion of the coastal commerce into Upper Osun during the seventeenth century. Consequently, Upper Osun with its weak political structures suffered from Ilesa's marauding activities aimed at furnishing the coast with human cargo. Yet Upper Osun also became an active trading center as the Bight of Benin experienced a major economic boom fueled by Portuguese commercial interests on the coast. It was in these contexts that Early Osogbo was established and developed into a successful frontier market during the seventeenth century, serving both the hinterland and the coastal traders. Ilesa coveted this fledging but promising market town. It is also logical to speculate that the political leaders of Early Osogbo sought the patronage and protection of Ilesa, and were willing to become the clients of a regional hegemonic power. This led to the formal takeover of Osogbo and its transformation into the frontier market of Ilesa during the early seventeenth century.

Thus, Early Osogbo did not start as a frontier town of the Ilesa kingdom. Rather, the kingdom absorbed Early Osogbo after immigrants from the periphery of the Ilesa kingdom had established the settlement, and once the strategic importance of Early Osogbo to the expansionist and hegemonic interest of Ilesa was realized. In fact, Osogbo was only one of the frontier markets that Ilesa controlled during the seventeenth century. Between Osogbo and Akure, for example (see figure 1.1), Ilesa dominated an important trade route that linked the coast with Upper Osun (central Yorubaland) during the seventeenth century.[20] Ilesa did not stop at establishing political control; it also integrated Osogbo into its regional ritual field. During the annual Obokun festival in Ibokun, a satellite Ilesa metropolis, Osogbo was required, and is still required, to send a white ram to Baloro, the priest of Obokun.[21] The Obokun festival celebrates the deified founder of the Ilesa kingdom and its ruling dynasty. By incorporating Early Osogbo into the annual worship of the most revered ancestor of the Ilesa kingdom, the political entrepreneurs in Ilesa succeeded in establishing an ideological basis for their hegemonic control over an important frontier town in the region.

For the same economic reason that Ilesa made incursions into Upper Osun during the second half of the sixteenth century, the expansionist Oyo Empire in the savanna also sought a stake in Upper Osun. Oyo initially sought to achieve its goal by displacing Ilesa's interests in the Upper Osun area through the military conquest of Ilesa. Relying on its cavalry, Oyo attacked Ilesa sometime in the second half of the sixteenth century, but Oyo's cavalry was rebuffed by Ilesa warriors, who had a better mastery of their rain forest environment in hand-to-hand combat and the use of clubs and swords than their savanna foes, who depended on horses ill suited to fighting in wooded areas.[22] The stalemate that followed the Oyo-Ilesa war later resolved in a truce that recognized Ilesa as a junior but independent partner of Oyo in the regional power structure. This perhaps gave Ilesa the opportunity to consolidate its control over Early Osogbo. Oyo, however, pursued alternative strategies in implanting itself in Upper Osun. It established a colony at Ede-Ile during the early seventeenth century, only 15 km southwest of Osogbo. This way, Oyo set itself up as a competing economic and political interest in Upper Osun but avoided a military confrontation with Ilesa. The latter held on to Osogbo as its political and economic frontier, but Oyo's military and colonial presence in Upper Osun drastically curtailed Ilesa's expansionist and predatory activities in the area.

Conclusion

Early Osogbo arose on the fringes of the older patrimonial states (e.g., Ile-Ife and Owu) and the new expansionist, hegemonic states (Ilesa and Oyo). It never achieved metropolitan state status. It was founded on pan-Yoruba institutional structures and political systems, in which a settlement was spatially characterized by a palace and a market site, and a coterie of hierarchical chieftains headed by a ruler. All these represent the "pre-existing conceptions of social order" that the frontiersmen brought with them.[23] But these are panregional Yoruba preconceptions, not limited to the metropolises. Early Osogbo was a product of internal Yoruba frontier migrations, but those migrations were not inspired by and did not come from any of the metropolises. It was only after the economic potential of Early Osogbo had been established that the metropolises of Ilesa and then Oyo began to take a critical interest in the new community and its environs. Early Osogbo did not operate independently of its regional cultural context, but neither was it dependent on borrowing from the metropolises. Rather, Early Osogbo combined the panregional cultural model of society with the new economic opportunities linked to the Atlantic trade in order to create a new identity. Consistent with Kopytoff's conceptualization of the frontier as a historical phenomenon,[24] a new society with its own rituals, deities, and social construction was created in Early Osogbo. While the new hunter-frontiersmen took over the leadership of the new community, they were not able to import the entire religious repertoire from their homeland. The Osun deity, which developed from an aboriginal group living in the area prior to the seventeenth century, became the patron/guardian deity of the fledgling settlement. The fact that the environment was new to the frontiersmen required that the native deity be invoked to guide the newcomers. That deity was Osun. However, the narratives also hint that adopting Osun as the patron/guardian deity of the new settlement offered some resolution to the initial conflicts between the newcomers and the autochthons. This is a common phenomenon in the frontier settlement history of Africa, whereby the autochthons supplied the religious and ritual infrastructure, personnel, and symbols, while the new, demographically and militaristically powerful outsiders assumed political leadership.[25] In a fashion similar to the use of the kinship metaphor between autochthons and latecomers in various political and historical contexts across Africa, Osun provides a seemingly seamless transition and a bridge between the aboriginal group(s) held together by kin relations and the new society in which sociopolitical relations became more contractual, institutionalized, formal, and instrumental.[26] This seamless transition, so eloquently depicted in the oral traditions, and even suggested in the profiles of the archaeological deposits, may be more apparent than real. The scope and forms of internal conflicts, if any, that might have preceded the unification of the aboriginal and the immigrant groups await further analysis of the oral traditions and the uncovering of alternative archaeological profiles.

However, returning to the question that I posed at the beginning of the essay, the archaeological evidence shows that Early Osogbo was not a cultural backwater or a mere distorted replica of a metropolis, drawing its energy from the cultures of the metropolitan centers such as Ile-Ife, Oyo, Ilesa, Owu, or Benin. Rather than looking toward the metropolises for its reproduction, it looked toward the nebulous theater of commerce 200 km away on the Atlantic coast, itself a new commercial frontier in the Yoruba region during the seventeenth century. The material evidence indicates that Early Osogbo was a thriving frontier commercial center, possibly producing glass beads, manufacturing dyestuffs and dyed fabric, and certainly establishing linkages with the regional commercial networks that focused on the Atlantic coast.

Both archaeological and historical evidence encourage us to move beyond a unilinear conceptualization of the frontier. Recent anthropological studies have defined frontiers broadly as places at the edge of cultural and/or political spheres, within which various overlapping political, economic, and cultural contacts take place.[27] These studies conceive the frontier as a porous and fluid spatial entity of unpredictable cultural-historical consequences. Early Osogbo fits this model. The frontiersmen who created Early Osogbo were not from a metropolis and were not originally sponsored by the metropolitan powers of the region. Rather, the opportunistic Ilesa kingdom annexed the settlement only after its commercial potential as a frontier market was realized. Due to this commercial potential, Upper Osun soon became a theater for the contestation of power between the Ilesa and Oyo polities. The study at Osun Grove invites us to pay attention to intrafrontier migrations as a useful means of understanding regional cultural changes and historical dynamics. The archaeological research at Osun Grove is beginning to shed light on how an internal Yoruba frontier was constituted, and it offers insights for revising Kopytoff's paradigmatic cultural-historical framework of the "internal African frontier." The archaeological evidence shows that Early Osogbo was not blindly copying the cultural repertoire of any of the known metropolises of the period in the Yoruba region. In fact, Early Osogbo was innovative as a frontier market town that experimented with new sources and directions of commercial relationships in the region. There is also no indication that Early Osogbo was technologically backward, compared to other known towns in the region. The likely production of glass beads in Early Osogbo would have made it an important economic center in the seventeenth century, given the importance of glass beads in the region's political economy and in the construction of symbols of power and elitism in Yoruba culture. In sum, rather than leading a life reflecting a conservative, rural subsistence economy, Early Osogbo diversified its economy and served as a center for cosmopolitan production and the consumption of goods (including the ideas and symbols associated with those goods) of external origin. Yet, for all its commercial success, Osogbo became stabilized as a small-scale polity within a geographical frontier. Even after the Early Osogbo settlement was abandoned in the eighteenth century, giving way to the new Osogbo town one kilometer away, the latter has retained a frontier mentality based in part on its crossroads location in Yorubaland.[28]

Notes

1.   I. Kopytoff, "The Internal African Frontier: The Making of African Political Culture," in *The African Frontier,* ed. I. Kopytoff, 3–81 (Bloomington: Indiana University Press, 1987).

2.   A. Ogundiran, "Chronology, Material Culture, and Pathways to the Cultural History of Yoruba-Edo Region, Nigeria, 500 b.c.–a.d. 1800," in *Sources and Methods in African History: Spoken, Written, Unearthed,* ed. T. Falola and C. Jennings, 33–79 (Rochester, NY: University of Rochester Press, 2003).

3. M. Breusers, "The Making of History in Colonial Haute Volta: Border Conflicts between Two Moose Chieftaincies," *Journal of African History* 40 (1985): 447–67; S. Green and S. Perlman, eds., *The Archaeology of Frontiers and Boundaries* (New York: Academic Press, 1999).

4. T. Champion, ed. *Center and Periphery: Comparative Studies in Archaeology* (London: Unwin Hyman, 1989); M. Rowlands, M. Larsen, and K. Kristiansen, eds., *Center and Periphery in the Ancient World* (Cambridge, Cambridge University Press, 1987); R. Santley and R. Alexander, "The Political Economy of Core-Periphery Systems," in *Resources, Power, and Interregional Interaction,* ed. E. Schortman and P. Urban, 23–49 (New York: Plenum Press, 1992).

5. C. Chase-Dunn and T. Hall, "Conceptualizing Core/Periphery Hierarchies for Comparative Study," in *Core/Periphery Relations in Precapitalist Worlds,* ed. C. Chase-Dunn and T. Hall, 5–44 (Oxford: Westview Press, 1991); C. Sinopoli, "The Archaeology of Empires," *Annual Review of Anthropology* 23 (1994): 159–80.

6. Kopytoff, "The Internal African Frontier," 8.

7. Ibid., 9–11.

8. For historical landmarks in long-term continental movements and migrations, see A. Stahl, *African Archaeology: A Critical Introduction* (Malden, MA: Blackwell, 2005).

9. J. Guyer, "Wealth in People, Wealth in Things—Introduction," *Journal of African History* 36 (1995): 104; J. Vansina, *Paths in the Rainforest* (Madison: University of Wisconsin Press, 1990), 262.

10. See, for example, A. Ogundiran, *Archaeology and History in Ilare District (Central Yorubaland, Nigeria), 1200–1900,* Cambridge Monograph in African Archaeology 55 (London: Archaeopress, 2002).

11. S. A. Falade, *The Comprehensive History of Osogbo* (Ibadan: Tunji Owolabi Commercial Printers, 2000), 18–19; Osogbo Cultural Heritage Council, *History of Osogbo* (Osogbo: Igbalaye Press, 1994); S. Wenger, *The Sacred Groves of Oshogbo* (Germany: Verlag für Wissenswertes, 1990).

12. The dating was completed in the laboratories of Beta Analysis Inc, Miami.

13. Interviews with the following: Owolabi Ayinde, Baba Isale Olosun, Osun Shrine, Osogbo Palace, August 4, 2004; Oba Oyewale Matanmi III, Ataoja of Osogbo, Osogbo Palace, June 24, 2003; Chief Gabriel Ojo, Ajagunna of Osogbo, Osogbo Palace, June 23, 2003.

14. Interviews with the following: the late Chief Ibilola Omileye, Yeye Osun of Osogbo, Osun Shrine, Osogbo Palace, June 25, 2003 and August 4, 2004; Osundara Efunkemi of Ola, Osun Grove-Osogbo, August 5, 2004.

15. Falade, *Comprehensive History,* 29.

16. A. Ogundiran, "Ceramic Spheres and Historical Process of Regional Networks in Yoruba-Edo Region, Nigeria, A.C. 13th–19th Centuries," *Journal of Field Archaeology* 28, nos. 1 and 2 (2001): 27–43; C. Sinopoli, *Approaches to Archaeological Ceramics* (New York: Plenum Press, 1991).

17. For a summary, see Ogundiran, "Ceramic Spheres." Also see B. Agbaje-Williams, *A Contribution to the Archaeology of Old Oyo* (PhD diss., University of Ibadan, Nigeria, 1983); R. Alabi, *An Environmental Archaeological Study of the Coastal Region of Southwestern Nigeria, with Emphasis on the Badagry Area* (PhD diss., University of Ibadan, Nigeria, 1998); G. Connah, *The Archaeology of Benin: Excavations and Other Researches*

in and around Benin City, Nigeria (Oxford: Clarendon Press, 1975); P. Garlake, "Excavations on the Woye Asiri Family Land in Ife, Nigeria," *West African Journal of Archaeology* 7 (1977): 57–95.

18.   For details, see Ogundiran, *Archaeology and History in Ilare District.*

19.   The Alawo of Awo's Papers, Alawo Palace, Awo, accessed May 6, 2004.

20.   J. Peel, "Inequality and Action: The Forms of Ijesha Social Conflict," *Journal of African Studies* 14, no. 3 (1980): 478–79.

21.   Interviews with the following: Chief Emmanuel Orisasunmi, Ibokun, September 7, 1991; Oba Oyewale Matanmi III, Osogbo, June 24, 2003.

22.   S. Johnson, *The History of the Yorubas* (Lagos, Nigeria: CSS Bookshops, 1921); R. Law, *The Oyo Empire c.1600–c.1836: A West African Imperialism in the Era of the Atlantic Slave Trade* (Oxford: Oxford University Press, 1977), 91.

23.   Kopytoff, "The Internal African Frontier," 33.

24.   Ibid., 25.

25.   See, for example, Vansina, *Paths in the Rainforest.*

26.   Kopytoff, "The Internal African Frontier," 59.

27.   B. Parker, "Toward an Understanding of Borderland Processes," *American Antiquity* 71, no. 1 (2006): 77.

28.   C. Adepegba, ed., *Osogbo: Model of Growing African Towns* (Ibadan, Nigeria: Institute of African Studies, University of Ibadan, 2005).

2

The Root Is Also Here

The Nondiaspora Foundations
of Yoruba Ethnicity

OLATUNJI OJO

This chapter is a contribution to the debate on the origin of pan-Yoruba ethnicity. There are two points of view. One is that an age-old ethnic consciousness existed, deriving from the supranational state (Lucumi or Nago) headquartered at Ile-Ife, from which other communities derived their ancestry, related political systems, and linguistic affinities.[1] A more widespread view counters this, tracing the ethnic consciousness to the era of the Atlantic slave trade, when it developed among enslaved Yoruba speakers in the diaspora. This view contends that, until the nineteenth century, Yorubaland was divided into several ethnicities, which underpinned the massive scale of warfare and enslavement in the region during the century. But as Yoruba-speaking people who were sold into the Atlantic trade distinguished themselves from people of other cultures, there evolved, through a process of ethnogenesis, the Nago and Lucumi nations in the Americas (especially Brazil and Cuba) and the Aku (later the Yoruba) nation in Sierra Leone.[2] That is, enslaved Yoruba speakers, like other migrants, searched for those who shared with them certain familiar identifiers: for example, religion (Orisa and Islam), urbanism, language, political organization, and certain facial markings, and formed a cohesive nationalism or Yoruba ethnic consciousness. Liberated slaves who returned home (and their outgrowth, the Lagos intelligentsia) introduced Yoruba-ness to those left behind. Their efforts were complemented by those of Christian missionaries and British colonialists, who, because this new identity met their idea of "nationhood" and a new sociopolitical order, propagated it.[3]

This chapter seeks to modify the two views. Contrary to the first, the "making" of the Yoruba was less simple or traditional than it was complex and the result of invention. While not underestimating diasporic innovations, this chapter analyzes those nondiaspora factors that shaped the evolution of Yoruba ethnicity. It must be pointed out that the emergence of national and cross-political, otherwise called pan-ethnic, sentiments among speakers of the Yoruba language in the diaspora did not lead to a complete cessation of their previous parochial alliances. In Brazil, for instance, where the Nago uprising of 1835 has been highlighted as one symbol of ethnic consciousness, court records show that pan-Yoruba identity was not wholly accepted by all.

In spite of the outward manifestation of a Yoruba identity, the revolt shows that the identity was not fully entrenched in the mores of the Africans. Sub-ethnic differences in the Yoruba homeland re-echoed in Bahia and manifested themselves in the survival of identities such as those of Oyo, Ijesa, Ketu, Egba, and Ijebu, among others. In Trinidad, the differences reverberated as Yoruba elements determined the ranking of the *orisa* and whether Sango (an Oyo cult) was superior to other *orisas* or not. When Nago slaves in Bahia were asked to define their origins, they used appellatives such as Nago-Ba (Egba), Nago-Jebu (Ijebu), Nago-Gexá (Ijesha), and others. This process is interesting because it shows that these people accepted the Brazilian term Nago while at the same time maintained, through usage within the group, the names they considered more representative of their ethnicity. Antônio, a Nago and one of the court witnesses, identified himself as Egba. While referring to Islamic items found among the objects in the possession of the slaves owned by his master, he stated that he believed they belonged to the slave Joaquim, who was also Nago, because "he cooked lamb, which he killed at Pai Ignácio's home, where other blacks from Joaquim's country got together, since, although they are all Nago, each has his own country." During the trial, Carlos, a Nago-Jebu slave, complained of the air of superiority of literate (Muslim) Nagos "who can read, and who took part in the insurrection [for they] would not shake hands with nor respect outsiders." Apparently, the "outsiders" in this case were the non-Muslims (often non-Oyo), and they were derogatorily called *gafere* (Yoruba: *keferi*, Arabic: *kafir*, i.e., nonbelievers). Another slave, Jose, "claimed to be an Ijebu, that is Nago-Jabu," while an ex-slave, Sabina, referred to a black woman named Edun as a Nago-Ba (Egba). Another Jose, after ten years in Brazil, continued to insist he was from the Egba-Yoruba nation, and yet another Jose identified himself as Oyo. These distinctions (and denials, perhaps), while they were natural in the face of possible long terms of imprisonment and severe punishments for the rebels, did suggest that though Brazilians and non-Yoruba slaves referred to the speakers of the Yoruba language as Nago, the Yoruba viewed the term as being too broadly applied and not a true reflection of their ethnic identity.[4] Such debates and shifts between a strictly communal/political and a more all-embracing ethnic identification among the diaspora Yoruba were also at play in the homeland.

Diasporic and homeland Yoruba faced related challenges—warfare, enslavement, and population displacement, life in refugee camps, and villagers' movement into cities, which necessitated adjustments to existing ideologies. Like those who were sold to the Americas or were resettled in Sierra Leone, slaves kept in the Yoruba homeland, people who fled from slave raiders, and even those whose villages were not attacked also suffered from a range of problems: the possibility of capture, separation from families and communities, loss of loved ones, long journeys to port towns, and a sense of alienation in slaving societies or safe zones, all of which could be compared with the dangers of the Middle Passage across the Atlantic. Both those who were sold away and those who were not had access to common cultural/ethnic resources with which to adapt to the challenges of slavery. These cultural artifacts were simultaneously molded into a meaningful ideology, which became Yoruba ethnicity. With regard to these shared experiences and experiments, the recommendations of returnee slaves were meaningful, marketable, and acceptable in the homeland. Sometimes the new concept of ethnicity was refined and reexported to invigorate a budding Yoruba diaspora culture.[5] Ethnic "molding" involved serious restructuring of existing practices and the invention of traditions to legitimize the new ideology. Due to the availability of source materials for the nineteenth century, and to the fact that most Yoruba slaves were enslaved, exported, and repatriated during the nineteenth century, the two viewpoints on the origin of pan-Yoruba ethnicity have largely revolved around what happened during that century. Hence, I have chosen the same century for the basis of my modification, and I intend to show that the history of the Yoruba region during this time is central to the birth of an ethnic consciousness. The chapter is divided into three sections. The first discusses the political conflicts that engulfed the Yoruba region during the nineteenth century and how these linked ethnic factionalization with slaving operations. The next section assesses the impact of warfare, the most important results of which were population displacement and the conversion of freeborn people to slaves and refugees. The final section examines the resources that were available to forced migrants and the way they wove these resources into unified and transnational cultural symbols.

Frontiers of Slavery: The Political Implosion of Yorubaland

From about the middle of the eighteenth century, the Oyo kingdom, the most powerful Yoruba state and a state that had some political leverage over the Yoruba region, began to suffer from internal decay. The decay stemmed from a series of constitutional crises, provincial revolts, and elite factional fighting. While these points have received extensive scholarly attention,[6] what concerns us here is to analyze the role that slavery played in the collapse of the Oyo kingdom. As a frontier state located in the guinea savanna, Oyo became a trading as well as a producing state, carrying out wholesale trade between its neighbors in the Central Sudan and those located further south, in the forest belt. Especially because Oyo's rise to power coincided with the era of the Atlantic slave trade, the trade in slaves was central to Oyo's strength. Effective participation in the Atlantic trade, however, was dependent on Oyo's ability to raise a strong military force and defeat its forest neighbors. Here, trade with the Central Sudan in horses was also significant. Due to the activities of Oyo's cavalry force, not later than the 1730s, Dahomey conceded to Oyo access to the port of Ouidah. But this was only a temporary victory. Cavalry warfare was less effective in the forest than in the savanna, so it did not take long before Dahomey challenged Oyo's hegemony and forced Oyo to move its trade first to Porto Novo and sometimes to Badagry in the 1750s. By the 1790s, Oyo was in search of a new outlet to the sea beyond the Dahomeyans' reach. Even a though a new port was opened at Lagos, Oyo was too weak to control it. Instead, the major actors were traders from the coastal states of Ijebu, Egba, and Awori. It has been suggested, and rightly, that the loss of control over the slave trade heightened Oyo's internal divisions.[7]

Oyo's crisis accelerated during the nineteenth century with the warring factions calling on outside support, especially from the Sokoto jihadists. Because many of Oyo's slaves were from the Central Sudan, they used the influx of Muslims and Hausa soldiers into Ilorin to escape and blend in with free Hausa. The rise of Ilorin as a sanctuary emboldened not only slaves but also Yoruba Muslims, who seized on the religious fervor of Sokoto to rebel against Oyo authority. From 1817, therefore, the crisis expanded into a jihadist war, and by 1830, the greater part of Old Oyo had been destroyed and some of its territory incorporated into the Sokoto Caliphate. The warfare in Oyo had an adverse impact on commerce and state relations in Yorubaland. Political instability coupled with poor socioeconomic relations between Sokoto and Oyo led to the reorganization of trade routes and the diversion of trade into non-Oyo territories.[8]

The jihad meant that not so many slaves were now coming from the Central Sudan and new slaves had to be sought from within Yorubaland. In essence, demographic movements and the rise of brigandage altered the ethnic composition of Yoruba towns and of the slaves sold from within the region. The emergence of Lagos as West Africa's leading port drew Yorubaland even more intimately into the slave trade. The closeness of Lagos spread the frontiers of slave raiding further into the interior, thereby increasing the level of violence associated with slave recruitment.[9] The simultaneous impact of the jihad and the rise of the port of Lagos is attested in Samuel Johnson's observation that "confiscation and slavery for the slightest offence became matters of daily occurrence."[10]

Warfare and slave raids and the attendant movement of population had far-reaching consequences for the Yoruba region. Refugee movements, provincial uprisings, and Islamic militarism spawned a generation of armed brigands, consisting of Muslim militants, the *jama'a*, and thugs, the *Ògo wẹẹrẹ* (young glories).[11] The collapse of the Old Oyo kingdom accelerated the political crisis in Yorubaland and exposed the intensity of "ethnic" rivalries among Yoruba states and the rate at which one group would recruit slaves from among the others. One result of this was increased military professionalism, which contributed to greater social and economic devastation. As J. F. A. Ajayi has remarked, "bands of immigrants, particularly of the warrior class, began to roam the countryside restlessly, living off the land, intervening in local disputes, acting as mercenaries and sometimes initiating quarrels of their own."[12]

The Yoruba wars, and the general raids for slaves to which they gave rise, added their own element to the character and nature of the slave trade and slaveholding. They intensified the competition for able-bodied men and women and led to economic and political competition. Commercial accumulation later underscored the general social disturbances that characterized eastern Yorubaland in the nineteenth century. Even after the legal abolition of the Atlantic slave trade, the succeeding "legitimate" commerce in nonhuman commodities created an unprecedented demand for land, markets, and labor. Hence, warfare became a political means of coping with new economic demands. Slaves, refugees, and brigands spread the frontiers of political instability, which in turn forced the relocation of trade routes. The pace of political and economic transformation followed the direction of the trade routes, creating new urban centers, political alliances, and conflicts. Refugees followed trade routes to places of safety while soldiers and brigands followed similar routes for raids and kidnapping activities. Pressures on land exerted by incoming refugees and the evolution of a culture of excessive consumption or entrepreneurship of violence by some freebooters began to affect the political and economic lives of host towns. In turn, these problems heightened ethnic divisions and social tension, leading to new demographic shifts and sociopolitical problems.

Ethnic and Demographic Factors in the Yoruba Slave Trade

Slave recruitment during this period was not simply a question of one Yoruba enslaving another. Although people in the Yoruba region spoke mutually intelligible dialects, shared various cultural traits, and had a nostalgic attachment to Ile-Ife, the true picture until about 1890 was that of a region of multiple ethnicities. Hence slaves were recruited from among the Yagba, Owe, Ijumu, Bunu, Oworo, Owo, Akoko, Ekiti, Igbomina, Ijesa, Ife, Ilaje, and Ondo in the east; the Oyo, Owu, Egba, Egbado, Awori, and Ijebu in the center; and the

Sabe, Ketu, Anago, Idaisa, Manigri, Isa, and Ana in the west,[13] with slaves from one district (ethnic group) sold to holders in other districts.[14]

As refugees fled in search of safe havens, they carried with them the spirit of exclusive nationalism. People were classified according to their ethnicities, represented by body scarification (facial markings), religious beliefs, food culture, dialects, and cultural identifiers that distinguished between sexes, age groups, vocations, and residence (metropolitan versus provincial and city versus country). Thus, in explaining the pattern of slave recruitment, a certain Chief Ifabiyi of Egba laid out what amounted to a Yoruba conception of "legal" and "illegal" enslavement. He described the "legally" enslaved as people "bought," "captured in wars," or "received as gifts from friends in far away country." On the contrary, the wrongfully enslaved were "our own people," "waylaid" or "kidnapped" by the "wicked people of our own tribe." In the final analysis, to the Yoruba, slaves were outsiders who belonged to "tribes" other than those of their owners.[15]

By 1826, the larger parts of the Oyo, Owu, and Egba kingdoms were either destroyed or engulfed in conflict. Warfare was contagious. It spread to Egbado in the late 1820s, and eastern Yorubaland and the coastal region in the 1840s. Warfare started with Oyo in the 1770s and persisted in scattered parts of Yorubaland through the 1890s. With frequent fighting, whole communities were scattered within and beyond the territory of modern Yorubaland.[16]

Despite the apparent diversity and even extreme disunity, the effects of the slave trade, warfare, and demographic fluidity produced so complex an ethnic mix that Yoruba ethnic boundaries overlapped in many sectors. These factors complemented the broad linguistic and cultural links that had evolved over centuries. Intermarriage, population mixture, and fellow feeling developed among people from different towns and districts among the Yoruba groups and between them and their non-Yoruba-speaking neighbors. All this intermixture laid the basis for cultural affinity and the formation of supraethnic networks.

In spite of the Yoruba crises, or what some Church Missionary Society (CMS) agents termed the "age of confusion," the refugees were not a randomized lot. Although some fled as individuals, many people moved in groups.[17] All of them "struggled to hold on to what they could of old identities and patterns of living." They carried with them into slavery and refugee camps "the springs of social identity" in their names, praise poems, body marks, diets, dialects, political structure, and religious practices. Wherever people settled, they looked for others who shared or recognized these markers.[18]

After the fall of their towns in the 1820s, refugees from about 153 Egba towns and villages, joined by the remnants of Owu and, in 1862, Ijaye, converged on Abeokuta, as well as on nearby Awori, Ondo, Ife, Ibadan, and Ijebu villages.[19] Rather than melding into a new identity, almost all of the Egba villages were reorganized into separate wards, each under its own chief, and these chiefs were subgrouped under the four most senior chiefs: the Alake, Osile, Agura, and Olowu.

In some instances, refugees settled in hitherto unoccupied territories, by seizure, purchase, or negotiation. Attacks on northern Ekiti and Ookun districts induced a southward movement of population with the result that people who were originally Nupe, Yagba, and Ijumu migrated into Ekiti. For instance, around 1844, the remnants of the Iye population from Yagba moved into Ekiti where they established the town of Ayede.[20] Similarly, Omu, an Ijumu town, and remnants of two Yagba villages moved into an Ekiti forest hitherto used as a hunting ground by Ijelu farmers, who had themselves relocated from Ijumu in the 1810s. Omu and Ijelu, which were separated by a distance of about seventy miles in 1840, were by 1860 separated by less than two miles. In the fall of 1875, Ibadan soldiers mistook the two villages for one.[21] In the same vein, Nupe raids drove occupants of Iyemero, Iporo, Ipere, and Epe villages southward to Ijero-Ekiti, and Iyemero tradition shows that the town was peopled by remnants of the population of twenty-two towns.[22] In Akure district, refugees from Akoko, Ekiti, and Owo joined forces with the people of Ode Oja to form the new town of Ita Ogbolu.

The immigrants into Ekiti also included traders, soldiers, administrators, and their dependents from Benin. These colonists set up farms in the forest straddling the Akure-Idanre-Owo border and occupied what is now called the Ọgbọn Ado (Edo quarter) of Ado-Ekiti. Similarly, refugees and slaves captured by Benin forces from Ado villages were settled at Ikere, where they established Ogotun, Afao, Are, Iluomoba, and Agbado quarters, all named after their previous towns. As late as 1933, Ado emigrants still constituted one-fifth of Ikere's population.[23] The mixture of population in the far northeastern districts of Okun, Akoko, and Owo along the Yoruba, Edo, Nupe, Igbira, and Igala border was more complex. Refugees from neighboring districts moved into this area, formed semiautonomous communities, and retained their languages or dialects, some of which are distinctly Nupe, Igala, Yoruba, or Edo (see table 2.1).[24]

Nearer the coast, the former Idoko, Ifore, and Oka groups were totally assimilated into Ondo and Ijebu; by 1886, the only traces left of them were the rituals associated with Orisa Idoko and the installation of the Ondo king.[25] Although Okeigbo was originally Ondo, by 1860 its inhabitants were predominantly Ife and Owu and settlers from other Yoruba districts.[26] The most devastated area, in terms of population, was the Oyo kingdom. In western Yorubaland, Oyo refugees moved to occupy the central forest region, thereby displacing or settling among the Egba, Ijesa, and Ife, with the result that by 1840, towns such as Osogbo and Igbajo (Ijesa), Ibadan and Ijaye (Egba), and Apomu, Ikire, Ipetumodu, Yakoyo, Modakeke, and other Origbo villages (Ife) had become Oyo towns. Although the Oyo refugees forced out many members of the previous population, many remained behind,

Table 2.1. Ethnic composition of some Yoruba towns

TOWNS/Families	Origin	TOWNS/Families	Origin
LAGOS		IPETU-IJESA	
Oba, Eletu Iwase,		Elebedo	Ileoluji
Asogbon & Eletu		Apare & Odo Ise	Efon-Alaaye
Odibo	Benin	Elekute	Aramoko
Onilegbale	Benin/Ijebu	Ejemu	Benin
Oniru	Keta	Osolo & Ojoko	Idanre
Onisemo	Ilaro	Odole	Aramoko
Modile	Egba	Onikotun	Ogotun
Oluwa	Badagry/Gun		
Onisiwo & Egbe	Aja/Gun	EKITI	
Eletu Ijebu and		Odigbo & Uri of	
Onimole	Ijebu	Igede	Erijiyan
Faji	Mahin	Asawo of Igede	Oye
Olorogun Adodo	Benin/Ijo	Ekerin of Esure	Oyo
		Ubamewa of Igbemo	Ise
IBADAN	Egba, Oyo, Ijebu,	Alakoto of Ode	Ise
	Owu, Ife, Ijesa	Uro of Ode	Ikole
EPE	Ijebu/Awori	Ulisa of Agbado	Ise
		Emure of Agbado	Emure
IGBAJO		Emure of Owo	Emure
Obala OkeOja	Ado-Ekiti	Epinmi & Idogun	
Aworo Ogun & Aro	Ado	of Lasigidi	Akoko/Owo
Obala, Leise,		Isije of Egbe	Ogbagi
Eyesorun	Aramoko	Abon of Igbaraodo	Ilesa
Saloro, Eesawe, & Ese	Ijero	Itaogbolu	Owo/Akoko
Eleyele, Olodu,		Igbogun of Iju	Benin
Obaloja	Ijero	Ogotun of Ikere	Ogotun
Elemikan	Ire	Agbado, Afao, &	
Osunji & Anigbedu	Ido	Igbemo of Ikere	Ado kingdom
Agbore	Okemesi	Idemo of Ado	Akoko/Owo
Lowa Ikan	Owo	Ogbonado of Ado	Benin
Odofin Ikan	Efon	Ikoyi of Ikole	Oyo
Aro Mayan, Kojodun	Nupe	Ijesa-Isu of Ikole	Ijesa
Enuromi & Oloje	Nupe	Ayesan of Ondo	Ijesa
		Egbeoba of Ayede	Ikole
IPETU-IJESA		Ijoka of Akure	Owo
Apoti	Obo-Ekiti	Igiso, Oritagun,	
Ikeji-Ile	Apa-Ekiti	Ijemikin of Akure	Benin
Oke-Owa	Omuo-Ekiti		

Source: Ademola Fasiku, *Igbajo and Its People* (Lagos: Writers' Fraternity, 1995); James Ogun-julugbe, *The History of Ipetu-Ijesa* (Ibadan: University Press, 1993); and David O. Asabia and J. O. Adegbesan, *Idoani Past and Present* (Ibadan: Ibadan: University Press, 1970). Ekiti and Nupe immigrants constitute 17.5 percent of Igbajo's 103 compounds.

and every new town became an amalgam of people from several prewar "ethnicities." Ibadan is a classic example, with its initial population made up of
Oyo, Owu, Egba, Ife, and Ijebu settlers.

Slaves constituted an important category, not just because their stories
were similar to those of their Atlantic counterparts but because they outnum-
bered the free in some communities. Musin near Lagos, according to Sandra Barnes, was populated by a mixture of Awori, Bini, Nupe, Dahomeyan,
and hinterland Yoruba groups,[27] with the last three categories arriving originally as slaves. The populations of Old Oyo, Lagos, Abeokuta, and Ibadan
were ethnically diverse and socially stratified with the quota of slaves (perhaps with some exaggeration) estimated at about 66 percent of the Oyo
population in 1830, 50–90 percent of the Lagos population of 25,000 in
1858, and half of the Ibadan population and about a third of the Abeokuta
population in the mid-nineteenth century.[28] The slave population is also
interesting because Yoruba towns drew their dependent workers from a wide
geographical region: Ibadan from northeastern Yorubaland; Lagos, Ijebu,
and Abeokuta from all over Yorubaland, but also heavily from the Central
Sudan; and Ilorin from northeast Yorubaland and Hausaland. Between 1844
and 1876, Ibadan's raids in northeastern Yorubaland captured thousands
of slaves.[29] Because these were long campaigns, slaves were constantly led
into the city of Ibadan in droves. David Hinderer, a CMS agent, wrote that
Ibadan's "population [about 100,000] had been augmented . . . by immigrants from the provinces [and] by the thousands of slaves brought in annually."[30] The demographic preponderance of eastern Yoruba slaves persisted
into the 1870s. On his visit to the city of Ibadan in 1877, Rev. James Johnson
noted the prevalence of Ijesa slaves and their dialect, and the popularity of
the Ijesa dialect even among many free citizens.[31] It is no wonder that most
Ibadan slaves soon assumed an Ijesa identity. Isaac Akinyele, the local historian of Ibadan, confirmed Johnson's observation on Ijesa slaves and the Ijesa
dialect. In Akinyele's words, the Ijesa phrase "Oyo kabi onia" became the
password among the slaves of Ibadan in the nineteenth century, "and it was
not uncommon for a free born to mingle with the slaves of a powerful chief
in order to share of the great privilege that was theirs."[32]

Orisa and the Making of Yoruba Ethnicity

The most significant symbol of the Yoruba diaspora is religion—Santeria
(Cuba), Candomble (Brazil), Sango or Orisa (Trinidad), and Egungun
(Sierra Leone). But this had its parallels, even antecedents, in the home-
land. A byproduct of population networking was the evolution of a "unified"
Yoruba Orisa religion. Prior to and alongside Christianity, which is well doc-
umented as having facilitated Yoruba nationalism in the diaspora, people in

the homeland were also united through pan-ethnic religious fraternities and cults such as Oro, Ifa, Egungun, and Ogboni. These cults had members from all over Yorubaland, whose allegiance to each other transcended ethnic and political hostilities. Immigrants came with their *orisa,* thereby expanding the religious repertoire of host societies.

Prior to 1800, elements of Orisa religion could be geographically located as follows: Ogboni/Osugbo and Oro (Egba and Ijebu), Ebora and Imole (northeast area), and Sango and Egungun (Oyo). As late as August 1859, when Charles Gollmer of the CMS visited Ketu, he did not see any sign of the Ogboni or Oro cults, which were very powerful in Egba.[33] In 1877, Charles Phillips noted Ondo's first contact with the Sango cult. But this regional compartmentalization or localization of Orisa worship ended with the mass disruption and admixture of Yoruba population that led to religious realignments and spiritual reformation. In a persuasive article, Peter Morton-Williams opines that Oro and Ogboni were introduced into New Oyo from the south during the nineteenth century. He bases his conclusion on a close examination of the political roles of cult organizations among the Egba and Oyo-Yoruba. In Oyo, Morton-Williams discovered, the *alafin* did not control the Oro organization, and the cult also lacked the political role it had in Egba and Ijebu.[34] We might suggest that the relative newness of the Oro cult in Oyo was responsible for its location outside the Oyo power calculus.

The Ogboni or Osugbo cults[35] originated as the meeting points for the Egba and Ijebu aristocracy, and in so doing served political and economic purposes. The southward movement of northern Yoruba population into the forest region that was the original homeland of the Egba and Ijebu resulted in the absorption of the immigrants into the Ogboni and Osugbo cults. Moreover, because members of the Ogboni had a mastery of the religious rituals of the forest region, the immigrants, even when they controlled political positions, allowed the "aborigines" to retain their religious posts. The same phenomenon is demonstrated in the early years of Ibadan when Oyo settlers overpowered and expelled many Ijebu, Ife, and Egba residents. Yet they yielded religious functions to an Ife chief, Labosinde, whose family has ever since held the Oluwo title. By the 1870s, Ogboni had spread to eastern Yorubaland through returnee ex-slaves and military apprentices. Among these were leading soldiers like Ogedengbe (Ilesa), Fabunmi (Okemesi), Aduloju (Ado-Ekiti), Fajembola Olugbosun (Egosi), and Lisa Edun (Ondo), whose membership of Ogboni facilitated the signing of nonaggression pacts and ensured martial solidarity between Ibadan chiefs and some of these warlords. This in turn, it is speculated, is responsible for Ogedengbe and Aduloju's initial reluctance to join the anti-Ibadan war in 1878. In essence, Ogboni appears to have complemented the Yoruba belief that any war chief who ordered the death of his equal or a king would suffer a similar fate at an early date.[36]

If Ogboni and Oro spread northward and eastward, the Egungun and Sango cults, like Islam, moved in the opposite direction. Egungun's *oriki* locates its origin around the Yoruba-Borgu border, thus suggesting that its homeland was Nupe, from which it spread to Yorubaland during the sixteenth century when some members of the Oyo elite lived in exile at Igboho.[37] Prior to 1817, the Oyo population lived closer to the Niger than now, and even after they left the area, the Niger/northern factor manifested itself in various ways. For instance, in 1857 near Jebba, a Yoruba-speaking priest was called to appease the local Ketsa deity, which was believed to be responsible for a shipwreck, even though Yoruba was no longer the language of the region.[38] Over the years, however, among the Oyo, Egungun became the ancestral spirit through which the dead communicated with the living. As Oyo people pushed into the southern forests, they carried with them their Egungun. From Oyo, Egungun spread to Igbomina—tradition says it extended to Omu Aran to support an unpopular monarch.[39] Oyo people also took Egungun to Egbado, Egba, Ijebu, Awori, and Dahomey.[40] Akinyele traces the spread of Egungun to Remo in the military activities of Oluyole of Ibadan (ca. 1833–47), but Oyin Ogunba thinks Remo received Egungun from Egba while Ijebu Igbo received it from Ibadan.[41]

There were times when Egungun spread through other means than Oyo immigrants or people influenced by them. In Lagos for instance, Egungun seems to have appeared with waves of immigrants into the town. In the 1790s, John Adams noted visitations of Egungun (Adam's devil) from across the lagoon, thereby implying the cult's existence on the Lagos (Awori) mainland.[42] However, John Losi, a local historian, traced the origin of Egungun to the first decade of the nineteenth century, when the children of the reigning king, Adele, introduced the cult into the palace. The fact that Nupe slaves and Islam also became notable aspects of Lagos life during this time could have meant that Central Sudanese elements were the leading spirits behind Lagos Egungun. Interestingly, Adele is noted as being a leading slave trader who had a number of Nupe slaves in his service.[43] A third tradition points to Fon/Gun culture in the popularization of Egungun in Lagos. The Fon influence is also linked to Adele, who in earlier years had lived in exile in Badagry, during which time he interacted extensively with Porto Novo and Ouidah, where Egungun, especially the Zangbeto, was central to royal control. This tradition is corroborated by a British trader who reported the presence of Mahi (Dahomeyan) traders and slaves in Lagos during the first decade of the nineteenth century.[44] This meant that captives taken from the Dahomeyan hinterland were sent first to Porto Novo for onward transmission to Lagos, where many were retained locally and others sold into the Atlantic trade, probably as "Nago" slaves. Thus, the recourse to Egungun (whether from Dahomey or Nupe), Islam, and slaves (all foreign elements) was representative not only of Adele's tumultuous reign as king but of the heterogeneity of post-1800 Lagos. During the nineteenth century, Ibadan, Ilorin, and Nupe expansion, through soldiers and returning captives, spread Egungun Alaso, as opposed to the preexisting Egungun Elewe, to Ife, Ijesa, and Ekiti. As rich chieftains imported textiles from Oyo, Nupe, and Ilorin and across the Atlantic, Egungun that had textile masks (Egungun Alaso) became more powerful and prestigious than those with masks of grass or leaves (Egungun Elewe). In effect, by the middle of the nineteenth century, Yorubaland had evolved into a unified Orisa world. So while previous scholars have emphasized the importance of Islam and Christianity, one must add "Orisa" as the third religion that created the Yoruba.

Religious restructuring and the survival of new cults were predicated on the availability of ritual guides—priests. One solution to the problem of availability was the expansion of priestly offices through which culture entrepreneurs were appointed to oversee new cults. Through this means, strangers, including slaves, were admitted into the ritual assemblage of host societies. Yoruba traditions show how expert strangers introduced new beliefs and served as pioneer priests in new religious houses. In the eighteenth century, Oyo authorities sent, in addition to the *ilari* (political agents), the *alágbàà* (Egungun priests) and *oje* (Egungun worshippers) to its provinces to help organize the Egungun cult. In Ondo, slaves and ex-slaves were pioneer converts to Islam and a few *orisa* cults. In 1877, Phillips described this phase:

> Ondos are purely heathens . . . . [I h]ave only seen five resident Mohammedans in the whole country since I came [in 1877] . . . . Ondos have many idols in common with other Yoruba tribes e.g. Ifa, Ogun, Sango. It is remarkable that the priests of those idols are chiefly slaves from the interior countries [*sic*].[45]

In the absence of any known cases of cult slavery in Ondo, Phillips' statement should be taken as reflecting either the newness of some of the *orisa* or the expertise of slave-priests, which was great enough to displace existing priests.

The Yorubanization of *orisa* worship necessitated adjustments to existing rituals, the religious calendar, and the ranking of the gods. Information on Ayede-Ekiti illustrates some adaptations that Yoruba people made to meet the realities of politico-religious shifts. Soon after Esubiyi emerged as Ayede's chief around 1850, he began a process of power concentration and weakening of the prior Owa dynasty. By allying himself with Ibadan warlords, he secured support against Ilorin and Nupe, staved off Ibadan raids, and as Ibadan's agent in the Niger district was given a free hand in the region. Friendship with Ibadan was legitimized by Esubiyi's conversion from the local Yagba-based Orisa Oju'na to his patron Oluyole's Oyo-based Yemoja cult. In addition to being a deft move to suppress cults that were associated with the previous dynasty,[46] the elevation of Yemoja to the status of royal cult ritually bonded Ibadan (Oyo) and Ayede (Yagba/Ekiti). Lisa

Edun Kolidoye's contacts with Ibadan leaders resulted in the introduction of a few neo-Oyo practices into Ondo. These involved, for example, three Muslim slaves who pioneered Islam in Ondo.[47] The earliest recorded Sango practices in Ondo also revolved around the Lisa's household. In the late 1870s, signs of religious tension were apparent in the town, as residents, especially priests of local cults, blamed Sango worshippers for the outbreak and spread of smallpox and for defrauding those afflicted with the disease.[48] Consequently, there was an uproar, in which the expulsion of Sango adherents was demanded. According to an eyewitness,

> Ondo head priests of different fetishes assembled at the market with loads of charms to denounce any Ondo who would hereafter worship Sango. Authorities thought this would check the smallpox epidemic. The epidemic did not stop for weeks and Sango devotees gathered at Lisa's house to sing, dance and drum in the town in triumph.[49]

The choice of the Lisa's house for Sango's "dance" most probably represented the cult's quest for local support. This would seem to have succeeded, for barely three months after the anti-Sango protest, Ondo authorities made a sacrifice to Sango, hoping it would end the epidemic.[50] The activities of religious entrepreneurs contributed to the birth of a pan-Yoruba Orisa identity.

At other times the promotion of an *orisa* was a response to the realities of demographic shifts. Certain cults, having lost most of their followers or priests, went into oblivion or lost their status and privileges. In other cases, new *orisa* had more adherents and, when these included powerful chiefs, could displace existing ones. Okeigbo, originally an Ondo farmstead, had by the 1860s been transformed into a heterogeneous town composed largely of Ife, Oyo, and Owu immigrants. Consequently Oranyan and Anlugbua, introduced by Ife and Owu settlers respectively, became the leading *orisa*.[51]

Women, Marriage, and Yoruba Creolization

On its own, the availability of culture entrepreneurs was not enough to ensure religious survival. Survival also required the presence of prospective converts. Here, interethnic marriages, particularly involving slave wives, were central to the evolution of the Yoruba ethnic identity. Unlike Christianity and Islam, which reserved very little space for women in their sacraments, and virtually no role in leadership positions, the Orisa religion and its spread depended strongly on the involvement of female worshippers. Women were priestesses, temple cleaners, dancers, praise singers, cooks, and the wives and mothers of current and future converts. Indeed, it might not be out of place to suggest that religious adherence was deeper among Yoruba women than among men during the nineteenth century. A study of Christian missionary papers, the richest source on the Orisa religion, reveals a record of numerous female Orisa adherents, sometimes carrying multiple *orisa* symbols on their bodies. One of the earliest references in the literature to female adherents concerns the marriage in the sixteenth or seventeenth century between Alafin Oluaso of Oyo and Arugba Ifa (carrier of Ifa's calabash), an Awori woman. When the couple's son became the *alafin*, Arugba introduced Ifa and related cult objects (Aje, Opon, Ajere, Osun, Elegbara, and Iroke) into Oyo.[52] In addition, after nearly twenty-five years in Sierra Leone, William Moore Odusina returned to Abeokuta in 1851 and was reunited with his relatives, from whom he had been separated when their town, Isaga, fell in 1824.[53] Moore's mother, who had been enslaved at the fall of Isaga, was soon afterward ransomed by her brother and uncle and taken to Oba, a neighboring village. Around 1826, Oba fell and she was recaptured and sold to an Ijebu woman. As her mistress was wicked, she fled, and through the help of a guide left Ijebu for an Egba town. Here, however, her guide proved treacherous and wanted to sell her, so she appealed to local chiefs for protection. Afraid to commit herself to another guide, and not daring to leave the town alone, she remained there for many years. At length this town too was destroyed, and she was captured for the third time, brought back to Ijebu Ode, and sold to a man. After a while, her former mistress found her, and begged to buy her former slave again, intending to sacrifice her. The master refused. When he died, Moore's mother, together with the rest of his property, was shared among his relatives. Because her primary inheritor lived away from home, she came under the immediate supervision of a man who confined her and two other slaves in a house, with the idea of sacrificing them at a funeral.[54] In confinement she faced two possibilities. She could either be sacrificed or be dedicated to clean the shrine of an *orisa*.[55] But she was lucky; one of the Ijebu whose children she had catered for, seeing the danger she was in, smuggled her to an Abeokuta village to join her primary inheritor. Having gone through these ordeals, which spanned a quarter of a century, not to mention long periods of illness, she believed she owed her safety to her *orisa*. It does appear that during her ordeal, she had collected several *orisa;* thus it was no surprise that while going to meet her son around 1852, she traveled with "a bag of idols."[56]

The patronage of multiple *orisa* was replicated in various large households. As slave women were incorporated, through marriage, into the community and gave birth to children, a gradual creolization of Yoruba society evolved. This shift or transformation did not take place at the same speed in every case. The households of soldiers and chiefs, with their multitudes of people, changed faster than others. On a visit to the chief of Igbotako, an Ikale town, in the early 1930s, Edward Ward, a Catholic priest, met "a number of aged Ondo women" who had been captured as "part of the spoils of war of an inter-tribal war of the past." When he asked them if they desired to return to Ondo, one of them replied, "*Me fe lo pada si Ondo mo. Igbotako ni ile me nissiyi* [*sic*]—I do not want to return to Ondo. Igbotako is my home now." Soon after this exchange, Ward also learnt from a priest in the Ondo church that a good many Ikale women who had been taken in wars lived in Ondo.[57]

Interethnic marriages had a long precolonial history. The history of Samuel Crowther, the celebrated Yoruba slave turned CMS priest and cultural nationalist, shows that on his father's side, he claimed descent from "Ketu"; his grandfather, *bale* of Awaye-Petu, had migrated into Osogun during the eighteenth century.[58] His mother, Afala, had more distinguished roots, being descended from Alafin Abiodun (1770–89), the last great ruler at Old Oyo.[59] By Yoruba custom, Crowther should have been ethnically "Ketu" but in 1837, at the age of thirty-one, he described himself as from the "Eyo (Oyo) country."[60]

Other examples of interethnic marriages abound; their products often utilized their multiple roots. Notable products of interethnic marriages included Lagos kings: Osinlokun (who had an Ijebu mother), Akintoye (with an Owu mother) and Kosoko (with a Mahin mother). Alliances with the mothers' towns were useful as these chiefs fought to secure themselves in power. They regularly called on their mothers' "kin" for support or used their mothers' towns as sanctuaries.[61]

Interethnic or slave marriages appear to have developed in military towns more frequently than in other places. Because of its military achievements, Ibadan attracted aspiring soldiers, many of whom were young, single men. From Ibadan's early years, slaves of both sexes were acquired from such political units as Egba and Owu. Though we do not have statistical evidence, sources indicate that Ibadan soldiers were particularly interested in capturing female slaves for the purpose of marriage. Before 1840, the new colonists at Ibadan took many Egba female captives as wives. Such women became the mothers of the first generation of Ibadan-born children.[62] Indeed, by the third quarter of the nineteenth century, the practice of soldiers going to war to capture female slaves for the purpose of marriage had developed to a remarkable extent. According to Johnson, the great men of Ibadan added the fair young women captives to their harems while the young men saved themselves the expenses of a dowry by making wives of any woman that came into their hands.[63] The importance of female slaves becomes even clearer when we consider the frequency with which Ibadan chiefs fought to keep their women. For example, in 1893, the Ibadan authorities forwarded a petition to Governor George Denton of Lagos objecting to a resident European officer. A portion of the petition reads: "we fear our wives will be taken by the soldiers which will be a source of great offence to us."[64] It may be that female captives were more likely to be retained (as wives) while the men were more easily sold off.

In addition to integrating captive women, some people deployed aesthetics to alter ethnic identification. In Yorubaland, body (especially facial) scarification was related to social status and citizenship. Body scarification reflected memories that had to be repressed or concealed because of their violent or controversial implications. An 1898 court case from Ondo confirmed this. On March 18, Okolu of Ijesa accused Chief Otunba of Italemo ward of seizing his sister, Osun, and her daughter in 1894. Both mother and child had managed to escape from captivity in Ikale in 1895 but were recaptured by the accused. As a form of forcible integration of slaves, Otunba made Osun a wife, but rather than treating her as such, he forced her to work daily on his farm. Additionally, the accused tried to conceal the identity of Osun's daughter by tattooing Ondo marks on her face, thereby imposing a major feature of Ondo ethnic identification.[65] Even when there is inadequate information about how many children were assimilated by means of scarification, the evidence suggests that it was a widespread practice. In 1878 and 1880, James Johnson, himself a product of a bi-ethnic marriage (he had Ijebu and Ijesa parents), remarked that it was a "common practice among Oyo and Egba widows to buy slave children on whom they imposed their ethnic marks."[66] Marking such children was carried out to incorporate them into the adopting family/community/ethnicity. Although they were slaves, such children occupied positions that were higher than those of other slaves. They were classified as *eru ibile* (home-born slaves), and could hold family land in their own right. Other slaves depended on their owners.[67] Ondo sources reveal the prevalence of slave wives, and show that by the 1930s, children from dual or multiple backgrounds, including second and later generation slaves, came to dominate the town's administration. An official wrote: "probably at least half of the prominent citizens of Ondo . . . are descendants of slaves. Many have titles. The president of Onisere native court is the son of a slave."[68] A notable example of multiple backgrounds is that of Folayegbe Akintunde-Ighodalo, born in 1924. Her paternal grandfather, Makinde, had settled in Ife territory after the destruction of Old Oyo in the 1820s. Around 1850, he joined Derin Ologbenla's army and settled in the Odo Bada ward of Okeigbo. At roughly the same time, Akinlalu, who would become his father-in-law, had also fled, in his case from Ogbomoso to Ibadan, settling in Oje quarter. As the Yoruba wars continued, some people from Oje migrated to Okeigbo, perhaps initially as soldiers in the powerful Ibadan army. Eventually they settled at Ita Otun ward of Okeigbo. One of them was probably Akinlalu, whose daughter married Makinde. Their son, Akintunde Olojomo, who became Folayegbe's father, was born around 1885. Folayegbe's mother, Sarah Ogunkemi, was the daughter of Adelekun Ajero of the Ile Balagbe household in Ita Orisa ward, Okeigbo, whose father was Owa Aponlese of Ilesa. Sarah's mother, Adetola, was one of the elder daughters of Ologbenla through his wife Safunke, herself the daughter of the Olu-koro of Ikoro-Ekiti. From these two lineages we see one that derives from what was probably a military/refugee family, while the other originated from Ekiti and Ijesa women who were captured in the wars of the 1850s. These multiple ethnic backgrounds were reflected in religious and lin-guistic practices associated with the upbringing of Folayegbe and her par-ents. For example, while a Muslim uncle, Belo Aromoye, raised Olojomo, Folayegbe's mother frequently mocked her husband with songs in the Ekiti dialect. So during my interview with Folayegbe Akintunde-Ighodalo, when I asked her about her ethnic background, she responded: "You want to know if I am an Ondo or not . . . . I do not know where my Ondo starts or where my Ekiti, Oyo, or Ife stops. That is why I am the Wabodu of Ile-Ife and the Iyalode of Okeigbo."[69]

Harmonizing/Syncretizing Yoruba Historical Narratives

The reconfiguration of Yoruba society was incomplete until it was his-torically rationalized and legitimized. Thus, historical narrative (*itan*) among the Yoruba, Apter argues, follows a discursive strategy. It traces the multiple explanations for relocations or migrations: wars, quests for resources, epidemics, and family and communal disputes. In the discur-sive realm, narratives resituated these relocations within a "unifying" net-work of "mythos-history."[70] The narratives reformulated Yoruba historical genealogies to accommodate multiple traditions and new realities. Such a process seeks to include new members and their culture, and reorder the society into a meaningful and easy-to-explain schema. By proposing a community formed out of many, *itan* works on producing local as well as global nationalisms.[71]

A pointer to a sense of ethnic nationalism in the *itan* is the widespread tradition of Yoruba origin in Ile-Ife or the geographical east. The idea of common descent from Ife apparently preceded the nineteenth-century dispersal of the Yoruba. In 1812, Sultan Bello of Sokoto, drawing from Islamic traditions, located the Yoruba "eastern homeland" in Arabia, some-times Iraq.[72] In Oyo, however, the east was Ile-Ife, "where their ancestors came from."[73] Although, Ile-Ife was also said to be the "home of man-kind—white and black," there is no doubt that Yorubaland was the central focus of humanity for Oyo—just as Israel was the focus of Jewish biblical tradition. This was made clear in 1825, when Alafin Majotu described Oyo, Ijebu, Benin, and Ketu as "brothers who descended from the same father, Nupe," and in 1830 as "the four pillars of the world."[74] The term "brother" (Yoruba: *arakunrin, ebi*) and the phrase, "four pillars of the world" (*igun [opo] merin ti o so ile aye ro;* the four corners [pillars] that hold the world together) are significant because they suggest a sense of affinity and group awareness among people living within the "walls." Moreover, the fact that during the time in question (the 1820s), Oyo, Benin, Ijebu, and Ketu controlled the northern, eastern, southern, and western extremities of the Yoruba-speaking region, and Majotu's location of Borgu, Dahomey, and Nupe, despite their various links with Oyo, beyond the "four pillars" lead one to assume that the people of Oyo knew that the "brothers" had more in common with each other than with their neighbors to the north and west. Although the origins of Bello's and Majotu's stories/traditions are not known, so that it is unclear whether one influenced the other, nevertheless, it is evident that the name "Yoruba," by which Oyo and related language speakers were known, derived from the Central Sudan. How then do we explain its acceptability among the people that were later called "Yoruba"? Did the Yoruba *ulama,* with allies in the Muslim world, push this project? Sadly, the writings of the early Yoruba *ulama* have not survived, but it would appear that they sold the term "Yoruba" to Sierra Leonians and made it preferable to the British/CMS "Aku" or "Eyo."[75]

A more important point is that this Yoruba tradition of a common origin preceded the diasporic pan-Yoruba consciousness and therefore developed independently of it. It was a unity that originated in Africa and was then taken away into the diaspora, where, aided by the European notion of a territorial and linguistic nation, it developed into full maturity. Ife-centric traditions were regurgitated from various points of view by Yoruba exiles. Samuel Crowther, writing in the 1840s, and traditions collected at Ibadan, Ile-Ife, Modakeke, Oyo, Okeigbo, and Ijebu at various times between 1851 and 1886 agreed to the brotherhood (*ebi*) of Yoruba kings—their descent from a single father, Okanbi or Oduduwa.[76] On June 4, 1851, a few months after he settled in Ibadan, David Hinderer, the first European in the town, wrote in his diary:

> three days journey east from here [Ibadan] is the large and famous town of Ife . . . famous as being the seat of idolatry, all the multiple idols of this part of the country are said to emanate from the town . . . and all people of this country and even whitemen spring from the town.[77]

Other traditions describe Ife as the "cradle of the race," the "home of ancestral gods," the "power from which they inherit the spirit of war and war banner," the "father of all our kings," and the "conservators of the world."[78] Put together, these epithets could be said to have drawn upon an older one, which in itself came out of the harmonization of a sequence/series of imagined or real historical events. In particular, traditions of Ile-Ife ancestry were recorded three or four centuries after Ife had lost its political power. This seems to suggest a long tradition of ethnic/cultural affinities among those who look to the city for relevance. During the nineteenth century, imagination was turned into reality.

Transatlantic Contributions to the Evolution of Yoruba Ethnicity

If Yoruba ethnic consciousness was developing, though haphazardly and slowly, in the Yoruba homeland, the return of liberated slaves of Yoruba origin from Sierra Leone and the Americas, starting with the expulsion of Nago and Muslim freedmen from Bahia after 1835, took the evolution and maturing of this identity to new heights. Even though we have shown above that the Yoruba diaspora community was not unaffected by communal divisions back at home, nonetheless, it was relatively detached from the intractable wars raging in the homeland for most of the century. In particular, except for the Egba, whose new home at Abeokuta near the Atlantic coast enabled their returnees to travel home, most other returnees from inland districts settled in Lagos, barred by insecurity and fear of reenslavement from heading to their old homes in the hinterland. This fear would account for the large numbers of Brazilian-Yorubas or Aguda in the modern Republics of Togo and Benin and of the Oyo, Ijesa, and Ekiti in Lagos.[79]

Another opportunity for the concretization of Yoruba ethnicity in Lagos was the British takeover of the port town in 1851. From this time onward, Lagos became a sort of a "no-man's-land," with the new British administrators depending heavily on the returnees for labor and services needed by the British in their effort to penetrate the Yoruba, later Nigerian, hinterland. These returnees, who later formed the nucleus of the Nigerian educated class or "new elite," seized upon their association with the government to further advocate a national (Yoruba) identity. Indeed, when Yorubaland was integrated into the new state of Nigeria in 1900, and there was increasing competition for government positions and commerce with non-Yoruba elements, the propagation of Yoruba identity became inseparable from the very survival of the Lagos-Yoruba new elite.[80] As Robin Law and Karin Barber have demonstrated clearly, these elite members were the pioneers of Christianity, a new religion independent of the sociocultural restrictions of the previous era. From the Christian churches also came the first generation of teachers and school pupils who were trained to be national heroes—writers and students of "national histories," and a national (Yoruba) language. The translation of the English Bible into Yoruba (actually into Oyo/Egba dialects) and the teaching of this language in schools furthered the development of a Yoruba identity. In effect, what emerged in Lagos was a pan-Yoruba identity stronger than anything that existed either in the diaspora or in the hinterland.[81] Interestingly, several of the traditions upon which the "national histories" were based were collected from local historians, usually elders who had not crossed the Atlantic. The elders confessed to transcommunal bonds such as military alliances, myths of common origin, and bonds facilitated by ritual associations.[82] By the 1920s, not so many educated or noneducated members of the elite would dispute the "fa(mo)(bro)therhood" of Ile-Ife in relation to other Yoruba districts.

Another contribution of the new elite group was their role in ending the century-long Yoruba wars. St Paul's Church, Breadfruit, Lagos, the biggest Anglican congregation in Nigeria (then and now) was the forum for Yoruba nationalist discussions throughout the second half of the nineteenth century. It was here that the Ijesa Association, composed of Ijesa emigrants from Sierra Leone and the Americas and those who, although captured and sold into slavery were not exported out of Lagos, Ijebu, or Abeokuta, was formed in 1852. However, the association in alliance with Ekiti citizens of similar backgrounds became transformed into the Ekitiparapo society around 1876, as a platform for an Ekiti/Ijesha uprising against their Ibadan (Oyo) overlord.[83] Thus, between 1852 and 1876, this association forged an alliance that transcended the hostilities between Ekiti and Ijesa people in the hinterland. Also, members of this association reached out to their non-Oyo counterparts in Lagos to forge an anti-Ibadan (Oyo) coalition that oversaw the prosecution of the Kiriji war, 1878–93, while at the same time talking with the Oyo to work out a possible resolution of the conflict.[84] What could be adduced from the evolution of the Lagos Yoruba was an ethnogenetic process in which liberated slaves of Yoruba origin pursued parochial interests and at the same time gradually came together for broader, "national" (pan-Yoruba) interests. These moves helped to persuade the combatants in the interior to give up their differences and work more on issues and ideas that bound them to people beyond their immediate political affiliation. Here one could invoke Sandra Barnes and Robin Law's findings on the religious dynamics of Lagos and Ouidah, respectively. They opined that cultural heterogeneity should not be taken to imply that foreigners were not assimilated into host societies. Though the perpetuation of ethnically specific ancestral cults served in various ways to maintain a notion of cultural diversity, to the extent that these cults involved public displays and popular participation, their operation also served to promote feelings of homogeneity.[85] It could thus be argued that by around 1900 (and indeed today), while membership of Oyo or Ekiti or other subgroups was not synonymous with acceptance of a Yoruba identity, membership of any of these subgroups was not incompatible with belonging to the Yoruba nation.

Conclusion

If diasporic Yoruba resorted to their "national spirit" as a "refuge" from slavery, what did those in the homeland do? Put differently, why were the latter receptive to an "imported" ethnic ideology? Population displacement forced Yoruba speakers, regardless of social status and residence, to adjust to new circumstances, fall back upon familiar practices, and borrow from neighbors toward meeting new realities. We saw this with the fashioning of new political systems and religious rituals, the emergence of multiethnic cities and kingdoms, and the diffusion of refugee and slave cultures beyond their home countries. The spread of Yoruba "ethnic" consciousness received a boost with the repatriation of ex-slaves. As in the homeland, the diasporic slaves were also initially split along pre-Yoruba ethnic lines. With time, however, they came together, partly as a counterpoise to other, non-Yoruba-speaking groups and as a survival mechanism in the life of bondage. Thus, we can argue that a complex web of cultural intermixture and wide-ranging social and ethnic relationships was being woven by events that took place in the Yoruba country at the same time as the diasporic Yoruba were active. Indeed, while Samuel Crowther and other CMS missionaries were writing about "Yoruba" history, the region was slowly evolving the potential for some semblance of unity and ideological communication that would be both meaningful and effective. In other words, some of the declarations by Crowther and other returnees could be understood and accepted by a broad spectrum of the peoples in the region because the new ideology drew upon certain existing and commonly shared beliefs there. These shared beliefs were fed into Yoruba consciousness in Lagos, the hinterland, and the diaspora to soften whatever historical misgivings were at work.

Notes

1.   Biodun Adediran, "Yoruba Ethnic Groups or a Yoruba Ethnic Group? A Review of the Problem of Ethnic Identification," *Africa: Revista do Centro do Estudos Africanos de USP* 7 (1984): 57–70

2.   John D. Y. Peel, "The Cultural Work of Yoruba Ethnogenesis," in *History and Ethnicity*, ed. Elizabeth Tonkin, Maryon McDonald, and Malcolm Chapman, 198–215 (London: Routledge, 1989); and John D. Y. Peel, *Religious Encounter and the Making of the Yoruba* (Bloomington: Indiana University Press, 2000), 278–309; Robin Law, "Ethnicity and the Slave Trade: 'Lucumi' and 'Nago' as Ethnonyms in West Africa," *History in Africa (HA)* 24 (1997): 205–19; and Robin Law, "Yoruba Liberated Slaves Who Returned to West Africa," in *The Yoruba Diaspora in the Atlantic World*, ed. Toyin Falola and Matt D. Childs, 349–65 (Bloomington: Indiana University Press, 2004).

3.   Robin Law has been prolific on this subject. See the following works by Law: "The Heritage of Oduduwa: Traditional History and Political Propaganda among the Yoruba," *Journal of African History (JAH)* 14, no. 2 (1973): 207–22; "How Truly Traditional Is Our Traditional History? The Case of Samuel Johnson and the Recording of Yoruba Oral Tradition," *HA* 11 (1984): 195–221; "Local Amateur Scholarship in the Construction of Yoruba Ethnicity, 1880–1914," in *Ethnicity in Africa: Roots, Meanings and Interpretations*, ed. Louise de la Gorgondière, Kenneth King, and Sarah Vaughan,

55–90 (Edinburgh: Centre of African Studies, University of Edinburgh Press, 1996); "Constructing 'A Real National History': A Comparison of Edward Blyden and Samuel Johnson," in *Self-Assertion and Brokerage: Early Cultural Nationalism in West Africa*, ed. Paulo F. de Moraes Farias and Karin Barber, 78–100 (Birmingham: Centre for West African Studies, 1990). See also Michel Doortmont, "The Invention of the Yoruba: Regional and Pan-African Nationalism versus Ethnic Provincialism," in Farias and Barber, *Self-Assertion and Brokerage*, 101–8; and Karin Barber, "Translation, Publics, and the Vernacular Press in 1920s Lagos," in *Christianity and Social Change in Africa: Essays in Honor of J. D. Y. Peel*, ed. Toyin Falola, 187–208 (Durham, NC: Carolina Academic Press, 2005).

    4.   "Devassa do levante de escravos ocorrido em Salvador em 1835," *Anais do Arquivo do Estado da Bahia* 38: 7; Joao J. Reis, *Slave Rebellion in Brazil: The Muslim uprising of 1835 in Bahia* (Baltimore: John Hopkins University Press, 1993), 110–54; Reis, "Ethnic Politics among Africans in Nineteenth Century Bahia"; and Maria I. C. de Oliveira, "The Reconstruction of Ethnicity in Bahia: The Case of the Nago in the 19th Century," in Paul E. Lovejoy and David Trotman, eds., *Trans-Atlantic Dimensions of Ethnicity in the African Diaspora*, 158–60 (London: Continuum, 2003).

    5.   Lorrand J. Matory, "The English Professors of Brazil: On the Diasporic Roots of the Yoruba Nation," *Comparative Studies in Society and History* 41, no. 1 (1999): 72–103; and Stephan Palmié, "The Cultural Work of Yoruba Globalization," in *Christianity and Social Change in Africa: Essays in Honor of J. D. Y. Peel*, ed. Toyin Falola, 43–82 (Durham, NC: Carolina Academic Press, 2005). Also see Kristin Mann and Edna G. Bay, eds., *Rethinking the African Diaspora: The Making of a Black Atlantic World in the Bight of Benin and Brazil* (London: Frank Cass, 2001).

    6.   Samuel Johnson, *The History of the Yorubas from the Earliest to the Beginning of the British Protectorate* (Lagos, Nigeria: CSS Books, 1976 [1921]), 178–283; Bolanle Awe, "The Rise of Ibadan as a Yoruba Power 1851–1893" (DPhil diss., Oxford University, 1964); J. F. Ade Ajayi and Robert Smith, *Yoruba Warfare in the Nineteenth Century* (London: Cambridge University Press, 1964); Stephen A. Akintoye, *Revolution and Power Politics in Yorubaland, 1840–1893: Ibadan Expansion and the Rise of Ekitiparapo* (London: Longman, 1971); Robin Law, *The Oyo Empire c.1600–c.1836: A West African Imperialism in the Era of the Atlantic Slave Trade* (Oxford: Clarendon Press, 1977), 245–302; Robin Law, "The Constitutional Troubles of Oyo in the Eighteenth Century," *JAH* 12 (1971): 25–44; Adeagbo Akinjogbin, "The Prelude to the Yoruba Civil Wars of the Nineteenth Century," *Odu*, 2nd series, 1, no. 2 (1965): 24–46; Abdullahi Smith, "A Little New Light on the Collapse of the Alafinate of Yoruba," in *Studies in Yoruba History and Culture: Essays in Honour of Professor S. O. Biobaku*, ed. Gabriel Olusanya, 42–71 (Ibadan, Nigeria: Ibadan University Press, 1983); and Joseph A. Atanda, "The Fall of the Old Oyo Empire: A Reconsideration of Its Causes," *Journal of the Historical Society of Nigeria (JHSN)* 5, no. 4 (1971): 477–90.

    7.   Peter Morton-Williams, "The Oyo Yoruba and the Atlantic Slave Trade, 1670–1830," *JHSN* 3, no. 1 (1964): 24–45; and Law, "Constitutional Troubles."

    8.   Hugh Clapperton saw many Fulani cattle camps located between Egbado and Old Oyo. See James B. Lockhart and Paul E. Lovejoy, eds., *Hugh Clapperton into the Interior of Africa: Records of the Second Expedition 1825–1827* (Leiden: Brill, 2005); Richard Lander, *Records of Captain Clapperton's Last Expedition to Africa*, 2 vols. (London: Henry Colburn and Richard Bentley, 1830).

9.   See David Eltis and David Richardson, "West Africa and the Transatlantic Slave Trade: New Evidence of Long-Run Trends," in *Routes to Slavery: Direction, Ethnicity, and Mortality in the Transatlantic Slave Trade*, ed. David Eltis and David Richardson, 16–35 (London: Frank Cass, 1997); Robin Law, "Trade and Politics behind the Slave Coast: The Lagoon Traffic and the Rise of Lagos, 1500–1800," *JAH* 24, no. 3 (1983): 343–48; Robert S. Smith, *The Lagos Consulate, 1851–1861* (London: Macmillan Publishers, 1978); David Eltis, Paul E. Lovejoy, and David Richardson, "Ports of the Slave Trade: An Atlantic-Wide Perspective," in *Ports of the Slave Trade: Bights of Benin and Biafra*, ed. Robin Law and Silke Strickrodt, 12–34 (Stirling, UK: Centre for Commonwealth Studies, University of Stirling, 1999); Caroline Sorensen-Gilmour, "Slave-Trading along the Lagoons of Southwest Nigeria: The Case of Badagry," in Law and Strickrodt, *Ports of the Slave Trade*, 72–95; Kristin Mann, "The Original Sin: British Reform and Imperial Expansion at Lagos, "in Law and Strickrodt, *Ports of the Slave Trade*, 169; David Eltis, "The Diaspora of Yoruba Speakers, 1650–1865: Dimensions and Implications," in Falola and Childs, *Yoruba Diaspora*, 17–39; Paul E. Lovejoy, "The Yoruba Factor in the Trans-Atlantic Slave Trade," in Falola and Childs, *Yoruba Diaspora,*, 40–55; and Morton-Williams, "The Oyo Yoruba and the Atlantic Slave Trade," 45.

10.   Johnson, *History*, 188.

11.   Ibid., 193–221.

12.   J. F. A. Ajayi, "The Aftermath of the Fall of Old Oyo," in *History of West Africa*, vol. 2, ed. J. F. A. Ajayi and Michael Crowther (London: Longman, 1976), 145.

13.   Ikale is a mixed region of Yoruba and Niger Delta settlers. "Ekiti" refers to the multiple chiefdoms inhabiting the hilly region east of Ilesa, north of Ondo and southwest of the Niger confluence. The name "Ekiti" in the nineteenth century was used to include Efon, Ado, and "Ibodo." Yagba, Ijumu, Oworo, Owe, Akoko, and Owo were collectively called "Kakanda" (by the Hausa) or "Ibodo" (by the Edo). The inability of these chiefdoms to form centralized states was not unrelated to their location in hilly regions not conducive to human movement. Furthermore, they were bordered by the more powerful Edo, Nupe, Ilorin, Ijesa, and Ibadan, who frequently preyed on them. See William H. Clarke, *Travels and Exploration in Yorubaland, 1854–1858*, ed. J. A. Atanda (Ibadan, Nigeria: Ibadan University Press, 1972); C. A. Hone and D. Hone, eds., *Seventeen Years in the Yoruba Country: Memorials of Anna Hinderer Gathered from Her Journals and Letters* (London: The Religious Tract Society, 1872); and Daniel J. May, "Journey in the Yoruba and Nupe Countries in 1858," *Journal of the Royal Geographical Society (JRGS)* 30 (1860): 212–33.

14.   On Yoruba ethnic wars, see Edward Roper, "What I Saw in Africa: Sketches of Missionary Life in the Yoruba Country, Part II," *Church Missionary Gleaner (CMG)* 3, no. 27 (March 1876): 35; Rowe to Derby, May 18, 1888, encl. 1 in no. 8, C5144, British Parliamentary Papers (PP) read at the Ohio University Library, Athens, OH; J. F. Ade Ajayi, "Nineteenth Century Wars and Yoruba Ethnicity," in *War and Peace in Yorubaland 1793–1893*, ed. Adeagbo Akinjogbin, 9–19 (Ibadan, Nigeria: Heineman Educational Books, 1998); and Niyi Oladeji, "Language in Ethnic Rivalries: An Analysis of Ethnocentric Use of Yoruba in Nineteenth Century Yorubaland," in Akinjogbin, *War and Peace*, 451–61.

15.   Roper, "What I Saw in Africa, Part II," 35. See also Henry Townsend, Journal for the Quarter Ending June 25, 1847, CA2/085b, Church Missionary Society

Archives (CMS), University of Birmingham, UK; and E. Adeniyi Oroge, "The Institution of Slavery in Yorubaland with Particular Reference to the Nineteenth Century" (PhD diss., University of Birmingham, UK, 1971), 113–33. For a broader debate, see Robin Law, "Legal and Illegal Enslavement in West Africa in the Context of the Trans-Atlantic Slave Trade," in *Ghana in Africa and the World: Essays in Honor of Adu Boahen*, ed. Toyin Falola, 513–22 (Trenton, NJ: Africa World Press, 2003).

16.   R. and J. Lander, *Journal*; Phillip D. Curtin, "Joseph Wright of the Egba," in *Africa Remembered: Narratives by West Africans from the Era of the Slave Trade*, ed. Philip D. Curtin, 317–33 (Madison: University of Wisconsin Press, 1967); Edward Irving, "The Ijebu Country," *Church Missionary Intelligencer* (*CMI*) 7 (1856): 65–72, 93–96, and 117–20; M. Akin Mabogunje and J. Omer-Cooper, *Owu in Yoruba History* (Ibadan, Nigeria: Ibadan University Press, 1971); Wande Abimbola, "The Ruins of Oyo Division," *African Notes* 2, no. 1 (1964): 16–19; Robin Law, "The Owu War in Yoruba History," *JHSN* 7, no. 1 (1973): 141–47; and J. F. Ade Ajayi and Stephen A. Akintoye, "Yorubaland in the Nineteenth Century," in *Groundwork of Nigeria History*, ed. Obaro Ikime, 299–300 (Ibadan, Nigeria: Heinemann, 1980); and Ajayi, "Aftermath of the Fall of Old Oyo."

17.   Isola Olomola, "Demographic Effects of the Nineteenth Century Yoruba Wars," 371–79, and Gabriel O. Oguntomisin and Toyin Falola, "Refugees in Nineteenth Century Yorubaland," 381–98, both in Akinjogbin, *War and Peace*.

18.   Peel, *Religious Encounter*, 49–50.

19.   Irving, "The Ijebu Country"; A. H. Dulton, "Reports on Orile-Owu Chieftaincy Dispute, January 10, 1938," Ibadan Prof 1/1/135, Nigerian National Archives Ibadan (NNAI); Mabogunje and Omer-Cooper, *Owu in Yoruba History*; and Rasaki Akinwale, "The Resettlement of Owu Ipole 1909–1919" (MA thesis, University of Ibadan, Nigeria, 1987).

20.   See May, "Journey in the Yoruba and Nupe Countries"; N. A. C. Weir, Intelligence Report on Itaji District of Ekiti Division, para. 3, 1934, CSO 26/1/29800, NNAI.

21.   Oba Ajibade Iyanda, Owajumu of Omu, "Coronation Speech," May 27, 1989.

22.   T. B. Bovell Jones, Intelligence Report on Ijero District, 7, Ondo Prof 1/1/906, vol. 1, NNAI.

23.   See reports by N. A. C. Weir, all in NNAI: Intelligence Reports on Ado District of Ekiti Div., 1933, CSO 26/1/29734; Intelligence Report on Ogotun District of Ekiti Div., 1934, CSO 26/1/29762; and Intelligence Report on Ikere District of Ekiti Div, 1933, CSO 26/1/29799.

24.   Intelligence Report on Akoko District, 1–10, enclosed in Joseph H. Beeley, Intelligence Report on Owo and Ifon Districts (1934), CSO 26/1/29956, NNAI.

25.   Michael C. Adeyemi, *Ondo Kingdom: Its History and Culture* (Ibadan, Nigeria: Bounty Press, 1993), 15, 48, 71–72; Johnson, *History*, xx; Peter Lloyd, "Osifekunde of Ijebu," in Curtin, *Africa Remembered*, 222–87; Brand to Russell, December 31, 1860, FO 84/1115, Public Record Office (PRO), London; and Charles Phillips, "Address Delivered at Missionary Meeting Held in the Schoolroom," Faji, Lagos, February 28, 1879, Phillips 1/3/3, NNAI (hereafter Phillips, "Address").

26.   Phillips, journal, January 29, 1977. Bishop Samuel Charles Phillips Papers, Kenneth Dike Memorial Library, University of Ibadan, Nigeria.

27.　Sandra Barnes, *Patrons and Power: Creating a Political Community in Metropolitan Lagos* (Bloomington: Indiana University Press, 1986), 23, 27–36.

28.　R. and J. Lander, *Journal*, 181; Campbell to Clarendon, March 27 and 28, 1858, FO84/1061, PRO; and Oroge, "Institution of Slavery." Also P. Amaury Talbot, *The Peoples of Southern Nigeria: A Sketch of Their History, Ethnology and Languages With an Abstract of the 1921 Census* (London: Frank Cass, 1969 [1926]), 124; R. L. V. Wilkes, "Intelligence Report on the Central Awori Group in the Ikeja and Badagry District of the Colony," CSO 26/29939, NNAI; and "Notices of the Villages," G3/A2/0/191, CMS.

29.　Campbell to Clarendon, December 7, 1855, FO 84/976, PRO; and Johnson, *History*, 324 and 381.

30.　David Hinderer to Henry Venn, October 26, 1855, CA2/049b, CMS.

31.　Report of James Johnson, August 1877, CA2/056, CMS.

32.　Isaac B. Akinyele, *Iwe Itan Ibadan ati die ninu awon ilu agbegbe re bi Iwo, Osogbo, Ikirun*, 4th ed. (Ibadan, Nigeria: Board Publications, 1980 [1911]), 209

33.　See Charles Gollmer, extracts from journals for July and August 1859, in Charles H. Gollmer, *Charles Andrew Gollmer: His Life and Missionary Labours in West Africa*, 2nd ed. (London: Hodder and Stoughton, 1889), 146.

34.　Peter Morton-Williams, "An Outline of the Cosmology and Cult Organization of the Oyo Yoruba," *Africa* 34, no. 3 (1964): 243–64. On the spread of Oro, see R. Braithwaite Batty, "Notes on the Yoruba Country," *Journal of the Royal Anthropological Institute of Great Britain and Ireland* 19 (1890): 160–64.

35.　By the 1850s, Ogboni had taken root among the Oyo elite of Ijaye and Ibadan. See Adolphus Mann, Journal, October 16, 1854, and March 29, 1855, CA2/066, CMS. On Ogboni, see Leo Frobenius, *The Voice of Africa: Being an Account of the Travels of the German Inner African Exploration Expedition in the Years 1910–1912*, vol. 1 (New York: Benjamin Blom, 1968 [1913]), 172–73; S. O. Biobaku, "Ogboni: The Egba Senate," *Proceedings of the III International West African Conference, Ibadan, 12–21 December 1949* (Lagos, Nigeria, 1956), 257–63; Babatunde Agiri, "The Ogboni among the Oyo-Yoruba," *Lagos Notes and Records* 3, no. 2 (1972): 50–59; and J. A. Atanda, "The Yoruba Ogboni Cult: Did It Exist in Old Oyo?" *JHSN* 6, no. 4 (1973): 365–74.

36.　Johnson, *History*, 241, 443, 446; and Anthony O. Oguntuyi, *Aduloju Dodondawa* (Akure, Nigeria: Aduralere Press, 1950), 29.

37.　Solomon Babayemi, *Egungun among the Oyo Yoruba* (Ibadan, Nigeria: Board Publications, 1980). Also see Johnson, *History*, 160–61; Peter Morton-Williams, "The Egungun Society in South Yoruba Kingdoms," *Proceedings of the III International West African Conference, Ibadan, 12–21 December 1949*, 91; R. S. Smith, "The Alaafin in Exile," *Journal of African History* 6, no. 1 (1965): 63; and Joel A. Adedeji, "The Origin of Yoruba Masque Theater," *African Notes* 6, no. 1 (1970): 80–85.

38.　Samuel Crowther and John C. Taylor, *The Gospel on the Banks of the Niger: Journals of the Native Missionaries Accompanying the Niger Expedition of 1857–1859* (London: Frank Cass, 1968 [1859]), 117.

39.　This might be a euphemistic reference to the mobilization of Oyo power/support and the monarch's creation of a parallel power base over which he alone had control.

40.　J A. Adedeji, "The Alarinjo Theatre" (PhD diss., University of Ibadan, Nigeria, 1970), 144–87.

41.   Akinyele, *Iwe Itan Ibadan*, 47; and Ogunba, cited in Babayemi, *Egungun among the Oyo Yoruba*, 28.

42.   See John Adams, *Remarks on the Country Extending from Cape Palmas to the River Congo* (London: Frank Cass, 1966 [1823]), 96–105.

43.   John B. Losi, *History of Lagos* (Lagos, Nigeria: Tikatore Press, 1914), 19. On Adele, see Robin Law, "The Career of Adele at Lagos and Badagry, c. 1807–c. 1837," *Journal of the Historical Society of Nigeria (JHSN)* 9, no. 2 (1978): 35–59.

44.   See G. A. Robertson, *Notes on Africa* (London: Sherwood, Neely, and Jones, 1819), 286–88.

45.   See Phillips, "Address," 1/3/3, NNAI.

46.   Andrew H. Apter, *Black Critics and Kings: The Hermeneutics of Power in Yoruba Society* (Chicago: University of Chicago Press, 1992), 36–54.

47.   Charles Young, Journal, September 6, 1879, G3A2, 1880/125, CMS.

48.   See journals of Young and Phillips from Ondo, 1876–79, CA2/078, CMS, and CA2/098, CMS.

49.   Phillips, Journal, January 11, 1879, Phillips 1/3/1, NNAI.

50.   Phillips, Journal, April 25, 1879, Phillips 1/3/1, NNAI.

51.   On Anlugbua, see Mabogunje and Omer-Cooper, *Owu in Yoruba History*.

52.   Johnson, *History*, 158–59.

53.   Moore, Journal, in Mary Barber, *Oshiele or Village Life in the Yoruba Country* (London: James Nisbet & Co., 1857), 55.

54.   On human sacrifice, see my "Slavery and Human Sacrifice in Nineteenth Century Yorubaland—Ondo c.1870–1894," *Journal of African History* 46, no. 3 (2005): 379–404.

55.   Two of her associates were sacrificed to Osun. Cult slavery in Yorubaland is yet to be studied.

56.   The use of a plural term signifies the multideity nature of Yoruba religion. See Barber, *Oshiele*, 125–36; Gollmer, Journal, September 15, 1856, in *Charles Andrew Gollmer: His Life and Missionary Labours*, 123–24. Thomas B. Wright, a CMS agent in Lagos, also noted a woman whose house was destroyed by thunder: "This woman's room is filled with every kind of rubbish—calabashes of every description, & pots of various kinds—every one of which is a representative of an Orisa." Wright, Journal, May 1, 1867, CA2/097, CMS. See also Karin Barber, "Oríkì, Women and the Proliferation and Merging of Orisa," *Africa* 60, no. 3 (1990): 313–37.

57.   Edward Ward, *Marriage among the Yoruba* (Washington, DC: Catholic University of America, 1937), 15.

58.   Samuel Crowther, "Report of Visit to Ketu in 1853," *CMI* 4 (1853): 243–52.

59.   Samuel Crowther, "Journal of an Overland Route Journey, December 1871–February 1872," CA3/04, CMS.

60.   Samuel Crowther to the Rev. William Jowett, Secretary of the Church Missionary Society, Fourah Bay, February 22, 1937, "Detailing the Circumstances Connected with His Being Sold as a Slave," *Church Missionary Record*, 8 (October 1837): 217–23. See also *Journals of the Rev. James Frederick Schön and Mr. Samuel Crowther, who with the Sanction of Her Majesty's Government Accompanied the Expedition to the Niger in 1841* (London: Frank Cass, 1970 [1842]); Herbert Macaulay, "The Romantic Story of the Life of a Little Yoruba Boy Named Adjai," *Nigeria Magazine*, 24 (1946),

169–79; and J. F. Ade Ajayi, *Christian Missions in Nigeria: The Making of a New Elite, 1841–91* (London: Longman, 1965).

61. Losi, *History of Lagos,* 22 and 33.

62. Johnson, *History,* 226.

63. Ibid., 324–26. On Ijaye, see ibid., 236.

64. Ibid., 638.

65. Traveling Commissioner, Journal, March 18 and 22, 1898, Ondo Div 8/1, NNAI. For Ijesa marks on Idoani people, see David O. Asabia and J. O. Adegbesan, *Idoani Past and Present* (Ibadan, Nigeria: Ibadan University Press, 1970), 5–6.

66. James Johnson to Wright, Annual Report, June 21, 1878, and January 1880, CA2/o56, CMS.

67. Teslim O. Elias, *Nigerian Land Law* (London: Routledge, 1951), 139; and E. O. Oloyede, "The Laws Relating to Children and Young Persons under the Customary and Statutory Laws of Nigeria" (PhD diss., University of London, 1970), 209–10.

68. R. Foulke-Roberts (District Officer, Ondo), cited in Secretary Southern Provinces to G. C. Whiteley, Chief Secretary, March 17, 1937, CSO 26/11799, vol. IV, NNAI.

69. Interview with Chief Felicia Folayegbe Ighodalo, Agbowo, Ibadan, August 26, 1999. Wabodu is the senior female title in Derin Ologbenla's family at Ile-Ife. See also LaRay Denzer, *Folayegbe M. Akintunde-Ighodalo: A Public Life* (Ibadan, Nigeria: Sam Bookman Publishers, 2001), 5–10.

70. Apter, *Black Critics and Kings,* 1–30.

71. J. D. Y. Peel, "Between Crowther and Ajayi: The Religious Origins of the Nigerian Intellectuals," in *African Historiography: Essays in Honour of Jacob Ade Ajayi,* ed. Toyin Falola, 64–79 (London: Longman, 1993); and Doortmont, "Invention of the Yoruba."

72. Muhammad Bello, *Inf aq al-mays ur,* ed. C. E. J. Whitting (London: Luzac, 1951 [1812]).

73. R. and J. Lander, *Journal,* 171; and Charles Phillips, Journal, January 15, 1878, Phillips 1/3/3, NAI; and "Report of Second Visit to the Camps," encl. 6 in no. 33, Evans to Granville, August 24, 1886, C4975, LX, PP.

74. See Clapperton, Journal, January 25, 1826, in Lockhart and Lovejoy, eds., *Hugh Clapperton.* See also R. and J. Lander, *Journal,* 168.

75. See John Raban, *Vocabulary of the Eyo or Aku Language, a Dialect of Western Africa,* 3 vols. (London: Richard Watts, 1830–32).

76. Samuel Crowther, *A Vocabulary of the Yoruba Language* (London: Seeleys, 1843).

77. David Hinderer, Diary, June 4, 1851, CA2/049, CMS.

78. See Adeagbo Akinjogbin, introduction to *The Cradle of a Race: Ife from the Beginning to 1980,* ed. Adeagbo Akinjogbin, xi–xv (Port Harcourt, Nigeria: Sunray Publications, 1992).

79. See Benjamin Campbell (Consul of Lagos) to Lord Clarendon, June 5, 1857, #11, PP, vol. 63; and Lorenzo Turner, "Some Contacts of Brazilian Ex-slaves with Nigeria, West Africa," *Journal of Negro History* 27, no. 1 (1942): 55–67.

80. See Obafemi Awolowo, *Path to Nigerian Freedom* (London: Faber, 1947).

81. See note 4, above.

82. See Johnson, *History,* vii–viii.

83.   See Akintoye, *Revolution and Power Politics,* 80–82.

84.   R. A. Olaniyan, "War Termination and Conflict Reduction in Yoruba Military Tradition"; Stephen A. Akintoye, "The British and the 1877-93 War in Yorubaland"; and S. O. Arifalo, "The Educated Elite in the Search For Peace," all in Akinjogbin, *War and Peace,* 263–306. See transcripts of peace negotiations in CMS (Y) 1/7/5, NNAI, and "Correspondence Respecting the Wars between Native Tribes in the interior and Negotiations for Peace Conducted by the Government of Lagos," 1887, C4957, PP; and "Further Correspondence," 1887, C5144, PP.

85.   Sandra Barnes, "The Organization of Cultural Diversity in a Pre-colonial Community of West Africa," paper presented at the annual meeting of the African Studies Association, 1991; and Robin Law, *Ouidah: The Social History of a West African Slaving "Port" 1727–1892* (Athens: Ohio University Press, 2004), 91–92.

3

Settlement Strategies, Ceramic Use, and Factors of Change among the People of Northeast Osun State, Nigeria

ADISA OGUNFOLAKAN

In an attempt to extend the frontiers of Yoruba archaeology, between 1992 and 1994 I undertook an archaeological survey of northeast Osun State, Nigeria (see figure 3.1) with an emphasis on Ila-Orangun, Oke-Ila, Oyan, Asi, and Iresi, with a view to making the area known archaeologically. Hitherto, the area had been left unexplored by archaeologists. Most work done in southwestern Nigeria has concentrated on Ile-Ife, Benin, Old Oyo, and Owo, with their art works in bronze, terracotta, and wood. In Yorubaland, there are areas other than Ife, Old Oyo, and Owo that are prominent and vital to its history and archaeology. It is this notion that prompted me to start an archaeological exploration in northeast Osun State.

Previous archaeological work in this area is scarce. The only related investigation is that of P. A. Allison, who observed and photographed a head from Ikirun that was similar to an Ife head.[1] My decision to work in northeast Osun was also informed by the desire to locate potsherd pavements in other Yoruba towns besides Ile-Ife, where the well-known Luwo-type potsherd pavements are found. These pavements cover almost the entire town of Ile-Ife. They are made primarily of potsherd laid on edge and either in a herringbone design or in a straight row. The tradition is credited to Luwo, the only known female ruler in Ile-Ife.

The northeast part of Osun State under investigation comprises the notable ancient and historical towns of Igbajo, Ikirun, Iragbiji, Iresi, and Ajaba, the last-named being a town that links the southern and northern parts of Yorubaland. Between 1992 and 1994, I carried out a survey of parts of this study area with visits to Oyan, Asi, Asaba, Ila-Orangun, Oke-Ila, and Iresi, among other places.[2] In addition, Jere Akpobasa carried out an archaeological survey of Ila-Yara, an abandoned settlement of the Ila people and probably

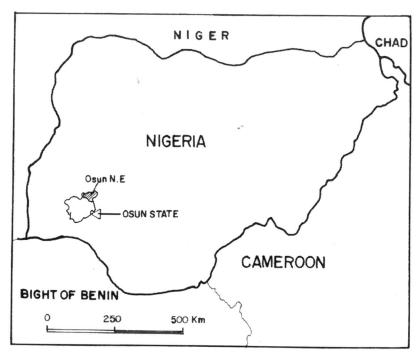

Figure 3.1. Southwestern Nigeria showing the study area. Credit: Adisa Ogunfolakan.

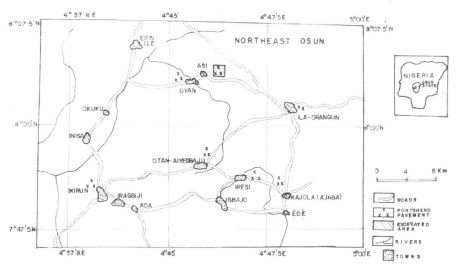

Figure 3.2. Northeast Osun. Credit: Adisa Ogunfolakan.

their second point of settlement after leaving Ile-Ife.[3] This settlement derived its name from the remains of the defense trench and the embankment. *Yara* in Yoruba means trench (see figure 3.2).

The northeast Osun area lies between latitudes 7°50' and 8°05' N and longitudes 4°40' and 4°50' E. The region covers six state local governments, namely, Boripe, Boluwaduro, Ifelodun, Oke-Ila, Ila, and Odo-Otin. The area is inhabited by members of the Oyo Yoruba dialectal group and by Igbominas who occupy the Ila and Oke-Ila region. In the southwest of the area, especially, some inhabitants are speakers of Yoruba dialects that are neither Igbomina nor Oyo but are greatly influenced by the Ijesa dialect. This dialectal influence is most pronounced in Igbajo, Iresi, and Otan-Ayegbaju. L. Lanlehin and S. Aina[4] remark that "Otan-Ayegbaju has been dominated by the Ijesa and the Oyos, hence their accents strongly influence the Otan dialect and ethnic affinity."

The study area could very broadly be divided into three parts according to the dialects of the people (see figure 3.2). These are as follows: the Igbomina group of the Ila region, consisting of Ila-Orangun, Oke-Ila, and Ajaba; the Oyo-speaking group, which includes Oyan, Ikirun, Iragbiji, and other places; and a third group, consisting of Igbajo, Iresi, and Otan-Ayegbaju, which has a pronounced Ijesha-influenced dialect rather than an Oyo dialect.[5] There has been considerable dialectal influence from outside, and in fact, the Igbajo dialect is an agglomeration of Yoruba dialects. The dialectal diversity might have come into being at a late stage, particularly after the Yoruba wars of the nineteenth century.

The northeast Osun topographical region is undulating and it features a muddy terrain and a rocky ridge that runs in a north-south direction. The area is well drained by numerous but small seasonal streams and rivers that have their sources in the hills near which most of the towns in the region are situated. Most of the streams dry out in the dry season. Some of the streams bisect towns: the Afo River bisects Ikirun town and the Isoko River virtually splits Iresi town into two. These streams later merge to form a large river known as Oyi in the Ila region and Osun in the Ikirun area. Some of the towns in this area could not spread outward because of the rocky hills and they have had to spread in line with the length of the hill. Most of the inhabitants of this area are farmers planting cocoa, orange trees, kola, and some subsistence crops like yams (mostly in the Ila, Iragbiji, and Igbajo zone). The tree crops are found in the lowlands and the valleys through which streams run.

The people of northeast Osun are united by overlapping sociocultural institutions, historical traditions, religion, and worldview. The intermingling of the people, especially during and after the Yoruba wars of the eighteenth and nineteenth centuries, made them into one subgroup of the Yoruba entity. How has the dispersal of people influenced the growth of cities in this area? What has been its influence on the dialect and the sociocultural affinities of the people? These remain important questions to answer. To do so, the archaeologist has to look for material culture to decipher the meanings of the minds and hands of the people who produced this culture.

Potsherd Pavements in Yorubaland: A Review

As earlier stated, one of the aims of this project is to identify potsherd pavements in the northeast Yoruba area. But first, it is important to provide a general review of the pavements that are found elsewhere in Yorubaland. Much has been written on potsherd pavements in Yorubaland, and they have long been the subject of debate among scholars from diverse fields. Potsherd pavements are most frequently found in Ile-Ife, where they covered almost the entire town.[6] This led Ekpo Eyo to divide the history of Ife into the pre-pavement, pavement, and post-pavement eras.[7] Frank Willett was the first to uncover a potsherd pavement when he excavated the Ita-Yemoo and Catholic Road pavement sites in 1957 and 1958.[8] Peter Garlake[9] and Ekpo Eyo,[10] respectively, excavated the pavement sites of Obalara's Land and Lafogido Street in the ancient town. Eyo's excavation led to the establishment of a new chronological framework for Ife as against Willett's preclassical, classical, and postclassical Ife. Graham Connah also came across a pavement in Benin.[11] Since the Ile-Ife pavements were excavated, more work has been done to identify potsherd pavements in other parts of Yorubaland. This includes investigations of pavements at Imesi-Ile, Itagunmodi near Ilesa, and Ilare, and the excavation of pavement sites in the Ijesa zone.[12] One must also note that the occurrence of potsherd pavements is not limited to the Yoruba region of Nigeria alone; such pavements also occur in Togo and the Benin Republic.[13]

As in the Yoruba and non-Yoruba centers mentioned above, my own research in northeast Osun State has led to the discovery of potsherd pavements, at places such as Oyan, Asi, Ila, Iresi, Otan-Ayegbaju, Ila-Orangun, Oke-Ila, Iragbiji, Ikirun, and the Ajaba site where I am currently working. In addition, I have located pavements in Ilesa town, Ishan-Ekiti, Owo, and Osu, and at CAC Street, Ilaje.[14] In order to understand the spread of potsherd pavements in other West African countries, I visited the town of Notse in Togo (about 161 kilometers north of Lomé, the capital), where I observed two different structural layout systems: the flat laid system and the edge laid system. I observed that the flat laid system is ideal in a sandy area, while the edge laid system is ideal for a region with compact clayey soil.[15] Most of the pavements identified in Yorubaland are made of potsherd laid on edge in either a herringbone or a straight row design.[16] The early Ife pavements were made solely of potsherds, but later included stone, cobblestones, and even fragments of an Olokun beads crucible.[17]

It is true that a great deal of research has been carried out on the pavements, but none of it has addressed the issue of the pavements' functionality. Therefore, in 1988, I started working on the nature, function, and spatial configuration of the pavements.[18] Potsherd pavements are an important aspect of ancient Yoruba culture, their construction perhaps demonstrating the sophistication of Yoruba civilization at the time.[19] Most of the pavements identified in Yorubaland have shown evidence of an advanced sociopolitical system. They reveal collective work in their construction, not single-person production as in the construction of the terracotta or bronze figurines.

The Technology of Potsherd Pavements

Evidence abounds in the ancient town of Ile-Ife of metal, ceramic, and stone artifacts, proving that Africans had well-developed technologies long before the era of European colonization. Her Majesty Queen Luwo, the twenty-first *ooni* (ruler) of Ile-Ife, is believed to have conceived, designed, and supervised the construction of the paved walkways popularly known as *apaadi Luwo* (Luwo's potsherd pavements). If they were originally meant to pave the way for the queen so as not to soil her feet and dress during the rainy season, by the fourteenth and fifteenth centuries, *apaadi Luwo* had become part of the architectural heritage of the Ife people.

According to oral tradition,[20] the pathway or the courtyard to be paved would be prepared by leveling the ground. The potsherds were then prepared by breaking them into pieces. The soil was then well kneaded to make for a good sub-base providing the working platform. The soil base was mixed with residual water from the palm-oil industry (*omi-eku*) and left to ferment for two to three days. In the absence of residual water from the palm-oil industry, the soil was mixed with palm oil. Where there was no palm oil, the soil was left to ferment longer, say, for one week. Mixing the soil with *omi-eku* or palm-oil was done to provide uniform heating when the pavement was being "baked."

After the base was prepared, the potsherds were then stuck into the prepared soil and arranged in whatever design was desired, be it herringbone or straight row design. The pavement was left to dry out before being "baked." In the baking process, dry wood and shrubs were packed on top of the pavement and set on fire. As pointed out elsewhere,[21] the choice of material in the later stages of the evolution of potsherd pavements in Ile-Ife may have depended on the choice or social status of the client. A pavement observed at Owode Street in Ile-Ife was designed with fragments of an Olokun crucible in a special arrangement of seven pottery rows to three rows of crucible fragments.

I observed, when cutting through a section of a Luwo potsherd pavement, that the design features qualify it as an example of what today is regarded as a rigid pavement. The wearing course, which is the layer of sherds embedded in the soil sub-base, was designed without any allowance for small deformations at the surface. The well-kneaded soil sub-base provided the working platform. This provided the strength of the pavement and protected it from deterioration.

In the process of establishing the technology of this pavement, and in order to test the authenticity of the oral history collected on the pavement technology, I replicated the pavement by paving round a stone statue at the modern house of a prominent Ile-Ife chief (the *aro*). I used laterite mixed with cement (lime) rather than the ordinary laterite mentioned in the oral tradition. This was because we could not "bake" (fire) the pavement because it is in an enclosed area. In addition, to compare the strength of ancient pottery with sherds from modern pots, I paved two different points at Chief Eluyemi's house in Ile-Ife (late Chief Eluyemi was then director general of the National Commission for Museums and Monuments), one using the ancient sherds collected from a pavement area in the town, and the second using sherds from contemporary pots from Ipetumodu, a town about 14 kilometers from Ile-Ife. It is believed that Ife itself did not produce utility pots; Ife imported and continues to import pots from Ipetumodu. Ife is well known for its ritual pots, however.

The result of this test shows that the pavement made from ancient potsherds withstands human traffic, while the pavement made from contemporary sherds is already wearing away, even though the level of the human traffic on it is lower than on the ancient potsherds pavement. This, then, suggests that pots made in ancient times were better fired than contemporary pots, or that the pottery shards used in ancient pavements were from used pots that might have been re-fired several times as a result of use. In addition, a replica of this pavement was made in a 2 ft x 4 ft wooden box that is on display in the gallery of the Natural History Museum, Obafemi Awolowo University, Ile-Ife, Nigeria.

Archaeological Reconnaissance

In continuation of my previous archaeological survey of part of northeast Osun (e.g., Ila-Orangun, Oyan, Asaba, Asi, and Iresi), I carried out an excavation of the pavement site at Ajaba. Before beginning this work, we made several visits to Ajaba to familiarize ourselves with the people and the topography of the area. Since we had our principal informant (Pa Popoola) with us, we had an amicable encounter with the people. Both oral and written evidence were examined thoroughly; thereafter; we embarked on the location, identification, and documentation of archaeological/cultural sites.

There are peculiar problems in carrying out an archaeological survey in a tropical rainforest environment, because of the poor visibility and difficulties in movement that often impede access to the surface archaeological features. Movement and visibility during the rainy season were made extremely difficult by the heavy undergrowth and multilayered tree canopies in the study area, especially in the Ajaba, Iresi, and Igbajo zone. However, in open areas, visibility was good and movement was easy, and I was able to identify and collect archaeological materials. Erosion has greatly affected cultural features. The topography of the area allows erosion annually to wash away cultural materials from the soil. I examined only visible features like cultural mounds and refuse mounds. These consist of accumulated debris and remains from domestic and public areas within a settlement; they constitute a reliable context from which to obtain a broad and long-term range of cultural materials reflecting various aspects of a community's activities.

Geophysical Methods of Archaeological Prospecting

Geophysical methods of archaeological prospecting are well known and have been used for about four decades.[22] In northeast Osun State, this was the first time the method had been employed to identify archaeological sites. Virtually the entire range of geophysical methods was used in our investigation. The usefulness of magnetic methods in archaeological surveying cannot be overemphasized. The technique adopted is popularly known as magnetometer profiling, and it involves the accurate measurement of the earth's magnetic field at closely spaced points. Magnetometer profiling is inexpensive, nondestructive, and a very cost-effective method of acquiring useful information about the environment, especially in locating small ground structures that could be of great archaeological interest. The points that gave positive readings during the geophysical survey correspond to the area where we found concentrations of pavements during the excavation.

The Survey

Our survey was conducted with the assistance of a colleague from Germany, Fred Fielberg. An archaeological survey demands a variety of procedures, such as selective surface collection, the complete collection of visible materials, collection along systematic transects, a combination of systematic and random sampling according to a superimposed local or regional grid, and collection around specific cultural or landscape features. However, the value of a survey depends on the level of detail recorded and the nature of the archaeological records being surveyed.

As suggested earlier, conducting an archaeological survey in the forest zone is tedious, especially during the rainy season when the forest becomes denser. However, this is the period when most of the potsherd pavements are exposed and in many cases washed away. In Ile-Ife, most of the terracotta and bronze heads were discovered after a heavy rain.[23] Art works like these are washed away from their primary context, redeposited, and covered with soil. This is probably why it has become difficult to find such works of art in their primary context. Our major survey took place during the dry season, from October to March. This is the best time to enter the forest, as visibility is somewhat better. In the northern part of the study area, that is, the Ila-Orangun and Oyan axis, visibility is improved by the yearly burning of the bush. According to information from Chief Adeyemi, *balogun* of Oyan, the Fulani cattle herders set the bush (elephant grass mostly) on fire to provide green grass for their cattle during the dry season. Within one week of the bush being set on fire, fresh shoots of grass appear. With the bush burned and the cattle eating the shoots, a clear view of what is on the surface is produced. Unfortunately, damage is often done to artifacts, especially those made of organic materials and even ceramics as a result of trampling by cattle.

Our survey was also made difficult because of religious-cultural factors. For instance, we were not allowed to enter a certain shrine until a particular time or until certain rituals were performed. Furthermore, we could not enter some shrines and groves or sacred forests unless the chief priest was there. At times, certain females are not allowed to approach a shrine or grove. You may well make endless appointments to visit a grove or shrine without success. In a situation where you have limited time or resources, all this makes things difficult. For example, at Ire, I made several appointments with the then *aree* of Ire, Oba Omotoso, to no avail. Even the last and most successful appointment was not totally successful, as the *oba* was hosting a crucial meeting at the time. By the time of our next appointment, he had "gone into the roof" (*oba w'aja*): that is, he was dead. This disrupted our work and put it on hold.

In some cases, the owner of the area will want his son or daughter to be present before a survey can be carried out. To the owners, such children are their "eyes": they are educated and whatever they say is final. But a son or daughter who is not knowledgeable about archaeology will not own up to his or her ignorance of what the archaeologists want to do and will only complicate matters. When we were surveying a cocoa farm within Ajaba abandoned settlement, the son of the owner of the farm told his father we were looking for gold and not for cultural remains and subsequently requested money before allowing us to continue our work. It is the belief of the people that any activities carried out on their farmland are tantamount to the taking over of their land from them. They do not want to compromise any of their economic gains for sociocultural gains. They do not understand that actually there is economic value in exposing the cultural-historical relics in their areas.

Many of the archaeological/historical sites are within built-up areas. My main focus was on Ajaba, Igbajo, Iragbiji, and Iresi. A visit was also made to Ire and Otan-Ayegbaju, where potsherd pavements have been reported. Yoruba oral histories, especially settlement histories, often said that the people left Ile-Ife or their former place of abode because of a chieftaincy dispute or in a bid to found another settlement. In doing this, either they followed the instruction of the Ifa oracle or simply moved in the direction they felt would suit them. In addition, at each place of settlement or at their final place of settlement, either the immigrants met aboriginal settlers or various subgroups accidentally stumbled upon each other after they had settled. According to Chief Lemikan, smoke from a fire was usually a sign of the presence of another human settlement.[24] In Ila-Orangun, Oyan, Asi, and Oke-Ila, the instructions of the Ifa oracle were employed in the location of settlement sites. But in the case of the Igbajo people, the choice of their former settlements was not made by following the instructions of the oracle.

During the survey, surface materials were collected, and features were photographically documented. At Iree, near Otan-Ayegbaju, I was informed of the presence of a potsherd pavement. My informant was a student at Osun State Polytechnic in Iree, to whom I had earlier shown a pavement in Ile-Ife. On investigation, we found that the Ire pavement is typical of the well-known Ife type with a herringbone design. The pavement site was in a town known as Ayekale, which was destroyed during the Fulani wars of the early nineteenth century. According to the *baale* (chief) of Ayekale, his great-grandfather was responsible for the construction of the pavement. Unlike the people of the surrounding towns and villages, the people of Iree claim no direct link with Ile-Ife. According to the late *aree* of Iree, Oba Omotoso, the people of Ire came from Ipee in Kwara State of Nigeria in the early nineteenth century (presumably during the Fulani wars). They first settled at Oke-Ipole (on a hill) and later moved down the hill. Annually, they celebrated the Odun Oke Ipole, that is, the Ipole Hill festival. The festival precedes the Egungun festival in the town.

Excavation

In 1994, the potsherd pavement site at Kajola (Ajaba) along the Iresi-Ajaba road was noted and earmarked for further investigation including excavation (see figure 3.3). That year, the pavement was exposed in the middle of the road leading to Iresi from Ajaba because of the yearly grading of the road by a heavy machine. Later, in 1996, when we visited the site, the pavement earlier exposed in the middle of the road had been totally destroyed.

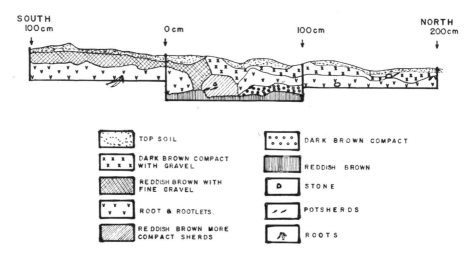

Figure 3.3. Stratigraphy of the western wall of the site. Credit: Adisa Ogunfolakan.

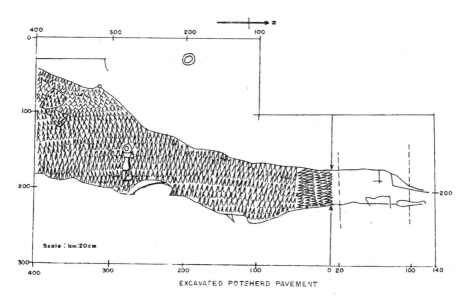

Figure 3.4. Potsherd pavement. Credit: Adisa Ogunfolakan.

The destruction of the pavement as a result of road construction allowed erosion to create mini-gullies on the road, though also exposing more pavement and scattered pottery along the road. By July 1997, more areas of pavement were exposed toward the northern end of the road leading to Iresi. It was then decided that the pavement be opened up so as to determine its extent, design, and orientation, and the materials used in it. This would help determine its relevance and relationship to the abandoned site and to the known pavement sites of Ile-Ife, Ila-Orangun, Iragbiji, and other known sites within the study area.

The pavement is part of Ajaba abandoned settlement. It is located to the northwest of Ajaba town, about 200 meters from the middle of the town's market, and about the same distance from Aba Paanu village. The whole site was initially a sacred grove. According to the *owaloja* of Kajola, Oba Jacob Adedotun Adetoyese, people started encroaching on the grove for their farming and most importantly for the exploitation of timber. By 1997, almost three-quarters of the grove had been cultivated. A marginal portion is now left as *igbo-riro,* that is, uncultivable land, or *igbo-risa,* forest of demons.

From the appearance of the exposed pavement, it seemed that the road cut across the pavement. The road must have cut it into two, thereby exposing pavement and pottery of different sizes, shapes, and thickness. In addition, a pot (*ajere*), probably embedded in the center of the pavement and badly crushed by heavy traffic, was retrieved. The pot was in an inverted position with a small iron hoe at its mouth. From our findings, it appears more than one person at a time was working during its construction, as the pavement was pointing in different directions (east-west and north-west orientations) (see figure 3.4). This implies that several people were working at the site at the same time, facing in different directions but all meeting at a point to produce uniform paving.

Pottery

In describing other archaeological materials from this study, our focus is on the decorative motifs and the technological attributes of ceramics. At present, no analysis has been carried out on the pottery. In all, 354 potsherds were recovered from the excavation and from surface collection. In the excavation, the bulk of the pottery was found in layers one and two (see table 3.1). The concentration of pottery at these levels could be due to disturbance as a result of the yearly grading of the road, which must have removed a great deal of soil from the upper layers, resulting in the loss of much information and many cultural materials. Mat-impression is the most important decoration and it is represented on almost half of the total number of shards recovered from the excavation. Other forms of pottery include plain, weathered, and twisted-cord-decorated pottery (see table 3.2).

Table 3.1. Artifacts from excavation

Artifacts	Layer 1 (0–10 cm)	Layer 2 (10–20 cm)	Layer 3 (20–30 cm)	Total
Pottery	147	88	20	255
Stone	8			8

Table 3.2. Pottery: decorative types

Decorative types	Layer 1	Layer 2	Layer 3	Total
Mat impression	54	42	8	104
Twisted cord	21	14	3	38
Plain	42	11	2	55
Weathered	30	21	7	58
Total	147	88	20	255

In Yorubaland, clay pots have been given different names to distinguish their uses: the *ape* (cooking pot), *amu* (water jar), *isaasun* (soup-pot), *oru* (kettle), and so on. It has been claimed that decorating the bodies of pots adds aesthetic value and represents cosmological and religious concepts, and that similar decoration on different pots expresses coherent underlying perceptions, accounting for cultural continuities in an art form.[25] These underlying perceptions are today the major preoccupation of archaeologists. While, in Ife, clay was used to produce famous images and pots for ritual purposes, in other areas and, most importantly, in the study area, pots became important utilitarian items in people's homes. Because pottery has often been preserved, archaeologists have been using it to help them understand different aspects of the life-ways of people in those periods for which there are no written records.

The interrelatedness of pottery decoration and symbolic structures justifies the widespread use of decoration as the prime index of ethnicity preserved in the archaeological record. Ceramic attributes were used in drawing inferences on the cultural-historical relationships among the people of northeast Osun and between them and the people of other parts of Yorubaland, most especially Ile-Ife. No standard regional typological scheme has been developed for describing ceramics in Yoruba archaeology. This is usually blamed on the inadequacy of ethno-archaeological research on Yoruba pottery.[26] However, the lack of a common front among archaeologists in describing and analyzing ceramics may have been the cause. Each researcher tends to use his or her own procedure, depending on what he or she is aiming at.

Ceramic stylistic attributes are used to draw inferences about relationships among the settlements in northeast Osun and between them and Ile-Ife. Any study of ceramics should be considered from two viewpoints: (1) the technology, and (2) the characteristics. The objective of my analysis has been to elucidate the technology of the pottery, the method by which clays were prepared, shaped, finished, and fired. Characterization involves an examination of ceramic properties with a view to isolating material of different origins and ultimately establishing the sources of these materials. In our study, this was done by physically examining the fabrics of the ceramics obtained from the study area, which can be classified into two types: coarse-grained pottery and fine-grained pottery. These different pottery textures were found at all the sites, the coarse type being more pronounced at Ajaba. Also, the shards from the pavement at Ajaba were found to be thicker than the shards from other sites. Their thickness ranges from 0.3 in to 1 in. In Yoruba pottery, thick pots (*ikoko*) are always meant for storage, while thin-body pots (*ape*) are used for cooking, frying, or fetching water.

The sources of pots are at times recognizable from the color, form, design, or decorative motifs of the pots. For instance, pots from Ilorin are quite different from those from Ipetumodu, near Ile-Ife. While the Ipetumodu pots are brown in color, those of Ilorin are lighter; and the Isan-Ekiti pots are dark brown and mostly burnished. The color of the pots may at times depend on the color of the local clay. From the colors and textures of most of the pots from northeast Osun, it looks as if they come from the same sources. A total of 89.1 percent of the excavated shards are of coarse fabric and only 10.9 percent are of fine fabric. Sixty percent of the shards from the cultural mound around the site are of coarse-grained fabric and the rest are of fine-grained fabric. Since coarse wares vary petrologically from site to site and sometimes within the same site as a result of the use of different raw materials, the occurrence of coarse-grained shards within this region without significant differences, with the exception of contemporary pottery shards from Iresi rock shelter and the Kiriji War site at Igbajo, shows the homogeneity of the tradition and its interrelatedness.

The fabric of the pots is thus the first attribute to be studied. The second attribute is the decorative motifs. There are variations in motifs—pots may show the maize-cob, mat-impression, double-twisted-cord, grooving, grooving/painted, and multiple grooving types of decoration, and some are plain. Of all these decorative motifs, mat-impression is the one that occurred in all the sites. In earlier work in this region (Ila-Orangun, Oyan, Asi, Iresi, and Ajaba),[27] mat-impression was found in 80 percent of the decorative motifs. But it is interesting to note that in the excavated pottery, there is no maize-cob decoration, which indicates that the site might have been occupied prior to the sixteenth century, since maize was introduced to West Africa only in that century.

Discussion and Conclusion

The origin of the present Yoruba population is still a contentious subject. Some traditions speak of Ife as the original center of the world; others give accounts of migration, generally from the east, sometimes giving Mecca as the place of origin and ascribing the cause of migration to conflict between paganism and Islam.

In the words of Mabogunje and Omer-Cooper:[28]

> Whatever the origin of the Yoruba dynasties, the picture of dispersal from Ife, whether as the primary or secondary centre is now almost universally accepted. This picture is expressed in terms of family genealogy as the movement of individual descendants of Oduduwa to become the founders of different towns. Tradition of descent from the universal ancestor at Ife was jealously maintained and the prestige of a ruler depended on his seniority within this quasi-mythical descent system. No ruler could lay claim to the full mystique of kingship unless he could show that he derived his crown by direct descent from Ife or that his ancestor had received it from one who could trace his descent in this way.

The original pattern of settlement was in the form of a series of autonomous city-states, each ruled by a king possessing the full attributes of royalty, and the kings were roughly equal in prestige. The city-state pattern is a striking feature of Yoruba sociopolitical organization. The urban nature of the Yoruba may be due to trade. Local trade between producers of different types of agricultural produce and artisans in the towns, trade between neighboring towns, and longer-distance trade between coastal and forest areas and the inland savanna regions often played an important role in the life of the Yoruba towns. Unfortunately, the archaeology of Ife is still poorly studied in relation to the origin of the city and the Yoruba as a whole. However, recent archaeological evidence from other parts of Yorubaland providing a relationship with Ile-Ife (the pavements, for example) is a welcome development.

Certainly, the identification of potsherd pavements in the majority of the towns in northeast Osun has opened up more lines of investigation as to the relationship of the area with Ile-Ife. The pavements also suggest interactions or migrations of people within this area. From Oyan to Ajaba to Iragbiji, the pavements bear the same design feature, the pot embedded in their center, as is found in Ile-Ife. They are also practically all of herringbone design. The pavement in Ila-Orangun is remarkable, as it is flush with the lip of the pot in the Ife tradition, and the pavement's lines circle round the pot.

The pot embedded in the center of the pavements in Ile-Ife has been linked to ritual and sacrificial functions.[29] It is not likely that most of the pavements in northeast Osun were linked to similar functions, except, perhaps, for the pavement at Ajaba. The pot embedded in the center of the Ajaba pavement is unique in that it is a perforated pot (*ajere*) with a small hoe at its mouth. The pots embedded in Ife pavements are not perforated. In addition, the Ajaba pot is in an inverted position with the hoe covering its mouth. The pavement at Ajaba may have served as a ritual place and at the same time as a courtyard pavement. As Garlake remarked, "the presence of altars, shrines or libation receptacles in the courtyards did not preclude their being used for ordinary domestic chores, nor does it in the courtyards of Yoruba compounds today."[30] The grinding-stone balls placed on the Ajaba pavement also suggest domestic use. In addition, the iron hoe found at the lip of the pot is significant. Garlake came across metal objects during his excavation of Obalara's Land, but these metal objects were not associated with the pot embedded in the center of the pavement. I asked a *babalawo* (Ifa diviner) in Ile-Ife, Chief Fatoba Olabampe, about the significance of the *ajere* pot with a hoe in its mouth, and learned that it was meant for protection against theft in the compound. It is common to have sacrificial materials packed in a pot and buried in the foundation of a house before the commencement of the building. One example is the *itele* (underlay) pot found under my family house in Ile-Ife.

It is interesting to note that the potsherd from most of the northeast Osun pavement sites are the same in terms of fabric content. They are of coarse fabric with mica inclusion. This may imply that the pottery was all produced using similar clay obtained within the region or it may indicate that the communities traded with the same people for their pottery. Whatever the case, the clay material must have been from the same sources. No site of pot production has been found in the area. It has been suggested that northeast Osun mostly procures its pots from Koro-Ekiti, Ishan-Ekiti, and other towns in Igbominaland.[31]

The mass movement from Ile-Ife to the east and north of Ife, and the southeastern drift of the Oyo in their expansionist wars of the eighteenth and early nineteenth century, influenced the attributes of the ceramics of Ilare in the northern Ijesa area, the northern Igbomina area, and Ila Yara (on the periphery of the study area).[32] This conclusion has also been reached in previous studies conducted in Yorubaland,[33] in which similarities in the decorative motifs of pottery from Ife, Owo, and Benin have been used in elucidating the influence of these powerful polities. There is continuity in the ceramic attributes that were established in Ife during the tenth and eleventh centuries at Ita Yemoo and that continued till the sixteenth century in the Woye Asiri and Obalara's Land sites, and until the seventeenth and eighteenth centuries in the Lafogido and Odo-Ogbe sites.[34] Ife influence appears to have spread to the northeast Osun area, as the ceramic attributes (both in the potsherd pavement and the ordinary pottery) found in this area are the same as those of Ife. The Ajaba site is yet to be dated. However, we can use dates from neighboring Ila Yara (fourteenth to seventeenth centuries) and Ilare (fourteenth to nineteenth centuries),[35] where similar potsherd pavements and ceramics have also been found.

The intermediate period of Ife (ca. 1400 AD–1600 AD) was a period of sociopolitical change throughout Yorubaland. It witnessed large-scale migration of people toward northern and eastern Yorubaland as a result of economic and political pressure, the establishment of new settlements, the overrunning of older communities, and the waging of wars in the need and desire for economic stability, political power, and territory.[36] The people of Ede and others from northeast Osun were among those who migrated from Ife, settling at different places before arriving at their final settlement. They did not settle without bringing with them a significant aspect of their culture. The potsherd pavement is a material indicator of movement or cultural interaction, and the pavement may well have been part of the cultural attributes the people brought from their original home to the study area.

Archaeological research in the northeast Osun area is ongoing. More intensive research work on the Ajaba abandoned site, with careful analysis of surface and excavation materials, would provide a better ground for comparison with materials from large political centers such as Ile-Ife. Future research in the area will contribute more knowledge not only of northeast Osun's own history but also of the history of the interrelationships between Yoruba groups.

Notes

1.   P. A. Allison, "A Terra-Cotta Head in the Ife Style from Ikirun, Western Nigeria," *MAN* 193/94 (1963): 156–57.

2.   Adisa Ogunfolakan, "Archaeological Survey of Osun North East of Osun State, Nigeria" (master's thesis, University of Ibadan, Nigeria, 1994).

3.   Jere Akpobasa, "Settlement Studies of Ila-Yara, Osun State: An Ecological Approach" (master's thesis, University of Ibadan, Nigeria, 1994).

4.   L. Lanlehin, and S. Aina, eds., *The History of Otan-Ayegbaju* (Ibadan, Nigeria: Secre-Print, 1995).

5.   Ibid.

6.   Adisa Ogunfolakan, "Luwo Potsherd Pavement: A Unique Aspect of Ife Culture," *Journal of Arts and Ideas* (Obafemi Awolowo University, Ile-Ife, Nigeria) 3 (2000): 88–97.

7.   Ekpo Eyo, "Odo Ogbe Street and Lafogido: Contrasting Archaeological Sites in Ile-Ife, Western Nigeria," *West African Journal of Archaeology* 4 (1974): 99–109.

8. Frank Willett, *Ife in the History of West African Sculpture* (London: Thames and Hudson, 1967).

9. Peter Garlake, "Excavation at Obalara's Land, Ife: An Interim Report," *West African Journal of Archaeology* 4 (1974): 111–48.

10. Eyo, "Odo Ogbe Street."

11. Connah, *The Archaeology of Benin* (Oxford: Clarendon Press, 1975).

12. Babatunde Agbaje-Williams, "Potsherd Pavements and Early Urban Sites in Yorubaland, Nigeria: A Consideration," paper presented at the 14th biennial conference of the Society of Africanist Archeologists, Syracuse University, Syracuse, NY, June 1998; see also Akin Ogundiran, *Archaeology and History in Ilare District (Central Yorubaland, Nigeria) 1200–1900 AD*, Cambridge Monograph in African Archaeology 55 (London: Archaeopress, 2002); A. Siyanbola, "An Archaeological Investigation of Imesi-Ile" (BA project, Department of Archaeology, Obafemi Awolowo University, Ile-Ife, Nigeria, 1988).

13. Nwanna Nzewunwa, "Prehistoric Pavements," *West African Journal of Archaeology* 19 (1989): 93–116.

14. Ogunfolakan, "Luwo Potsherd Pavement," 2000.

15. Ibid.

16. Garlake, "Excavation at Obalara's Land."

17. Ogunfolakan, *Luwo Potsherd Pavement in Ile-Ife: 30 Years of Nigerian Independence* (Moscow: Academy of Sciences, 1987).

18. Ogunfolakan, "Archaeological Survey."

19. Babatunde Agbaje-Williams, "Potsherd Pavements and Early Urban Sites in Yorubaland, Nigeria: An Interim Report," *Nigerian Field* 66 (2001): 93–104.

20. Ogunfolakan, "Luwo Potsherd Pavement," 2000.

21. Ogunfolakan, *Luwo Potsherd Pavement*, 1987.

22. S. Gaber, A. El-Fiky, S. Abou Shagar, and M. Mohamaden, "Electrical Resistivity Exploration of the Royal Ptolemic Necropolis in the Royal Quarter of Ancient Alexandria, Egypt," *Archaeological Prospection* 6 (1999): 1–10.

23. Eyo, "Igbo'Laja, Owo," *West African Journal of Archaeology* 6 (1976): 37–59.

24. Chief Lemikan of Igbajo, personal communication (1997).

25. N. David, J. Sterner, and K. Guaya, "Why Pots Are Decorated (with Comments)," *Current Anthropology* 29 (1989): 365–89.

26. Phillip Allsworth-Jones, "Continuity and Change in Yoruba Pottery," *Bulletin of the School of Oriental and African Studies* 59, no. 2 (1996): 312–22; see also A. Fatunsin, *Yoruba Pottery* (Lagos, Nigeria: National Commission for Museums and Monuments, 1992).

27. Ogunfolakan, "Archaeological Survey."

28. A. Mabogunje and J. Omer-Cooper, *Owu in Yoruba History* (Ibadan, Nigeria: Obafemi Awolowo University Press, 1971).

29. Eyo, "Odo Ogbe Street"; Garlake, "Excavation at Obalara's Land"; Willett, *Ife in the History of West African Sculpture.*

30. Garlake, "Excavation at Obalara's Land."

31. Aribidesi Usman, Jonathan Aleru, and Raphael Alabi, "Sociopolitical Formation on the Yoruba Northern Frontier: A Report of Recent Work at Ila-Yara, North Central Nigeria," *Journal of African Archaeology* 3, no. 1 (2005): 139–54.

32. Ibid.; Akin Ogundiran, "Settlement Cycling and Regional Interactions in Central Yoruba, a.d. 1200-1900: Archaeology and History in Ilare District, Nigeria" (PhD diss., Boston University, 2000).

33. Eyo, "Odo Ogbe Street"; Garlake, "Excavation at Obalara's Land"; Willett, *Ife in the History of West African Sculpture.*

34. Ogundiran, "Settlement Cycling"; Usman, Aleru, and Alabi, "Sociopolitical Formation."

35. Ogundiran, "Settlement Cycling"; Usman, Aleru, and Alabi, "Sociopolitical Formation."

36. Robert Smith, *Kingdoms of the Yoruba,* 2nd ed. (London: Methuen, 1969); Usman, Aleru, and Alabi, "Sociopolitical Formation."

4

Precolonial Regional Migration and Settlement Abandonment in Yorubaland, Nigeria

Aribidesi Usman

Introduction

Migrations have been part of human endeavor since humans' emergence as a species. As Tessie Naranjo put it, "People have moved from place to place and have joined and separated again throughout our past, and we have incorporated it into our songs, stories, and myths because we must continually remember that, without movement, there is no life."[1] The formation of a cultural group (e.g., family, clan, tribe, ethnic group, nation, state) in the past as well as in the present is the consequence of a dynamic and selective process of aggregation, identification, and differentiation.[2] Africa has been a "frontier continent"—the center of population movements of different kinds, ranging from the protohistoric Bantu dispersions to the local movements immediately before colonialism.[3]

Humans have left their original homes for various reasons. Now as in the past, population movements have occurred as a result of famines, civil wars, ethnic rivalries, political persecution, and conflicts between societies. There have been forced migrations in which the migrants have played no role in the decision to move or in the choice of the final destination. In all these instances, displaced people have had to face the problem of forging a new life in a new environment sometimes completely different from the one they have left behind. Migrations affect both the migrants and the hosts. Migrants can stimulate further migration by the displacement of indigenous population through warfare, which leads to an alteration in sociocultural and political characteristics.

Migration has remained an important topic of study in geography, demography, and genetics. The geographic and demographic models emphasize causal factors, transportation costs, and information exchange. It is assumed that migration is most likely to occur when "push" factors at the point of origin combine with "pull" factors at the destination and with acceptable transportation costs to cause the decision to migrate.[4] The application of geographic and demographic models of modern human population movement to the past has been a contentious issue. One view is that the behavioral processes of migration functioned in the past as they do in the present.[5] Others regard migration as a "density-dependent phenomena" that did not occur in Stone Age economies but only in the protohistoric and historic periods.[6]

The geographical and demographic models stress individual decision making in the migration and movement of population. Concepts such as "migration stream" and "return migration" were developed to characterize modern urban or rural-urban migration in which the individual or family acts as the migratory unit. However, in the prehistoric period and also today, while individuals have made decisions about their movements based on the information available to them, the group's decision has been more important than any individual's needs or desires.[7] Among African societies, when populations move into frontier areas, they do so in groups, not as individuals, because individuals are embedded within the corporate groups of which society is composed.[8]

There has been an increasing interest among archaeologists in the use of migration as an explanatory framework.[9] This new interest is attributed to the current focus on interregional interaction, the formation of broad-based theoretical frameworks such as world systems theory, and the increased interest in ethnicity and historicity that evolved in the last decades of the twentieth century.[10] Also, models developed in other fields are being applied to archaeological problems. For example, following the geographic and demographic models, a distinction has been made between short-distance and long-distance migration. Short-distance migration involves moves "within an information field that represents habitually interacting social groups," as in a change of residence at marriage. Long-distance migration involves movement across an ecological or cultural boundary and involves migratory patterns such as "migration streams," "leapfrogging," and "return migration."[11]

This chapter looks at past regional migration, settlement abandonment, and settlement dynamics in Yorubaland in the period between the eleventh century and the early twentieth century (AD 1000–1900). The focus here is on south-north migration, although north-south population movement also occurred (see figure 4.1). The fourteenth to twentieth centuries are divided into the Late Formative Period (AD 800–1000), the Classical Period (AD 1000–1400), the Intermediate Period (AD 1400–1600), the Old Oyo Period (AD 1600–1800), and the Revolutionary Period (AD 1800–1900). Each of these periods involves one or more episodes of migration and settlement abandonment. It is important to note that those Yoruba people who

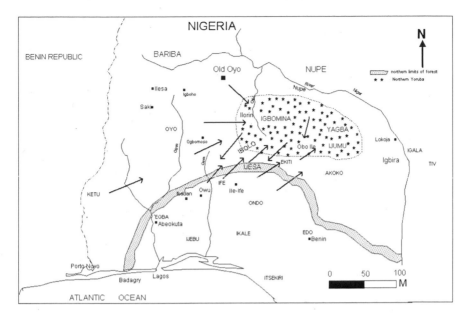

Figure 4.1. Migration and population movement in Yorubaland. Arrows indicate direction of movement (south-north, north-south). Credit: Aribidesi Usman.

claim descent from Ile-Ife or Old Oyo, for example, did not leave those centers all at once. While some had already settled in northern Yorubaland before or during Oyo's political suzerainty, others left their areas of origin during the eventful period of Alafin Abiodun, which ended in 1789. Some started to flee from the Old Oyo area even before Alafin Aole was forced to commit suicide in about 1796. The breakup of the Old Oyo Empire around 1837 also led to the movement of some refugees from the capital and its immediate surroundings toward northern Yorubaland in search of safety. I have used multiple sources of information—oral tradition, ethnohistory, linguistic data, and archaeological data—to explain the causes and effects of migration and settlement abandonment in the period before colonialism. I also attempt to show how we can identify migration and social groups in the archaeological record. The data presented in this chapter come mostly from my research work in northern Yorubaland since 1994, which has identified more than fifty abandoned sites in and around the Ilorin, Igbomina, and Ibolo areas.

Study Area

Southwestern Nigeria includes areas from the Slave Coast east to the Niger Delta, extending 320 km inland to the Niger where it flows southeast to join the Benue, and extending to the border of the Benin Republic. Yoruba-speaking populations occupy most of southwestern Nigeria, along with their neighbors to the east, the Edo or Bini. Major kingdoms in the area, such as Oyo, Ife, Ijebu, and Benin, had clearly been flourishing for many years by the time the European "explorers" arrived on the coast in the mid-fifteenth century. As one goes toward the north, into central Nigeria, one finds other Yoruba people, who are divided into groups including the Igbomina, Ekiti, Ibolo, Ilorin, and Ookun. They have shared boundaries and interacted with non-Yoruba neighbors such as the Igbira, Igala, Gbari, and Nupe. The northern Yoruba people are characterized by small-scale political structures described as "mini-states,"[12] "village group" or "town" polities,[13] and "chiefdoms."[14] Many of the traditions of the areas in which small-scale polities have prevailed suggest that sociopolitical changes, through amalgamation, occurred during precolonial times, often under the pressure of external aggression. Also, the rise of Oyo contributed to the growth or emergence of some localized polities in the area[15] (see figure 4.1).

The Yoruba people are generally believed to be immigrants into their present area. Most Yoruba groups have a set of traditions that locate the ancestral home of the people in areas outside their present abode. The people who now constitute the northern Yoruba claim to have arrived in the area at different times in history and from various places. The Kabba people probably came from Ile-Ife and then moved northeast through Ekiti; the Ijumu claim Ile-Ife origin; while the earliest Bunu settlers may have come from the Ekiti area.[16] The oral traditions of the ruling houses in Ila in Igbomina claim a link with Oduduwa and Ile-Ife as the original home.[17] Like Ila, the Igbomina communities of Omu-Aran, Oko, Omupo, Olla, and Alaabe also claim in their oral tradition to have migrated from Ile-Ife, while the Oro-Ago people (especially the Ajagun group) claim to have come from Ketu. The Ilorin, Ibolo, and Igbomina units such as Ipo, Esie, Ilere (including Agunjin), Esa, Aun, and Erese trace their ancestry to Old Oyo. These groups may also include some migrants from Ile-Ife.[18] However, some people have claimed autochthonous origins in their present locations. The tradition of Oba, in Igbomina, suggests that it was at Oba that the world was created. The generic *oriki* referring to the *oloba* as "Ọmọ ẹrẹ," meaning "offspring of the mud," may reflect an indigenous origin in Igbomina.[19]

The different versions of the migration stories of northern Yoruba people can be interpreted as an indication of distinct phases of migration from different areas and at different periods, a long history of cohabitation, and the bonds of domination, conquest, and exploitation during the nineteenth century.[20] Since the traditions often point in the direction of Ile-Ife or Old Oyo, it is difficult to determine in most cases whether the original homes mentioned refer to these centers or simply to settlements in close proximity to them. This is a major reason why the period of arrival at places people now occupy may not be easy to be put in chronological order. However, the events that made each group leave might help to determine their lineage and/or their genealogical group.

Migration and Population Movement

Most often in African oral tradition, a small set of "push" factors—witchcraft accusations, persecution, disputes over political issues, adventurous hunting and trading for new game or profits, overpopulation, warfare—have been used to explain the movement of people from their original homes to other places. It is therefore important to understand the conditions at the places of origin. Information on these is drawn from Ile-Ife, Benin, and Old Oyo because they are regarded as the primary dispersal points for most Yoruba groups. Also, archaeological research has been very successful in these areas, and data are more abundant than for other areas. It is equally important to know what makes a place attractive to immigrants and consequently a potential destination. This is what has been termed the "pull" factor for migration.[21] For example, why did immigrant groups from the south choose to migrate to northern Yorubaland?

A critical issue in the decision to migrate is access to information about potential destinations. What kind of information was available to migrants prior to their migration and how was this information disseminated? Before the fifteenth century, northern Yorubaland was only sparsely populated. Early small-scale migrations may have set the stage for the substantial migrations witnessed from the fifteenth century and especially the sixteenth and seventeenth centuries. The concept of the "familiar area" discussed with regard to migration in palaeolithic Europe may be applicable to the Yoruba regional phenomenon. A "familiar area" is larger than the home range of any single individual. It is the largest region within which populations can comfortably operate when environmental conditions allow.[22]

Late Formative Period (AD 800–1000)

Although very little information is available on the preclassical period, it is characterized by transitions from village polities and village confederacies to centralized polities with central capitals.[23] At Ile-Ife, the period was marked by conflicts between the supporters of a confederacy and the supporters of a centralized political structure. The success of the Oduduwa group, which favored centralized power, and the dismantling of the old structure led to the abandonment of many settlements in the Ile-Ife area. In the Ijesa and Ekiti areas, these events are associated with the foundation of towns and dynasties and are often reenacted in annual rituals of origin, indicating groups that moved from Ile-Ife and established new settlements in different parts of the Yoruba region.[24]

Classical Period (AD 1000–1400)

The Classical Period was marked by political consolidation, stability, and the efflorescence of material culture in the Yoruba-Edo region.[25] The material culture of the Classical Period includes stone sculptures, potsherd pavements, glass beads, city walls, terracotta figures, and copper-alloy sculptures.[26] The spread of the sociopolitical and material culture innovations of this period in the Yoruba and Edo regions was probably achieved through population movements and intersocietal networks of elites, economic relations, and cultural imitation.

Stone figures of humans from the Ore grove in Ile-Ife and Eshure in the Ekiti area are illustrative of the early manifestations of figurative human sculptures in honor of deceased political figures in the Yoruba region.[27] Obatala, the last of the rulers who derived their political mandate from the sociopolitical structures of the earlier period at Ile-Ife, is associated with the early trends in artistic representations of human figures in the Yoruba worldview.[28]

Courtyard floors and roads in the Yoruba and Edo regions were paved with potsherds arranged on their edges in herringbone patterns. At Ile-Ife, these were credited to Luwo, a female *ooni* or ruler.[29] Only a powerful political authority would embark on potsherd pavement construction given the intense labor involved. The general notion is that the pavements served as pathways along which the king passed to prevent falls.[30] Further studies have produced other functions (e.g., political, religious, and environmental).[31] Some of these potsherd pavements, which are associated with the "medieval" (or classical) layers, contained potsherds with maize (*Zea mays*) impressions. Since maize was not introduced to West Africa prior to the sixteenth century, it appears that the Classical Period extended up to the sixteenth century. Radiocarbon dates from the thirteenth to the fourteenth centuries have been obtained from charcoal samples associated with potsherd pavements at Old Oyo, Benin, and Itagunmodi (Ijesaland).[32]

The first substantial migration of people from the southern Yoruba area probably took place during the Classical Period. The foundation of some settlements in Ipo, Isin, and Ila in Igbomina is a consequence of the migrations during this period. For some groups from the politically advanced south, the preference for the north of the Yoruba area as their destination may have been in response to its abundant resources. Northern Yorubaland provided a better environment for hunting game than the forested south. Iron ore was also available in the area and facilitated smelting and smithing in the precolonial period.[33] It has been suggested that iron and other goods in Igbomina drew people from Ijesha, Oyo, and Ilorin.[34] By the thirteenth century, large-scale ironworking had intensified at Oba-Isin.[35] The occupation of the Olupefon site in Ipo occurred in the early fourteenth century. Oral tradition says the founder, Olupefon, whose name is synonymous with the settlement and his profession (that of a hunter), came to the Igbomina area to hunt game, especially buffalo.[36] The tradition of Ila-Orangun claims that the founder, Ajagunla, and his mother, Adetinrin, were at the head of a migrant group that left Ile-Ife in about the twelfth century AD. Archaeological excavations have placed the original occupation of Ila-Iyara, former site of Ila-Orangun, at between the late fourteenth and the early fifteenth century.[37]

The Classical Period witnessed the region-wide emulation of Ife's, Old Oyo's, and Benin's elite subcultures by their subordinate polities. For example, stone sculptures in naturalistic human forms like those at Ile-Ife are found at Esie, Ijara, Ofaro, and Pee in Igbomina.[38] Terracotta pieces associated with the Esie collection have produced a TL (thermoluminiscence) date of AD 1100.[39] However, it has been suggested, speculatively, that the stone figures belonged to a cultural milieu whose foundations were laid independently of Ile-Ife between AD 800 and AD 1000.[40]

Potsherd pavements have been found in the Igbomina areas of Ipo, Oro, Aun, Ila-Orangun, Isin, Ajaba, Oyan, and Asi, and in the neighboring town of Iresi (see figure 4.2). In construction and function, the pavements are similar to those at Ile-Ife, at Old Oyo, and in the Edo region. Like the Ile-Ife pavements, the potsherd pavements at Ila-Orangun and Aun are designed in the herringbone pattern, while a pot is embedded in the middle of the pavement at Ila-Orangun.[41] At Oke-Ola Oro, the potsherd pavement situated within the Oro central market is a combination of potsherds and cobblestones like some of the pavements at Ile-Ife.

As is the case in most of these northern Yoruba centers, the present inhabitants have very little direct connection with the potsherd pavements. The people of Asi, for example, claim that they found the pavement at the site when they settled there, and the location of the pavement is referred to as "Aganju Oba Tapa" (the palace courtyard of Nupe's king), a king known in the tradition as Ajangidi.[42] Like the inhabitants of Asi, the people of Aun, in northeast Igbomina, remember little about the potsherd pavement located in the village. The Aun people came from Old Oyo (Oyo Ile) in the early seventeenth century and lived at two settlements, Aun I and II, before the current village was founded in 1971.[43]

The founder of Oke-ola Oro in Igbomina, Adetutu Ariyunbole, came from Ile-Ife and lived at different places, such as Kanko, before he finally settled at Oke-ola Oro. A small structure that formerly occupied the Oro central market site at Oke-ola was called "Isẹsi Oba" ("ibi ti Oba sọ do si,"

Figure 4.2. Potsherd pavement at Aun, Igbomina. Credit: Aribidesi Usman.

that is, "where the king settled").[44] The potsherd pavement found in the area is linked to Adetutu Ariyunbole as part of his palace architecture. Our informant, Abdul Rahman Afolabi, gave some insight into the significance of the potsherd pavement at Oro central market. He called it "dressing terrazzo," and described it as "nkan àrà, ọla ni wọn fi nsé," meaning, "a remarkable feature, serving as an attribute of wealth."[45]

Unlike potsherd pavements at Ile-Ife, Old Oyo, and Benin, no date is available for potsherd pavements in northern Yorubaland. Two suggestions can be offered here with regard to these pavements. First, the immigrants into northern Yorubaland brought the idea of potsherd pavements from Ile-Ife, Old Oyo, or the Edo region after the fourteenth century. Other groups who arrived in the region, probably from the seventeenth century AD, displaced these immigrants. Second, the idea of constructing potsherd pavements in northern Yorubaland may be independent of migrants from the southern Yoruba centers. The examples from Asi, at least, suggest that groups other than Yoruba may have been involved in the construction of potsherd pavements. However, it is clear that potsherd pavements in northern Yorubaland, as in the large political centers of the south, were architectural features connected with palaces, religious centers/shrines, or chiefs' houses.

Intermediate Period (AD 1400–1600)

This was the period when the foundations of the Oyo and Benin states were laid, and military expansion and territorial control were intensified. The fifteenth century saw a general population increase and migrations to the northern frontier of the Yoruba lands as a result of factional competitions and conflicts. The immigrants included members of specialized professions: blacksmiths, iron smelters, wood carvers, leather workers, diviners, medicine men, royal families, and career warriors. The increasing occupation of the Igbomina area (Ipo, Ilere, and Ila) during the fifteenth century was a consequence of this migration process.

According to Ila oral traditions, a certain Amota led his followers from Igbo Ajagunla (the site where Ajagunla was born after the migrating party left Ile-Ife) to Ila-Iyara.[46] The arrival and occupation of settlements by Ila people must have been met with resistance from the "indigenous" groups. Such encounters may have been violent, or compromises may have been made that probably involved the subordination of "indigenous" groups to new centers of authority. The emerging polity of Ila-Iyara was further faced with the growing and competing polities on the frontier, such as the Owu, Ijesha, and Benin kingdoms. Owu was among the earliest polities to develop a cavalry force in the savanna.[47] In addition, the growing importance of the Atlantic trade and the increasing use of horses in warfare in the West African savanna may have forced many weaker and even powerful groups to seek protection.[48]

Large-scale ironworking and the importance of the Ogun deity in northern Yorubaland increased with the arrival of immigrants during this period. The use of iron probably went beyond mainly domestic or economic purposes to include military and political uses. Iron ore deposits in the area facilitated smelting and smithing, which left traces on the landscape in the form of quarries, slag mounds, smelting furnaces, tuyeres, pieces of iron, smithing workshops, and shrines linked to Ogun.[49] Most people who currently live in northern Yorubaland and have strong traditions of iron smelting trace their ancestral homes to eastern or southern Yorubaland, but also northwestern Yorubaland, particularly the Oyo area. According to Owa (Owa Onire and Owa Kajola communities) tradition, the founder, Ajiboye, left Old Oyo accompanied by his supporters, a chieftaincy staff of office (*owa*), and a symbol of the deity of Ogun.[50] Another story says that a "man came from Irè in the present Ondo State to practice his profession of blacksmithing and to stay on a hill where he could find iron ores for his job."[51] Important clues can also be found in the meaning of "Owá" and "Irè," two terms that are often associated with this region. Although Ilere tradition sees "Owa" and "Irè" as meaning, literally, "You come," and "profit" or "gain," respectively, the term "Irè" may be significant in an examination of the migration history of this Igbomina group from Irè and the connection with Ogun cult. Irè town, which is located in eastern Yorubaland, is the center of the Ogun cult,[52] where it may be that a "branch" of the Ogun cult, known as Ogun Onirè, originated.[53] Irè is synonymous with Ilérè or "Ilé-Irè" (home of Irè), an area in northern Yorubaland where Owa Onire and Owa Kajola are presently located.

Ogun, god of iron in the Yoruba pantheon, was an important deity before the arrival of the Europeans and was as prominent among the Igbomina as among the Oyo.[54] The northeastern Igbomina area including Ilere has a rich oral tradition on the mythology of Ogun and its association with the earth tradition. This fits well with the Yoruba myth of Ogun's disappearance by sinking into the earth, and with the close association of the Idoma earth cult with hunting.[55] A cave shrine situated about 2 km northeast of Ofaro I (a former site of Owode Ofaro) and 1.5 km from Owa Onire has been used to explain the tradition of ironworking and the Ogun legend in Ilere. According to oral tradition, Ogun, accompanied by his dog, visited the Owa and Ofaro communities in the past.[56] At the end of the visit, which lasted several days, Ogun advised the people to always reach out to him whenever they were in need. Ogun then disappeared through the cave known to the local people as "àjà ilẹ̀" (underground tunnel). The cave was later converted into a shrine dedicated to the worship of Ogun, until the seventeenth century when the two communities were abandoned (see figure 4.3).

An inspection of the cave surface showed rock fragments and pieces of pottery that suggest human activities. Also, pick marks on the roof and pieces of hematite stone may be associated with past mining for ironstone. The cave was an extension of a large iron-bearing hill known to the people as "Epa Ogun," which literally means "path of Ogun." It appears ironstone was mined in the cave and then transported to other places where smelting and smithing were then carried out (see figure 4.4). A test excavation of one square meter in the cave conducted in 2003 recovered pottery and small charcoal pieces at a depth of 0.3 meters. The charcoal has helped in dating the human use of the cave to 410±60 BP, calibrated at AD 1420 to AD 1640 (Beta 202615). This date is contemporaneous with habitation settlements in the area such as Ikotun (former site of Owa), dated to AD 1386–1671, and Ofaro I (former site of Owode Ofaro), dated to AD 1505–95 and AD 1620–1810. The cave, with a ceremonial function and a connection to the mythology of Ogun, is similar to evidence from elsewhere in Yorubaland and in West Africa, where forges are likened to earth shrines and the smith's status is likened to that of the earth priest.[57]

The Ogun personified in the Ilere tradition may be connected with the introduction of iron or ironworking in the area. The presence of a cave with evidence of mining, and probably ritual, directly tied the deity to a historical event or activity. Iron was revolutionary in the lives of Africans, as it brought

Figure 4.3. Entrance of cave shrine. Credit: Aribidesi Usman.

Figure 4.4. Interior of cave shrine. Credit: Aribidesi Usman.

important changes to societies. In Yorubaland, a conventional pattern for dealing with extraordinary phenomena like iron, culture heroes (e.g., the ironworker, the pioneer in ironworking), or anomalies in nature was to deify them. The genesis of Ogun quite likely involved a deification that grew out of a set of commonly held notions about the mystical properties of iron and the individual who made or used it.[58]

Old Oyo Period (AD 1600–1800)

Several writers have referred to the large population concentration in the northern part of Yorubaland during the period before the fall of the Old Oyo Empire. Samuel Johnson remarked that prior to the Yoruba ethnic wars, the majority of the Yoruba people lived in the towns of the plain, "the towns in the forest lands being small and unimportant, except for the town of Owu."[59] Hugh Clapperton in his journal indicated that the Old Oyo and Ilorin areas had populations of more than 20,000 people, compared to Badagry and Shaki in the south, which fell below 20,000.[60] Large migrations of people from the south to the north occurred during the Old Oyo period, and it seems that a sociopolitical "pull" factor was the cause. The immigrants may have been encouraged by the defeat of Nupe in the early sixteenth century and the establishment of Old Oyo authority in the area; and second, by the growing peripheral centers in the area, which might offer both security and good socioeconomic prospects. The Old Oyo authorities may have encouraged people to settle in the area as a way of solidifying Old Oyo's hold over the territory and building future alliances against Nupe expansion.

Old Oyo's expansion from the sixteenth century onward increased the tempo of the population influx into the northern Yoruba region and contributed to the displacement or partial absorption of the indigenous population. The incessant friction between the Nupe and the Yoruba during this time (which most often resulted in military incursions into Igbominaland) has been seen as "frantic efforts by the Nupe to regain the territory."[61] This scenario can be best understood in terms of what has been called the "action space" of warfare, a geographic model discussed by Ekanade and Aloba:

> As the population of the different core areas of the hypothetical communities increase both over time and space, expansions would generally be towards the unoccupied frontiers between any two contiguous communities .... Increased population pressure in the frontier area may rapidly deplete the available resources and members of the different communities may want to lay exclusive claims on parts of the frontier for the benefit of their own members .... Intercommunity competition for territorial units along their common frontiers may lead to war or violence.[62]

Thus, competition over space or resource use, or revenge for lost territory, was probably one of the causes of Nupe's aggression in Igbomina from the late eighteenth century onward. The need by one group to control resources or to attack a neighbor may be motivated by either internal or external forces acting on politico-economic systems and institutions.

The Old Oyo period witnessed changes in settlement patterns (especially an increase in site size as a result of aggregation), the emergence of chiefly authority, and increased regional interaction. The movement of immigrants toward the north led to considerable internal sociopolitical changes, as new settlements were formed or old settlements were abandoned or became more aggregated, leading to centers of unprecedented magnitude, which probably dominated other settlements. It appears that the competition between Old Oyo and Nupe, which led to the consolidation of Igbomina under the former, may have stimulated rapid settlement growth in the area. The emergence of large sites such as Okegi, Gbagede, Igbo-ejimogun, and Ila-Iyara in Igbomina is related to the complex demographic, economic, and political developments of this period.[63]

The towns established in northern Yorubaland replicated the physical characteristics of towns in the south. The most important of these features were walls or ramparts, which were built around settlements. The enclosing walls of Gbagede and Iyara in Ipo are 3.4 km and 2.8 km long, respectively, while the Ila-Iyara wall in Ila-Orangun is 9.2 km long.[64] Walls with three or more entrance gates are associated with linear ditches. Beside their defensive function, walls are important records of urban transitions with the potential to inform us about the making of urban cultures. The enclosure walls are a physical manifestation of the internal sociopolitical changes in the periphery. The settlements in the periphery constructed enclosed walls and evolved toward increasingly "centralized" control and "hierarchy" in response to large population concentrations.

Revolutionary Period (AD 1800–1900)

The nineteenth century (AD 1800–1900) has been described as a "Revolutionary Century."[65] The first half of the century was associated with the collapse of the Old Oyo Empire, followed by regional internecine warfare; the emergence of new political formations; the massive dislocation of populations, forcing people to move from the north to the south; and extensive enslavement and the transportation of war captives to the New World, especially the Caribbean and Central and South America. Warfare, either for political or economic reasons, was the main cause of migration and population movement during the first half of the nineteenth century.

The political decline of Old Oyo from the late eighteenth century onward began with an internal political crisis, of a kind that tended to afflict all major West African states.[66] The crisis in the Old Oyo metropolis made Old Oyo's northern frontiers vulnerable to external attacks. From the mid-eighteenth century, slave raiding, both for export and for domestic use, was a major preoccupation of the Nupe with regard to northern Yorubaland and probably accounted for the frequent raids on the Yoruba during this time. These raids continued well into the nineteenth century, when Fulani conquest (or rule) was imposed on the northern Yoruba. Nupe raids were "smash and grab" operations, with little consideration for long-term exploitation or permanent political control over the defeated people. The Nupe raids became particularly noticeable under three notable Nupe kings: Etsu Jibrilu (1744–59), Majiya I (1769–80), and Mu'azu (1780–95).

The revolt of Afonja was the final blow to Old Oyo's supremacy and territorial control and later led to the internecine Yoruba wars and the resulting massive population displacement. In the early nineteenth century, Afonja, the *aare-ona-kakanfo* (military commander) of the Old Oyo Empire who was based in Ilorin, revolted against Old Oyo, having failed in his bid for the throne. In 1817, he lured the jihadists in Ilorin and slaves of northern origin living in Oyo-Ile (the Old Oyo capital) to his side, and made them into a formidable force known as the *jama'a* (congregation of the faithful). The Fulani jihadists in Ilorin later turned against Afonja and succeeded in eliminating him in ca. 1823–24. The jihadists took control of Ilorin, which became an outpost of the Sokoto Caliphate.[67] From about 1825 until it was defeated at the battle of Osogbo in 1840, the emirate of Ilorin destroyed most of the northern Oyo towns.[68] The Fulani raided the city of Oyo-Ile itself, cut off its supplies, and forced the *alafin* to abandon the city in 1837 and seek a new capital at Ago Oja, later named (New) Oyo. The collapse of Old Oyo led many people to become refugees. Most of them migrated southward, while others went eastward and northward, taking up residence outside their original homes, in Igbomina and Ekiti towns and villages, in search of safety.[69]

Under Fulani rule in Ilorin, expansionist wars against the Igbomina, the northern Ekiti, and other groups in northern Yorubaland continued. Slaves were an important product of Ilorin's early expansionist wars, which had been started by Afonja.[70] Ibadan, often in competition with Ilorin for control of the area, emerged as the most powerful state in Yorubaland, and by 1875 was master of most of the communities in the northern part of Yorubaland.[71] In the late 1840s, the Ibadan armies moved northeast through the Ekiti area and conquered most of the Igbomina towns to the north, south, and west, and stationed their *ajele* (local warlords and tax collectors) there.[72] A nineteenth-century observer wrote that "all the Efon, Ijesa, and Akoko territories had now become a field for slave hunting for any number of men who could bind themselves together for an expedition."[73]

People captured in the Nupe, Fulani, and Ibadan wars but not retained as domestic slaves of the war chiefs were sold to Lagos for guns and powder. On the Slave Coast in the nineteenth century, traders from a number of nations traded slaves and shipped exports primarily to their own countries' settlements in the Americas, but Portuguese from Brazil and native-born Brazilians dominated the trade. In the final three decades of the trade, Spanish Cuba became a major market. Yoruba male and female captives turned up in Haiti, Brazil, and Cuba.[74] The Yoruba of Cuba were called "Lucumi." "Ulkami" may be a word of Gun (a language of the Ewe group) origin and be cognate with Lucumi, which has been found to be a Cuban name for the Yoruba.[75] Lucumi is said to be derived from an Ijesha salutation (*oluku-mi*, "my friend") and dates from the mid-nineteenth century, when it was given by fellow slaves to Ijesha slaves captured by raiders from the newly founded town of Ibadan and shipped at the very end of the slave trading period to Cuba, one of the last importers of slaves.[76]

In response to the Nupe, Fulani, and Ibadan military aggression, some people retreated from the northern Yoruba grasslands to the towns of the neighboring forest belt, while new towns such as Ibadan and Abeokuta grew up as gathering places for refugees and became militarily strong. Other groups moved to new, more easily defended hill sites within the northern Yoruba grasslands. People from Osi-Opin, Saki, Ila-Odo, and Old Oyo itself settled on the Ilere hill in the northeastern Igbomina area. The northeastern Igbomina communities (e.g., Ilere) resorted to moving their settlements onto rugged hills, situated in naturally fortified positions, and built houses on and between rock outcrops. The new settlements are generally called *ori oke* or *oke*, referring to a hilltop. The hilltop facilitated a commanding view of approaching invaders and restricted enemies' advances. The people of Isin found their way to Ogba Irobi, an inaccessible, securely hidden, and forested gorge on the extreme northern fringe of their homeland.[77] In the Yagba and Ijumu area in northeast Yorubaland, the Nupe destroyed settlements and forced the inhabitants to flee their homes and seek refuge in great discomfort on hills and mountains. Some Yagba people were separated from their families and clans and taken to the Nupe towns of Lafiagi/Pategi, where they have remained till today.[78]

Some communities moved to join others at existing settlements. Safety in numbers is undoubtedly a benefit of aggregation, as larger settlements are not as open to raiding as are smaller, dispersed settlements. The present Oko town in Igbomina was an aggregation of seven communities representing Odo-Oko, Iwoye, Idemorun, Inisan, Akowaro, Odo-aba, and Irapa. Oke-Ode, a northern Igbomina town located on a hill, became a large refugee center for people displaced by the Ibadan army between 1850 and 1860. The Oro Ago town became a temporary refugee center for people from Omu-Aran and its environs. Babanla in the Ilere area was also an important center for war refugees, who were attracted to the settlement by the military prowess and popularity of its ruler, Abogunrin. Also, following the destruction of their towns and realizing the need to unite in order to fight, some people from the Igbomina towns of Omu-Aran, Oko, Ola, Rore, Aran Orin, and Ipetu as well as adjacent Ekiti towns (e.g., Iloffa, Odo Owa, Ekan, and Erinmope) moved to Ajo and lived there between 1878 and 1898.[79]

The interethnic wars of the nineteenth century between the Yoruba and Fulani/Nupe altered the political arrangements in northern Yorubaland. As villages allied or amalgamated for the purpose of defense, the traditional base of authority was readjusted to accommodate other men, particularly military leaders, brought into prominence by the war. For example, in Isin, military prowess and the claim of an Ife pedigree enhanced the status of the *olusin* of Isanlu, and encouraged the people to flock to him for protection. Consequently, the *olusin* emerged as the principal ruler in a rapidly expanding Isin, though he had to share the throne with descendants of two of the absorbed settlements and recognize the other displaced chieftains as members of the *olusin's* council of chiefs.[80]

In the Esisa area, several autonomous settlements existed by the beginning of the eighteenth century. These included Oke Ayin, Aworo-Ona (Oganyin), Aiyetoro, Isaoye, Omugo, Iraye, Oke Daba, Okerunwon, Okeluworo, Ilafe, Okemure, Okewa, and Awu. Each of these settlements jealously guarded its independence until the crises of the nineteenth century forced them into some sort of political alliance, which gave rise to Oro-Ago. The people of Oro-Ago claimed to be the earliest settlers among the groups, but this claim was probably due to their early military success in the area, which led their leader, Ajagun, to emerge as the head of the Esisa area.[81] In another area, the ruler of Oke-Ode, who offered protection to other groups during the turbulent years of the late eighteenth through the nineteenth centuries, was accepted as the military leader of the people, thus overshadowing in importance the rulers of Ora and Owa Onire, who hitherto had had preeminence over the others.[82]

Events associated with the second half of the nineteenth century included the movement of settlements from their hidden positions as peace returned to the area, the introduction of Christianity, the advent of "legitimate" trade, and the advent and impact of British colonial rule. While settled conditions resulting from the penetration of colonial administration from 1900 onward provided the stimulus for movement from the hills in a number of cases in the Western Region of Nigeria, the downhill movement of people had started before the penetration of Europeans into Yorubaland. The inhabitants of the hill settlements had already been faced with challenges. Some of these challenges have been identified as shortages of farmland, long journeys to and from the fields, isolation, congestion, and limited possibilities for physical expansion.[83]

The European presence provided a final push in the process of the downhill movement of settlements. This movement took place during two periods. The earlier of the two came in the middle decades of the nineteenth century, closely following the end of the Fulani and Ijaye wars, while the later period followed the introduction of British administration in the early decades of the twentieth century. For example, some Ilere communities in Igbomina such as Aafin, Alaabe, Ofaro, Okegbo, Oreke, and Agunjin moved in two stages before setting up their present settlements. The oral tradition of these communities suggests a general inadequacy of land for farming and expansion on the hilltops. The Ofaro, Aafin, Alaabe, and Agunjin moved from their hilltop sites to the foot of the hills in the mid-nineteenth century, and from the foot of the hills to their present settlements in the 1930s. Even though war had subsided by the mid-nineteenth century, the people were still very concerned about safety, and this continued to play a significant role in their choice of settlements. The Alaabe community, for example, chose the foothill site known to the people as "Aya Oke" (hill crest) or "Alaabe Keji" (Alaabe II) because it was less stony than the hilltop site (Alaabe I) but close to it, and therefore the hilltop site could provide an immediate refuge in case of a sudden attack.[84] Ilere communities like Owa, Ikosin, Oke-Oyan, Obirin, and Idoba came directly from their hilltops to found their present settlements in the 1940s. The Agunjin community left its hilltop site (Oke-Agunjin) in 1919, at the same time as the Oke-Ode people moved downhill to their present settlement.

The earlier choice of an inaccessible site for settlement represented a nice balance between the need for defense and the other needs of the community, which could be disturbed by a change in any conditions.[85] Such a change appears to have occurred with the end of the Fulani wars and the defeat of Ijaye. A downhill movement of settlements, which reduced the need to carry food supplies for the village up a steep hill and removed the need for the daily trek down to the fields and back again in the evening, must have been an attractive possibility. But the possibility of further attacks had to be weighed against these advantages. It is not surprising therefore that some villages moved only to the foot of their hill or that others remained on their hill sites.

The decisions to move settlements seem to have been taken by the village communities. In the early twentieth century, the colonial administration played an active role in the final settlement relocation by working through the authority of the traditional chiefs. However, the final decision rested with the local people, and disagreements over the choice of migration or the potential destination often occurred, leading to settlement fragmentation. In Ilere, the decision to abandon the old Oke-Oyan site in 1948 led to a disagreement over the choice of location of the new settlement. The result was the establishment of two separate settlements, Idera and new Oke-Oyan, in different locations. Other factors, such as new religions (Christianity and

Islam), influenced the decision to migrate and the structure of the new settlement. During the move from the hilltop of Owa Orioke to the present settlements, the Owa people split into religious camps—Muslim and Christians—and established separate settlements (Owa Onire and Owa Kajola) that mostly followed religious lines.

Migration and Social Groups in the Archaeological Record

The greatest challenge in studying the evidence for migration in precolonial Yorubaland is identifying social groups in the archaeological record. Pottery styles have proven to be the most important material evidence for addressing the issue of cultural boundaries. The diagnostic elements that characterized the ceramic assemblages in the northern areas of the Yoruba-Edo region included burnishing, basting, twisted-string roulette decoration, scallops, brush marking, carved roulette chevron (zigzag) motifs, dot punctates, shell-edge impressions, striation (wiping), perpendicular incisions, and incised geometric symbols consisting of cruciform, triangular, and square motifs (see figure 4.5).

In western Igbomina (e.g., Ipo, Erese), the earliest snail shell-edge decorated pottery, a common pottery type at Old Oyo (but also found in small quantities at Ile-Ife), dates from the fourteenth century.[86] The presence of this decorative style suggests that Old Oyo or Ife elements had spread to the area by that time, or that some form of social relations (probably intermarriage) had been formed between Old Oyo or Ife and people who settled in the western Igbomina area. In northeastern Igbomina (e.g., Ilere, Isin, Esisa) during the same period, snail shell-edge decorated pottery was absent. Instead, the pottery was dominated by a type of decoration called "wiping"[87] or "striation."[88] Ila, the most southerly Igbomina center, lacked the snail shell-edge decorated pottery, the popular pottery type at Old Oyo. The pottery types from Ila-Iyara probably fall within the range of Ife-Benin decorative types rather than the Old Oyo range.[89]

Many changes in utilitarian ceramics that began during the fourteenth century came to florescence in the seventeenth century. Archaeological data from Igbomina suggest that large-scale Yoruba immigration northward in the sixteenth century was preceded by smaller-scale immigration and/or ceramic style emulation.[90] As indicated by the Gbagede, Obaloyan II, and Apateki sites in Igbomina, Old Oyo pottery types, such as the circle stylus, the scallops, and the brush mark incisions that were absent from the early period in Igbomina, became evident. As in the pre-Oyo period, twisted-string roulette designs continued to be the dominant decoration. Snail shell-edge decorated pottery, which first appeared in Igbomina in the fourteenth century, became the predominant pottery type during the seventeenth century, and for the first time (e.g., at the Okegi site), this type surpassed time-honored

b. scallops-punctation

a. snail shell-edge

c. twisted string roulette   d. striation or "wiping"

Figure 4.5. Some types of pottery decoration mentioned in the text.
Credit: Aribidesi Usman.

decoration styles like the twisted-string roulette (see figure 4.5).[91] Also, the circle stylus, a decorative motif common to Ife[92] but less well known in Igbomina before the seventeenth century, was common during this time. The scallop (or impressed arc) is another important Old Oyo decoration type that became very frequent at Gbagede during this period.

It is significant that large quantities of gray/black ware found at Old Oyo are similar to ceramics found in Esie (western Igbomina) and Ilorin. The coloration of *isaasun* and other small domestic and ritual pots such as *oru, ajere, konjo, awo kutupu,* and *fitila* is a dark brown in Ogbomoso, Ilorin, and Igbomina, a coloration produced by the smoke from burning grass and from basting with the liquid produced from *Parkia biglobosia* seed pods. This similarity in pottery making, according to some accounts, is traceable to contacts with Old Oyo during the reign of Alaafin Abiodun (1775–1805).[93] It is also claimed that some of the female potters in Oyo-Ile (the capital of Old Oyo) settled in or were taken to Ilorin after the collapse of the city, and that these potters brought their traditions with them.[94]

Compositional analysis using instrumental neutron activation (INAA) was performed on some excavated pottery and clay samples from northern Yorubaland.[95] The goals of quantitative analysis are to identify ceramic groups that enable meaningful archaeological interpretations, to link ceramics of unknown provenance to raw clay sources and previously established groups, or to determine that a group assignment is not possible.[96] The compositional analysis of excavated pottery from western Igbomina indicates that snail shell-edge pottery, the common Old Oyo type, was locally manufactured in the western Igbomina area. The major northeastern Igbomina decorated pottery type, featuring "wiping" or "seriation," was produced in the area by potters using similar local clay resources. The fact that "wiping"-decorated pottery was produced in this area as early as the late fourteenth century suggests that this type of pottery must have been very old, and was probably a local innovation by the early settlers in the area. In northeastern Igbomina, groups such as those of Esisa did not share the "wiping" pottery type. The archaeological sites in the area (e.g., Ajagun, Oke-Odia) contained mostly pottery with twisted-string roulette decoration. The ancestors of the people of Ajagun and Oke Odia (Obobo) came from Ketu and Old Oyo, respectively, during the seventeenth century.

Although ceramic production may have been much more fluid in the past, as is the case with the "ethnic" attribution of motifs, the presence of some southern Yoruba pottery types in northern Yorubaland may indicate the presence of immigrant elements in the society. The simultaneous use of new pottery design elements and old types may reflect the arrival of new immigrants and the presence of exchange networks involving groups outside northern Yorubaland. Pottery designs can be purposefully manipulated to define and maintain social relations.[97] Changes in ceramic design and the frequent appearance of certain decorative motifs indicate not only the contribution of ideas from new social groups but also the dominance of certain social groups over others. Design techniques and the probable imitation of Old Oyo styles may be a consequence of marriages contracted with distant groups to reinforce alliances, or the arrival of new migrants. Migrants from Oyo, Ife, and other centers in Igbomina produced ceramics by replicating design styles common at their original homes. It also appears that the integration of the periphery (Igbomina) by the state (Old Oyo) involved shared stylistic elements, especially in terms of ceramics, which are clearly evident during the relevant period.

Conclusion

This chapter has made several contributions to the study of migration and population movements in precolonial Yorubaland. The first is a clear documentation of population movements into northern Yorubaland from southern, eastern, and central areas, and the sociopolitical and cultural implications of this. The second lies in the opportunity to reconstruct and to identify social groups in the archaeological record. An attempt is made in the chapter to divide migration and population movements into different periods and identify the various causes or factors that triggered them. A study of northern Yoruba narratives of origin reveals that most of the reconstituted villages and towns in the region were set up as a result of migrations from elsewhere. By 1940, only a few villages were located on their pre-eighteenth-century sites. As one travels around the villages and towns in northern Yorubaland today, one finds relics of abandoned habitations, important reminders of the chaos and devastation of the last two centuries.

The nature of prehistoric Yoruba population movements may be mirrored in the massive relocation of population that was documented in Yorubaland during more recent periods. For example, during the late nineteenth and early twentieth centuries, the people of many hilltop villages in Yorubaland moved to more convenient areas, and it appears that such communities moved as groups. These events show that Yoruba people could move in groups of some size, and suggest that community coherence may have been characteristic of periods before the nineteenth century.

Was enough information available to the southern Yoruba population prior to AD 1500 to allow them to evaluate the northern Yoruba area as a possible destination? Two scenarios might be considered. First, people moving back and forth between north and south must have known the north well enough to understand its potential as a possible new home. Second, groups of migrants from the south may have established residence in the northern Yoruba area before the fourteenth century and maintained ties with the south, providing the south with information about the possibilities of life in a new region. Relationships between the south and the north may have become established over long periods of time, providing knowledge of possible destinations for migrants.

One question concerns the scale of nineteenth-century migrations. The study suggests that this population movement had a profound effect on northern Yorubaland. The Igbomina, especially those in the northeastern part, had lived in settlements that had changed little since they were founded. It seems the out-migration witnessed in the region in the nineteenth century ended whatever social, political, or demographic gains the region had recorded in the previous centuries. There was overall population redistribution as some of the displaced population from towns in northern

Yorubaland moved further south to swell the populations of towns favorably placed for defense in the border country between grassland and forest, such as Ilesha, Ife, Osogbo, Iwo, Ibadan, and Abeokuta.

Northern Yorubaland is well suited to studies of precolonial migration. It lies between several broad culture areas (Yoruba, Nupe, Borgu, Ebira, etc.). The differences between these cultures are sometimes so distinct that comparisons can be made. For example, archaeological work in northern Yorubaland has identified some patterning in decorated ceramics that suggests the existence of multiple cultural groups in the area. More work is needed on the Yorubas' relationships with the Bariba of Borgu and neighboring areas to the north and with the people of Nupeland to the east. The extent of the Nupe influence on the Yoruba is not clear, as Nupe never established any sustained or long-term political control over the Yoruba. It has been suggested that answers to the problem of cultural affinities could still be provided through intensive archaeological work, complemented by ethnographic studies within the various culture areas, which may provide typological affinities and at least suggest the directions of cultural relationships.[98]

Notes

1.   Tessie Naranjo, "Thoughts on Migration by Santa Clara Pueblo," *Journal of Anthropological Archaeology* 14 (1995): 247–50.

2.   Thomas Levy and Augustin Holl, "Migrations, Ethnogenesis, and Settlement Dynamics: Israelites in Iron Age Canaan and Shuwa-Arabs in the Chad Basin," *Journal of Anthropological Archaeology* 21 (2002): 83–118.

3.   Igor Kopytoff, "The Internal African Frontier: The Making of African Political Culture," in *The African Frontier*, ed. Igor Kopytoff (Bloomington: Indiana University Press, 1987), 7.

4.   Catherine Cameron, "Migration and the Movement of Southwestern Peoples," *Journal of Anthropological Archaeology* 14 (1995): 104–24.

5.   David Anthony, "Migration in Archaeology," *American Anthropologist* 92 (1990): 895–914.

6.   Geoffrey Clark and J. M. Lindly, "On Paradigmatic Biases and Paleolithic Research Traditions," *Current Anthropology* 32, 5 (1991): 577–87.

7.   See Cameron, "Migration and Movement," 112.

8.   Kopytoff, "Internal African Frontier," 23–25.

9.   Anthony, "Migration in Archaeology," 895–914; see also Geoffrey Clark, "Migration as an Explanatory Concept in Paleolithic Archaeology," in *Journal of Archaeological Method and Theory* 1, no. 4 (1994); Clark and Lindly, "On Paradigmatic Biases," 577–87; Marcel Otte and Lawrence Keeley, "The Impact of Regionalism on Paleolithic Studies," *Current Anthropology* 31 (1990): 577–82; Irving Rouse, *Migrations in Prehistory* (New Haven, CT: Yale University Press, 1986); Olga Soffer, "Migration vs. Interaction in Upper Paleolithic Europe," in *Cultural Transformations and Interactions*

in Eastern Europe, ed. John Chapman and Pavel Dolukhanov, 65–70 (Brookfield, VT: Avebury Publishing Company, 1993).

10.   Anthony, "Migration in Archaeology," 897; Cameron, "Migration and Movement," 111.

11.   Anthony, "Migration in Archaeology," 901; Cameron, "Migration and Movement," 112.

12.   Ade Obayemi, "The Yoruba and Edo-Speaking Peoples and Their Neighbors before 1600 a.d.," in *History of West Africa,* vol. 1, 2nd ed., ed. J. F. A. Ajayi and M. Crowder (Ibadan, Nigeria: Longman, 1976), 255–322.

13.   S. F. Nadel, *A Black Byzantium: The Kingdom of Nupe in Nigeria* (London: Oxford University Press, 1942).

14.   Timothy Earle, "Chiefdoms in Archaeological and Ethnohistorical Perspective," *Annual Review of Anthropology* 16 (1987): 279–308; see also Timothy Earle, "The Evolution of Chiefdoms," *Current Anthropology* 30 (1989): 84–88; Robert Cameiro, "The Chiefdom: Precursor to the State," in *The Transition to Statehood in the New World,* ed. G. D. Jones and R. R. Kautz (New York: Cambridge University Press, 1981), 37–79.

15.   Robin Law, *The Oyo Empire c. 1600–c. 1836* (Oxford: Clarendon Press, 1977), 106; for further information, see C. S. Burnett, Assessment Report, Ajasse-Po District, Offa Division, SNP 7/13, 4702/1912, 11, Nigerian National Archives Kaduna (NNAK); H. B. Hermon-Hodge, *Gazetteer of Ilorin Province* (London: Allen and Unwin, 1929), 37.

16.   Daryll Forde, *The Yoruba-Speaking Peoples of South-Western Nigeria* (London: International African Institute, 1969), 74.

17.   John Pemberton and Funso Afolayan, *Yoruba Sacred Kingship* (Washington, DC: Smithsonian Institution Press, 1996), 17; A. Adetoyi, *A Short History of Ila-Orangun* (Ila-Orangun, Nigeria: Iwaniyi Press, 1974), 9.

18.   Aribidesi Usman, "State-Periphery Relations and Sociopolitical Development in Igbominaland, Northcentral Yoruba, Nigeria" (PhD diss., Arizona State University, 1998); see also Aribidesi Usman, *State-Periphery Relations and Sociopolitical Development in Igbominaland, North-Central Yoruba, Nigeria,* British Archaeological Report International Series 993 (London: John and Erica Press and Archaeopress, 2001); P. O. A. Dada, *A Brief History of Igbomina (Igboona)* (Ilorin, Nigeria: Matanmi Publishing Company, 1985).

19.   Adesina Raji, "Aspects of the Early History of the Northcentral Yoruba," *West African Journal of Archaeology* 27, no. 1 (1997): 41–49.

20.   Toyin Falola, *Yoruba Gurus* (Trenton, NJ: Africa World Press, 1999).

21.   Cameron, "Migration and Movement," 111.

22.   Clark and Lindly, "On Paradigmatic Biases," 581.

23.   Akinwumi Ogundiran, "Chronology, Material Culture, and Pathways to the Cultural History of Yoruba-Edo Region, 500 b.c.–a.d. 1800," in *Sources and Methods in African History: Spoken, Written, Unearthed,* ed. Toyin Falola and Christian Jennings (Rochester, NY: University of Rochester Press, 2003), 43.

24.   Ibid., 44.

25.   Ibid., 46.

26.   Ekpo Eyo, "Recent Excavations at Ife and Owo, and Their Implications for Ife, Owo, and Benin Studies" (PhD diss., University of Ibadan, Nigeria, 1974); also

Ekpo Eyo, "Odo Ogbe Street and Lafogido: Contrasting Archaeological Sites in Ile-Ife, Western Nigeria," *West African Journal of Archaeology* 4 (1974): 99–109, and "Igbo'Laja, Owo," *West African Journal of Archaeology* 6 (1976): 37–58; Peter Garlake, "Excavations at Obalara's Land, Ife, Nigeria," *West African Journal of Archaeology* 4 (1974): 111–48, and "Excavations on the Woye Asire Family Land in Ife, Western Nigeria," *West African Journal of Archaeology* 7 (1977): 57–96; Frank Willett, *Ife in the History of West African Sculpture* (London: Thames and Hudson, 1967), 70.

27.   Frank Willett and A. Dempster, "A Stone Carving in an Ife Style from Eshure, Ekiti, Western Nigeria," *MAN* 1 (1962): 1–5.

28.   O. B. Lawuyi, "The Obatala Factor in Yoruba History," *History in Africa* 19 (1992): 369–75; Willett, *Ife in the History of West African Sculpture*, 122–23.

29.   Eyo, "Odo Ogbe Street," 99–109; Ogundiran, "Chronology," 50; Adisa Ogunfolakan, "Archaeological Survey of Osun North-East, Osun State, Nigeria" (master's thesis, University of Ibadan, Nigeria, 1994).

30.   Ogunfolakan, "Archaeological Survey."

31.   Ogundiran, "Chronology," 50–51.

32.   Robert Soper, "Archaeological Work at Old Oyo," unpublished report, Department of Archaeology/Anthropology, University of Ibadan, Nigeria, 1975; Graham Connah, *The Archaeology of Benin* (Oxford: Oxford University Press, 1975), 32, 35; Babatunde Agbaje-Williams, *Archaeological Investigations of Itagunmodi Potsherd Pavement Site, Ijesaland, Osun State, Nigeria, 1991/92* (Ibadan, Nigeria: IFRA Publication, Institute of African Studies, University of Ibadan, 1995).

33.   Jonathan Aleru, "Archaeological Sites in Igbominaland, North-Central Yorubaland, Kwara State, Nigeria: The Need for Systematic Archaeological Research," *West African Journal of Archaeology* 22 (1993): 37–50; David Aremu, "Archaeological Reconnaissance and Excavation on Ipole Hilltop, Obo-Aiyegunle" (master's thesis, University of Ibadan, Nigeria, 1984); also David Aremu, "The Archaeology of Northeast Yorubaland with Emphasis on Early Techniques of Metal Working" (PhD diss., University of Ibadan, Nigeria, 1991); Usman, *State-Periphery Relations*, 2001.

34.   William H. Clarke, *Travels and Explorations in Yorubaland* (1854–1858), ed. J. A. Atanda (Ibadan, Nigeria: Ibadan University Press, 1972).

35.   Jonathan Aleru, "Thin Section Spectrographic and Petrographic Analysis of Pottery from Igbominaland, North Central Yorubaland," *West African Journal of Archaeology* 30, no. 2 (2000): 67–80.

36.   Usman, "State-Periphery Relations," 1998; also Aribidesi Usman, "A View from the Periphery: Northern Yoruba Villages during the Old Oyo Empire, Nigeria," *Journal of Field Archaeology* 27, no. 1 (2000): 43–61.

37.   Aribidesi Usman, Jonathan Aleru, and Raphael Alabi, "Sociopolitical Formation on the Yoruba Northern Frontier: A Report of Recent Work at Ila-Iyara, North Central Nigeria," *Journal of African Archaeology* 3, no. 1 (2005): 139–54.

38.   Phillip Stevens Jr., *The Stone Images of Esie, Nigeria* (New York: Africana Publishing, 1978); B. R. Hallam, "Excavation of a Shrine at Ijara Isin, Kwara State: Preliminary Report," *Confluence* 1 (1978): 26–35 (a publication of Kwara State Council for Arts and Culture, Ilorin, Nigeria); Usman, *State-Periphery Relations*, 2001.

39.   Stevens, *Stone Images*, 41.

40.   Henry Drewal, *Yoruba: Nine Centuries of African Arts and Thought* (New York: Center of African Art in association with H. N. Abrams, 1989), 88.

41. Ogunfolakan, "Archaeological Survey."

42. Ibid.

43. Oral interview with Chief James Akanbi Dada, the Asiwaju of Aun, aged 68 years, Ilorin, Kwara State, March 20, 2003.

44. Oral interview with Prince Abdul Rahman Afolabi, 75 years old, Okeola Oro, Kwara State, May 9, 2003.

45. Ibid.

46. Pemberton and Afolayan, *Yoruba Sacred Kingship*, 17; Adetoyi, *Short History*, 9.

47. Pemberton and Afolayan, *Yoruba Sacred Kingship*, 38.

48. Susan McIntosh and R. J. McIntosh, "From Stone to Metal: New Perspectives on the Later Prehistory of West Africa," *Journal of World Prehistory* 2, no. 1 (1988): 89–113.

49. Usman, *State-Periphery Relations*, 2001.

50. Oral interview with Oba Lawal Fabiyi II, the Onire of Owa Onire, aged 71 years, Owa Onire, Kwara State, October 1988.

51. Dada, *Brief History*, 21.

52. Denis Williams, *Icon and Image: A Study of Sacred and Secular Forms of African Classical Art* (London: Allen Lane, 1974), 84.

53. Kevin Carroll, *Yoruba Religious Carving* (New York: Praeger, 1967), 79.

54. Robert Smith, *Kingdoms of the Yoruba*, 2nd ed. (London: Methuen, 1976).

55. Robert Armstrong, "The Etymology of the Word 'Ogun,'" in *Africa's Ogun: Old World and New*, 2nd ed., ed. Sandra T. Barnes (Bloomington: Indiana University Press, 1997), 29–38.

56. Oral interview with Oba Lawal Fabiyi II, the Onire of Owa Onire, aged 71 years, Owa Onire, Kwara State, October 1988; oral interview with Mr. Oyedunmola, the ruler of Owode Ofaro, aged 85 years, Owode Ofaro, Kwara State, November 1988.

57. Alex Okpoko, "The Early Urban Centers and States in West Africa," *West African Journal of Archaeology* 17 (1987): 243–65; L. M. Pole, "Decline or Survival? Iron Production in West Africa from the Seventeenth to the Twentieth Centuries," *Journal of African History* 23, no. 4 (1982): 503–13.

58. Sandra Barnes, "The Many Faces of Ogun," in *Africa's Ogun: Old World and New*, 2nd ed., ed. Sandra T. Barnes (Bloomington: Indiana University Press), 1–28.

59. Samuel Johnson, *History of the Yorubas from the Earliest Times to the Beginning of the British Protectorate* (London: G. Routledge, 1921), 93.

60. G. J. Afolabi Ojo, *Yoruba Culture: A Geographical Analysis* (London: University of London Press, 1967), 106; for more information on this, see Hugh Clapperton, *Journal of a Second Expedition into the Interior of Africa, from the Bight of Benin to Soccatoo* (London: J. Murray, 1829).

61. Cornelius Adepegba, "Ife Art: An Enquiry into the Surface Patterns and the Continuity of Art Tradition among the Northern Yoruba," *West African Journal of Archaeology* 12 (1982): 95–109.

62. Olusegun Ekanade and Oluwole Aloba, "19th Century Yoruba Warfare: The Geographer's Viewpoint," in *War and Peace in Yorubaland 1793–1893*, ed. A. Akinjogbin, 21–31 (Ibadan, Nigeria: Heinemann, 1998).

63. Usman, "View from the Periphery," 43–61; see also Usman, Aleru, and Alabi, "Sociopolitical Formation," 139–54.

64.   Usman, *State-Periphery Relations*, 2001; Usman, Aleru, and Alabi, "Sociopolitical Formation," 139–54.

65.   Steven Akintoye, *Revolution and Power Politics in Yorubaland, 1840–1893* (New York: Humanities Press, 1971).

66.   J. D. Fage, *A History of Africa* (London: Hutchinson, 1978), 282.

67.   J. F. A. Ajayi and S. A. Akintoye, "Yorubaland in the Nineteenth Century," in *Groundwork of Nigerian History*, ed. Obaro Ikime, 280–302 (Ibadan: Heinemann, 1980).

68.   J. F. A. Ajayi and Robert Smith, *Yoruba Warfare in the Nineteenth Century* (Cambridge: Cambridge University Press, 1964).

69.   Joseph Atanda, *The New Oyo Empire: Indirect Rule and Change in Western Nigeria, 1894–1934* (London: Longman, 1973).

70.   Johnson, *History*, 200.

71.   Ajayi and Akintoye, "Yorubaland," 290.

72.   Akintoye, *Revolution and Power Politics*, 58–59; K. V. Elphinstone, *Gazetteer of Ilorin Province*, New Impression (London: Frank Cass, 1972), 17–18.

73.   Johnson, *History*, 323.

74.   Robert Thompson, *Flash of the Spirit* (New York: Vintage Books, 1983), 17.

75.   William Bascom, *Shango in the New World* (Austin, TX: African and Afro-American Research Institute, 1972), 13.

76.   Peter Morton-Williams, "The Oyo Yoruba and the Atlantic Trade, 1670 to 1830," in *Forced Migration*, ed. J. E. Inikori (New York: Africana Publishing Company, 1982), 169; William Bascom, "Two Forms of Afro-Cuban Divination," in *Acculturation in the Americas*, ed. Sol Tax (Chicago: University of Chicago Press, 1952), 13.

77.   Funso Afolayan, "War and Change in 19th Century Igbomina," in Akinjogbin, *War and Peace*, 77–90.

78.   Joseph Omoniyi, "Literary and Historical Reflections on the Yagba Protest Movement against Nupe Hegemony before 1939," in *Northeast Yorubaland: Studies in the History and Culture of a Frontier Zone*, ed. A. Olukoju, Z. O. Apata, and O. Akinwumi, 16–24 (Ibadan, Nigeria: Rex Charles Publication, 2003).

79.   Daniel Babalola, *Igbomina Art and Culture: An Introduction* (Zaria, Nigeria: Division of Art History, Ahmadu Bello University, and Okinbaloye Commercial Press, Ilorin, Nigeria, 1998), 18–19.

80.   Afolayan, "War and Change," 81–82.

81.   Elphinstone, *Gazetteer*, 43.

82.   Afolayan, "War and Change," 82.

83.   Michael Gleave, "Hill Settlements and Their Abandonment in Western Yorubaland," *Africa* 33 (1963): 343–52.

84.   Oral interviews with Pa Maliki Aremu, 72 years old, and Mr. Suberu Oluode, the head of the hunters, 56 years old, Alaabe village, Kwara State, February 10, 1990.

85.   Gleave, "Hill Settlements," 349.

86.   Usman, *State-Periphery Relations*, 2001.

87.   Graham Connah and G. S. Daniels, "Mining the Archives: A Pottery Sequence for Borno, Nigeria," *Journal of African Archaeology* 1, no. 3 (2003): 39–76.

88.   Aleru, "Thin Section Spectrographic Analysis," 67–80.

89.   Usman, Aleru, and Alabi, "Sociopolitical Formation," 139–54.

90. Usman, *State-Periphery Relations*, 2001.

91. Ibid.

92. Garlake, "Excavations on the Woye Asiri Land," 57–96.

93. Gbadegesin Ajekigbe, "Pottery Making in Ilora and Its Relationship with Old Oyo Pottery Finds," in *Historical Archaeology in Nigeria*, ed. K. W. Wesler, 99–141 (Trenton, NJ: Africa World Press, 1998), 1.

94. Frank Willett, "Investigations at Old Oyo, 1956–57: an Interim Report," *Journal of the Historical Society of Nigeria* 2 (1960): 59–77.

95. Aribidesi Usman, R. Speakman, and D. Glascock, "An Initial Assessment of Prehistoric Ceramic Production and Exchange in Northern Yoruba, North Central Nigeria: Results of Ceramic Compositional Analysis," *African Archaeological Review* 22, no. 3 (2005): 141–68.

96. Michael Glascock, "Characterization of Archaeological Ceramics at MURR by Neutron Activation Analysis and Multivariate Statistics," in *Chemical Characterization of Ceramic Pastes in Archaeology*, ed. H. Neff, 11–26 (Madison: University of Wisconsin Press, 1992).

97. Ian Hodder, *Symbols in Action: Ethnoarchaeological Studies of Material Culture* (Cambridge: Cambridge University Press, 1982); H. M. Wobst, "Stylistic Behavior and Information Exchange," in *Essays in Honor of James B. Griffin*, ed. C. E. Cleland (Ann Arbor, MI: Anthropology Paper no. 61, Museum of Anthropology, Ann Arbor, 1977).

98. Ajekigbe, "Pottery Making in Ilora," 135.

5

Migrations, Identities, and Transculturation in the Coastal Cities of Yorubaland in the Second Half of the Second Millennium

An Approach to African History through Architecture

BRIGITTE KOWALSKI OSHINEYE

Introduction

Studies of African architecture are rare, and many lacunae remain in the few works in this area. The architecture of African historical centers is in peril, and historical buildings are being destroyed as a result of economic activities, development projects, and land speculation. For example, the majority of the finest historical buildings on Lagos Island have been demolished and replaced by modern towers that reflect the current dynamism of the city.

Built during the nineteenth and twentieth centuries, these historical structures, called Afro-Brazilian buildings, are generally associated with colonial architecture. However, on closer examination, the word "colonial" appears justified only in reference to the features of colonial Brazilian architecture that distinguished the buildings. This architecture owes its features to freed slaves returning from the Americas. These ex-slaves, most of whom resettled in the societies from which they had departed, especially in the coastal region of West Africa, introduced new ways of life and new architectural styles acquired from the lands of their sojourn overseas. By examining patterns of international and interregional migration and of settlement, it is possible to detect and understand the cultural mix that contributed to and enriched Yoruba culture in the coastal region, especially in terms of architecture.

Using concrete examples, genealogical inquiries, narratives of travelers, and historical essays, this chapter[1] demonstrates the way in which the architectural features of the Afro-Brazilian buildings bear out the dynamism found in the population and encode its economic and cultural transformation.

Background

Narratives of nineteenth-century travelers mention new architectural features found along the coasts of Africa. For example, according to l'abbé Laffitte in 1860,

> les maisons des nègres libérés au Brésil marquent un progrès sensible sur la maçonnerie indigène . . . . on voit à la solidité des murs, à leur élévation, à l'aménagement intérieur, que son exil temporaire au milieu d'un peuple civilisé lui a été quelque peu profitable.[2]

Prior to the emergence of these new styles of building, slave traders on African coasts were generally lodged in traditionally built houses and compounds. For example, the first house occupied by Francisco Felix de Souza in Ouidah, as shown in figure 5.1, was a traditionally designed structure.

By the middle of the nineteenth century, new architectural features appeared in the coastal cities of the Slave Coast.[3] These new features constitute physical evidence of the new dynamics in the composition of the population that settled on the coasts. The change in population was tied to the onset of colonialism, the major event of the nineteenth century. After four centuries of trade with European and American nations, Africa began to come under the rule of Europe, which partitioned the continent between its great powers, France, Great Britain, Portugal, Germany, and Italy. On the Slave Coast, Lagos became in 1861 the first city to be annexed by Great Britain, following the treaty of 1851. The annexation of Badagry occurred in 1863, and in 1882, Porto Novo came under the protection of France. The following decades witnessed the expansion of British and French rule within the continent. Given the increase in the numbers of Europeans living in West Africa, it would seem reasonable to attribute to them the new architectural style that began to emerge during this period. Nonetheless, a closer examination of the emerging architecture reveals important structural and decorative features that require some explanation.

The Europeans designed colonial architecture for Africa and created special plans for their new colonies. For instance, the verandas running around the buildings of King's College in Lagos[4] and the palace of the governor in Porto Novo are typical of the colonial architecture designed for Africa. A study of colonial buildings, however, has shown that only a few of the buildings

Figure 5.1. First house occupied by Francisco Felix de Souza, Brazilian slave trader settled in Ouidah in 1800. The compound and house are traditional in manner, materials, techniques, and plan. Credit: Brigitte Kowalski Oshineye.

in the coastal regions actually corresponded to the colonial architectural plan.[5] Most of the buildings involved designs and features that not only deviated from the colonial style proposed for Africa but also deviated from traditional African architecture, while others revealed links to the colonial architectural style designed for Brazil.

If colonialism changed the economic and political structures of the African continent, a careful examination of the patterns of architecture will show that the abolition of the slave trade probably contributed more to influencing the structural landscape and producing cultural changes than colonialism did. The argument of this chapter is that the emergence of new cultural groups in the coastal regions of West Africa resulted from the slave trade and its abolition and was connected with the emergence of new cultural features found in the architecture of the coastal cities of Africa.

In sum, there are various sources for the differing architectural patterns of the Afro-Brazilian style on the coast of West Africa. The observed styles are connected with the different cultural and ethnic origins of the people who converged in the coastal region due to the abolition of slavery and the inception of colonization. The chapter will show how this mixture of people produced "creolized" architectural styles. The next section describes the different architectural styles found in this region.

Architectural Features: Plans and Decorations

The study of Afro-Brazilian houses in Porto Novo, Lagos, Badagry, and Abeokuta reveals different styles in plan and decoration. There are three identifiable architectural plans. These are the classical Brazilian type, the Badagry type, and the Yoruba-Brazilian type. These plans were used in building one- or multiple-story houses.

Structures built according to the classical Brazilian plan have a front and a rear veranda, and a central parlor. Rooms are situated on each side of the parlor, with openings to the parlor and onto the front veranda. In general, the access to a one-level house is through a door open in the front veranda. For all one- and multiple-story houses, another access to the residential area is created in the middle of the rear veranda. In buildings with two or more stories, the first floor is used as a store. For multiple-story houses, two types of plan exist, one with a front and a rear veranda, the other without the front veranda. The classical Brazilian plan is well represented in Porto Novo and Lagos; a few such structures exist in Badagry and in Abeokuta.

The second type of architecture is the Badagry style. In contrast to the classical Brazilian style, the parlor of the Badagry type is in the façade and it opens onto rooms situated at the back of the house. A porch in the middle of the façade gives access to the parlor, which itself opens to a corridor or passage located on the right or left of the building. The same type of plan is used for single- and multiple-story houses. As in classical Brazilian buildings, the first floor is occupied by shops. Access to the next level is through a door on one side of the building that opens directly onto the street. This corridor leads from the front door to the courtyard behind the building. A staircase located in the corridor gives access to another corridor at the next level. In this corridor, a door opens onto the front parlor of the residential area. The parlor is always situated in front of the building and it faces the street. The other rooms are placed at the back of the house, behind the parlor, facing the courtyard. This building style is well represented in Badagry and Lagos, and less so in Porto Novo.

The third type of plan is called the Yoruba-Brazilian style. This type is characterized by a central corridor that traverses the entire house, ending up at the courtyard that is situated behind the building. The corridor contains a door that opens onto the front parlor. In the front parlor, two doors lead to rooms situated at the back of the house. This same template is used on each side of the building. In many instances, this type of house combines retail and residential sections. These two areas are separated by a corridor. The living area has a parlor whose front portion opens onto the street and onto rooms located in the inner courtyard, at the back of the building. The other part is the shop. It opens onto the street through a large door and it has a room at the back that is used for storage. Both single-story and

and multiple-story houses follow the same plan, except that multiple-story houses have a staircase in the middle of the central corridor that leads to the higher levels. This architectural style includes features from the Badagry plan, as well as features from several other cultures including those of Yorubaland and Brazil. The last houses, built around 1935–50, are little different and are organized around a long central corridor opening onto all the rooms. This Yoruba-Brazilian type is well attested in Lagos and Badagry; it is very frequent in Egbadoland and Egbaland, and has been seen in Ado-Odo, Ilaro, Oke Odan, and Abeokuta.

The following section describes the pattern of decoration that accompanies the styles of construction. The first type, exemplified by the Water House (see figure 5.2), could be described as the Brazilian style. Other houses that illustrate this decorative pattern are the Branco House in Porto Novo and the Doherty House in Lagos. The decoration is specific to Brazil, and the façade reproduces the decoration of Bahian buildings in Brazil.

The second type, unlike the traditional pattern, is flowery in nature. It has been called "Lagos flower" by Joann Shaw;[6] however, I prefer to refer to it as the Badagry type because of its prevalence in Badagry. Although this type appears in Lagos, it seems to have been adopted from Badagry and its environs. Almost all the buildings in Badagry and the villages around it have a flower pattern situated in the middle of the running molding surrounding the window. This decorative design has green leaves, red or blue petals, and a yellow heart; it incorporates bright colors that enhance its appearance. A sample of this pattern is seen on the Arigbawonwo House (see figure 5.3), and it is also found on the Layode houses in Badagry. This decorative type is enriched by new designs from Europe. The European features include the cross of David, shells, and ribbons. The main characteristics of the style are the little flower carved in plaster at the top of the window and the leaves at each corner of the running ornament surrounding the window.

In Abeokuta and its environs, especially toward the south, the most frequently found style is the Yoruba-Brazilian style. This involves a mixture of Brazilian and European decorative arts as well as other influences that remain to be determined. This third style appears to be an interpretation of the Brazilian style by Yoruba craftsmen. This Yoruba-Brazilian style includes various decorations, including figurative or geometrical symbols with Islamic references, especially toward the end of the period, that is, 1930–45. This Yoruba-Brazilian style was favored in the hinterland, but with slight regional variations. The Yoruba-Brazilian decoration in Abeokuta is different from that of Osogbo. The existence of this third style underscores the appropriation of the style and the incorporation of new designs into Yoruba culture.

Figure 5.2. Water House in Lagos Island, Nigeria. One of the most famous and most typical buildings in the Brazilian style of the Slave Coast. Credit: Brigitte Kowalski Oshineye.

Figure 5.3. Arigbawonwo House in Badagry, Nigeria. The front façade presents all the typical decorations of the Badagry Brazilian style: porch, flowers carved at the top of the running molding surrounding the windows, and a base with engraved and painted designs. Credit: Brigitte Kowalski Oshineye.

Architectural Features, Urbanism, and Cultural and Economic Changes

The different types of Afro-Brazilian architecture are indicative of the different sources of influences on the style. In addition, the differences reflect the changing composition of the population in Yorubaland at this period. The evolution of Afro-Brazilian architecture attests to the economic changes occurring in the coastal region between 1840 and 1950.

Given their close resemblance to buildings in the colonial style in Brazil, the majority of the Afro-Brazilian buildings are evidence of the return of freed slaves and ex-slaves from Brazil to Africa. This return was propelled by the "Revolt of the Malés" in 1835 in Bahia. The government of Bahia, frightened by several insurrections of slaves and freed slaves in Brazil, made many arrests and finally decided to send back to Africa the "undesirable slaves" as was reported in 1835:

> bannir tout Africain libre suspect, . . . 150 de ces Africains ont été envoyés à la côte d'Afrique, aux frais de la dépense publique; 120 d'entre eux ont été bannis comme suspects, et les autres sont une partie de ceux pris dans le trafic de contrebande.

The first shipment of people back to Africa contained insurgents, suspects, and individuals who had been freed from the prohibited trade in human cargo. Subsequent shipments included Afro-Brazilians, for whom, due to the political upheaval, the situation in Bahia had become quite insecure. They voluntarily chose to leave, as was explained in the same report:

> Le résultat immédiat de cette mesure a été le départ volontaire de beaucoup d'autres Africains. Davantage encore se prépare à quitter notre territoire.[7]

Further evidence of this exodus showing that wealthy members of the Afro-Brazilian community became worried and boarded ships to take them back to Africa is also found in this report. This report shows that wealthy members of the Afro-Brazilian community became worried and boarded ships to take them back to Africa:

> Nous avons appris qu'un nombre considérable d'Africains libres, deux à trois cents, étaient sur le point d'embarquer pour la côte d'Afrique, et qu'un vaisseau britannique avait été affrété par eux pour cinq contos de reis (875 livres sterling à l'époque), pour les convoyer au lieu d'où ils sont venus, un point nommé Onim (Lagos) . . . . Une enquête nous a montré que l'entreprise était dirigée par un Noir libéré, qui faisait partie de la cargaison d'esclaves amenés ici par l'Emilia en 1821. Ayant acquis une certaine aisance parmi ses concitoyens émancipés, il l'a utilisée pour les engager à retourner en leur pays natal.

Pour faciliter l'opération, il a vendu divers esclaves, sa propriété personnelle, et donné la liberté à six autres qui devaient l'accompagner. [8]

As seen above, some of the freed Afro-Brazilian slaves were wealthy individuals, who owned businesses and slaves in Brazil. The status and quality of life of these wealthy individuals were significant factors influencing the manner of their settlement once they arrived back in Africa. In addition to wealth and status, these people had also acquired in Brazil a new culture, knowledge, and skills that they later introduced to the various parts of Africa to which they relocated.[9] Among these returnees were craftsmen and farmers, who created new economic activities in Africa and contributed to the transformation of the coastal cities, their preferred place of settlement. Their return was soon to be favored by the colonial administration.

Ce qui est appelé par erreur la partie brésilienne de cette capitale, composée de marchands, négociants, artisans, marins, laboureurs, ouvriers et autres représentants de la communauté avancée, ordonnée, active, stable et respectable, présente un exemple de citoyens généralement dignes de louanges. Pour un pays comme l'Afrique occidentale, le développement de nouveaux intérêts agricoles et, en conséquence, de ses plans économiques est de la plus grande importance; aussi le rapatriement de ses artisans et agriculteurs qualifiés est-il particulièrement souhaitable.[10]

The freed slaves coming back to the coast at first built traditional houses. In Porto Novo, the first house occupied by Bambeiro Paraiso (his surname is indicative of his profession, that of a barber) was built with traditional techniques and materials. A few years later, he built for his son an Afro-Brazilian house in brick, following the classical Brazilian pattern. The professions of the father and son as barber and tailor, as well as their knowledge of the Portuguese language and foreign cultures, made them well accepted and soon indispensable to traders. As a result, they became wealthy and were able in a few years to build for themselves prestigious houses in the coastal cities.

According to Edgar Foa, by the end of the nineteenth century, the Afro-Brazilians had not only become settled but had become integrated with the class of Portuguese that included slave traders of different origins and mulattoes:

à Whydah, à Lagos, à Porto Novo, des noirs brésiliens . . . occupent actuellement le même rang que les mulâtres réellement brésiliens et sont entre le blanc et l'indigène . . . . Ils ont un peu voyagé, un peu vu et fréquenté l'Europe, copié ses usages; il ne leur reste plus du noir que la couleur. Ils vivent comme les étrangers, en dehors des détails pénibles des lois indigènes, et sont, enfin, fort heureux dans leur pays où leurs parents ont tant souffert.[11]

In Lagos, the Afro-Brazilians, who were also called Aguda, settled in the Portuguese Quarter. The name was changed to Brazilian Quarter at the end of the nineteenth century. The foreign culture of the Aguda and their economic power gave them a special place in African society. They became servants of African kings, and later of the colonial administrations. In Porto Novo, d'Albeca noted, concerning their position within the circle of African elites during the second part of the nineteenth century, that

> ils ont des factories et tiennent souvent en échec des maisons européennes. Les José Marcos, Ignacio Paraiso, Bakari, etc., sont des notables, riches, considérés et très prisés du roi indigène Toffa, auquel ils prêtent de l'argent.[12]

Porto Novo (Benin Republic)

In Porto Novo, as shown in figure 5.4, the wealthy Afro-Brazilian merchants settled near the lagoon and enjoyed unhindered access to the Atlantic. Their settlements were also near the king's palace. The Afro-Brazilian buildings from this era are still standing today, and their styles correspond to the description provided by Lieutenant Gellé:

> partie basse peuplée de petits traitants étrangers et d'afro-brésiliens. Ces derniers développent un habitat qui se distingue des concessions africaines en rez-de-chaussée: des maisons à étages apparaissent dans la ville aux couleurs vives et aux formes et aux plans inspirés des habitations bourgeoises du Brésil.[13]

According to Lieutenant Gellé, the Afro-Brazilian community had introduced the Afro-Brazilian style, which soon became a symbol of a certain social position. Thus, it was adopted by the elite of the African society: "Certains dignitaires du royaume se font édifier des maisons semblables à celles des 'brésiliens,' notamment le roi dans ses deux palais."[14]

Famous masons, such as Senior Lazaro Borges da Silva, Senior Francisco Nobre, and Senior Juan Baptist da Costa, all contributed to enriching Lagos Island with new architectural features. Master carpenters, such as Senior Balthazar dos Reis in Lagos, gave a new impulse to Yoruba woodwork and introduced a new repertoire of furniture and designs that became popular in local high society. These craftsmen were so famous that they were called in to build in different cities of the coast. For example, the Great Mosque of Porto Novo, shown in figure 5.5, was erected by Afro-Brazilian craftsmen from Lagos. By the middle of the nineteenth century, when European administrations and traders settled in the various coastal cities to develop the legal trade based on palm oil and palm kernels, they found in existence convenient houses and a pool of craftsmen for their needs.

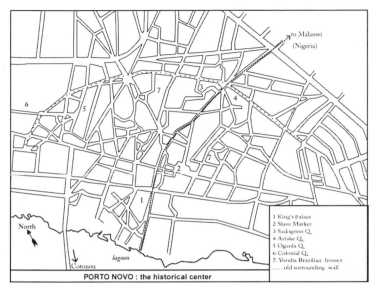

Figure 5.4. Plan of Porto Novo, Benin Republic. A street has replaced the wall surrounding the city. The returnees settled first between the lagoon and the king's palace (1), then Afro-Brazilian buildings followed the road from the lagoon to Malanwi, in the direction of Yorubaland. The Colonial Quarter (6) was situated outside the surrounding wall, and a quarter for colonial officials was erected by Afro-Brazilians in Oganla (5). Credit: Brigitte Kowalski Oshineye.

Figure 5.5. The Great Mosque of Porto Novo, Benin Republic. The Great Mosque was built after a visit to the Central Mosque of Lagos and by the same master masons. The decoration is very close to the Baroque style in Brazil; the plan adopts the pattern of a Christian basilica. Credit: Brigitte Kowalski Oshineye.

In Porto Novo, an entire quarter was built by Afro-Brazilian investors to lodge colonial administrators and officials. Oganla Quarter, shown in figure 5.4, was situated close to the Colonial Quarter. Oganla Quarter contained Afro-Brazilian style residences that were rented out to colonial administrators. As is confirmed by family records, the name of the quarter, Oganla,[15] which means "big chief" and refers to the chief colonial officer, is indicative of the successful integration of the Brazilian community into Yoruba culture. Aguda adopted Yoruba names in order to reconnect with their African roots.[16] The giving of Yoruba names to quarters underscores the importance of the trade link between Yorubaland and Porto Novo and the preferred trade routes before the colonial borders became fixed.

In Porto Novo, the preferred relationships between countries at an earlier period are revealed by the road bordered by classical Brazilian buildings, noted as 1, 2, 3, and 4 in figure 5.4. This road was probably the trade route connecting traders in Yoruba cities of (what is now) Nigeria with Porto Novo before colonial rule. This road linked the east of the town of Porto Novo to the lagoon. It was connected to Malanwi and to the Yoruba cities of Ado-Odo, Ilaro, and Abeokuta, and it went through Porto Novo, passing through two quarters, Attake and Sadognon Haoussa. In Porto Novo, the road then passed the big market, the major slave market of the Slave Coast, and the king's palace, ending at the lagoon. Porto Novo is situated at a crossroads between Yorubaland and the Atlantic ports. To the east, the lagoon links Porto Novo to Badagry and to Lagos; to the west, Porto Novo is linked to Ouidah and the ports of the Slave Coast.

The distribution of the different Afro-Brazilian styles reflects the economic changes following the settlement of new population groups from the nineteenth century to the beginning of the twentieth century.[17] The political and economic changes caused by French rule are illustrated by the residential Afro-Brazilian buildings in Porto Novo. Trade buildings adopting French architectural features were built close to the lagoon between the king's palace and the Colonial Quarter. These new architectural features reveal the transfer of power from the king to the French administration. The construction by the French administration of a bridge and a railroad connecting Porto Novo to Cotonou underscores and illustrates the colonial preferences in terms of trade routes.

Subsequent to the development of agricultural production imposed by colonial rule, houses of the Badagry style are found located behind the slave market, on the eastern side of the road to Yorubaland, as shown in figure 5.4. These buildings were occupied by Yoruba families from Oyo, such as the Olatunji and Balogun families. Buildings of the Yoruba-Brazilian style are located between Oganla Quarter and the former Brazilian Quarter. Many of the Yoruba families had resided in other cities of the Slave Coast, such as Badagry, before settling in Porto Novo.[18] The distribution of the different styles seems to be indicative of the waves of Yoruba migrations from inland, following the fall of the Oyo Kingdom. The observed pattern of migrations is connected with the development of trade. It illustrates the participation of Yoruba people in economic activities and reflects the changes in economic organization that were occurring during the nineteenth century and at the beginning of the twentieth century.

Badagry

Evidence of Yoruba merchants in Badagry is found in family histories. Initially, Yoruba migration to this region was associated with the fall of the Oyo Kingdom in 1831, and then associated with an increase in the exportation of agricultural products. Badagry settlements were organized into quarters, each of them headed by a chief. Jegba Quarter was headed by the Akran from Ketonou, a little village near Porto Novo in the Benin Republic. Boekoh Quarter was headed by the Mobbe family. His first chief, Boe, came from Whydah in the Benin Republic, at the time of the invasion of the city by the Dahomey Kingdom in the second quarter of the eighteenth century. Possukoh Quarter was headed by the Possu, issued from Dahomey Kingdom, and settled in Badagry during the eighteenth century. These chiefs lived in Afro-Brazilian house types that combined a classical Brazilian plan with patterns of decoration from different Afro-Brazilian types.

The Yoruba, who came from inland during the nineteenth century, settled in all the quarters. Initially, these migrants came with specialized skills such as tailoring, but they soon turned to trading. Their houses correspond to the Badagry type. In the majority of cases, stores and shops were built close to the house. Other migrants adopted the Yoruba-Brazilian type, which contained a central corridor dividing the building into two halves. One half was residential and the second half served as shops and stores. The combination of residential areas and shops seems to have been utilitarian and driven by trading activities.

Despite the Afro-Brazilian elements in the buildings and their influence on architecture in Badagry, no Afro-Brazilians can be located in the town. A study of the houses provides a probable reason for their absence. In Badagry, the houses suggest an evolution from the classical Brazilian type to the Badagry type. Mobee House presents a classical Brazilian plan. But an elaborate porch is placed in the middle of the front façade, introducing a new item, usually seen on the Badagry type. A similar porch is found on the Layode houses on the Marina, but it opens directly onto a parlor replacing the front veranda, and the rooms are located at the back of the building. This is the Badagry type.

The Badagry plan incorporates the traditional Yoruba style. It has a front veranda that has an opening to rooms situated at the back of the building.

The front veranda of the traditional Yoruba plan is replaced by a front parlor in the Badagry and Yoruba-Brazilian types of the Afro-Brazilian style. In the Badagry and Yoruba-Brazilian types, the front parlor that replaces the front veranda is closed. Its façade has Brazilian features and it includes a decorated porch that gives access directly to the road. The importance given to the decoration of the porch and façade can be related to the symbolic representation of the wealth of the owner within traditional Yoruba architecture. A closer look at the Alafia Compound in Badagry confirms the connection with traditional Yoruba culture. For example, the trade buildings of the compound are placed in such a way that they surround the courtyard. At the end of the courtyard are rooms for the employees. These rooms were built to have an open veranda in front of them. This spatial organization is directly tied to the traditional Yoruba impluvium and it differs from a Brazilian compound, which is surrounded by trade buildings and has a family house located in the middle of the courtyard.

Family records such as that of the Alafia family also help to explain the transformation from the Brazilian to the Yoruba-Brazilian architectural style in Badagry. According to the descendants of the family, the original Alafia got his surname through the Yoruba salutations he received from white traders who were unable to remember his name. He came to Badagry as a tailor because of the depression in the Oyo Kingdom in 1831. Gradually, he got into trade and sold palm oil and palm kernels, and became wealthy. The personal story of Alafia illustrates the history of the Yoruba community and its participation in the legal trade during the nineteenth century. Displaced from the Yoruba kingdoms, Yoruba people moved to the south and took part in the economic activities of the coastal cities. Gradually, they became middlemen in the distribution of agricultural products, replacing the Afro-Brazilians, who had left Badagry to invest in the international trade concentrated in such big centers as Lagos and Porto Novo. Yoruba settlement in the coastal cities is connected with new architectural features that combined Brazilian styles with other influences that seem to have come from Yorubaland.

Abeokuta, Egbaland, and Egbadoland

The Yoruba-Brazilian type is prevalent in Badagry, Lagos, and Abeokuta, and in villages between Badagry and Abeokuta. By the use of colonial reports and travelers' narratives, these architectural types may be connected with another group of freed slaves who came from Sierra Leone during the nineteenth century. Called Saro in Lagos and Abeokuta, these people were emancipated by the British who were charged with the enforcement of the treaty abolishing the slave trade.

The captured ships were redirected to the new colony of Sierra Leone, where the enslaved people were set free and joined the population of the new colony that had been created in 1787. The inquiries of the Select Committee of Sierra Leone mentioned the return of many of them in the second quarter of the nineteenth century.

> On estime qu'entre 1839 et 1842, près de 500 d'entre eux quittèrent Sierra Leone. Ceux qui débarquèrent à Badagris s'en tirèrent relativement bien, mais la plupart de ceux qui allèrent à Lagos furent volés par les chefs esclavagistes locaux, et s'échappèrent vers Abéokuta avec les quelques vêtements qu'ils avaient pu sauver.[19]

The contribution of the Saro and Aguda to the elaboration of the Afro-Brazilian style becomes quite evident in Abeokuta, a town with a variety of Afro-Brazilian buildings. R. F. Borghero, who visited the town in the middle of the nineteenth century, described it as a traditional Yoruba town: "Souvent les maisons des Egbas sont de forme carrée, avec une cour au milieu."[20] This suggests that the new architecture must have appeared in Abeokuta after the middle of the nineteenth century. Benjamin Campbell, consul in Lagos, testified that Brazilians from Lagos asked for his permission to move inland in 1859. The migrants wanted to return to the land of their origins, according to the consul's report:

> plusieurs Africains self emancipated des Brésils ayant, après leur arrivée dans ce pays, manifesté le grand désir de retourner en leurs anciens pays dans le Youraba (Yorouba), Houssa (Haoussa) et Nuffé (Tapa).[21]

The Aguda joined the Saro and Yoruba who settled in Abeokuta after the creation of the kingdom in 1830. The transformation of Abeokuta is due to the Saro and Aguda. The architectural features reveal various building styles, such as a wooden house in Agoba Oja Quarter (see figure 5.6). Wooden houses were not built traditionally in Yorubaland or in Brazil.

The Red Book of West Africa and families' narratives tell of the varied origins of freed slaves, for example the Vaughans in Lagos, whose

> business was established in 1873 by [the man] whose name it bears, Mr. J. C. Vaughan, an American citizen, who was born at Camden, South Carolina . . . . it has been under the sole control of his son, Mr. J. W. Vaughan, who was born in Abeokuta in 1866.[22]

In Sierra Leone, emancipated African slaves called "recaptives" joined a population settled there by the British abolitionists. This population was composed of poor Africans from Great Britain, Nova Scotians, black Loyalists

Figure 5.6. House in Agoba Oja Quarter in Abeokuta is unusual, probably due to the returnees from Sierra Leone. Credit: Brigitte Kowalski Oshineye.

from the American War of Independence, and Maroons from Jamaica. The freed African slaves were welcomed by the Anglican mission and they participated in the expansion of the territory of the new colony. Most of them became itinerant merchants trading with the interior. Some of them achieved important positions in international trade. For instance, H. W. Macauley, during the inquiries of the Select Committee, declared:

> les Africains libérés faisaient le commerce avec plus de bénéfice que les march-
> ands blancs . . . car déjà depuis de nombreuses années, ils avaient peu à peu
> réussi; beaucoup d'entre eux sont bons commerçants. Et après avoir renvoyé
> hors du marché les maroons et les colons, ils renvoient maintenant graduelle-
> ment les commerçants blancs.[23]

Nineteenth-century travelers described Freetown, the capital of the new colony, as European, or Nova Scotian, or Caribbean.[24] In fact, the buildings in Freetown reflected the varied origins of the people who settled there. The architectural plan for Sierra Leone, described by Sylvie Kande,[25] cor-responds to the shotgun houses that were first built in Haiti and then in the south of the United States of America. The relationship to shotgun houses involves the corridor that traverses the whole building and serves the rooms on each side. The evolution of the Yoruba-Brazilian plan may be explained by the return of the Saro to Badagry and Abeokuta, cities that were assuming importance as a result of a mixed settlement.[26] However, the contribution of the Saro to the Yoruba-Brazilian style remains to be clearly defined. A study of foreign architecture in Sierra Leone would be of great importance in this regard.

Considering the importance of the Saro community in Yorubaland and the community's origin, there are two possible reasons or groups of reasons for their influence on Brazilian Yoruba architecture. First, many houses on the Slave Coast reveal that Afro-Brazilian masons were able to build on demand. They were able to adapt the plan to the compounds and were also able to create different kinds of designs. Freed Africans in Sierra Leone were trained in masonry and carpentry, according to a colonial record: "J'ai bien sûr fait le compte pour les bâtiments dans les villages séparément et avec le nombre d'artisans que nous formons parmi les nègres capturés."[27] They were also familiar with the knowledge of the brick-making technique that was characteristic of Afro-Brazilian architecture.

> un africain libéré de Bathurst avait essayé de faire des briques de glaise à Mandinari. Il a réussi, et maintenant il les produit, à 50 shillings les mille . . . . L'homme en cuit un millier à la fois, dans une termitière creuse.[28]

Second, Saro craftsmen may have been able to join the group of Afro-Brazilian masons in Yorubaland. The integration of the members of the Saro community into the elite society of the coastal cities and their contribution to cultural changes were reflected in their position in Lagos at the beginning of the twentieth century. Allister Macmillan[29] noted in 1920 that Mr. I. A. Cole, born in 1862 in Lagos, had opened a technological institute:

> as a builder and contractor Mr. Cole has done much for the improvement of Lagos and among the buildings erected by him are Elephant House . . . I.D. Hospital in Egye, Bishop's Court, offices of Lagos Stores, Messrs John Holt & Co's stores, and numerous staff quarters for various firms in Lagos, Kano, Zaria, and Ibadan.

Many Saro were originally Yoruba taken into slavery in the first half of the nineteenth century. The social position that they acquired in Sierra Leone gave them the opportunity to return empowered to their original country. Upon their return, most of them took Yoruba-style names such as Bankole or Giwa. They probably contributed to the introduction and development of new architectural features in Afro-Brazilian architecture.

The special designs in Abeokuta testify to the successful integration of the Afro-Brazilian style into Yoruba culture. One example is a house situated at the entrance of Abeokuta on the road from Lagos. The flower design found

Figure 5.7. House situated at the entrance to Abeokuta, on the road from Lagos, Nigeria. The decoration is typical of the Yoruba Brazilian style, and is representative of the integration of styles and the creation of new designs by local craftsmen. The flowers on the capitals of the colonnade show an interpretation of a design particularly appreciated in many cities of the Slave Coast. The shape of the porch is also characteristic of the Yoruba Brazilian style. Credit: Brigitte Kowalski Oshineye.

on the capitals of the front veranda (see figure 5.7) seems to be an interpretation of the flowers on the capitals of Branco House (see figure 5.8) in Porto Novo. In Abeokuta, craftsmen seem to have enriched the Afro-Brazilian repertoire with special features, decorating features such as porches and wooden doors with new designs, such as heraldic items. The particular attention given to these architectural elements is connected to traditional Yoruba art. Pillars, wooden doors, and decoration emphasized the social position of the owner of the building in traditional Yoruba society.

Several villages on the road from Badagry to Abeokuta appear to have been important crossroads on different axes linking Porto Novo, Badagry, Lagos, and Abeokuta. The beautiful and important buildings in Afro-Brazilian style found in these villages are indicative of their economic importance. In Ado-Odo, for example, there is a quarter that was built in Afro-Brazilian style. The decoration of the buildings reveals the entire repertoire of new designs adopted between the end of the nineteenth century and the second half of the twentieth century. A surprising feature is a house (see figure 5.9) that looks like a palace. A front veranda with sculpted wood pillars is characteristic of a traditional Yoruba palace, but here the pillars are replaced by a multicolored colonnade in Afro-Brazilian style. The fine treatment of the

Figure 5.8. Capital of Branco House in Porto Novo, Benin republic. Characteristic of the classical Brazilian style, here, the "prototype" of the flowers seen on the house in Abeokuta is in stucco. Some later examples were observed in cement in Porto Novo and Badagry. Credit: Brigitte Kowalski Oshineye.

Figure 5.9. Akindele House in Ado-Odo. The front façade is reminiscent of a Yoruba palace with its columns replacing the traditional carved pillars, as in the Bale's Palace in Lagos. The multicolored decoration in cement is characteristic of the Yoruba Brazilian style. The carved door with blazon and the porch topped by a crown surrounded by leaves are new features. These designs are observed from Badagry to Abeokuta. Credit: Brigitte Kowalski Oshineye.

carved door reminds one of the carving and significance of the door in Yoruba traditional art. This building, because of its magnificence, illustrates the contribution of Brazilian features that serve to reflect the importance, social position, and wealth of the owner in accordance with Yoruba traditions and patterns. Islamic inscriptions were also found on the front doors of some houses, just as houses in Lagos had Yoruba proverbs or sentences about the family inscribed on their front doors.

Lagos

As the capital of Nigeria under colonial rule, Lagos attracted traders from all the neighboring cities including Porto Novo, Abeokuta, and Badagry. A mixed community emerged, related by marriage and trade and linking various cultural groups whose members recognized themselves first as Yoruba people. The urbanization of Lagos during the nineteenth century reflected the varied ethnic composition of the population. The quarter of the indigenes surrounded the king's palace, and outsiders occupied the rest of the island. The outsiders' areas included the Brazilian Quarter, the Saro Quarter, the Missions Quarter, the Colonial Quarter, and the Marina, which was settled by traders. Today, the Brazilian Quarter on Lagos Island reflects this cultural mix. Its buildings reflect all the Afro-Brazilian types. Their mixed origin is revealed by family names, for example, King-Tinubu or Bankole-Wilson.[30] The magnificence of the buildings in Lagos revealed the dynamism of the city then, just as the glass towers do today. Unfortunately, most of the Afro-Brazilian buildings have disappeared.

Afro-Brazilian architecture was effectively introduced by freed slaves who came from different places such as Brazil and Sierra Leone. But the Afro-Brazilian architecture in Yorubaland reflected a mixture of influences, from Brazil, Sierra Leone, and Yorubaland. It also reflected the economic and political contributions of a mixed African community, for example, Aguda, Saro, and Yoruba. The following description of the Elephant House on Lagos Island confirms the social position of the local traders and, more importantly, of the new class of merchants (composed of Aguda and Saro and Yoruba on the eastern Slave Coast) who were competing with European companies:

> To one unversed in local affairs, the appearance of the mansion suggests that it is the abode of some great man of state or some wealthy foreigner, as though no son of the people could attain to a position commensurate with that indicated by so grand a dwelling.[31]

Furthermore, the buildings in Lagos illustrate the integration of new population components, Aguda and Saro, into the local elite and underscore their association with large African families such as Akitoye and Akerele.

Conclusion

Afro-Brazilian architecture, by its different patterns and designs, revealed the new religions and behaviors of its population. Conversion to Islam and Christianity is suggested by the erection of mosques and churches as well as by the designs on the front façades that reflected both local and international events. The distribution of the different styles is related to the settlement patterns of the freed slaves along the Slave Coast. For instance, while Aguda settled in all the coastal cities of the Slave Coast, Saro preferred to settle in its eastern part. This choice can be explained by the pursuit of the illegal slave trade in the western part at the time of their return. Ouidah was the major port for the illegal trade and Saro, as they knew English, were often seen as British spies in the town. There may be a second reason for their settlement in the British colony. Ex-slaves, captured and brought into slavery by the slave traders of Ouidah or Aneho or Agoué, Saro were afraid to be recaptured.

The development of the Afro-Brazilian style also reflects the relationship between the colony and its metropolis. From 1920 to 1950, the Afro-Brazilian style adopted European architectural features. This was the period of European rule. The borders of each colony were fixed, and roads and railways started to be built. Buildings in the western part of the Slave Coast, from Aneho to Porto Novo, included French-type decorations and styles. In the same way, patterns and styles from England and from other British colonies were introduced into the eastern part of the coast. The introduction of European features confirms the integration of African elites into international business and their access to European commodities. Children were sent to famous schools such as Fourah Bay College in Freetown or King's College in Lagos, and later to England or France: "Mr. Pearse is the proud and happy father of four children—three girls and a boy. The two eldest girls are at school in England."[32] Active participation in business turned the Aguda-Saro community into powerful traders and investors, who introduced new architectural features.

> At the time of writing Mr. Thomas is on a visit to Europe, which may result in the [extension] of the scope of his operations in European and American centres . . . .
>
> The head office of the business comprises a large three-storied building in William Street . . . . On the Marina at Elegbata, Itolo, Offin, and Idunmagbo are other stores . . . . Branches of the business are established at Agege, Agbado, Agbessi, Alagaba, Abeokuta, Ileigbo, Ikirun, Ilorin, Kani, Lafenwa, Lalupon, Owowo, Opeji, Olodo and Osogbo, with an agency at Zaria and factories at Iwo, Ede, and other stations . . . also at Calabar and in the Cameroons, with probable extensions to Sierra Leone and Gold Coast . . . . he owns [a model

farm] in Nigeria. The farm is under the supervision of an American and his wife . . . . In addition to the large number of his native employees, Mr. Thomas has eight Europeans in his service in Nigeria.[33]

This emerging Yoruba identity was modified and enriched by the different cultures brought with them by Yoruba and freed slaves returning to Yorubaland.

Contemporary Yoruba identity is a mix of influences woven together over time. Architecture provides useful information on the process of introduction and appropriation of external cultures, as well as on the social mutations of new architectural patterns in Yoruba territory. The study of Afro-Brazilian architecture makes it possible to determine how Yoruba people integrated foreign influences to create an original culture. It also reveals that African cultures and arts have been evolving through time because of migrations, transculturation, and reactions to historical events. Thus, African architecture demands the attention of the liberal arts, as it is a significant source of information on African history, on the construction of present-day African identities, and on world history.

Notes

1.   This chapter follows on from a previous study of the Afro-Brazilian architectural heritage on the Slave Coast and refers to an aspect of my current research, the origin of the emancipated slaves who resettled in the Gulf of Guinea and their impact on Yoruba culture and history. Using architecture as evidence of cultural interactions, my research, using historical, linguistic, and oral inquiries as well as architectural evidence, has the purpose of clarifying the history of Africa and its diaspora during the period from the slave trade and its abolition to colonial rule, in the area from Zinder (a Hausa city-state) to the Gulf of Guinea (the Yoruba kingdoms and their neighbors) and the Atlantic ocean and the lands bordering it (the U.S. South, the Caribbean islands, and Brazil). My research focuses on the history and the cultures of the African diaspora, and the participation of the returnees in the economic and social changes created by British and French rule over the Yoruba kingdoms. The influence of each component of population in the Gulf of Guinea under colonial rule informs my research on the links established in the Atlantic world by the African diaspora, with particular attention to the role of Sierra Leone in the process of cultural interaction and political change in Africa during the nineteenth century.

2.   M. l'abbé Laffitte, *Le Dahomé, souvenirs de voyage et de mission* (Tours, France: Alfred Mame et Fils, 1873). "The houses from the freed Negroes from Brazil demonstrate reasonable progress on the indigenous masonry . . . We can see by the strength of the walls, by their elevation and interior planning, that their temporary exile among civilized people was somewhat beneficial for them."

3.   Alain Sinou, *Porto Novo, ville d'Afrique Noire*, Collections Architectures traditionnelles (Paris: Parenthèses-Orstom, 1988).

4.   K. Akinsemoyin and A. Vaughan-Richards, *Buildings Lagos* (Lagos: 1976).

5.   J. Poinçot, A. Sinou, and J. Sternadel, *les villes d'Afrique Noire entre 1650 et 1960. Politiques et opérations d'urbanisme et d'habitat*, Collection Analyses et Documents (Paris: Orstom-Aca, Documentation Française, 1989).

6.   Cited in J. Soulillou, ed., *Rives Coloniales, Architectures, de St Louis à Douala*, Collection Architectures Traditionnelles (Paris: Parenthèses-Orstom, 1993), 265.

7.   J. Jackson to Palmerson, Rio, March 5, 1886, quoted in Pierre Verger, *Flux et reflux de la traite des nègres entre le Golfe du Bénin et Bahia de Todos os Santos du XVIIe au XIXe siècle* (Paris: La Haye Mouton, 1968), 358. "Banish all suspected freed Africans . . . 150 of these Africans were sent to the African coast, at the cost of the public expenditure. 120 of them were exiled as suspects and the others were part of those who were caught for smuggling"; "The immediate effect of this measure was the voluntary departure of many other Africans. More still prepare to leave our country."

8.   Ibid., 362. "We have heard that a considerable number of freed Africans, from two to three hundred, were about to embark for the African coast, that they leased a British vessel for five contos de reis to take them to the place they came from, a place called Onim (Lagos). . . . An inquiry has shown that the enterprise was directed by a freed Black, who was part of a load of slaves brought here by Emilia in 1821. Having acquired a definite affluence among his freed fellow countrymen, he has used it to encourage them to go back to their native land. To facilitate the project, he has sold different slaves, his own property estate, and has set free six others who have to go with him."

9.   Milton Monteiro Ribeiro, "Agoudas, les 'brésiliens' du Bénin—Enquête anthropologique et photographique" (PhD diss., Ecoles des Hautes Etudes en Sciences Sociales, Marseille, November 1996).

10.   Letter of the governor of Lagos, captain Alfred Moloney, *Lagos Observer*, June 18, 1887, quoted in Verger, *Flux et reflux*, 622. "What is called by mistake the Brazilian part of the capital city, which is made up of merchants, bargainers, craftsmen, sailors, farmers, workmen, and other representatives of this advanced community, orderly, active, stable, and respectable, presents an example of praiseworthy citizens. For a country like West Africa, the development of new farming interests and economic plans are of great importance, therefore the repatriation of these skilled craftsmen and farm workers is particularly desirable."

11.   Edgar Foa, *Le Dahomey, Histoire, géographie, mœurs, coutumes, commerce, industrie, expédition française (1891–94)* (Paris: Hennuyer, 1895), 210. "In Whydah, Lagos, and Porto Novo, Brazilian Blacks . . . actually occupy the same rank as mulattos really Brazilians and are between the white and the native. They have traveled a little and have seen a bit of Europe and copy their uses; they remain black only by their color. They are living like foreigners, besides the painful details of the native laws, and are, at last, very happy in their country where their parents had suffered so much." The Portuguese language was the lingua franca on the African coast at the time of the slave trade, so the slave traders settled in Africa were assimilated into the Portuguese group. Ollivier de Montaguère, son of the director of the French fort of Whydah and an active private slave trader on the coast, was called da Oliveira.

12.   A. d'Albeca, *Les établissements français du golfe du Bénin* (Paris: Librairie Militaire de L. Baudoin et Cie, 1889). "They have factories that often frustrate European

companies. Jose Marcos, Ignacio Paraiso, Bakari, etc., are notables, rich, esteemed, and very prized by the native King Toffa, to whom they loan money."

13.   Lieutenant Gellé, "Notice sur Porto Novo," *Revue Maritime et Coloniale* (Paris) 10 (March 1984). "[The] low part [of the city] is populated by small foreign merchants and Afro-Brazilians. The latter develop a habitat that is distinguished from the African concessions in the ground floor: story houses appear in the town with vivid colors and patterns and plans inspired by the middle-class dwelling in Brazil."

14.   Gellé, "Notice sur Porto Novo." "Some dignitaries of the kingdom make them build houses similar to those of the Brazilians, notably the king and his two palaces."

15.   *Oga* means chief, and *nla* means big, in Yoruba. The name of the quarter refers to the colonial Resident, who was the "big chief" of the town, in opposition to the king.

16.   Freed slaves from Brazil on their return chose to settle down in their original countries. As they had lost all their possessions in Africa, they settled in coastal cities. Most of the Aguda on the Slave Coast were originally from Yorubaland and Hausaland.

17.   Robin Law, ed., *From Slave Trade to "Legitimate" Commerce: The Commercial Transition in Nineteenth-Century West Africa* (Cambridge: Cambridge University Press, 1995).

18.   Oral inquiries among members of Yoruba families in Porto Novo, 2000.

19.   Quoted in Verger, *Flux et reflux*, 618. "We estimate that between 1839 and 1842 around five hundred of them left Sierra Leone. Those who discharged at Badagry got away relatively well but most of those who went to Lagos were robbed by the local slave trader chiefs and ran away to Abeokuta with the few wraps they could save."

20.   R. F. Borghero, *Journal de Francesco Borghero, premier missionnaire du Dahomey, 1861–1965*, Documents rassemblés et présentés par Renzo Mandirola et Yves Morel (Paris: Karthala, 1997), 188. "Frequently, Egba houses are square shaped with a courtyard in the middle."

21.   Quoted in Verger, *Flux et reflux*, 617. "Several self emancipated Africans from Brazil, after their arrival in this country, demonstrated a strong desire to return to their former countries in the Youraba (Yoruba) Houssal (Hawsa), and Nuffé (Tapa)."

22.   Allister Macmillan, *The Red Book of West Africa* (Ibadan, Nigeria: Spectrum Books, 1920, new edition 1993), 108.

23.   H. W. Macauley, quoted in Verger, *Flux et reflux*, 556. "The freed Africans made the trade with better results than the white merchants . . . because over a number of years, they had, little by little, begun to succeed; many of them are good traders. And after dismissing the maroons and the settlers from the market they now gradually send back the white merchants."

24.   Sylvie Kande, *Terres, urbanisme et architecture "créoles" en Sierre Leone, XVIIIe–XIXe siècles*, Collection racines du présent (Paris: L'Harmattan, 1998), 232–33.

25.   Ibid., 241.

26.   For Badagry, see Verger, *Flux et reflux*, 558.

27.   Governor MacCarthy, quoted in Kande, *Terres, urbanisme et architecture*, 228. "Of course I have done the count for the buildings in the villages separately and with the number of craftsmen that we educate among the captured Negroes."

28.   W. Singleton, report of W. Singleton's visit to Africa. Account of a visit to the Gambia and Sierra Leone, 18–23, 25–66, in London Yearly Meeting of the Religious Society of Friends (London: Harvey, Darton & Co., 1822), quoted in Kande, *Terres, urbanisme et architecture,* 228. "A freed African from Bathurst has tried to make clay bricks at Mandinari. He has succeeded, and now he produces them, at fifty shillings per thousand. . . . The man fires a thousand at a time in a hollow termite mound."

29.   Macmillan, *The Red Book of West Africa,* 110.

30.   K. Akinsemoyin, *Who are Lagosians?* (Lagos: Nigerian Security Printing and Minting Co., 1979); oral inquiries in Lagos, 2000.

31.   Macmillan, *The Red Book of West Africa,* 97.

32.   Ibid., 97.

33.   Ibid., 95.

Part B

Movements and Identities

6

Squatting and Settlement Making in Mamelodi, South Africa

Gerald Steyn

Introduction

South Africa's constitution grants all its citizens the right to decent housing. But the end of apartheid did not stop some of the most visible expressions of segregation—shantytowns. In fact, the explosive growth of illegal squatter settlements on the peripheries of South African cities seems irreversible. Authorities react to the inevitable socioeconomic stress and unhealthy living conditions by building hundreds of thousands of small, identical, freestanding, subsidized houses. This is a questionable policy, due to the costs and sheer numbers of buildings involved, and because such Western-style suburbanism generally perpetuates urban sprawl, as well as social and economic fragmentation. Environmentally, economically, and socially sustainable strategies must arguably be informed by, and possibly aligned with, data on the dynamics of migration and the consequent patterns of shantytowns. The purpose of this chapter is to report on a study carried out to investigate the impact of migration—the fact that all residents are from somewhere else—on the form and function of an informal settlement, using an illegal shantytown in Mamelodi, South Africa, as a case study. It hopes to offer a tentative theory of settlement by exploring the relationships between (1) the demographic profiles of migrant households, including their origins and expectations; (2) the form of a squatter settlement; and (3) the way such a settlement actually functions as a setting for social and economic activities. It is well known that a shantytown, like all built environments, both shapes and responds to behavioral patterns, but when the study was initiated, it was not clear whether the shantytown's form and function were the direct and inevitable manifestations of existential realities—culturally value-free responses to poverty, marginalization, and lack of resources—or manifestations of an indigenous system of knowledge and consequently the expression of an intrinsic African urbanism.

Context and Research Plan

This chapter explores the relationships between migration and form in illegal squatter settlements, using a portion of Mandela Park in Mamelodi, South Africa, as a case study. It commences with a brief description of the context and research plan, followed by the analysis in three parts: (1) demographics; (2) form; and (3) function. These inform a tentative theory of informal settlement, the aim of this chapter.

Squatters are people who occupy land, often illegally, outside the formal housing delivery system. Such squatter camps, also called informal settlements or simply slums, generally have a bad reputation, and images of unhealthy, polluting, crime-ridden, and seemingly inhuman shantytowns are justifiably upsetting. But apparently nearly 80 percent of the poorest people in the least developed countries are living in shantytowns.[1]

The Gauteng region of South Africa, which includes Johannesburg and Pretoria, is the economic dynamo of sub-Saharan Africa, and it is not surprising that it is an attractive destination for migrants. At least one-fifth of Gauteng's population lives in informal dwellings.[2]

There are currently two schools of thought. They can conveniently be called the school of *eradication* and the school of *celebration*. An important proponent of the second stream is David Dewar of the University of Cape Town, who believes informality should be celebrated.[3] He maintains that informal settlement is the only practical solution to housing the poor. Good public transport, access to economic opportunities, and professional and constitutional support for the incremental improvement of public spaces could offer enormous advantages, many more advantages than simply providing houses for free.

Students from the Tshwane University of Technology and the Hogeschool van Utrecht have been doing intensive research in Mamelodi, situated toward the east of Pretoria, for the last three years. The research site, referred to as Mandela Park, is an illegal informal settlement whose residents started to invade land allocated for a major arterial road around 1997.

Although shaped by apartheid-era spatial planning doctrines, Mamelodi is spatially part of Pretoria, rather than simply a satellite city (see figure 6.1). Here, rapid urbanization is mainly due to migration from rural areas and illegal migration from other African countries. Contrary to popular belief, rural-urban migration is not due only to rural poverty but often also to the perception that the city offers more social and recreational variety. For many rural adolescents, surviving in the city for some time before returning home is also a form of initiation into adulthood.

Urban growth is also due to natural population increase. Individuals and young families have to move out of formal-sector houses belonging to parents or grandparents when conditions become overcrowded. There is a long

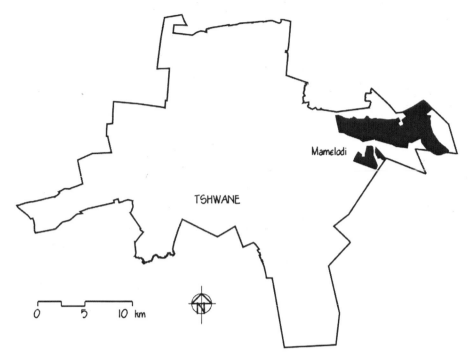

Figure 6.1. The center of the Tshwane Metropolitan Area with Mamelodi shaded. Credit: Gerald Steyn.

waiting list for subsidized houses, with the result that even households with steady incomes sometimes resort to land invasion. Finally, there are also those who have good jobs in the city but travel to their rural homes each weekend. For them, a shack is a conveniently cheap temporary shelter.

It is puzzling that, in spite of the fact that all the residents are from somewhere else, and in spite of the wide range of reasons for living there, Mandela Park, like most shantytowns, is an amorphous landscape—an agglomeration of similar shacks (see figure 6.2). There is no diversity at all. In adjacent areas, however, where squatters have been granted secure tenure and the sites are serviced, shacks have sometimes been replaced by mansions, obviously expressions of wealth. Also noticeable in these adjacent areas is the expression of the occupants' individual aesthetic taste.

The aim of this chapter is, therefore, to try and determine whether the form and function of the illegal settlement under study are the direct and inevitable manifestations of existential realities—culturally value-free responses to poverty, marginalization, and lack of resources—or manifestations of an indigenous system of knowledge and consequently the expression of an intrinsic African urbanism. The research involved a triangulation

Figure 6.2. The amorphousness of shantytowns. Credit: Gerald Steyn.

of literature reviews, interviews with residents and other stakeholders, and observation and recording of behavioral and physical patterns. Comparative analyses were used for integration and interpretation.

Demographics

Key Survey Results

Seventy people were interviewed; we estimate this number to be about 30 percent of the adult population. The data reveal a large proportion of young nuclear families and single parents. Sixty-five percent have earnings below the official poverty line (which is about $2,400 per year), but 76 percent state that their circumstances have improved since moving to Mandela Park. A total of 52.2 percent claim to be unemployed, but many of these receive child and/or disability benefits. Thirty percent are employed, 10.6 percent are self-employed, and 10.3 percent are housewives and students. Since the survey involved a relatively small portion of the population, these figures cannot be considered conclusive. They are, however, a reasonable indication of a demographic trend.

Figure 6.3. A well-kept shack as a permanent home. Credit: Gerald Steyn.

Housing Perceptions

Most residents perceive a definite progression from a rural homestead to a shack to a small, subsidized one- or two-roomed house to a bonded house (a conventional house financed through mortgage bonds). But while some residents clearly consider the squatter settlement as a transit camp, others regard it as a permanent home (see figure 6.3). Most are extremely proud of their houses and the yards and public spaces are kept clean, in spite of there being no municipal waste removal.

Modes of Transport

None of the residents interviewed own cars. Surprisingly, only 0.5 percent use bicycles, although a number of informal workshops repair them. Fourteen percent use the train service, 13 percent use the public bus service, and 27 percent use minibus-taxis (see figure 6.4). Many people rely mostly on walking (35 percent).

Figure 6.4. Minibus-taxis. Credit: Gerald Steyn.

Residents' Likes and Dislikes

The surveys showed that inhabitants appreciated the cheap shelter and the ubiquitous minibus-taxis. Most respondents considered the streets safe for children, many enjoyed the community spirit and associated street life, and some commented on the low levels of crime. Nearly all, however, complained about the lack of economic opportunities, civic amenities, and services. Many complained about having to walk long distances, and others commented on the lack of trees and parks. Surprisingly, very few commented on the quality of shelter, in spite of an almost uniformly low level of climatic comfort. Rural thatched mud houses are known for their climatic fit, and it can only be deduced that the respondents feel that the economic advantages of living in the city outweigh the poorer physical performance of shacks.

Form

Morphology

The site is located in a road reserve between a formal-sector housing scheme to the east and a school to the west. The settlement consists of alleys, lanes, and small patches of open ground. The layout is certainly informal and organic but organized by a distorted grid of lanes and alleys. All buildings have timber frames clad in flat or corrugated iron sheeting and sometimes wooden boarding. Houses range from about 12 square meters in size, and are rarely larger than 30 square meters. They occupy plots of about 100 square meters (see figure 6.5). There are a number of pit latrines and standpipes, which are often shared by a number of shacks.

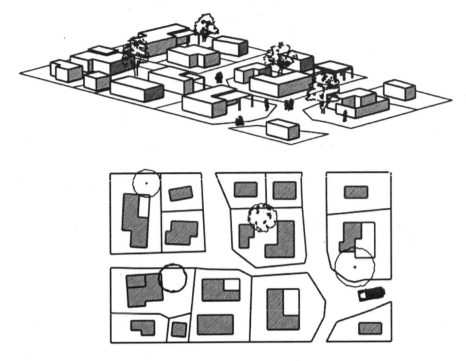

Figure 6.5. Plan and isometric view of a fragment to show morphology.
Credit: Gerald Steyn.

Land Use

Mandela Park has a low coverage at 26 percent, but a high density at more
than 90 units per hectare and at least 340 people per hectare. What is surprising is that space is available for more building, but that the rate of occupation seems to have been stabilized. The area is consequently much less
crowded than some other informal settlements with densities of 740 people
per hectare; this has been described as "a common Third-World density."[4]

Function

The right to occupy land, the construction of shacks, and general conduct
are governed by a strict set of rules enforced by a ward committee established by consensus. This is a different dispensation from the household and
clan leadership by elders found in rural areas, or the election of party-politi-
cal representatives in formal townships.

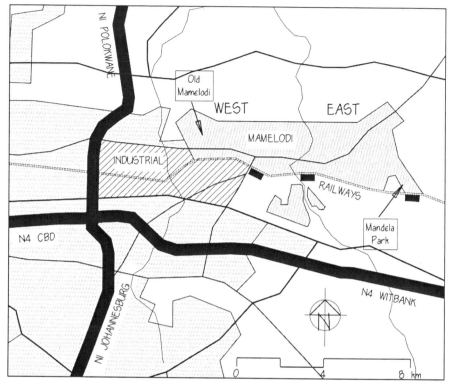

Figure 6.6. Locality plan. Credit: Gerald Steyn.

It seems as if the locality of the settlement directly influences the way it functions. While Old Mamelodi, a 1950s model township, relates directly to major industrial districts, Mandela Park is simply too remote from such employment opportunities, and residents have to be much more self-sufficient (see figure 6.6). Instead, Mandela Park seems to relate more directly to its rural hinterland than to the adjacent township.

The market street with its "spaza" shops—small kiosks selling basic necessities and providing basic services—is a major feature in Mandela Park. For many people, life depends on self-sufficiency—these people include hawkers, small traders, artisans, technicians in home industries, and even subsistence farmers. Front gardens, streets, alleys, spaza shops, and shebeens are true social spaces and intensely inhabited (see figure 6.7).

Toward a Theory of Informal Settlement

People come from the adjacent township five kilometers away, they come from rural villages a few hundred kilometers distant, or they travel a thousand

Figure 6.7. Inhabited social space. Credit: Gerald Steyn.

or more kilometers from Zimbabwe, Zambia, and Malawi. Still, when they occupy the land, they adopt a common spatial and technological expression, a morphology that broadly resembles a denser form of rural settlement but is constructed with materials salvaged from urban, industrialized society. We were sensitized to this phenomenon by Henry Matthews and Bashir Kazimee, who write that "in Third-World cities, we no longer see urbanization of the rural migrants, but rather a growing ruralization of the cities."[5]

Our tentative theory is that, although the squatters face an insecure future due to the constant threat of eviction, they still manage to maintain a dignified existence and a reasonable—albeit rather precarious—standard of living because they have adopted the paradigm of that ancient guardian institution, the African village. This would explain the uniformity. Building forms developed slowly and incrementally over very long periods and became culturally embedded once an appropriate solution for a certain set of circumstances had been found (see figure 6.8). This pattern seems to be what we are witnessing here. This phenomenon does not imply a rejection of Western urban forms; in fact these are readily embraced by higher-income people. The community-based social organization, the lack of infrastructure, and the need to build with found materials simply demand a response that evolved from an indigenous knowledge system.

Figure 6.8. A traditional Swazi homestead. Credit: André Roodt.

This theory can be partly substantiated by the physical characteristics of Mandela Park. Its pattern of lanes and alleys, created without any professional intervention, has nothing in common with the pattern of its closest neighbor, Old Mamelodi, which is the archetypal "garden suburb" mutation. However, it is conceptually very similar to that of Lamu, off the coast of Kenya, a historical but still functioning Afro-Arab town (see figure 6.9). But what is truly surprising is that the permeability (walkability) offered by the streets of Mandela Park is nearly identical to that of Seaside, Florida, the quintessential "new urban" town![6] Considering a 400 x 400 meter fragment, with 400 meters the distance comfortably walked in five minutes, it was found that the squatter settlement had 4,374 meters of streets compared to Seaside's 5,182 meters, 12 access points into the settlement compared to Seaside's 11, and 44 intersections compared to Seaside's 52! Simplistic comparisons of form (see figure 6.10) and spatial organization (see figure 6.11) demonstrate a clear conceptual similarity to rural settlements.

Precolonial African urbanism is dominated by the concept of the village, and cities like Kano, Zaria, Benin City, and Old Oyo are unquestionably collections of villages, each with strong rural characteristics. It could well be that such ancient and collective memories are the major forces shaping informal settlements.

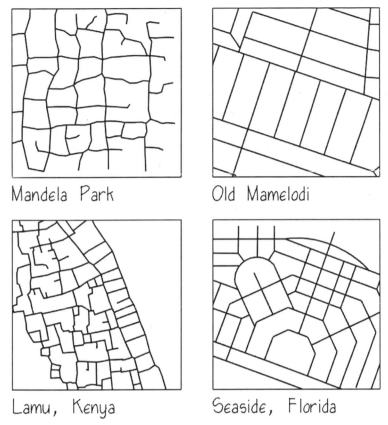

Figure 6.9. A comparison of street configurations. Credit: Gerald Steyn.

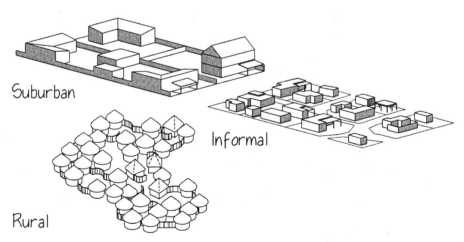

Figure 6.10. A comparison of form to explore scale. Credit: Gerald Steyn.

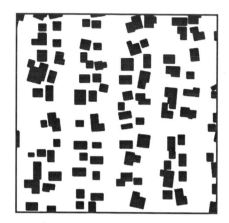 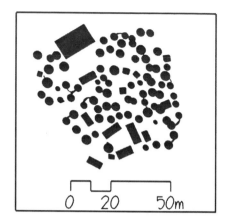

Figure 6.11. A comparison of spatial organization. Left: Mandela Park; right: a rural settlement. Credit: Gerald Steyn.

Conclusions

The way an illegal settlement looks and the way it works do not seem to be simple, purely practical, value-free responses. On the contrary, form and function seem to reflect embedded values that have been part of sedentary sub-Saharan village culture, arguably for nearly 2,000 years. But the spatial organization of Mandela Park cannot be considered a direct replica of rural forms; rather, with its rectangular-shape houses and its fairly straight alleys and streets it syntheses rural and urban spatial forms. It is in reality a new and innovative form of spatial organization, structurally aspiring to an urban form, while receiving inspirations from and retaining elements of rural forms.

Some illegal settlements provide a satisfactory home for many people, in spite of poverty, marginalization, and a lack of resources. It is doubtful if squatting will ever be eradicated. A more meaningful course of action seems to be to celebrate and facilitate informality! A true African city will always be heterogeneous. It will have different types of buildings and neighborhoods for people with different means and expectations. That diversity must be appreciated. What is extremely important is that low-income people should not be restricted to the peripheries of our cities but should rather be accommodated in mixed-use, mixed-income settings closer to places of economic opportunities, in numbers that would ensure political critical mass and a viable local economy. Interdependence already exists, and our cities and architecture must reflect it.

Notes

1.   United Nations Human Settlements Programme, *The Challenge of Slums: Global Report on Human Settlements 2003* (London: Earthscan, 2003).

2.   Susan Brown and Alta Fölscher, eds., *Taking Power in the Economy: Gains and Directions* (Cape Town: Institute for Justice and Reconciliation, 2004).

3.   David Dewar, "Transforming Housing Environments through Design," keynote address, 33rd International Association for Housing Science (IAHS) congress on housing, University of Pretoria, South Africa, September 27–30, 2005.

4.   Rajeev Kathpalia, "Beyond Sustainable Cities: Applied Strategies for Regional Sustenance," 7th Commonwealth Association of Architects (CAA) general assembly and conference, University of the Free State, Bloemfontein, South Africa, 2003.

5.   Henry Matthews and Bashir Kazimee, "The Quest for Shelter: Squatters and Urbanization throughout the World, in *The Built Environment: Creative Enquiry into Design and Planning*, ed. Tom Bartuska and Gerald Young, 129–39 (Menlo Park, CA: Crisp, 1994).

6.   Peter Katz, ed., *The New Urbanism: Toward an Architecture of Community* (New York: McGraw-Hill, 1994).

7

"Scattering Time"

Anticolonial Resistance and Migration among the Jo-Ugenya of Kenya toward the End of the Nineteenth Century

Meshack Owino

There are countless numbers of works on the subject of African resistance to the coming of colonialism,[1] yet only a select few deal with the extent to which resistance changed African demography. Only a few studies focus on the aftermath of African resistance, on the new migration and settlement patterns that emerged during and after colonial resistance. Most works on African resistance to the colonial invasion tend to focus on the preparations for resistance, the nature of resistance movements, and the immediate outcome; they rarely focus on the long-term fortunes of those who were scattered and displaced during resistance. Studies of resistance are often characterized by assumptions, for example, the assumption that after the failure of an attempt at resistance, the defeated people fled. This assumption is made without any detailed examination of how people fled, where they fled to, and why. A cursory examination of the existing materials on African movements and migrations during colonial conquests reveals many such assumptions, characterized by vague and imprecise terms and phrases such as the following: "and they were scattered to the four winds"; "and after the defeat, the leader and his community then fled"; "and the battle was over, and the resisters dispersed"; "and they were defeated, and after that they fled." Little context is provided, and little is said about why a resisting leader and his followers chose a particular area for sanctuary. This failure by major studies of African resistance to look at the migration, movement, and settlement patterns that emerged during and after resistance has created a lacuna in our understanding of colonial invasions and of African resistance. The scholar looking at these materials becomes frustrated by the paucity of information on why leaders and their communities chose a particular area in which to hide from colonial invaders, how they moved there, what happened to them there, whether or not they tried to come back to their homeland, and with what result. What one finds in these works are in fact more and more questions begging for answers. They are questions that can be answered only if studies dealing with the impact of colonialism on African migration and settlements contextualize their analyses by rigorously focusing on movement patterns before and after resistance, on why and how leaders and their people moved to new areas of settlement, on whether or not they tried to come back, and on their fortunes in doing so. By focusing on events during and after resistance, scholars can help fill in yawning gaps in our knowledge of population movements in Africa during the colonial period. This knowledge is integral to a comprehensive understanding of African agency during resistance to the colonial invaders.

A study of the Jo-Ugenya resistance and subsequent migration to the neighboring territories of Gem, Alego, Samia, and Manyala (also known as Bunyala) can help answer some of these nagging questions on the experience and fortunes of African colonial resisters, and on demographic changes in Africa during the colonial period. At the beginning of the colonial conquest, the Ugenya folk put up a spirited resistance in 1896 and 1897. The resistance wars resulted in the dispersal of the Jo-Ugenya from modern Uholo and South Wanga, specifically, Musanda valley, Machere, Mahondo, Bukura, Marama, and Butere, to new areas in Alego, Gem, Samia, and Manyala, where they established new settlements. Thus, one of the major outcomes of the Jo-Ugenya resistance to British colonialism was their dispersal from their homes to neighboring territories as refugees. There was a demographic shift in Ugenya after the resistance. Survivors of the anti-British resistance of 1896–97 fled to Alego, Gem, Samia, and Manyala, where a large number still live to the present day. The resistance therefore led not only to the dispersal and scattering of the Jo-Ugenya but also to a dramatic reconfiguration of the Ugenya social and political landscape. To save themselves from further bloodshed, a large number of defeated Ugenya warriors and their families moved out of their traditional settlements in modern South Wanga and Uholo and went elsewhere. After their migration, the Jo-Ugenya tried many times to come back to their land. They tried to use legal tactics as well as open defiance and protests to force the hand of the colonial government. Although a few Ugenya refugees came back to their homeland after several years, many others were unable to do so due to the opposition of the British colonial administration working in tandem with the Church Missionary Society (CMS) and the administration's Wanga allies.

What is significant about the Jo-Ugenya resistance to the British conquest, flight, and subsequent agitation for their land is that it highlights the plight and tribulations of Africans who were dispossessed of their land during the colonial invasion of Kenya. The Jo-Ugenya people were among thousands of Africans who were rendered landless when the British invaded Kenya and declared it their colony. The others included the Maasai, whose land was seized by the British in 1904 and 1911. There were also the Kipsigis and Nandi, whose fertile, arable lands in the Rift Valley of Kenya were seized by the colonial government and handed over to settlers who turned them into tea plantations. Then there were, of course, the Agikuyu, whose lands were also seized by the colonial state and handed over to white settlers. After repeatedly and unsuccessfully petitioning the colonial state for their land, the Agikuyu eventually resorted to war. The Mau Mau War was the Agikuyu way of saying that they had had enough of life as squatters while the colonial settlers grew wealthy from their land. This is the larger context within which the Jo-Ugenya people's demand for their land should be understood. It is also the context within which to understand the colonial government's reluctance to entertain the Jo-Ugenya demand for their land. The government reasoning was simple. If it accepted the Jo-Ugenya petition, other African communities would be encouraged to heighten their demands for their land. Another factor that the colonial government took into account while turning down the Jo-Ugenya petition was that during the Jo-Ugenya resistance, the government's ally, the Wanga, had quickly seized the vacated Ugenya territories, especially South Wanga. The colonial government was therefore reluctant to ask the Wanga to give the land back to the Jo-Ugenya, because it would offend an ally that had given considerable aid to the British during the early years of colonial rule in western Kenya. Thus the majority of the Jo-Ugenya refugees were unable to come back to Uholo and South Wanga after the resistance. There were just too many frustrating political obstacles in the way of those trying to come back to their homeland. This was particularly the case with respect to those who tried to come back to what is now Uholo and South Wanga only to find their land settled by new settlers from the Wanga Kingdom. The Jo-Ugenya refugees were thus forced to transform their sanctuaries in Alego, Gem, Samia, and Manyala into new homes. They became settlers. The scattering of the Jo-Ugenya during and after the resistance of the late nineteenth century thus became a permanent dispersal and migration. Home away from home became home, even as the refugees hankered for the day they would go back to their land.

The next question is the context in which the Jo-Ugenya migration and dispersal to Alego, Gem, Manyala, and Samia took place. This chapter addresses the question by examining, first, the coming of the British to Ugenya; second, the Jo-Ugenya resistance; third, the flight and dispersal of the Jo-Ugenya; and finally, the agitation of the Jo-Ugenya for their land.

The Coming of the British to Ugenya

The Jo-Ugenya are one of the thirty-six Luo "sub-tribes"[2] that are found in present-day western Kenya. During the nineteenth century, the Jo-Ugenya had a very strong military organization that over the years had enabled them to withstand and repel neighboring communities[3] such as the Wanga and foreign invaders such as the Arab-Swahili. In fact, report after report states that during the second half of the nineteenth century, the Jo-Ugenya were reputed to be a powerful military force, especially in their conflicts with the Wanga.[4] In their conflicts with the Arab-Swahili and their Wanga allies over land, livestock, and the slave trade, the Jo-Ugenya had done so well in repulsing their enemies that their warriors were beginning to appear within reach of the outskirts of the Wanga capital itself. The Jo-Ugenya were beginning to be very confident of their military prowess. They were poised to establish their hegemony over the Wanga when the British appeared in western Kenya and changed the emerging military and political configuration completely.

The Jo-Ugenya came into contact with the British during the latter half of the nineteenth century. These contacts were in connection with the British arrival and activities in Mumias (initially, Mumias was known as Lureko or Elureko), a major way station for the Arab/Swahili, the Europeans, and other foreigners who traveled between the East African coast and Uganda during the nineteenth century. Mumias, which was the capital of the Wanga Kingdom, is only a few miles from Ugenya. The visits by the Europeans to Mumias were at first insignificant, at least in the eyes of the Europeans themselves and the local people such as the Jo-Ugenya, because European interests at the time lay in Uganda rather than in western Kenya.[5] In the context of the European geopolitics of the time, the British were interested in Uganda because it was believed that whoever controlled Uganda would also gain supremacy over Lake Victoria, the Nile valley, and the lands bordering it.[6] Consequently, western Kenya served only as a backyard to British interests in Uganda, and Mumias merely as a way station between the Mombasa coast and Uganda.

In 1883, Joseph Thomson and his Maltese sailor-companion, J. Martin, made a momentous journey across Maasailand.[7] Thomson and his companion reached Mumias in December 1883 and stayed for two days only. Thomson's journey was significant to the Jo-Ugenya because he was the first European they had ever seen, as he passed through Ukwala in Ugenya on his way to Uganda. Two years later, in 1885, Bishop James Hannington passed through Mumias briefly on his way to Uganda. He hurriedly left Mumias for Uganda despite entreaties from Nabongo (King) Mumia of the Wanga to stay a little longer. Eventually Mumia assigned guards to escort him.[8] The bishop subsequently met his death at the hands of the Baganda for defying the injunctions of the *kabaka* (the Buganda king) prohibiting foreigners from entering the kingdom from the east.

The two journeys were typical of European ventures across Kenya into Uganda during the period of the European scramble for Africa. Such journeys and the activities of the Europeans who made them were crucial in terms of validating British claims to Kenya and Uganda in accordance with the "sphere of influence" doctrine of the Berlin agreement of 1884–85. Britain and Germany were the principal antagonists in the scramble for East Africa, and the presence of the mighty Germany in the region posed a considerable challenge to the British. The British government was therefore forced to increase and concretize its presence in the region before the Germans laid claim to the area.[9] In particular, the British increased their presence in Mumias, and befriended Nabongo Mumia of the Wanga. The growing importance of Mumias to the British arose, first, from its reputation as an old and reliable refreshment station for the Arab/Swahili and for European travelers. Second, Mumias was (and is) situated in a well-watered and fertile agricultural region from which supplies could easily be obtained. Third, it was located near an area where the River Nzoia could easily be forded. Finally, Nabongo Mumia was friendly and well disposed to Europeans,[10] and the Europeans regarded him as a dependable and reliable ally. With all these advantages, Mumias was attractive to the missionaries and to the Imperial British East Africa Company representatives and British government officials who invariably lodged there whenever they traveled between the Kenyan coast and Uganda.

Eventually, it was through Mumias that the influence of the British—hitherto confined largely to Uganda—slowly began to radiate into western Kenya. This influence increased with the signing in 1890 of the Heligoland Treaty, according to which the Germans formally recognized Uganda and Kenya as part of the British "sphere of influence." As a result of the treaty, the Jo-Ugenya unwittingly came under British jurisdiction. At the beginning, however, the government did not have a very visible presence in western Kenya. To begin with, Colonel Colville, the British government representative in Uganda, did not have enough manpower to monitor an area that was up to that point no more than a rest stop for European administrators and traders. He thus sent his valet, Frederick Spire, to represent him and establish a British administration post in Mumias in 1894.[11] Though Spire was only a valet, his appointment formally began the consolidation of British rule in Ugenya in particular and in western Kenya in general, with Mumias as its official administrative station.

Spire's tenure in Mumias was a very short one. In July 1895, he was replaced by Charles W. Hobley, who became the new subcommissioner of the area, now known as "Kavirondo." The orders of C. W. Hobley, the new subcommissioner of "Kavirondo," were as follows:

to relieve Spire, build a permanent station[,] generally establish an administration over the turbulent collection of tribes [*sic*], collectively known to the
coastal people as the Kavirondo.[12]

Hobley's arrival in Mumias considerably increased and added muscle to the
administrative presence of the British in western Kenya. For the first time,
the Jo-Ugenya began to take notice of the British presence in their region,
because Hobley's orders involved interfering in the internal affairs of the
Jo-Ugenya. These orders involved imposing an alien administration on a
people who were independent and who were not willing to be bothered by
outsiders. This added tension to an already fragile situation. The prospects
for war were very high, because the Jo-Ugenya would not be willing to give
up their independence and ascendant military status in the region easily.
The British, on the other hand, would not entertain any challenge to their
interests. Thus, what we had by the time the British were establishing their
administration in western Kenya in the late nineteenth century was a very
tense situation. The British were determined to fight and defeat all belliger-
ent local communities that challenged their authority in the region, while
local communities such as the Jo-Ugenya were determined to hang on to
their independence. What made the prospects for war between the British
and the Jo-Ugenya in particular very high was the fact that in the case of the
Jo-Ugenya, the British were, as we have already seen, very close to one of
Jo-Ugenya' perennial rivals, the Wanga. The Wanga had succeeded in establishing very close relations with the British ever since the Wanga had started
hosting various European visitors to western Kenya. In addition, according
to many Ugenya oral traditions, the Wanga allies of the British began incit-
ing the British against the Jo-Ugenya right from the beginning of the British
incursion into western Kenya, by telling them that the Jo-Ugenya were "a
very bad" people who should be conquered and defeated.[13] The oral traditions claim that the Wanga were the ones who instigated the "bad blood"
that developed between the British and the Jo-Ugenya. They claim further
that the main plan of the Wanga in orchestrating these conflicts was simple—to get the British to defeat their traditional Jo-Ugenya rivals once and
for all, and enable the Wanga to take over Ugenya territory.

However, although Ugenya reports tend to blame the Wanga for instigating
conflicts between the Jo-Ugenya and the British, a close reading of the available evidence suggests that other factors were also at play and bore considerable responsibility for the conflicts that emerged between the British and the
Jo-Ugenya. The British were establishing their hegemony in the region, and
were therefore not ready to tolerate anybody who stood in their way. They
fought and defeated the Bukusu of western Kenya in 1894 and 1895, when
their encroachment into the Bukusu territory was opposed by the Bukusu .
They fought the Nandi, also of western Kenya, in a long guerrilla war from

1890 to 1906 in a bid to suppress the Nandi resistance to their rule. They also fought and defeated the Turkana of Kenya. They fought and defeated the Abagusii of western Kenya. The British were fighting anybody who challenged their authority. This is the context within which the British war against the Jo-Ugenya should be understood. As we will see later in this chapter, the British were not being altruistic or charitable to the Wanga by taking their side in their long-running conflicts with the Jo-Ugenya; the British were simply using the Wanga to advance their own imperial interests in the region. Historians of Kenya have observed that there are two levels at which the British conflicts with the Jo-Ugenya can be viewed. At one level, the conflicts can be viewed as an attempt by the British to aid their allies, the Wanga, in a traditional military conflict with Jo-Ugenya. Margaret L. Otieno and others observe, for example, that when C. W Hobley mounted a punitive military expedition against the Jo-Ugenya in January 1897, it was in support of Mumia against the Jo-Ugenya, whose opposition to the Wanga had been organized by Gero and Obanda Ka'Nyang'inja.[14] At another level, the conflicts can also be viewed as part of an arsenal of strategies by the British to expand their empire in Ugenya and western Kenya as a whole.

In other words, the British were not supporting the Wanga blindly; they were doing it to advance their authority and control in western Kenya. They had their own motives. They wanted to expand their hegemony in the region and they were ready to join local potentates like Mumia of the Wanga to achieve that objective. In the words of the Kenyan historian Atieno Odhiambo, the British hoped to impose their administration on local people such as the Jo-Ugenya by expanding "the sub-imperialism of the Wanga."[15] John Osogo, another Kenyan historian, notes that the British-Wanga alliance was one through which the British expanded the influence of the Wanga while helping to fulfill their own colonial goal. In short, according to Osogo, the story of the Wanga Empire during the reign of Mumia is actually the story of the development of the British administration.[16]

The Jo-Ugenya Resistance to the British

In spite of their renowned military prowess and their successes against many foes over the years, the Jo-Ugenya did not want to fight against the British. Indeed, an analysis of their resistance shows that it started out inconspicuously and spontaneously. It was not something many Jo-Ugenya planned to do. Ugenya accounts constantly blame the other side for instigating the war. These accounts claim that the Jo-Ugenya were under express instructions from their elders not to fight the British. They claim that the main religious leaders (*jobilo*) of the Luo community had promulgated a major injunction among the Luo (thus including the Jo-Ugenya) expressly banning any type of military action against the British. Having prophesied the arrival of the British and understood the nature of their military power, the Luo religious leaders had advised the local people against fighting. They advised the Luo to avoid futile and unnecessary bravado against the British. They informed the Luo that the British were so powerful and their weapons so dangerous that any military altercation would only lead to unnecessary bloodshed among the local people. If anything, the *jobilo* advised the Luo to welcome the British, study them, and learn from them. B. A. Ogot refers to the advice of the *jobilo* to the community to "welcome the Europeans," and "live with them in peace."[17] There is evidence that some Jo-Ugenya *wasiande* (military commanders) were not happy with this injunction, but given the nature of Luo society, in which elders' words were the law, the commanders felt compelled to abide by the injunctions of the *jobilo*. As a result, many Jo-Ugenya started getting ready to welcome the British and live with them in peace, when unplanned events, miscommunications, and suspicions led to a deterioration in the relations between the Jo-Ugenya and the British. The deteriorating relations then evolved into a major conflict.

To understand the genesis of the misunderstandings and miscommunications that led to the Anglo-Ugenya War, one has to realize that the British arrived in Ugenya at a time of animosity and conflict between the Jo-Ugenya and the Wanga. Many Ugenya reports have claimed that there are direct links between these conflicts and the Anglo-Ugenya War of 1896 and 1897. They further claim that it was Nabongo Mumia, the ambitious king of the Wanga, who orchestrated the conflicts in order to take over Ugenya territory and extend his authority in western Kenya. These reports portray Nabongo Mumia as generally ambitious and hostile toward the Jo-Ugenya. Indeed, when the British arrived in western Kenya, they found Nabongo Mumia and the Jo-Ugenya in the middle of a conflict, a situation that, as we have already seen, the British were only too eager to exploit for their own imperialistic ends. Let us look a little more closely at what was happening with respect to this conflict by the time the British started venturing into the area. When the British arrived on the scene, they found the conflict going very badly for Nabongo Mumia. The Jo-Ugenya were gaining the upper hand. In a bid to turn his fortunes around, *Nabongo* Mumia cobbled together an alliance with Arab/Swahilis to fight the Jo-Ugenya. This did not work. Several times the Wanga–Arab/Swahili coalition engaged the Jo-Ugenya in skirmishes without defeating the Jo-Ugenya. Mumia became frustrated as the Jo-Ugenya warriors became bolder. He was rattled when Ugenya warriors started appearing on a regular basis at the gates of his capital, Mumias. It was during this period that the British arrived in Mumias. They found Mumia in a state of desperation. They found the Wanga–Arab/Swahili alliance that Mumia had established against the Jo-Ugenya crumbling and Mumia anxiously scouting for new allies.

Consequently, it was not surprising that Mumia started making requests for military assistance from the Europeans who were by then plying the route between the coast and Uganda. At first the Europeans largely ignored his requests. This was, as we have already seen, because the Europeans were mostly interested in Uganda. Furthermore, they also believed that Mumia was at the very least partly responsible for some of the friction with the neighboring communities against whom he needed the support. They contended, for example, that Mumia was abetting the activities of the Arab/Swahili slave merchants in Mumias, who were raiding the neighboring communities for slaves.[18]

The reluctance of the Europeans to become entangled in the local Wanga–Jo-Ugenya conflict soon ended, with the bankruptcy of the Imperial British East Africa Company and the takeover of the territory by the British government. The government began to argue that the territory should be made safe for caravans passing between the Kenyan coast and Uganda.[19] This inevitably required that local communities be brought under British control. This objective necessitated alliances with powerful regional chiefs, of whom Mumia was believed to be one.[20] The British therefore quickly ingratiated themselves with Mumia, established an alliance with him, and started helping him in his local military conflicts, one of which was against the Jo-Ugenya.

Most interview reports from Ugenya suggest that the first British military clash with Ugenya forces began purely by accident.[21] These reports claim that some time in December 1896, the British colonial administration summoned the Jo-Ugenya chiefs to a meeting at Manga Hills in Ugenya. Hobley, the head of the British administration in Mumias, wanted to use the occasion to demand the official submission of the Jo-Ugenya to British authority. As we have already seen, submitting to the British was something that the Jo-Ugenya themselves were anxious to do, having been directed to do exactly that by their religious leaders. On the eve of the meeting, however, Mumia, the king of the Wanga, decided to sabotage the meeting. According to Ugenya oral tradition, Mumia did this by clandestinely sending a subtle message to Ugenya, warning the Jo-Ugenya elders to take cover, because C. W. Hobley was allegedly planning to capture some of them during the meeting and use them as hostages to force the Jo-Ugenya to submit to colonial rule. Meanwhile, according to these traditions, Mumia then approached Hobley and told him that the Jo-Ugenya were a treacherous lot who should not be trusted. Mumia allegedly told Hobley that the Jo-Ugenya were in fact planning to kill him (Hobley at the scheduled meeting. He begged Hobley to be careful.

Unsure of the true state of affairs, but anxious to establish relations, both sides therefore arrived at the meeting place cautiously. They took precautions by arming themselves before going into the meeting. And in doing so, they unwittingly played into the hands of Nabongo Mumia, the crafty king of the Wanga. When the two parties arrived at the meeting, tensions and suspicions were very high, with both sides watching the other's moves very carefully. It was not lost on the Jo-Ugenya that C. W. Hobley arrived at the meeting with a large band of armed men. Hobley, on his part, observed that the Jo-Ugenya elders were surrounded by a large band of warriors. Both sides refused to come closer to one another, fearing an attack at any time, Mumia's warnings ringing in their ears. Hobley then ordered the Jo-Ugenya warriors to put away their spears, an order that was interpreted by the Jo-Ugenya elders as confirmation of the allegation that Hobley was planning to arrest some of them and forcibly march them to Mumias. When the Jo-Ugenya refused to disarm, Hobley began to believe Mumia's warnings that the Jo-Ugenya could not be trusted to maintain the peace. And then strange things began to happen. According to Ugenya traditions, a horse belonging to Hobley was speared to death by someone in the crowd.[22] In the ensuing melee, several people lost their lives as Hobley and his soldiers hurried back to Mumias. It is reported that Hobley went back to Mumias determined to come back and subdue the Jo-Ugenya. This was in December 1896. The following year, in 1897, the British administration in Mumias finally yielded to Mumia's persistent entreaties for military assistance against the Jo-Ugenya[23] by organizing an expedition.

In January 1897, Hobley organized a major expedition against the Jo-Ugenya. Hobley's company consisted of soldiers armed with an array of weapons, including machine guns (*bunde kamnara*).[24] Arriving in Anyiko, Hobley gave the Jo-Ugenya an ultimatum, saying that they must surrender. The Jo-Ugenya, having heard about the expedition, had repaired to a place called Anyiko. There they were split over exactly how to respond to Hobley's ultimatum. Should they fight back or should they heed the injunctions of the *jobilo* against fighting the British? One group, led by Osolo K'Otekra, a military commander, wanted the Jo-Ugenya to rise up and fight, but another, led by Gero K'Okado, felt that fighting would result in a massacre of hapless Ugenya people. But before the Jo-Ugenya could make up their minds, Hobley unleashed a volley of Maxim gun fire, demolishing a number of huts and killing a number of people. Hobley then marched into the village and arrested others.

The casualties included more than two hundred Jo-Ugenya warriors who were killed in the confrontation.[25] Ugenya livestock, crops, and other properties were confiscated. Many Jo-Ugenya fled from the scene. Musian Osolo K'Otekra was killed as he valiantly tried to swim across the River Nzoia to escape. As the British expedition fought its way back from Anyiko through Konjra, Ungas, and Tingare to Mumias, it forced numerous Jo-Ugenya to flee to Gem, Alego, Samia, and Manyala where they had relatives. According to Ogot:

Two hundred Luo soldiers were killed with a machine gun in one battle and the rest fled in all directions and took refuge in neighboring areas, especially in Alego and Bunyala.[26]

Ogot reports the findings of G. Were, to the effect that

After that Mumia brought Hobilo (Hobley) who succeeded in driving the Abageri (Kager—this was the main Ugenya clan fighting the Wanga) out of the lands that they had wrested from their enemies. And so the Abageri were dispersed and scattered to the four winds. Then the people of Mumia—Abashieni, the Abamarama and the Abarecheya—returned to their former territories.[27]

Apart from Osolo K'Otekra, one of the soon-to-be-famous victims of this war was Alfayo Odongo Mango. After the war, Odongo Mango, who was then a small child, and his mother fled to the neighboring Ulumbi in Gem.

Routed by the British in the confrontation, the Jo-Ugenya were emotionally, psychologically, and militarily traumatized and demoralized. Following the colonial conquest, many fled into exile where they formed minority groups.[28] The only person who did not flee during the battle at Anyiko was Gero K'Okado, one of the most senior elders in Ugenya. After demolishing the walls of Anyiko village and entering Gero's homestead, Hobley found Gero sitting by himself. As quoted by Ogot from a colonial source:

He sat outside his house, alone, in his bracelets and ornaments and waited, like a Roman Senator, for death. He was, of course, not killed.[29]

He was captured and taken to Mumias. Indeed, during the expedition to Anyiko, Hobley captured and arrested other influential community figures like Mulase K'Okwako and sent them to Mumias as hostages.[30] Hobley also decreed that the captives would not be released until Odipo K'Okwako, whom he was made to believe was the Ugenya chief, went to Mumias to make his people's official submission to British authority. This hostage-taking act on the part of Hobley forced the Jo-Ugenya to pledge their allegiance to the new order. The usefulness of the captives to the British in enforcing obedience from the Jo-Ugenya was noted by S. H. Fazan, a colonial government official, when he wrote that Gero was

not killed, but proved a very useful hostage, and by this means, the Wagenya [*sic*] were persuaded [*sic*] to come back to their homes.[31]

After the conquest, the British expediently participated in the peacemaking ritual of *ng'ado guok* (cutting a puppy) with the Jo-Ugenya.[32] This ritual was customarily used to formalize peace terms after a war, and the participation of the British, who ordinarily detested African customs, illustrates their insidious readiness to manipulate local belief systems to underwrite people's obedience to the colonial order. The Jo-Ugenya were obligated by the terms of this agreement to maintain peace, law, and order even as they seethed over the loss of their land.

After participating in the *ng'ado guok* ritual, the British started appointing headmen over the Jo-Ugenya. Odipo K'Okwako and Gero K'Okado were the first British-appointed headmen in Ugenya. Also, the British government established policies that would consolidate their administrative network in Ugenya. In March 1902, the eastern province of Uganda was transferred to the East Africa Protectorate. The following year, Odipo, the headman of north Ugenya, drowned, and after several years, he was replaced by his brother, Muganda K'Okwako, who was at that time an *askari* (policeman) in Mumias.[33] In 1908, North Nyanza was divided into subdistricts and administrative zones to improve the administration. Boundaries were defined in such a way that the Jo-Ugenya came under the direct control of Chief Mumia. Mumia's kinsmen were then appointed as headmen of the administrative zones with the support of Geoffrey Archer, the acting district commissioner.[34] Thus Munyendo became the headman of Buholo and South Ugenya, and, in November 1909, the government declared Mumia the paramount chief over Ugenya and the rest of Nyanza. These were far-reaching developments in Ugenya politics, because they limited people's ability to move and migrate in search of new land as they had done in the past. Since Mumia had been appointed as paramount chief of the whole area, the Jo-Ugenya found it extremely difficult to reclaim their land, especially as this land was now occupied by Mumia's subjects with his blessings.

One also has to understand the role of headmen and chiefs in colonial Africa to appreciate the way in which the appointment of Mumia's relatives as chiefs and headmen made it extremely difficult for the Jo-Ugenya refugees to come back from Gem, Alego, Manyala, and Samia to their land. First, as Mumia's relatives, the new headmen of Buholo and South Ugenya did not sympathize with the Jo-Ugenya demand for their land. Second, most of the new headmen in Ugenya, as in many other parts of colonial Africa, were selected on the basis of their ability to promote colonial policies in their areas of jurisdiction. Their sympathy for local grievances was never supposed to get in the way of implementing colonial policies. Even the appointment of Muganda K'Okwako, a Ja-Ugenya, as headman in North Ugenya was based on the assumption that he was "a known quality," having served the British dutifully as a policeman in Mumias under the watchful eye of Chief Mumia. Gero K'Okado and other headmen, then, were expected to be no more than cooperative administrative functionaries who would enforce colonial policies. Their action in implementing the colonial policies coming through

Mumias led to the control and curtailment of Ugenya migration and settlement. Like their counterparts elsewhere, the headmen were required to institute law and order. They were required to obey Chief Mumia, the most senior chief in the region, and to implement colonial directives. It is not clear whether the Ugenya headmen carried out these directives. But in a situation where the British were now in charge, the independence of the Jo-Ugenya came under severe checks; they could only move, migrate, and settle according to the terms defined by the British and their Wanga allies.

Displacement and landlessness were thus a major outcome of the Jo-Ugenya resistance. The problem was particularly acute in South Wanga and Buholo. The colonial administration not only prevented Ugenya refugees from coming back and reclaiming the areas they had fled from;[35] in addition, it handed their land to the Jo-Ugenya's most intractable rivals, the Wanga. When refugees like the young Odongo Mango came back to their land, they found it occupied by other people, specifically, the Wanga clans of the Abashieni, the Abakolwe, the Abamarama, and the Abarecheya. Ogot observes that Odongo Mango's family was thus forced to move out again:

> When Mango and his mother returned to their home at Uchirinya, they found it occupied by a Wanga clan called Wakolwe, and they therefore went to live with a relative, Opondo Komo, at Uuas village on the opposite bank of Kisama River.[36]

As a result of these administrative and political obstacles, the Jo-Ugenya elders began to work on alternative mechanisms to compel the government to let the displaced Jo-Ugenya refugees go back to their land. During the colonial period, they used legal and political means to challenge colonial rulings over their land. They hired numerous lawyers to appeal to the government on their behalf. They challenged the government at the *barazas* (Kiswahili: public meetings), the local native councils, and engaged missionaries in public arguments at various church gatherings over their plight. No forum was sacrosanct as far as their demand for their land was concerned. They accused the government of "stealing their land" and giving it to their enemies, the Wanga. But the government refused to heed their demands. The stock government response to Ugenya appeals for their land was that the land in question had been acquired by the Jo-Ugenya by military conquest, and they did not recognize conquest as a method of acquiring land. The Jo-Ugenya on the other hand argued that conquests were traditionally recognized as a legitimate method of acquiring land. They argued that this was how land had been acquired during the precolonial period, and that their rights should be honored because their conquests had taken place before the British arrived in the area. At the same time, the Jo-Ugenya launched a campaign for a chief of their own, hoping that if they gained their own chief they would be able to use him to petition the British. This was a change of tactics. The Jo-Ugenya were hoping that if a chief of their own was appointed, he would use his knowledge of the colonial administrative system to help them reoccupy their lost territories in modern South Wanga and Uholo. As B. A. Ogot observes, the "demand for a Luo chief in Buholo was only a small aspect of this inter-tribal conflict . . . . the Kager people [the Ugenya clan that was principally affected by the war] were demanding the whole of South Wanga, particularly the Musanda valley, Machere, Mahondo, Bukura, Marama, and Butere, which . . . they had conquered during the second half of the nineteenth century."[37]

In 1913, the Jo-Ugenya of Buholo appealed to Mr. H. Horne, the district commissioner of North Nyanza, for a chief of their own. In the same year, an Ugenya leader by the name of Omoro K'Omolo collected money from a number of Jo-Ugenya people and hired a lawyer to press the case for the Jo-Ugenya refugees to be resettled in their land. B. A. Ogot notes that the Jo-Ugenya even lodged appeals with the colonial secretary in London over their land. In 1932, the Jo-Ugenya of Buholo formed an association known as the Ugenya Kager Luo Clan South Bank of the River Nzoia Association (UKA). Mr. Joshua Elisha Obala was appointed as its secretary. The quest of the Jo-Ugenya had not changed: they wanted their land back. In the same year, the Jo-Ugenya, through the UKA association, hired R. R. Evanson to file an appeal with the government demanding their land back. In his appeal, Evanson explained the circumstances under which the Jo-Ugenya had lost their land, and outlined the reasons why the Jo-Ugenya felt that they should get it back:

> When Mr. Hobley and Mr. Spencer were disappointed in not seeing the peace party, they both set out to see what had happened, and a very large gathering awaited them at Manga . . . . there ensued a fight and Ugenya people were shot by Mr. Hobley and his *askaris* . . . . shortly after the fight described above, Chief Mumia provoked another battle at Anyiko, where there was a village populated by Ugenyans [sic] under an Ugenya chief named Gero son of Okado.[38]

In this abbreviated account of the two battles Evanson observed that the land was lost during the resistance to the coming of the British in Ugenya. He argued that the land belonged to the Jo-Ugenya. But the appeal, like the previous ones, was turned down, this time largely through the intervention of Archdeacon Owen, a British missionary with the CMS, who sided with the Wanga settlers already settled in the Jo-Ugenya areas of South Wanga. Evanson was told that the government could not interfere in land issues because these issues were governed by customary law. Unhappy with the ruling, the Jo-Ugenya continued to agitate. By this time Alfayo Odongo Mango had come of age and had become one of the leaders of the agitation. B. A. Ogot writes that Odongo Mango was so furious with the government ruling and particularly with the role of Archdeacon Owen in the affair that he decided to quit the Church Missionary Society to found his own church, the Holy Ghost Church (usually known as the Church of the Jo Roho). Admittedly, Alfayo Odongo Mango had many grievances against the government and the CMS, but it does appear that the ruling preventing the Jo-Ugenya from reclaiming their land in South Wanga was the last straw for him.[39]

Throughout the colonial period, the Jo-Ugenya continued to agitate for their land, even as the British government introduced measures that made it very difficult for people to migrate freely or acquire land through conquest as they had done in the past. The Jo-Ugenya continued to fight for their land even as they kept being told that they could not get it back. They continued to believe in their land as a right, and that is why they continued agitating for it. This constant agitation by the Jo-Ugenya for their land was not unique to them. Throughout Africa, we see dispossessed African communities doing the same thing. Land is dear to African peasants. It is their means of livelihood. The Maasai, Agikuyu, Kipsigis, and Nandi of Kenya agitated for their land during the colonial period, and continue to do so even today with varying results. The same struggle goes on in Zimbabwe, Namibia, and South Africa where Africans were thrown out of their land during the colonial period. Thus the Jo-Ugenya were not unique in mounting a vigorous struggle for their land. They were fighting for their land as a right, for their means of livelihood. Indeed, the Jo-Ugenya continued to fight for their land until the eve of independence when their struggle finally bore some fruit.

As part of the preparations for independence, the government of Kenya had formed the Kenya Boundaries and Delineation Commission to re-draw and re-demarcate Kenya's internal boundaries, taking into account the emerging political reality in Kenya. This was in 1962. The Kenya Boundaries and Delineation Commission traveled around the country, collecting views on boundary and land disputes. It was during this period that it came upon the long saga of the Jo-Ugenya campaign for their land. The members of the commission heard about the 1896–97 Ugenya resistance to the British. They heard about how the Jo-Ugenya who fled during the conflict were prevented from coming back to their land through the connivance of Nabongo Mumia, the church, and the early colonial administrators. They heard that this dispute was still fresh in the minds of many Jo-Ugenya, and especially that some of the Jo-Ugenya who were affected by the turmoil were still angry about it. They combed colonial archives and found testimonies to the effect that the dispute was causing a lot of friction between the Jo-Ugenya and the Wanga. The Kenya Boundaries and Delineation Commission felt that this state of affairs did not augur very well for the future of the soon-to-be independent Kenya. B. A. Ogot observes that, in 1962, the commission decided to transfer "several sub-locations to Kager [Jo-Ugenya] and their allies. The enlarged Buholo location was then transferred to Central Nyanza District," while Wanga remained part of North Nyanza District. The commission's decision was an important concession to the Jo-Ugenya. It went a long way toward assuaging the plight of the Jo-Ugenya. Although not all the Jo-Ugenya refugees were able to come back and not all of their land was given back, it was clear to them that the government was at least trying to make a concession to them. They also understood that this was probably the best deal they could ever get under the circumstances, considering the number of years that had elapsed since their dispersal. They therefore decided not to press their luck further with the commission, and decided to accept the land allocated to them. They decided to close the chapter on the land issue and started focusing their attention on the challenges of building the new nation of Kenya.

Conclusion

It is clear that when the British came to Ugenya, they created a major crisis that culminated in the dispersal of the Jo-Ugenya. They did not just conquer the Jo-Ugenya; they forced the Jo-Ugenya to scatter and then prevented them from coming back to reclaim their land. After the Jo-Ugenya had fled, their traditional territory was divided up among the Wanga and their allies. When the Jo-Ugenya tried to reclaim their land, they found it occupied, and their agitations for justice fell on deaf ears among the colonial administrators. In spite of legal and political efforts during the colonial period, they were unable to regain their land. They were dispersed and forced to settle in new territories. It was only on the eve of independence that some of them were able to reclaim some of their land from the Wanga. Although they did not win all their land back, they were at least successful in getting some of it back. Their struggles and agitations were therefore not in vain. They were partly successful.

Notes

Note on terminology: the term "Jo-Ugenya" refers to the inhabitants or people of Ugenya, while "Ugenya" refers to the territory or is used as an adjective. I owe my inspiration for the title of this chapter to John Lamphear's book, *The Scattering Time: Turkana Responses to Colonial Rule* (Oxford: Oxford University Press, 1992).

1.   The best book on African colonial resistance still remains A. A. Boahen, ed., *General History of Africa*, vol. 7, *Africa under Colonial Domination, 1880–1935* (London: Heinemann Educational Books, 1985). This book contains many chapters on African resistance, largely focusing on examples of resistance and their immediate aftermath. Other good chapters on African resistance can be found in B. A. Ogot, ed.,

War and Society in Africa: Ten Regional Studies (London: Frank Cass, 1972). Equally important is Shane Doyle's *Crisis and Decline in Bunyoro: Population and Environment in Western Uganda, 1860–1955* (Athens: Ohio University Press, 2006).

2.   E. E. Evans-Pritchard, "Luo Clans and Tribes" in *Rhodes-Livingstone Journal* 7 (1949): 24–40.

3.   H. O. Nundu, *Nyuolruok Dhoudi Mag Ugenya* (Nairobi: Kenya Literature Bureau, 1982); Margaret L. Otieno "The Biography of Ex-Chief Muganda Okwako, 1903–1952" (BA diss., University of Nairobi, 1972).

4.   J. R. Dealing, "Politics in Wanga Kingdom, c. 1650–1914," vols. 1–3 (PhD diss., Northwestern University, 1974); J. Osogo, "Historical Traditions of the Wanga," in *Hadithi I,* ed. B. A. Ogot (Nairobi: East African Publishing House, 1968), 32–46; J. S. Osogo, *Nabongo Mumia* (Nairobi: East African Literature Bureau, 1975); B. A. Ogot, *History of the Southern Luo,* vol. 1, *Migration and Settlement* (Nairobi: East African Publishing House, 1967); G. S. Were, *A History of the Abaluhya, 1500–1930* (Nairobi: East African Publishing House, 1967).

5.   B. A. Ogot, "British Administration in the Central Nyanza District of Kenya," in *The Challenges of History and Leadership in Africa: The Essays of Bethwell Allan Ogot,* ed. Toyin Falola and Atieno Odhiambo (Trenton, NJ: Africa World Press, 1971), 269; G. H. Mungeam, *The British in Kenya, 1895–1912: The Establishment of Administration in the East Africa Protectorate* (Oxford: Clarendon Press, 1966), 7. See also John Lonsdale, "The Politics of Conquest: The British in Western Kenya, 1894–1908," *The Historical Journal* 20, no. 4 (1977): 841–70; and John Lonsdale and Bruce Berman, "Coping with the Contradictions: The Development of the Colonial State in Kenya, 1895–1914," *Journal of African History* 20, no. 4 (1979): 487–505.

6.   R. E. Robinson and J. Gallagher, *Africa and the Victorians: The Official Mind of Imperialism* (London: Macmillan, 1961).

7.   PC/NZA.1/4, 1908–1909, Kenya National Archive (KNA); R. C. Bridges, "The British Exploration of East Africa, 1788–1885: With Special Reference to the Activities of the Royal Geographical Society" (PhD diss., University of London, 1963), 89; Mungeam, *The British in Kenya,* 2.

8.   Joseph Thomson, *Through Maasailand* (London: Sampson, Low, Marston, Searle and Ravington, 1962), 160; Osogo "Historical Traditions of the Wanga," 77; Osogo, *Nabongo Mumia,* 11.

9.   Charles W. Hobley, *Kenya from Chartered Company to Crown Colony* (London: Frank Cass, 1970), 68.

10.   Ibid.

11.   J. M. Lonsdale, "A Political History of Nyanza, 1883–1945" (PhD diss., Trinity College, Cambridge University, 1964), 98.

12.   Hobley, *Kenya from Chartered Company to Crown Colony,* 80.

13.   Reports based on interviews with many people in Ugenya. These include interviews with James Muga Muganda, age eighty, interviewed at Nyakenya sub-location, North Ugenya, March 23, 1991; and Zibedi Omondi Ndaga, age seventy-four, interviewed at Sigomre sub-location, Uhobo location, April 16, 1991.

14.   Margaret L. Otieno, "The Biography of Ex-Chief Muganda Okwako"; interview with Charles Oloo Meso, age seventy, Aoho sub-location, Ukwala location, March 1, 1991.

15. E. S. Atieno Odhiambo, "The Movement of Ideas: A Case Study of the Intellectual Responses to Colonialism among the Liganua Peasants," in *Hadith 6: History and Social Change in East Africa,* ed. Bethwell A. Ogot (Nairobi: Kenya Literature Bureau, 1976), 175.

16. Osogo, *Nabongo Mumia,* 18, 77.

17. Ogot, "British Administration in the Central Nyanza District of Kenya," 270.

18. Lonsdale, "A Political History," 101; Dealing, "Politics in Wanga Kingdom," 309.

19. Ogot, "Kenya under the British, 1895–1963," in *Zamani: A Survey of East African History,* ed. B. A. Ogot (Nairobi: East African Publishing House), 249.

20. Dealing, "Politics in Wanga Kingdom," 354–55; Osogo, *Nabongo Mumia,* 25, 26.

21. Interviews with James Muga Muganda, March 23, 1991; and Zibedi Omondi Ndaga, April 16, 1991.

22. Interview with Patrick Otieno Odhiambo, age sixty-five, Magoya sub-location, Uholo location, April 23, 1991. During an interview, Patrick Otieno Odhiambo asserted that the horse was speared by a Wanga soldier with the intention of sparking off the fighting. This claim was repeated by other interviewees.

23. PC/NN., 2/2, 1912–1918, KNA.

24. *Bunde* is a Kiswahili word meaning a "gun," while *kamnara* is a Luo corruption of the English phrase "Come near," coined due to the British habit of shouting "Come near, come near!" while brandishing a gun.

25. Interviews with Uduny Otieno, age seventy, Tingare sub-location, Uholo location, April 22, 1991; and Owino Orego, age sixty-four, Sigomre sub-location, Uholo location, May 8, 1991; DC/CN. 3/4, 1913–23, KNA; DC/CN. 3/4, 1913–29, KNA.

26. B. A. Ogot, "Reverend Alfayo Odongo Mango, 1870–1934," in Kenneth King and Ahmed Salim, eds., *Kenya Historical Biographies* (Nairobi: East African Publishing House, 1971), 91.

27. Ibid., 91.

28. DC/CN. 3/1, 1900–1910, KNA; DC/NNA. 3/3/6, 1929–30, KNA.

29. Ogot appears to have been quoting from S. H. Fazan, a colonial official in the area. For further information on this, see DC/CN. 3/4, 1913–23, KNA.

30. DC/CN. 3/4, 1913–23, KNA.

31. Ibid.

32. Interviews with James Muga Muganda, March 23, 1991; and Zibedi Omondi Ndaga, April 16, 1991; Hobley, *Kenya from Chartered Company to Crown Colony,* 368; Dealing, "Politics in Wanga Kingdom," 381.

33. Interview with Patrick Otieno Odhiambo, April 23, 1991; DC/NN. 3/1, 1900-16, KNA.

34. K. P. Lohrentz, "The Campaign to Depose Chief Mulama in Murama Location: A Case Study in Politics of Kinship," *Kenya Historical Review: The Journal of the Historical Association of Kenya* 4, no. 2 (1976); Osogo, "Historical Traditions of the Wanga."

35. DC/NN. 10/1/1, 1926–40, KNA; Ogot, "Reverend Alfayo Odongo Mango, 1870–1934," 90-91.

36. Ogot, "Reverend Alfayo Odongo Mango, 1870–1934," 91.

37. Ibid., 97.

38. R. R. Evanson was a lawyer that the Kager clan of the Jo-Ugenya hired in 1932 to represent them in a suit against the colonial government to recover their land in Buholo and Southern Wanga. DC/NN.10/1/1, 1926–1940, KNA.

39. For more on Reverand Alfayo Odongo Mango and the conflicts between the Jo-Ugenya and the British, see Cynthia Hoehler-Fatton, *Women of Fire and Spirit: History, Faith, and Gender in Roho Religion in Western Kenya* (New York: Oxford University Press, 1996).

8

Traders, Slaves, and Soldiers

The Hausa Diaspora in Ghana (Gold Coast and Asante) in the Nineteenth and Early Twentieth Centuries

Edmund Abaka

The African diaspora has become a focus of research by Africanists over the past two or so decades. Scholars have tended to equate the trading diaspora in Africa with voluntary migration. However, like the external diaspora, the diaspora in Africa resulted from forced migration as well. Ethnic groups such as the Hausa were involved in both voluntary and forced migration to modern Ghana. In all cases, these diasporic communities—the Yarse, Dyula, Fulani, and Hausa—kept ties with their homelands through extensive networks.[1]

The spread of Islam and Hausa culture has been attributed largely to the religiously inspired political conquests of the nineteenth century.[2] The contribution of the mercantile activities of the Hausa, Yarse, Dyula, and other communities has also been recognized.[3] However, there is a paucity of material in the extant literature on the totality of the diasporic experience of these groups in their host societies.

In this context, the present chapter addresses the role of the members of the Hausa diaspora in the history of the Gold Coast (Ghana) in two distinct phases—as traders and as soldiers. The chapter focuses on the voluntary and forced Hausa migration to, and activities in, the Volta basin in general and "Greater Asante" in particular. It posits that at the height of the Asante kola trade, the Hausa were a vital link in the desert-side trading venture between the Sokoto Caliphate, Asante, and the Volta-Afram basin. It also argues that during the period of the caliphate, not only did supplies of Hausa slaves enter the Atlantic slave trade network but also many of them wound up in Asante and the Volta-Afram basin, where they were utilized for all kinds of work.[4] Finally, during the early colonial period in Ghana, the Hausa became the fulcrum around which was created the famous Hausa constabulary or Gold Coast Constabulary, which the British used to consolidate their hold over the Gold Coast.[5] The West African Frontier Force was a progression from the Gold Coast Constabulary to a full-fledged military detachment. In the postindependence period, the Hausa constituted a large enough constituency that various political parties began to court their support. In this respect, this study differs from similar work on the Hausa or Wangara in other countries. As well, correspondence between the *asantehene*'s court and the Sarkin Zongo show that the Hausa constituted a large enough group to merit attention in Asante.

Hausa: Who or What?

The term "Hausa" has very varied definitions. On the one hand, it refers to the Hausa language. Apart from being spoken by a variety of people including Fulani and people from Bornu and Nupe, Hausa was also a trade language in the Central Sudan and along the trade routes of the Volta basin.[6] Consequently, Hausa was spoken by the people involved in cross-cultural trade, and people could pass as Hausa if they could partake in the trade discourse. Therefore, many slaves who were sold through the kola nut trade were classified as Hausa[7] because they had been part of the trade network and some of them had picked up a smattering of Hausa.

On the other hand, Hausa is a cultural term for the Hausa-speaking Muslim populations in northern Nigeria and the adjoining territories. These included mallams, religious students, and scholars who traveled from the Central Sudan to the Volta basin in the south and the Islamic world of North Africa, southern Europe, and Constantinople.[8] This definition does not include the non-Muslim Maguzawa of northern Nigeria.[9]

The term Hausa also refers to a geographical entity, the Hausa states. The seven original Hausa States (*Hausa bokoi*—Daura, Katsina, Kano, Rano, Zazau) as opposed to the seven "bastard" states (*banza bokoi*) legitimated the Hausa identity and became the organizing principle of migration to other parts of the Central Sudan, the Western Sudan, and the Islamic world. This geographical entity also encompasses the large assimilated populations of slave origin in Hausa communities.[10]

A diaspora maintains its membership, identity, internal divisions, language, religion, and cultural practices by subordinating all these elements to a common sense of identity. The Hausa diaspora in Ghana (the Gold Coast and Asante) was made up of slaves as well as freeborn members, that is, those who left their communities voluntarily. The communities they created, popularly known as *zongos*,[11] became Hausa and Muslim islands in the sea of the host communities.

The Hausa and Long-Distance Trade (*Fatauci*)

Hausa society and history have been characterized by spatial mobility. The foundation of the Hausa states, according to Hausa myths of origin, was enshrined in migration. Bayajidda, the Hausa hero, was supposed to have come from the east and sent his children out from Daura to establish their hegemony over the indigenous population.[12] Throughout their history, the Hausa have been known for their trading acumen and have migrated to create trade diasporas through long-distance trading (*fatauci*).[13] Since the fourteenth century, the Hausa have contributed to the political economy of Asante and the Gold Coast in various ways. Hausa merchants in Asante formed part of the broader commercial networks in West Africa. They provided the luxury goods needed by the Asante political elite, as well as the basic goods demanded by the populace as a whole. This led to the creation of various trade diasporas and settlements in trading centers such as Bonduku,[14] Kintampo,[15] Begho,[16] Gbuipe, Kafaba, Umfaha, and Yendi.[17] In the early nineteenth century, Salaga became the "grand emporium of the Inta Kingdom."[18] After the British invasion of Kumasi in 1874, Kintampo was established as an alternative trading center.[19] Some Hausa from Kunso resettled at Kintampo and helped to make it a vibrant trading center.[20]

Trade between Hausaland and the Volta basin dates back to the fifteenth century. In his *Sudanese Memoirs,* H. R. Palmer asserts that Sarkin Kano Abdullahi Burja dan Kanajeji (ca. 1438–52) "was the first in Hausaland to give Bornu *tsare* or *gaisua.*[21] He opened roads from Bornu to Gwanja. He was the first to own camels in Hausaland."[22] The beginnings of the kola trade to Bornu and Hausaland are obscure. However, Palmer indicates that kola nuts first entered Hausaland during the time of Queen Amina of Zazau in the early part of the fifteenth century.[23] It is very likely that the opening of the route from Bornu to Gwanja (Gonja) signaled the development of the kola trade with the Volta basin.[24] The accounts of Muslims in the Volta region of Ghana, which indicate that they moved to the area from Bornu and Hausaland before the establishment of the state of Gwanja, seem to point to the existence of an early involvement of Hausaland and Bornu in the kola trade with Asante and the Volta basin.[25] Abu Bakr al Siddiq, who was enslaved in the early nineteenth century, states that his father, a trader from Timbuktu, lived in Katsina for a while and moved as a trader to the Volta region.[26] Natron was one of the basic ingredients in food and medicinal preparations in Hausaland, and by the early nineteenth century, it was one of the most important items of trade to the coast and the Volta basin, where it was mixed with snuff.[27]

Even though Asante did engage in external trade, it was conducted in towns such as Salaga to the north of Kumasi. This continued from the mid-eighteenth century until the end of the nineteenth century. The exception to this rule was provided by the small but powerful and influential Muslim community resident in Kumasi.[28] Because Asante's trade was conducted largely in towns to the north of Kumasi, the kola trade to Asante became known in the Central Sudan as *fataucin Gonja*. In this context, "Gonja" referred to the Hausa trade diaspora involved in the kola trade—that is, the series of dispersed settlements of Hausa along the trade routes to the middle Volta basin.[29] The settlements were inhabited by people from Hausaland and Bornu who utilized kin networks to obtain access to local markets, capital, and information about the kola trade.[30] Thus, Hausa traders relied on a culture that transcended political and ethnic lines, and utilized Islam as a unifying ideology to facilitate business operations and guarantee warehousing facilities and credit.[31] More importantly, the Hausa trading settlements, united by language and religion, bridged the cultural and ideological gulf between the Hausa and the host societies, and provided the twin props of the trade, brokerage and agency, in Bonduku, Begho, Kafaba, Umfaha, Yendi, Salaga, Kete Krachi, Atebubu, Adawso, and coastal centers such as Cape Coast, Saltpond, and Winneba.[32]

The economic and ethnic heterogeneity of these towns and settlements gave them a distinctive character, different from the purely indigenous towns and settlements of the area. Laid out in a fashion similar to each other, these towns and settlements were always aggregations of wards, each ward inhabited predominantly by members of the same ethnic group, even though there were no sharp cleavages between the wards. Bonduku and Salaga had the appearance of a jumble of irregularly located compound houses;[33] in Kintampo, the compound houses were separated from each other with hedges that enclosed cultivated plots of maize, bananas, and pear trees.[34] Theophilus Opoku, the Akwapim evangelist, described the houses in Bonduku, Salaga, and Kintampo as

> round conical huts, of which more or fewer [than] ten to twenty huts, according to the size of the family and its possessions, are built together and separated from the rest by a wall or fence. These compounds are enclosed. The entrance is usually a larger hut, quite empty[,] with openings, one giving on the court, and the other to the street. The arrangement of huts in the compound is often haphazard; without much attention to regularity or beauty.[35]

In many of these trading centers, their geographical and political position, coupled with the entrepreneurial skills of the immigrants, fostered rapid growth. Hausa landlords (*mai gida*) provided accommodations and hospitality, bulked products entering the long-distance trade, collected and collated information about sources of commodities and market prices, helped with packing and storage, and offered short-term credit.[36] Most of the inhabitants of these diasporic communities were Muslim, used Hausa as their first language, and traced their ancestry to one of the Hausa cities. In spite of the fact that many Hausa were born in the diasporic settlements, they still considered themselves "strangers" in the new societies and identified more with their clients, distant trade centers, and Hausaland than they did with their adopted countries.[37] Similarly, the host communities regarded them as "strangers." Yet the influence of the Hausa in the diaspora was enormous.

Migrant Labor

In addition to long-distance trading, the Hausa have also been known for their involvement in dry-season migration for employment (*ci rani*), and have settled away from home.[38] From the 1880s onward, large numbers of Hausa were involved in seasonal migration to the cocoa-producing regions of Asante, Brong Ahafo, Akwapim, and Akyem to work as laborers during the cocoa-harvesting season. In addition, they served as porters. In fact, the bulk of the cocoa produced inland was carried by Hausa porters to the rail-heads and sometimes to the roadways.[39] John H. Harris stresses the Hausa role in cocoa porterage when he writes that

> The carriers are mostly Hausas, but the fame of the Gold Coast carrier traffic has spread far into the northern regions of Africa with the result that recognised caravan routes now come right down through the northern territories. These carriers, many of them from around and even beyond Lake Chad, drive herds of cattle down to the Gold Coast colony about the harvest time. They sell the cattle and then carry cocoa for the season. When the main harvest is over and there is little cocoa carrying, they will purchase loads of kola nuts which they carry back with them to the far interior and sell *en route* at a considerable profit. Thus, they make a three-fold financial return—on the sale of cattle, cocoa carrying, and the profits on the kola nut trade.[40]

The Hausa Police and the Colonial Administration

One of the major problems that bedevilled the early British colonial administration in the Gold Coast was the lack of a loyal, dependable force with which to maintain the security and defense of British possessions in West Africa in the nineteenth century. The British had no answer to the problem until ad hoc experimentation led to the solution in the form of the Hausa police force or Gold Coast Constabulary.[41] David Killingray argues that the origins of the Gold Coast police are to be found in a dual system of policing—an armed frontier police force designed to consolidate British political control over, first, the coastal towns and villages and later Asante and the Northern Territories, and a smaller, unarmed civil police force designed to extend British social control over the coastal towns and villages.[42]

Initially, the work of policing the British West African possessions was entrusted to the Gold Coast Corps. Unfortunately, relations between the corps and the colonial administration and garrison towns were, at best, tense. In 1862, when a soldier was flogged outside the gates of Cape Coast Castle for striking a girl with his musket,

> The men marched out of the castle with their band, and went to a place called Napoleon, *five miles distant from here, and situate in the bush.* The Government here (so called out of courtesy), consisting of three or four gentlemen, were exceedingly alarmed. Some chiefs and native gentlemen of Cape Coast succeeded at last in bringing back the mutineers, one hundred and seventy in number, and most of them have been sent up to Sierra Leone in a man-of-war. The castle is now garrisoned by some sailors and marines from vessels of war and Cape Coast Volunteers, a native force, who, although greatly despised and ridiculed sometime ago by some officers of the Gold Coast Corps, have rendered efficient service since the late mutiny.[43]

The *African Times* also reported that the soldiers of the Gold Coast Corps had committed outrages in the interior of the Gold Coast.[44]

In addition to the indiscipline, indiscretion, insubordination, and general inefficiency of the Gold Coast Corps, a further problem was that deaths due to disease were high.[45] The creation of a local force was thus born out of the need for a force to replace the Gold Coast Corps. And even with this need, the British did not have a clear-cut recruitment policy designed to enlist Africans. Reinforcements for the indisciplined Gold Coast Corps were often British deserters and members of other British units who were sent to West Africa as punishment.[46]

When the Gold Coast Corps was disbanded, units of the 4th West India Regiment under Lt. Col. Conran were sent to the Gold Coast, at a time when there were rumors of an Asante invasion of the coast in 1863.[47] In addition to the West India Regiment, the government raised a volunteer corps from the youth to help with the war effort.[48]

As the problem of a standing force adapted to the vicissitudes of the work on the Gold Coast continued to bedevil the colonial administration, the British resorted to enlisting men from the recaptives (rescued or liberated slaves) who were landed in Freetown.[49] To mitigate the recruitment problem, the soldiers of the West India Regiments were stationed on the West African coast, especially at Freetown, but the force was handicapped by the lack of availability of recruits. From the mid-nineteenth century onward, fewer and fewer recaptives were obtained. In addition, there were altercations between the soldiers of the West India Regiments and the people of the garrison towns.[50]

The armed Hausa police became, essentially, a solution to the problem of a dependable, efficient force on the Gold Coast as the enforcement wing of the colonial administration. The new forces were organized along paramilitary lines to play the dual role of a police force and an army. They were variously called constabularies or armed police or Hausa police.[51] They became a paramilitary force designed to suppress revolts and assert British control over the Gold Coast hinterland, especially after 1874. Many of the officers were European and came from a military background.[52] The type of European officers appointed to the force affected the type of recruitment to the rank and file.

The origins of the Gold Coast Constabulary arose out of the desire of the secretary of state for colonies in 1845 to establish a small police force of about 30–50 men, along the lines of the London police.[53] In 1855, Governor Benjamin Pine stressed the need for the establishment of an armed police force to maintain law and order.[54] Similarly, in the mid 1860s, Acting Governor Conran argued that a small, properly organized and well-armed police, stationed in the major towns of Cape Coast, Accra, and Annamaboe, would be more effective than a military detachment about three times its size.[55] These suggestions were given practical reality when Captain Glover raised a constabulary along the lines of the Lagos police.[56] This new police force was organized in 1865 along the lines of the Irish Constabulary.[57]

The major problem facing the new constabulary in the Gold Coast was the question of recruits. Since there was no consistent policy for building up the unit, the British relied on runaway slaves, especially from the hinterland (Hausa and Bornu slaves among others). While such people were eager to enlist, find a new career, or even gain revenge on their former masters, the freeborn were not keen on enlistment. This is vividly borne out by Richard Pine, who remonstrated to the under secretary for war and the colonies, Henry Labouchere, that nine out of every ten men who enlisted in the Gold Coast Constabulary were slaves. He pointed out the dangers inherent in such a system:

> First, the chiefs and upper class are deprived of their slaves without their consent and without remuneration. Secondly, these same slaves, generally bad characters, are sent back to them with red coats on their backs, to enforce the orders of Government; which, they, of course, do with all the insolence natural to their sudden change of fortune.[58]

Pine further noted that

> the Corps thus recruited is necessarily composed of the off-scourings of the country; of men who have plundered their masters or committed other atrocities. The conduct of such men acting as police may well be imagined. Whenever

they are sent into the bush on service, they pillage and maltreat people. Even the presence of the officers cannot restrain them. Every time I have taken an excursion into the interior accompanied by an officer and a few soldiers, well-founded complaints have been made of the lawless conduct of the men.

This is not all. Deserters from the Corps, and men discharged at the end of their term of service, for the most part, betake themselves to the bush. Besides plundering in the ordinary way, they not infrequently extort money under the name of fines which they impose on the people under the pretence that they are armed with the authority of the Government. They even form themselves and the refuse of the people around them, into armed bands.[59]

With the prospect of a British withdrawal from the Gold Coast following the recommendations of the parliamentary committee of 1865, British officials urged the creation of a local paramilitary force to handle all emergencies. However, no concrete action was taken until there was the threat of an Asante invasion in 1869. In 1871 and 1872, Governor Kennedy suggested the creation of a Hausa force; and by 1873, a force had been created along the lines of Glover's Lagos Armed Police, which was built around a core of runaway Hausa and Yoruba slaves. The rationale behind the creation of the Hausa force was that it was cheaper and more efficient than the Gold Coast Corps, especially for duties in the interior.[60] Ex-army officers from England and gazetted officers from the Caribbean were seconded to the force, and they transformed the Hausa police into a paramilitary force.

The Gold Coast Constabulary was an integral part of the British military expedition that invaded Asante in 1874. In the unsettled political climate in Asante and the Gold Coast after the British invasion of Asante in 1874, the Gold Coast Constabulary became the enforcer of British authority. Time and again, the constabulary was despatched to restore peace and tranquillity for trade purposes as well as to protect former vassals of Asante who had broken away and sought refuge in the British protectorate. For example, a detachment of the constabulary was despatched in 1888 to effect "the peaceful removal and internment in the protectorate of a body of Dadiassies or Kokofus who are alleged to be obstructing the trade route into Ashanti at a place called Essaman to the north of Prasu."[61] This detachment consisted of 175 Hausa under the command of the inspector general, Lt. Col. McInnis.[62] After the successful completion of the mission, the detachment of Hausa at Prasu was increased to thirty men but given instructions not to cross the Prah River.[63]

In the period of Anglo-German rivalry and the struggle for the control of the interior of the Gold Coast, the Hausa constabulary was used by the British to occupy Yeji and Salaga in 1897 to forestall a German occupation of those towns.[64] Inspector Aplin was instructed to sign treaties with the chiefs of Salaga and Yegi, and to leave a guard at Brumasi sufficient to oversee the British occupation.

Before 1874, recruits for the Gold Coast Constabulary were drawn largely from Nigeria. Most of them returned to Nigeria after the 1874 campaign against Asante, but others stayed behind as permanent members of the constabulary. The British were impressed by the way the Hausa constabulary members fought, and numerous citations attested to the bravery of the force. For example, one report stated: "My observations of the Hausa lead me to believe that if fanatical they are faithful and well-behaved . . . . They are fierce and intractable in warfare and look with contempt on Pagans."[65]

The question of recruits continued to bedevil the Gold Coast Constabulary. In fact, desertions from the constabulary continued to whittle down the size of the force.[66] To resolve this problem, an African officer, Abu Karimu,[67] Capt. Hay, Capt. Rupert La Trobe Lonsdale, and a Mr. Firminger[68] were sent on recruiting missions to Salaga.[69] Capt Hay was instructed "to endeavour not only to obtain a good supply of Hausas, sufficient to fill up our deficiencies, but to ensure if possible, a continuous [supply]."[70] Similarly, Capt. Lonsdale was instructed to explain to the Salaga authorities that

> this government has so high an opinion of the native of the Houssa country that it employs a military force recruited entirely from that district and in conversation with such Houssas as you may meet at Salagha, you should explain to them the advantages offered by employment in the Force.[71]

In actual fact, those members of the constabulary who were recruited in the Salaga area were Hausa only in terms of the broadest of definitions. In reality, they were composed of Zabrama, of Yoruba, and of Grushi (Gurunsi) and others from what became the Northern Territories.

By the time of the Yaa Asantewaa War in 1900, the British had upward of 700 Hausa soldiers ready for battle. After the suppression of the Asante revolt and defeat of Yaa Asantewaa in 1901, the Gold Coast Constabulary was renamed the West African Frontier Force, divided into units, and stationed in Kumasi. The Hausa constabulary continued to be a very loyal and dependable force throughout the colonial period. At independence the Hausa constituted an important core of the Ghanaian police and army. They were represented in the rank and file as well as in the officer corps. This continued in the postcolonial period and while it bred resentment from other ethnic groups it took a while before the numerical strength of the "Hausa" was appreciably diluted as a result of a gradual increase in the number of other ethnic groups represented in the armed forces.

In addition to continuing their role in the police and army,, the Hausa in the postcolonial period also became a large enough bloc to play an influential role in local affairs in Kumasi and other parts of the country. In the late

1920s the leaders of the Hausa diaspora and other "strangers" were "recognized" by the Gold Coast Native administration. In 1927, the Hausa headman or *Sarkin Zongo* was nominated by the chief commissioner, the British colonial official in Kumasi, to the Kumasi Public Health Board. Similarly, when Prempeh II became *asantehene* in 1935, the *Sarkin Zongo* or leader of the Hausa community was permitted to administer the affairs of the *zongo* and hold an informal court, under the direct, but remote, authority of the *asantehene*. Furthermore, the leader of the Hausa community was later asked to serve as one of the panel members on one of the *asantehene's* courts. The nascent political parties of Ghana also courted the support of the members of the Hausa and other diasporic communities in the country, especially after 1952 when the diasporic groups became increasingly active in politics. Between 1952 and 1955, many leaders of the Hausa diaspora allied with the *asantehene* against the Convention People's Party and some Hausas joined the Ashanti Party, the National Liberation Movement, which later became the United Party. Thus, during a period of tense political activities, amid threats of even secession in the pre-independence years, the Hausa diaspora became active in politics and many supported the anti-CPP faction. During this time, and even after Ghana's independence in 1957, the Hausa diaspora fielded candidates for positions on town councils.

Conclusion

This chapter has noted that Hausa migration to Asante and the Volta-Afram basin was both voluntary and forced. At the height of the Asante kola trade in the nineteenth century, the Hausa constituted a vital link between the Sokoto Caliphate, Asante, and the Volta-Afram basin. Kola was the lodestone that drew the Hausa over so many miles of rough terrain to Asante and the Volta-Afram basin. In the early colonial period, the Hausa constabulary was created to meet the exigencies of the day. The force enabled the British to consolidate its hold over the Gold Coast, Asante, and, later, the Northern Territories. Diasporic Hausa remained an important presence in the Gold Coast/Ghana in later years.

Notes

This is part of a larger project that benefited from a Bernadotte Schmitt Grant from the American Historical Association and a West African Research Association Post-Doctoral Fellowship for research in Ghana in 2006.

    1.   Abner Cohen, "Cultural Strategies in the Organisation of Trading Diasporas," in *The Development of Indigenous Trade and Markets in Africa*, ed. C. Meillassoux, 266–81 (London: Oxford University Press, 1971); Paul E. Lovejoy, *Caravans of Kola:*

The Hausa Kola Trade 1700–1900 (Zaria, Nigeria: Ahmadu Bello University Press, 1980); Philip Curtin, *Cross-Cultural Trade in World History* (Cambridge: Cambridge University Press, 1984), 15–59; J. Goody, "Ashanti and the Northwest," *Research Review*, Supplement no. 1, University of Ghana, Legon (1965); Ivor Wilks, "A Medieval Trade Route from the Niger to the Gulf of Guinea," *Journal of African History* 3, no. 2 (1962): 337–41.

2.   Murray Last, *The Sokoto Caliphate* (London: Longman, 1967); H. F. C. Smith, "The Jihad of Shehu dan Fodio: Some Problems," in *Islam in Tropical Africa*, ed. I. M. Lewis, 408–24 (London: Oxford University Press, 1966).

3.   For details of other communities, see Paul E. Lovejoy, "The Role of the Wangara in the Economic Transformation of the Central Sudan in the 15th and 16th Centuries," *Journal of African History* 19 (1978): 341–68; Jean-Louis Amselle, *Les négociants de la savanne: Histoire et organisation sociale des Kooroko (Mali)* (Paris, 1978), 25–48, 101–71; Robert W. Harms, *River of Sorrow: The Central Zaire Basin in the Era of the Slave and Ivory Trade, 1500–1891* (New Haven, CT: Greenwood Press, 1981).

4.   Marion Johnson, ed., *Salaga Papers* (Legon, Ghana: Institute of African Studies, 1966), vol. 1 (hereafter: SAL), SAL/4/1; SAL/8/5; SAL 17/11; SAL/18/5; SAL 21/2; SAL 39/1; SAL 41/3. See also Paul E. Lovejoy, *Transformations in Slavery. A History of Slavery in Africa* (Cambridge: Cambridge University Press, 1983); Paul E. Lovejoy, "Slavery in the Sokoto Caliphate," in *The Ideology of Slavery in Africa*, ed. Paul E. Lovejoy, 200–43 (Beverly Hills, CA: Sage, 1981).

5.   For the formation of the Gold Coast police, see Public Record Office, London (PRO) CO 96/4/9322, Sir Benjamin Pine to Labouchere, August 31, 1857; PRO CO 96/97/2305, R. Pine to Cardwell, February 4, 1865; PRO CO 96/98/12038, E. Conran to Cardwell, October 25, 1869. On January 24, 1876, , Malcolm J. Brown, acting colonial secretary, Cape Coast, announced the appointment of Captain Alfred Moloney, 1st West India Regiment, as acting police magistrate to replace Lt. Col. Strahan, 1st West India Regiment (PRO CO 991).

6.   Stephen Baier, "The Trade of the Hausa of Damerghou 1900–1930," paper presented at the 15th annual meeting of the African Studies Association, Syracuse, NY, October 31–November 3, 1973, 5. The Tuareg, for example, used the Hausa language in their trading contacts with the Kanuri-speaking people at Fachi and Bilma. See also Stephen Baier and Paul E. Lovejoy, "The Tuareg of the Central Sudan: Gradations in Servility at the Desert-Edge," in *Slavery in Africa: Historical and Anthropological Perspectives*, ed. S. Miers and I. Kopytoff, 391–411 (Madison: University of Wisconsin Press, 1977).

7.   This includes people from the Northern Territories of the Gold Coast, who were known as *ndonkofo* (sing. *odonko*) in contradistinction to the freeborn Akan.

8.   Nehemiah Levtzion, "Early Nineteenth Century Arabic Manuscripts from Kumasi," *Transactions of the Historical Society of Ghana* 8 (1965): 99–119.

9.   See Ludger Rueke, "Die Maguzawa im Nördlichen Nigeria" (PhD diss., University of Munster, Germany, 1967), translated.

10.   R. A. Adeleye, *Power and Diplomacy in Northern Nigeria, 1804–1906* (New York: Humanities Press, 1971); Last, *The Sokoto Caliphate*; Frank Salmone, "Becoming Hausa," *Africa* 45, no. 4 (1975): 410–25.

11.   The term *zongo* (or *zango*), as used in Ghana, refers to the residentially segregated quarters where strangers normally settle.

12.   M. G. Smith, "Historical and Cultural Conditions of Political Corruption among the Hausa," *Comparative Studies in Society and History* 6, no. 2 (1964): 164–94.

13.   Lovejoy, *Caravans of Kola*; Cohen, "Cultural Strategies"; Curtin, *Cross-Cultural Trade*; Harold Olofson, "Yawon Dandi: A Hausa Category of Migration," paper presented at the 14th annual meeting of the African Studies Association, Philadelphia, November 8–11, 1972.

14.   R. Austin Freeman, *Travels in Ashanti and Jaman* (London: Frank Cass, 1967), 206. According to Freeman, the inhabitants of Bonduku were mostly immigrants.

15.   L. G. Binger, *Du Niger au Golfe de Guinée par le pays de Kong er le Mossi* (Paris, 1892), 137.

16.   M. Posnansky, "Archaeological Aspects of the Bono Ahafo Region," in *Brong Akyempim. Essays on the History and Politics of the Brong People*, ed. K. Arhin (Accra, Ghana: Afram Publishers, 1979). Posnansky asserts that Begho was made up of three distinct quarters, those of the Brong, the *kramo* or Muslim trading community, and the Numu blacksmiths.

17.   SAL/22/1; K. Arhin, *West African Traders in the Nineteenth and Twentieth Centuries* (London: Longman, 1979); J. Goody, *The Ethnography of the Northern Territories of the Gold Coast West of the White Volta* (London: Hutchinson, 1971).

18.   T. E. Bowdich, *Mission from Cape Coast Castle to Ashantee* (London: J. Murray, 1819), 172; Capt. R. T. Lonsdale, "Report on a Mission to Kumasi, Salaga and Yendi, October 1881 to February 1882," in British Parliamentary Papers (PP), PRO London, C.3386. See also Ivor Wilks, *Asante in the Nineteenth Century: The Structure and Evolution of a Political Order* (London: Cambridge University Press, 1975).

19.   Lonsdale, "Report on a Mission," PP, C.3386; Arhin, *West African Traders*, 47–48.

20.   Brandon Kirby, "Report on Mission to Kumasi and the Interior Provinces of the Ashanti Kingdom," PP, C.4477.

21.   H. R. Palmer, *Sudanese Memoirs* (Lagos, 1928), vol. 3, 109.

22.   Ibid.

23.   Ibid.

24.   Ibid.

25.   M. A. Adamu, "A Hausa Government in Decline" (master's thesis, Ahmadu Bello University, Zaria, Nigeria, 1968), 57.

26.   Ivor Wilks, "Abubakar Al-Siddiq of Timbuctoo," in *Africa Remembered*, ed. Philip Curtin (Madison: University of Wisconsin Press, 1967), 159.

27.   E. W. Bovill, *Missions to the Niger*, series 4 (Cambridge: Cambridge University Press, 1966), 616; H. Clapperton, *Journal of a Second Expedition into the Interior of Africa from the Bight of Benin to Soccatoo* (London: John Murray, 1829), 59, 68.

28.   Ivor Wilks, "The Position of Muslims in Metropolitan Ashanti in the Early Nineteenth Century," in Lewis, *Islam in Tropical Africa*, 318–41; Wilks, *Asante in the Nineteenth Century*.

29.   Lovejoy, *Caravans of Kola*, 29; Cohen, "Cultural Strategies"; Curtin, *Cross-Cultural Trade*, 40; Abner Cohen, *Customs and Politics of Urban Africa: A Study of Hausa Migrants in Yoruba Towns* (Berkeley: University of California Press, 1969); Nehemiah Levtzion, *Muslims and Chiefs in West Africa. A Study of Islam in the Middle Volta Basin in the Pre-colonial Period* (London: Oxford University Press, 1968), 28–29.

30.   Lovejoy, *Caravans of Kola*, 31; Curtin, *Cross-Cultural Trade*, 40. See also Wilks, "Asante Policy towards the Hausa Trade in the 19th Century," in Meillassoux, *Indigenous Trade and Markets*, 124–39; Enid Schildkraut, *People of the Zongo: The Transformation of Ethnic Identities in Ghana* (Cambridge: Cambridge University Press, 1978); Cohen, *Customs and Politics*.

31.   Lovejoy, *Caravans of Kola*, 31.

32.   Ibid.

33.   SAL/19/2; Binger, *Du Niger*, 162. Binger described the houses as Mande and Dagomba type compound dwellings.

34.   Binger, *Du Niger*, 137.

35.   SAL/8/1.

36.   Lovejoy, *Caravans of Kola*, 31; Polly Hill, "Landlords and Brokers: A West African Trading System (With Notes on Kumasi Butchers)," *Cahiers d'études africaines* 6, no. 23 (1966): 349–66. For comparative purposes, see Mordechai Abir, "Brokerage and Brokers in Ethiopia in the First Half of the Nineteenth Century," *Journal of Ethiopian Studies* 3 (1965): 1–5; Philip Curtin, *Economic Change in Precolonial Africa: Senegambia in the Era of the Slave Trade* (Madison: University of Wisconsin Press, 1975).

37.   Lovejoy, *Caravans of Kola*, 32. Other trade networks, such as those of the Dyula/Juula, Yarse, Borgu, Wangara, and other merchants, all operated in the Volta basin, and their commercial activities overlapped with those of the Hausa in an interlocking grid that effectively linked the Volta basin with the Niger bend and beyond.

38.   Kenneth Swindell, "Farmers, Traders and Labourers: Dry Season Migration from Northern Nigeria, 1900–1933," *Africa* 54, no. 1 (1984): 3–19.

39.   John H. Harris, *Dawn in Darkest Africa* (London: Frank Cass, 1968), 255.

40.   Ibid., 256.

41.   British possessions at the time were restricted to the coastal areas of Sierra Leone and the Gold Coast littoral. The British forts in these areas were garrisoned by European troops. The period of formal expansion in the 1880s increased the size of British territory in West Africa. Therefore, there was a need to augment the small force of Europeans stationed in the forts and castles along the coast.

42.   David Killingray, "Guarding the Extending Frontier: Policing the Gold Coast, 1865–1913," in *Policing the Empire: Government Authority and Control 1830–1940*, ed. David M. Anderson and David Killingray, 106–25 (Manchester, UK: Manchester University Press, 1991).

43.   *African Times* (London), November 22, 1862, 51.

44.   *African Times*, November 22, 1862, 52; April 23, 1863, 113.

45.   James Africanus Horton, *West African Countries and Peoples* (Edinburgh: Edinburgh University Press, 1868), 97.

46.   See S. C. Ukpabi, "The West African Frontier Force: An Instrument of Policy" (master's thesis, University of Birmingham, UK, 1964). Ukpabi asserts that Capt. William Day organized a volunteer corps of Nova Scotians and maroons in Sierra Leone. But since the two groups had in the past shown open signs of hostility to each other, the government of the Sierra Leone Company and the European community were not happy at the prospect of relying on them for security.

47.   *African Times*, October 23, 1863, 40, 42; June 23, 1864, 152. See also Major W. F. Butler, *Akim-Foo: The History of a Failure* (London: Sampson Low, Marston, Low

& Searle, 1875), 66; Sir John Dalrymple Hay, *Ashanti and the Gold Coast: And What We Know* of *It* (London: Edward Stanford, 1874), 61.

48. *African Times*, April 23, 1864, 118.

49. Ukpabi, "West African Frontier Force," 456.

50. Horton, *West African Countries and Peoples*, 101.

51. PRO CO 96/43, Pine to Labouchere, Cape Coast Castle, February 10, 1858.

52. See PRO CO 99/1: Malcolm J. Brown, acting colonial secretary, Cape Coast, January 24, 1876, announced the appointment of Captain Alfred Moloney, 1st West India Regiment, as acting police magistrate to replace Lt. Col. Strahan, 1st West India Regiment; Captain Alfred Moloney, acting colonial secretary Cape Coast, August 16, 1876, announced the appointment of Mr. J. F. Lynch, late of the 13th Light Infantry, as acting inspector-general, Gold Coast Constabulary, by the secretary of state for the colonies; and Alfred Moloney, acting colonial secretary, Cape Coast, October 8, 1876, appointed Captain Craigge Halkett of the Fife Artillery Militia as artillery inspector of the Gold Coast Constabulary.

53. PRO WO 1/497, Stanley to Lilley, October 7, 1845; see also Killingray, "Guarding the Extending Frontier," 106.

54. PRO CO 96/4/9322, Sir Benjamin Pine to Labouchere, August 31, 1857.

55. PRO CO 96/97/2305, R. Pine to Cardwell, February 4, 1865; PRO CO 96/68/12038, E. Conran to Cardwell, October 25, 1869.

56. Lt. Col. C. S. Taylor, Regimental *History of the Nigerian Regiment of W.A.F.F.* (1944), cited in Samson C. Ukpabi, "Military Recruitment and Social Mobility in Nineteenth Century British West Africa," *Journal of African Studies* (Spring 1975): 87–107. See also David Killingray, "Guarding the Extending Frontier," In Sierra Leone, a frontier police was established in 1890. See Lt. R. P. M. Davis, *History of Sierra Leone Battalion of the R.W.A.F.F.* (Freetown, 1932). In Nigeria, the Royal Niger Company and the Niger Coast Protectorate also raised constabularies in areas under their protection. See Samson C. Ukpabi, "The Origins of the West African Frontier Force," *Journal of the Historical Society of Nigeria* 3, no. 3 (December 1966): 491.

57. See S. K. Ankamah, *Police History. Some Aspects in England and Ghana* (Ilford, UK, 1983).

58. PRO CO 96/43, Pine to Labouchere, Cape Coast Castle, February 10, 1858.

59. Ibid.

60. PRO CO 96/96/6426, Hennessey to Kimberley, May 31, 1872, enclosing a letter from Col. Forster, dated Elmina, May 27, 1872.

61. C.7917. Papers Concerning Gold Coast and Ashanti Affairs 1890–96, Gold Coast, Further Correspondence Relating to Affairs in Ashanti, PP.

62. Ibid.

63. C.7917. Gold Coast Correspondence Relating to Affairs in Ashanti, enclosure 2 in no. 3, W. B. Griffith to Lord Knutsford, PP.

64. Colonial Office African (West), 538, 69, enclosed in Governor's despatch dated Kumasi, August 16, 1897, in SAL/110/1; see also SAL/110/2; SAL/110/3; SAL 111/1; SAL 111/2; SAL/112/1; SAL/112/2; SAL/112/3.

65. NAG (Accra), ADM 1/470, Half-Yearly Report on the Gold Coast Constabulary, March 25, 1880.

66.   PRO CO 99/1, *Gold Coast Gazette,* 1876–1885. Names, descriptions, and ethnicities of the deserters from Elmina, Cape Coast, Keta, Adjuah, Addah, Accra, Winneba, Dixcove, Prasu, and other places were chronicled in the *Gold Coast Gazette.*

67.   SAL/16/6; SAL/54/4. Karimu was instructed to recruit Hausas as well as "bring down any Houssa deserters he might find on his road."

68.   SAL/73/1.

69.   SAL/59/1.

70.   NAG (Accra), ADM 1/469; ADM 1/470, Despatches to Secretary of State, Proposal to Send Officer to Salga to Recruit Housas, July 18, 1879.

71.   NAG (Accra), ADM 1/644, no. 144, Lonsdale's Instructions, enclosure in Despatch 264 of October 17, 1881; SAL/59/1.

9

Ethnic Identities and the Culture of Modernity in a Frontier Region

The Gokwe District of Northwestern Zimbabwe, 1963–79

Pius S. Nyambara

Introduction

Prior to the 1950s, the Shangwe provided the sparse population of the Gokwe region of northwestern Zimbabwe. The presence of the tsetse fly and the semi-arid conditions of the region had historically precluded settlement by large populations. However, in the post–World War II period, Gokwe experienced a large influx of immigrants, called Madheruka by the indigenous people.[1] There were a number of sources for the immigrants. The first and largest group was composed of between 10,000 and 12,000 "squatters" who were evicted by the state from Rhodesdale Crown Land.[2] Evictions from crown land were meant to clear the land of African "squatters" to make way for the large influx of white immigrants, most of whom were escaping postwar austerity in Europe. The population of white settlers in Rhodesia rose dramatically from 80,000 in 1945 to 219,000 by 1960. Although the majority of white settlers went to the major urban areas, many settled on the land.[3]

Subsequent immigrants to Gokwe, especially from the 1960s onward, came from different parts of the country and were largely "voluntary" immigrants. Gokwe was an attractive place for many immigrants due to its frontier nature. Some were drawn to Gokwe by dreams of wealth. Among them was an entrepreneurial class of people who had sufficient land in their home areas but were attracted by the prospects of securing more land, in order to engage in large-scale agriculture. Some had accumulated capital from formal employment and saw an opportunity to establish small-scale business enterprises such as grocery stores, grinding mills, and butcheries. Some came initially as civil servants and then decided to settle permanently in Gokwe. Others seem to have been drawn to Gokwe for political reasons: settlement there gave some people an opportunity to set themselves up as household heads, village heads, headmen, and chiefs. The majority of immigrants, however, especially in the 1960s and 1970s, were pushed to Gokwe by serious land shortages in their home areas. These immigrants included families in overcrowded reserves, especially in the southern parts of the country where land pressure had become severe, and, later, families that were removed wholesale from crown land with their chiefs by the state as a result of the implementation of the Land Tenure Act (LTA) of 1969. Other immigrants were drawn from former migrant workers who originated from neighboring countries, such as Mozambique, Malawi, and Zambia. After retiring from work, they wanted land to establish homes where they could spend the rest of their lives.[4]

The coming of the Madheruka in the 1960s coincided with the introduction of cotton cultivation in Gokwe by colonial agricultural officials, and the immigrants readily took to cotton cultivation while the indigenous people were reluctant to cultivate the new crop. This chapter uses the story of the development of cotton in the Gokwe region in the early 1960s as a window to explore the construction of ethnic identities during the colonial period. One of the central arguments is that there was clearly an interconnected process in Gokwe by which ethnic identities were constructed alongside the adoption of new economic practices. Colonial officials and Madheruka immigrants both disparaged the indigenous Shangwe people as "primitive," "backward," and "resistant" to change, while colonial officials regarded the immigrants as the embodiment of "modernization" and as model farmers to be emulated. The officials therefore concentrated their extension work among the immigrants, giving them the necessary technical advice and credit facilities.

Madheruka farmers dominated cotton growing partly because they brought the knowledge of commercial farming with them from their areas of origin. They also dominated the cooperative societies through which credit facilities and technical advice were channeled. Madheruka were themselves highly conscious of their "modern" status because of their exposure to the "modernization" introduced by colonial officials in their areas of origin. Some of them were already holders of master-farmer certificates.[5] Most of the immigrants had been associated with early nationalist political organizations in the 1940s and 1950s in their home areas; some had been wealthy tenants on European farms; and most of them had been exposed to missionary influence. This background was significant in that it made the immigrants conscious of themselves as different from the indigenous people.

This chapter seeks to critically address the following questions: What were the origins of the ethnic labels Madheruka and Shangwe? How widespread were the perceptions of Shangwe backwardness? Why did the immigrants call the indigenous people Shangwe, and why did the indigenous people call the immigrants Madheruka? Did each group accept these names? How rigid were these ethnic labels? Did they remain fixed or did they become fluid over time? Why and in what ways did colonial officials reinforce these ethnic categorizations? Did all the immigrants take to cotton growing and therefore become successful farmers as a result? Similarly, did all the Shangwe resist cotton agriculture and therefore remain "poor"? What was the role of ethnicity in the differentiation process? How did the guerrilla war of the 1970s, whose ideology was opposed to the colonial "modernization" agenda, affect ethnicity and the culture of modernity? By seeking answers to these questions, the chapter not only builds upon and contributes to the vast literature on cotton agriculture and differentiation but also contributes to the emerging literature on ethnicity in northwestern Zimbabwe.[6]

Shangwe and Madheruka: The Act of Naming Each Other

Two major developments promoted the introduction of cotton agriculture in the African reserves in colonial Zimbabwe during the early 1960s. One was that the government made serious efforts to promote cotton cultivation in ecologically suitable areas such as Gokwe. From the 1960s onward, agricultural demonstrators who in the early 1950s had been fully occupied with the implementation of the Native Land Husbandry Act (NLHA) reform (1951)[7] began to devote their attention primarily to progressive farmers.

The other major development was political. In 1965, Ian Smith announced the illegal Unilateral Declaration of Independence (UDI) from Great Britain. The imposition of sanctions on Rhodesia as a punitive measure had a devastating impact economically. Especially hard hit was the tobacco industry, which was one of the pillars of the Rhodesian agricultural industry. One way of beating sanctions was to institute a crop-diversification measure, and cotton ultimately emerged as one of the most important substitute crops. Seed cotton was required to feed a number of local spinning industries, which had emerged during and after World War II. UDI and the political and economic actions taken against the country, combined with the ensuing need for greater self-sufficiency, not only improved the local market for Rhodesian-grown cotton but made it possible to offer higher prices, especially in the period 1965–72.[8]

State agricultural officials introduced cotton agriculture in Gokwe in the early 1960s, and cotton quickly became the most important cash crop in the region.[9] While for the most part the Shangwe did not readily accept the new methods of agriculture, the majority of the immigrants were keener to cooperate with agricultural officers. As Eric Worby has observed, "It was as bearers of a new set of agrarian practices and as collaborators with district officials and extension workers in the articulation of a new discourse of development and modernity that the Madheruka were to have their greatest impact."[10] The sense of difference that the immigrants conveyed upon their arrival in Gokwe was largely a result of their exposure to the colonial agricultural programs introduced by the Native Department over a period of three decades beginning in the mid-1920s. Most of the immigrants originated from the southern part of the country, where policies of centralization and conservation had been implemented much earlier and with greater vigor, in the 1920s and 1930s.[11] Many of the immigrants had also been exposed to missionary activities, "which provided an institutional apparatus for the imposition of 'modern' disciplined habits and disposition."[12] Many had also been wealthy tenants on white land, large-scale cattle owners, and entrepreneurs. A good number had been political activists in the British African National Voice Association (Voice), led by Benjamin Burombo, and in the African National Congress (ANC), which succeeded Voice.[13] Because of this background, many immigrants were conscious of their progressive and modern status.

In contrast, the majority of the indigenous inhabitants of Gokwe had not been exposed to these forces of modernization. They had not seen agricultural demonstrators prior to the 1960s, and the first mission school was established in Gokwe only in 1963.[14] A delineation officer aptly summarized the thinking of colonial officials when he noted that the introduction of new settlers in Gokwe would "be one way of attack[ing local backwardness] . . . . This has the combined effect of bringing in capital investment, 'settler capital,' 'bush clearing' by the settlers as a deterrent to [the tsetse] fly, and perhaps of most importance, the introduction of people with fresh ideas and more sophisticated demands into areas where a catalyst is needed."[15]

The term "modernization" had very different meanings to the various actors in Gokwe: colonial officers, immigrants, and the Shangwe. Colonial officials conceptualized modernization as the process whereby "traditional" societies acquired attributes of "modernity" defined by their proximity to the institutions and values of Western and particularly Anglo-American societies. The term carried the assumption that modern meant being Western, and the acquisition of Western values provided a set of categories for ordering the present day of African societies by depicting modernization as an inexorable process of change toward modernity.[16] For colonial officials, cotton agriculture would transform "backward tribesmen" into disciplined, modern farmers. For the Madheruka immigrants, modernization was the act of adopting and mimicking Western values, whereas the Shangwe had never internalized the language of modernization. For them, modernization meant the unwanted intrusion of the state into their lives. In colonial eyes, the Shangwe were at best indifferent to the values of modernity promoted by colonial officials; at worst, they were hostile to these values. Those who

were stigmatized as Shangwe implicitly constituted "the anti-modern, a rhe-
torical foil against which progress and prosperity could be measured and
attained."[17] Colonial officials and immigrants alike disparaged the Shangwe
as primitive and backward. Stereotypes of the primitiveness of the indigenous people pervaded almost every aspect of their lives: house styles, clothing, hygiene, and gender relations.[18] The stereotypes also touched on ritual,
religion, belief, agricultural practices, cattle ownership, involvement in the
market, accumulation, the use of technology, and the consumption of manufactured commodities.[19]

The explanation for these perceptions must be sought in the construction of ethnic identities in colonial Zimbabwe. Shona speakers generally
regarded the Shangwe as "a kind of bastard, historically marginal to the
great Shona states of Zimbabwe's pre-colonial past and more recently,
diluted by thousands of immigrants of more authentic Shona and Ndebele
stock."[20] Colonial notions of Shangwe backwardness can be attributed to
the historical circumstances that placed the Shangwe on the margins of
the colonial administration because of their geographical isolation in the
remote northern areas of the country, which were not easily accessible to
colonial administrators and missionaries.[21] While missionaries had long
been present in many parts of Zimbabwe, where they competed to name
ethnic subjects and produce indigenous written languages, there were no
missionaries in the remote areas of Gokwe until the early 1960s. The Shangwe thus remained an ambiguous entity that never gained any currency at
the level of national politics.[22]

To be a Shangwe, in the eyes of the colonial officials and other Shona
groups, was to be "antimodern," "backward," and "primitive," while to
belong to one of the major Shona ethnic groups was "to embody a modern
style of being civilized."[23] The Shangwe, however, have identified themselves
with the major Shona groups and argued that the term Shangwe described
the place in which they lived rather than who they were. In fact, the Shangwe claim Rozvi origins and speak a Korekore dialect of Shona.[24] According
to Makaza Tawonesi, who claims to be indigenous to Gokwe, "There is no
ethnic group in Zimbabwe called Shangwe. Shangwe is just a place. As time
went on, people came to call us by the name of the place. We find it offensive to be called Shangwe."[25] Tawonesi, like many of the indigenous people
in Gokwe, claims that he is in fact a Rozvi, a member of one of the major
Shona groups.

The origins of the term Shangwe are not clear, but a number of versions
are given in various oral and written historical accounts. According to F.
Marr, the term Abashankwe was used by Ndebele to refer to the peoples of
Gokwe from whom they received a tribute in tobacco before the British conquest.[26] For Ndebele, then, "the term clearly served to locate a people who
stood in a particular spatial and political relation to themselves."[27] Barry

Kosmin cites a 1906 history, which claims that the name Shangwe was given to the people of Gokwe by the Rozvi *mambos* (the Rozvi rulers): *"Abashankwe,* meaning 'the people who live alone,' an apt description of a people cut off from the south by large areas of uninhabited country."[28]

To the indigenous people of Gokwe, the term Shangwe simply describes the frequent droughts and famines that often devastate the Zimbabwean plateau. Gokwe is generally a very dry area and prone to periodic droughts and famines.[29] Kosmin argues that "if this [the term Shangwe] has connotations with the Shona word *Shangwa,* famine or misery, it is also appropriate for the inhospitable region, with its endemic malaria and sleeping sickness."[30] David Beach has described the origins of the word in similar terms:

> *Shangw*[a] is a Shona word for drought, but it also means disaster or misery. Droughts . . . have been remarkably common on the southern Zambezian plateau . . . . But a mere shortage of rain is not the only thing that can produce *shangwa*. Rains that come too soon or too late, too much rain, locust plagues, or even frost and floods in some areas could destroy the crops of millet on which the people depended.[31]

Shangwe therefore signifies a place of drought.[32]

Shangwe people, on the other hand, call the immigrants Madheruka, "a term whose noun prefix (*ma-:* a class six plural form) classifies them not with persons at all but primarily with useful objects and undomesticated animals."[33] To understand fully the origins of this term, one should go back to the origins of the first group of immigrants in Gokwe in the early 1950s. The majority of the immigrants had resided in Rhodesdale Crown Land for generations.[34] In the postwar period, the colonial state, anxious to resettle ex-soldiers and to accommodate the increase in European immigration into the colony, evicted the squatters from Rhodesdale.[35] The evictions were carried out at short notice and the squatters were forcibly loaded into waiting government trucks and dumped in Gokwe and the neighboring Sanyati Reserve. The term Madheruka is "an onomatopoetic word intended to evoke the sound of the lorry engines that brought them to Gokwe."[36] According to Musingadzani Musakari, "the term *madheruka* refers to people who came from another place. They came in lorries and were dumped here by the whites. This is why they are called Madheruka."[37] Some claim that the word was derived from the Ndebele or Kalanga terms for "to descend"—*ukuehla* in Sindebele—meaning "those who descended from the vehicles."[38] However, the term came to be indiscriminately applied to all subsequent immigrants who came in the 1960s and 1970s.

Other informants claimed that the colonial district administrator coined the term Madheruka when he told the indigenous people, "You will soon be joined by some people who are coming to settle among you. They are called Madheruka. You should be careful of them because they will steal from you. They will bring a lot of cattle, some of which were stolen from Rhodesdale."[39] This statement demonstrates the role of the colonial state in reinforcing ethnic differences as part of the broader colonial agenda to divide and rule its subjects. Colonial officials worried that if politically minded immigrants were left to mix freely with unpoliticized Shangwe, the results could be politically explosive. Jocelyn Alexander and JoAnn McGregor emphasize this point when they argue that the colonial administrators "saw the evictees as dangerously political, as 'loud-mouthed gentlemen,' as a vociferous and truculent element. Administrators' efforts to prevent the two groups finding a common cause and joining together in political opposition led them to an inversion of previous tribal stereotypes."[40] Immigrants, however, objected to being called Madheruka and insisted that they belonged to genuine Shona groups. According to Nemadziwa Mupfugami, who came to Gokwe in the late 1970s, "I don't know of any people called by that name [Madheruka]. This is just a derogatory term intended to denigrate us."[41] Patrick Dube, another immigrant, vehemently objected to being called Mudheruka and asked, "How can I be a Mudheruka when I am a Zimbabwean citizen?"[42]

Some scholars have suggested that the term Madheruka is not an ethnic label since it collectively defined an amalgam of diverse peoples who originated in different parts of the country and therefore lacked a shared history.[43] But the use of the term Madheruka was the beginning of the ethnicization of immigrants. Gradually, the term assumed ethnic connotations, and the immigrants came to be regarded by others as well as by themselves as a distinct group of people, different in many ways from the people they found already settled in Gokwe.[44] The common denominator that came to identify the immigrants as distinct was their self-consciously progressive status, which became a critical part of their self-identity.

The ethnic categories Madheruka and Shangwe were therefore pejorative ways by which each group looked at the other: the one as rootless intruders, the other as impoverished people living in drought-stricken conditions. These notions converged nicely with European notions of modernity and backwardness. Colonial agricultural officials further reinforced these ethnic categories when they introduced cotton. Cotton growing and its accompanying agricultural techniques came to be identified with Madheruka master farmers, while, for the most part, the indigenous people were disparaged by colonial officials due to their reluctance to grow cotton. The following section will examine how colonial officials came to distinguish between backward and antimodern Shangwe and progressive Madheruka master farmers, thus reinforcing these ethnic categories.

Madheruka Master Farmers and Cotton

When colonial agricultural officers introduced cotton in Gokwe, they initially concentrated their efforts primarily on immigrant master farmers. Who were the master farmers and what were their origins? E. D. Alvord, an American Methodist missionary, who was appointed by the government in 1926 as agriculturalist for the instruction of natives, first introduced the master-farmer concept when he trained African demonstrators in various aspects of crop and animal husbandry and sent them into the reserves to teach peasants better farming methods.[45] According to T. O. Ranger, the demonstrators were selected from among the ranks of the mission educated and they naturally chose to work with similarly progressive farmers: "In its early years the demonstration scheme worked very much in the interests of the entrepreneurial minority."[46]

After the first master-farmer certificate was issued in 1933, the number of master farmers in the African areas as a whole increased. At the inception of the master-farmer scheme, the Native Department classified producers into four categories: ordinary native farmers, cooperators, plot-holders and master farmers.[47] By 1950, there were 1,665 master farmers, 37,591 plot-holders, and 55,694 cooperators. By 1965, the number of master farmers alone had increased to 14,626, yet they still represented only 3.2 per cent of all African cultivators. In the Umniati area of Gokwe, for instance, out of a total number of 1,796 farmers registered with the agricultural officer in 1968, 100 were master farmers, 80 were plot-holders, 277 were cooperators, and the rest belonged to the category of ordinary native farmers.[48] Except for two prominent women, the master farmers were immigrant male household heads.[49]

Melville Reid, the senior agricultural officer for Gokwe, introduced the first cotton plantings in 1963–64, on test demonstration plots (TDPs). Agricultural officers selected test demonstration plot-holders from among progressive farmers and members of cooperative societies who were considered "most suitable" and likely to carry out the recommendations of the agricultural officers "without tiring or losing interest." Out of the 84 "volunteers," 26 were selected, "preference going to Master Farmers, cooperative society members and other farmers of ability." The selected cultivators were provided with free seeds, fertilizer, pesticides, and sprayers by the Department of Agriculture, and the results of the TDPs were visibly displayed by public payouts in order to generate interest.[50] Justin Masewa, an agricultural demonstrator who began work in Gokwe in the early 1960s, was heavily involved in the early test demonstration plots. During the first year, he remembers that he began with three people: "Gibson Jeche, Martin Gumbo, and Musarurwa—all immigrants from Fort Victoria." The following year the number increased to twelve demonstration plot-holders.[51]

Further TDPs were set up in subsequent seasons to spread training in cotton growing to other parts of Gokwe. Colonial officers trained farmers, through meetings and field days, using handouts, discussion groups, visits, and talks by outstanding farmers. Early demonstration plot-holders received regular visits from Mr. Fitt, the cotton advisory officer, who was stationed at Gatooma Cotton Research Station; farmers, in turn, visited Gatooma regularly to acquire the necessary skills. TDPs also served as venues for field days, discussions, plot-holder training, and morale boosters for field staff and local cultivators, and they supplied vital localized information to farmers.[52] According to one agricultural officer, the idea behind the TDPs was to give keen farmers a half-acre plot each (1 hectare = 2.471 acres) to introduce the crop and better ways of increasing yields, with the hope that "others will follow if they wish."[53]

One of the villages most receptive to the introduction of cotton was MaCongress, a Madheruka village.[54] The founders of the village named it MaCongress because they were ex-ANC detainees who had been involved in nationalist political activities in their home areas in the late 1950s and had been arrested and detained at Kana in southeastern Gokwe when the government banned the ANC in 1959. When they were released in 1960, they decided to stay in Gokwe, where there was plenty of land, rather than go back to their home areas. They were not restricted to the standard ten-acre plot mandated by the NLHA but were allowed to choose as much land as they could use. Colonial officials feared that if they restricted the amount of land that politically minded ex-detainees received, the ex-detainees would probably threaten to go back into nationalist politics. In any case, the primary motive for their involvement in nationalist politics was the desire for more land. The majority had already acquired master-farmer certificates in their original home areas, so that when they settled in Gokwe they had a common goal: "to do our best in farming."[55]

The pioneers of MaCongress were Hlamba Moyo (who became the first village headman), Joseph Dube (who dominated the Munyati Cooperative Society as its manager), and Peter Katanda, all ex-detainees. Elliot Ncube, who came to teach at a nearby school, and Dennis Mguni soon joined them.[56] Hlamba Moyo acquired his master-farmer certificate in 1953 in his home area of Semokwe Reserve in Plumtree. Earlier, he had spent some years working in Johannesburg, South Africa. When he returned home in 1939, he worked as a storekeeper for a white man for ten years, before establishing his own store. He later sold the store and invested his money in agriculture. He was active in the first agricultural marketing cooperatives in his home area in the mid-1950s. When the ANC was established in 1959, he became the branch chairman. According to Hlamba Moyo, "cotton began here in MaCongress village, and everyone else followed our example."[57]

Joseph Dube had also acquired his master-farmer certificate in the early 1950s in his home area, Plumtree. He proudly described how easily he acquired the certificate. Dube had acquired his knowledge of basic land and animal husbandry in South Africa when he studied agricultural science and biology for the Junior Certificate, which stimulated his interest in farming. He never attended master-farmer courses, as was the normal procedure. Instead, the land development officer (LDO) simply asked him a few basic questions on animal and crop husbandry, and a few days later, Dube was called to the LDO's office to collect his certificate.[58]

In 1967, the agricultural officer for Umniati reported that MaCongress "is my model kraal and launching point for the whole area." The officer described the original founders of the village as "excellent farmers and most influential members in the area . . . . [they] comprise the bulk of Umniati Co-operative."[59] They were among the progressive farmers who were selected to participate in the cotton demonstration plots set up in Umniati in 1963–64. After that, they consistently planted large acreages to cotton and produced excellent yields. While the majority of the cotton growers grew an average of one to three acres of cotton, these leading farmers averaged between ten and fifteen acres and reaped profitable results.[60]

Profiles of prosperous Madheruka cotton growers were often provided in the widely read African newspaper, the *African Times*, as models to be emulated. For example, Mr. Mangwiro, a master farmer, began growing cotton in 1966–67. In his second season, he anticipated making a profit of Rh$300 from his five acres of cotton. The average height of his crop was over five feet. In addition to the labor of his own household, he employed four other people to assist with the picking, sorting, and baling of the cotton. He also grew maize, groundnuts, sorghum, pumpkins, sweet potatoes, and *rapoko*.[61] Another prominent farmer was Philemon Maguwe, a village headman and master farmer. In 1967–68, he had sixteen acres under cultivation, half of which were in cotton. The agricultural officer described Maguwe's crop of 16,000 lb as average. After various costs, such as spraying and the purchase of fertilizers, had been met, he expected to make a profit of Rh$400 on cotton alone.[62]

Some of the prominent Madheruka farmers, such as Peter Mazani of Ganyungu and Cornelius Ndiweni, who consistently produced good yields were recommended by the senior agricultural officer for the purchase of farms in the freehold African purchase areas, where plots varied from 500 to 800 acres.[63] The agricultural officer described Mazani as one of the best farmers in Ganyungu area. He owned twenty-one head of cattle, four calves, fifteen goats, farm implements—including two harrows, two planters, and two ploughs—a fenced home, and ten acres of fenced land, and he married four wives. In 1978–79, he made a profit of Rh$3,000 and in the following season his profit was slightly over Rh$3,117.[64] The agricultural officer described Ndiweni as one of the best farmers in Gokwe because he consistently produced good yields of cotton, maize, sorghum, and groundnuts and was a frequent winner at agricultural shows and a prominent leader of the farming community in the Munyati area.[65]

In the novel *Dew in the Morning*, Shimmer Chinodya gives a vivid description of a successful Madheruka master farmer named Mugowa:

> He was a very rich man. He owned two ploughs, two harrows and a tractor. He grew groundnuts and cotton and sunflowers in two huge fields . . . . He had built himself a fine brick and zinc house and had fenced off his huge fields in the fertile land near the vlei. Here the soil was black and crumbly, so damp that worms burrowed [in] it all year round. He kept his soil drugged with manure and fertilisers, so that even in bad years his mealies grew tall, and his acres went white with cotton bolls. He was one of those Derukas who enslaved the soil, overworked and underpaid their servants, and sent out huge herds of cattle to tax the humble meadows. In such homesteads, milk, eggs, vegetables, rice and green mealies were available at most of the year but human sweat oozed all year.[66]

Chinodya portrays Madheruka as hard working, enterprising, and innovative. They strove for the best in their agricultural activities. They possessed most of the critical resources necessary for successful farming: "huge herds of cattle," which provided draft power and manure; cash to purchase fertilizers and other inputs and to pay for hired labor; and "huge fields" of good-quality soil. They ate good food. But Chinodya is also conscious that these farmers thrived by exploiting their workers, whom they overworked and underpaid.

Justin Masewa, a demonstrator who worked in Gokwe in the 1960s and 1970s, described many Madherukas as expert farmers. "If one Madheruka came to settle in a predominantly Shangwe village, the rest of the village would look up to him. The Shangwe were excellent imitators. Immigrants came with the farming knowledge. Master-farmer training began in Fort Victoria in the south where most of the immigrants originated."[67] Shangwe refute this claim, however, and insist that "Madheruka did not come with the knowledge of agriculture. It was the white man rather than Madheruka who taught us better agricultural techniques."[68]

Shangwe "Resistance to Change": A Matter of Contrast?

In contrast to the above stories of Madheruka success, agricultural officers described the southern parts of Munyati area (Chisina, Mtanke, Blue Gums, and Chidoma) as largely inhabited by indigenous people, who were "backward" and "resistant to change." From 1963, reports of agricultural officers for these areas noted that there was "very little if any progress with cotton.

Progress is restricted to few villages and there [is] resistance to the use of fertilizers on the heavy soils." The officials disparaged the people as "resistant to change . . . and . . . not interested in change."[69] In his annual report for 1967, the agricultural officer in the area marshaled statistical evidence to demonstrate the reluctance of Shangwe to grow cotton. For instance, while immigrants in Ganyungu and Nyarupakwe grew some 550 acres of cotton in 1967, Shangwe in Chidoma grew only 20 acres, and no cotton was grown in Blue Gums. In the same year, out of a total of 422 registered farmers in the immigrant areas, about 40 percent were master farmers, whereas in areas inhabited by the Shangwe, out of 1,320 registered farmers, only about 3 percent were master farmers.[70]

In 1963, the agricultural officer lamented that "the majority of the people are originals and so disinterested in any form of progress . . . . I do not think anything will be achieved in this area for the next 5 or 6 years." Yet, he admitted, "rain is less than in other areas and crops are destroyed by elephants. Farmers are dissatisfied by the locality and wish to change." These southern districts were also described as "highly politically inclined and trouble brewing in the area will start here first," because the people were unhappy with the NLHA settlement "as they were used to shifting cultivation."[71] With reference to Blue Gums, the agricultural officer reported that

> Farmers are original inhabitants and see their lands and plots as a pleasant place to pass the time when on leave from mines and work. This means the wives and female relatives have to look after the land. The male population is young or old and so [is] not interested in any improvement. All suggestions made or carried out were received by females with great reluctance and as soon as husbands returned to work the smallest improvements were neglected.[72]

The agricultural officer described Chidoma, which forms the southernmost part of Munyati, and its people in similar terms:

> It is a very backward area and the population is disgusted about the resettlement since they are used to shifting cultivation. Livestock pressure is building up. There is some political activity in this area but rather infantile. They could easily be stirred to become hostile as they have hardly any education and are prepared to follow a leader. Moreover, they are regarded by the resettlers as a bunch of lowdown creatures and are not accepted in the newly formed communities.[73]

Some researchers in the 1970s further reinforced these stereotypes of Shangwe backwardness. In a research paper comparing the farming practices of indigenous Shangwe and immigrants in Gokwe, E. Nyangani repeated the old colonial perceptions:

The Shangwe are an almost illiterate and conservative tribe who have appreciated and assimilated very little from western cultures. The immigrants, though
semi-illiterate, show a relatively high degree of sophistication when it comes to
a comparison with the Shangwe. They have assimilated, in part or in full, many
aspects of western culture. The differences between the two are very much a
case of attitude towards cash incentives to satisfy certain desires. The indigenous seem to have very little needs and even less wants. They also tend to have
very little ranges of possible uses for cash.[74]

Nyangani went further, drawing comparisons between Shangwe and immigrants in nearly every aspect of their agriculture, from the size of their plots
to crop yields and cropping methods.[75]

Chinodya also gives a vivid description of the perceived contrast between
Shangwe and Madheruka:

The Newcomers brought a distinctive Deruka life-style based on shrewd hard
work. The ambition of every Deruka family was to build a good brick and zinc
house . . . . Derukas were generally great farmers. They cleared huge fields and
grew maize and groundnuts. A few started to grow sunflowers and cotton to
sell to the Grain Board. They kept many cattle, grew vegetables in the vlei gardens, dug fish ponds by the river and raised chickens. Some of them sold vegetables, milk and eggs. In contrast, the local people built their huts with grass
and poles, seldom bothering to plaster the walls with mud. Passing by these
huts, one could see sticks of firelight in the gaps between the poles. In the day-
time one saw few chickens, small kraals and small fields of maize and millet.
Many of the local people seemed to live from one day to the next, eating their
sadza, drinking their beer, and raising their children.[76]

Such views misrepresent Shangwe. In the first place, Shangwe distrust of the
rhetoric of modernity had nothing to do with an inherent hostility to economic change. Kosmin has demonstrated that Gokwe was home to a prosperous Inyoka tobacco industry from the middle of the nineteenth century
onward, and Shangwe paid tribute in tobacco to the Ndebele chiefdom.
After the arrival of the colonialists in the early 1890s, the Shangwe tobacco
industry expanded rapidly from 1903 to the early 1920s. European traders
became important middlemen, as they bought tobacco in bulk from Shangwe and sold it throughout the colony. In fact, the good price and the ready
market among Ndebele and European traders meant that the Shangwe had
little reason to turn to migrant labor in large numbers. They could easily
pay a large amount of their tax from tobacco sales. However, from 1922 to
1938, the industry went into decline, largely due to competition from manufactured cigarettes. Inyoka tobacco, which was used mainly for snuff, quickly
lost its market to the new urban trend of cigarette smoking. By 1938, the

Inyoka tobacco economy had virtually collapsed, and by the 1960s, all traces of Shangwe tobacco had gone.[77]

Nor was growing cotton a new concept to Shangwe. An indigenous cotton industry flourished in northwestern Zimbabwe prior to colonization. Thomas Huffman has used archaeological evidence to trace the existence of an indigenous cotton industry in Rhodesia to the Iron Age period. He argues that cotton growing, spinning, and weaving were well-developed industries among Africans in Rhodesia in general and in the Zambezi Valley (of which Gokwe is a part) in particular before the importation of European cloth.[78] The Shangwe were also renowned salt workers. They obtained salt from the Mapfungautsi plateau, processed it, and sold it across the Umniati River in Chwaya at a rate of one chicken in exchange for a dish of salt. Although this industry remained on a fairly small scale, it nevertheless attracted some European commercial interests at the end of the nineteenth century.[79] Shangwe also worked on colonial farms and mines, especially after the collapse of the tobacco industry, and when the colonial government introduced cotton in Gokwe in the early 1960s, Shangwe preferred to work for wages on Copper Queen (an African Purchase Farm Area) farms and at the state-run farm in neighboring Sanyati. They weeded and picked cotton, a crop that they were still reluctant to grow. But after independence in 1980, the number of Shangwe households growing cotton increased.[80]

Prior to the NLHA of 1951, the Shangwe had developed a viable economy suited to their locality. They cultivated the rich alluvial soils along the banks of the major rivers and they raised two crops a year. In addition, they hunted and gathered in the vast forests of the Umniati area. The NLHA forced the Shangwe to abandon these areas after they were relocated to upland areas in centralized villages alongside the immigrants. Naturally, Shangwe resented the move, for it deprived them of their best lands, which they had cultivated for generations.

The views of the agricultural officer on shifting cultivation echo many of the mistaken assumptions of colonial officials about the primitiveness and irrationality of African agriculture. The agricultural officer's views were similar to those of the colonial administrators who sought to contain and curb *citemene* (shifting) cultivation in what is now Zambia.[81] As Paul Richards has argued, "it would be perfectly reasonable to view shifting cultivation not as a problem but as a resource," citing many of the agro-ecological and socioeconomic benefits of shifting cultivation in sub-Saharan Africa in general.[82] The Shangwe did not resist economic change per se. Rather, they resisted certain agricultural techniques. For instance, they resisted the use of fertilizer because they had developed their own method of enriching the sandy soils without costly fertilizers. The practice of shifting cultivation was well suited to the regeneration of soil fertility. Consider the following remarks made by an observer in Gokwe in the early 1980s on the merits of shifting cultivation:

> The Gusu sands running west of Gokwe growth point out into Kana have inherently low fertility . . . but [are] ingeniously managed by farmers using the following indigenous technique: after planting two years in succession, fields are fallowed for 2 to 3 years (the fields are not stumped) allowing the bush to regenerate. Then the bush is cut and ploughed back into the soil before planting again.[83]

Studies of Gokwe have concluded that too much fertilizer in the black earth produced tall plants with few cotton bolls that were more difficult to spray and pick, a fact that the agricultural officers did not take into account when indiscriminately recommending fertilizer use.[84] Frank Nyathi, a retired agricultural officer who worked in this area in the 1960s, revealed that one of the first problems he encountered was resistance to the use of fertilizer by the indigenous people, because, they said, fertilizer increased the need for weeding. "They only agreed to the use of fertilizer after seeing the profits generated by their immigrant neighbors . . . who used fertilizers."[85]

Following the opening of the Empress Mine in southeastern Gokwe at the turn of the twentieth century, many Shangwe men worked for wages in the mine for various lengths of time every year and thus provided their families with an alternative source of cash. In the absence of most men, cotton growing was a heavy burden on the women and children who remained at home. This probably explains why women in particular resisted the introduction of cotton, as the agricultural officer observed. There is a large body of literature on the reasons why cotton growing is especially onerous in agricultural regimes that are chronically starved of labor, particularly in households that export migrant labor.[86] There is clear evidence that most of the households in areas predominantly settled by indigenous people in the southern parts of Umniati concentrated their efforts and resources on food crops rather than cotton. Figures for crop production given by the agricultural officer referred to above for the period 1966–70 clearly indicate that the area was more suited to maize production than to cotton. Reports during the 1960s indicate that Shangwe produced more maize than the northern areas and sold maize to the mine compounds at the Empress Mine.[87]

The straightforward and uncritical contrast between the Shangwa and the Madheruka described by Nyangani and Chinodya is problematic in that it tends to simplify a very complex picture. Not every Madheruka household took to cotton growing and became prosperous. The Madheruka may have felt modern, but they were on uncertain ground when it came to access to land, as the indigenous people considered themselves the owners of the land. Alexander and McGregor have noted that "the evictees' claim to superiority did not . . . rest on a firm institutional basis,"[88] partly because "they occupied a land which was already imaginatively possessed by someone else in ritual terms."[89] Shangwe rainmakers were some of the most powerful figures in society and considered themselves the owners of the land and guardians of the sacred pools, wetlands, animals, and shrines.[90] According to one informant, Madheruka "came begging for land like little children. If we had plenty of good land we would give them, but sometimes we gave them the poorest land."[91]

There is evidence suggesting that a significant number of indigenous people already possessed sizable herds of cattle and cultivated huge areas prior to the coming of the immigrants. A few indigenous people had already accumulated the signs of wealth recognized by the immigrants, and some others quickly took on the "modernizing" agenda—particularly the use of draft power and maize cultivation—and invested in education, houses, clothes, and other signs of progress.[92] Nor did all Shangwe object to growing cotton. Stories of successful Shangwe cotton growers make it difficult to generalize about Shangwe resistance to cotton growing and agricultural innovations in general. Musakari Musingadzana, a senior Shangwe village head, was one of the founding members of the Umniati Producers' Cooperative in the early 1960s. He began growing cotton as soon as the crop was introduced, starting with five acres and increasing the area under cotton cultivation with time. By 1970, Musingadzani had married four wives and acquired several head of cattle. He had worked in the cities of Kwekwe and Bulawayo for ten years as a cook before settling down to engage in cotton growing.[93]

In areas where the rate of labor migration among the men was low or insignificant, as in Nemangwe in northern Gokwe, some Shangwe households actually responded to cotton growing with great enthusiasm. In 1970, Derek Bates, who worked in Gokwe as senior agricultural officer between 1966 and 1976, remarked on the Shangwe of Nemangwe: "It should be noted that cotton was grown with great success in the Nemangwe area where the people were almost all the indigenous VaShangwe tribe."[94] In Nemangwe, the number of immigrants was "of little significance" because the area had not yet been opened to settlers as it was far to the north, away from the main road system and still largely infested by tsetse fly. Many of the people who took to cotton growing in the early years of its introduction were therefore indigenes.

When agricultural extension work first began in Nemangwe in 1962, Chief Nemangwe was the first participant. The local extension officer described him as "a very keen person and through the examples he set helped the people and the extension worker a great deal." "[T]he people were not quite sure of this crop during the first two seasons . . . but suddenly during the third season they caught on and the acreage increased rapidly." Indeed, acreages grew rapidly from 78 acres in 1965–66 to 381 in 1967–68. The number of cotton growers also increased from 39 to 112 during the same period. The average yield per acre increased from 700 lb to 800 lb. Some farmers whose management of the crop was of a good standard produced cotton yields in excess of 2,300 lb per acre in the 1966–67 season. The Nemangwe Cooperative Society bought its first tractor in 1965 for plowing and for transporting cooperative members' produce to the market,[95] and almost all the cotton growers were said to be using fertilizers on their crops.[96] Throughout the 1960s and into the 1970s, the Shangwe of Nemangwe were consistently growing large acreages of cotton and producing high yields.

The Guerrilla War and the Attack on Modernity

The success that was experienced by some Gokwe farmers in the 1960s and early 1970s was not sustained for long. From the mid-1970s, there was a general decrease in the area planted to cotton, from 19,459 hectares in 1973–74 to 13,861 in 1975–76, and to a low of 7,791 in 1978–79. Cotton production fell correspondingly, by 66 percent, from 18,000 tons in 1977–78 to 7,500 tons in 1978–79. The decline was partly due to lower producer prices relative to the rising costs of production and partly due to a lack of credit facilities through cooperative societies. After 1969, there was increasing abuse of the loan system, resulting in no loans being given from 1970 until 1973–74.[97] In addition, there was a serious drought in 1973. Uncertain rains, the lack of credit, and price uncertainty led to a drop in production.

More significantly, at the height of the guerrilla war, "the discourse of modernity was tainted by its association with the Rhodesian state, and many agricultural officers and Madheruka alike were either killed or fled to the towns in advance of the guerrilla forces."[98] Peasant farmers in many parts of Gokwe ceased growing cotton altogether; they were warned by the guerrillas to stop growing the crop because, the guerrillas alleged, the government was using the money generated from cotton to buy arms.[99] Advisory services broke down as extension officers were withdrawn from the field and operated from the safety of the urban areas.[100] Cotton yields fell from 800–900 kg/acre to 600–800 kg/acre at the peak of the war.[101]

Norma Kriger has argued persuasively that the guerrilla war heightened tensions within rural communities. In particular, the war presented an opportunity for the less well-to-do to vent their resentment of the uneven distribution of wealth.[102] Successful farmers were killed simply because they were better off than most people. One village head, for instance, described how he and his wife were beaten by a youth who accused him of "being a good farmer" and of using local medicines—witchcraft having been prohibited by both the state and the guerrillas—that enabled him "to farm better than others."[103] The targeting of those who were better off was clearly motivated by the perception that these people were collaborators. As one of Kriger's informants told her, "those master farmers who survived had to drop their standards if they didn't want to be killed. Master farmers were taken as associates of the government. They were adhering to government orders."[104]

Kriger's observations are pertinent to understanding African nationalism in Zimbabwe. Her analysis suggests that the liberation war can best be understood by paying close attention to the class composition of the countryside. Ian Phimister similarly argues that at the height of the guerrilla war in the 1970s, strains began to show in the broad anticolonial alliance of the rural people and that the liberation movement as a whole was increasingly being pulled in opposite directions by different social and political interests.[105] Not only did the guerrilla war present an opportunity for the less well-off to vent their resentment against the wealthy, but it also heightened generational and gender tensions. It created opportunities for women to assert greater control over their lives. The war also gave youths an opportunity to carve out greater independence from the authority and control of their parents and elders. It is within this broader context of the struggles within the struggle that the attacks unleashed upon the wealthy peasants by the poor should be understood. In Gokwe, the most common targets of attack by the guerrillas and the youth were Madheruka master farmers. They were seen as collaborators with the colonial regime because of their association with its modernization agenda.

A clear example of class tensions within rural communities at the height of the guerrilla war in 1978 was the killing of Nyambira Maheremende, one of the most prominent and successful immigrant farmers in the Umniati area, by the guerrillas.[106] Nyambira was the first member of the Umniati Cooperative Society when it was formed in 1962. He was a master farmer in his own right and had won many prizes for his agricultural activities. Although it was alleged that he was killed for objecting to his son's marriage to a Shangwe woman whom the son had impregnated, there is also a popular belief that he was killed because some Shangwe who were jealous of his success "sold him out" to the guerrillas. Nyambira "owned several herds of cattle and he had built for himself a five bed-roomed house like that of a white man. It was all fenced and gated. He had an orchard of oranges, mangos, peaches, etc. The man was a hard worker."[107] People who were closely related to Nyambira charged that the real reason he was killed was that he had been "showing too much enthusiasm for the white man's new methods of agriculture."[108] If it is true that Shangwe had a hand in this, then clearly the war period highlighted both class and ethnic tensions within rural society, as Kriger has argued.

Another example of the attacks on Madheruka master farmers was the fact that in 1979 alone, the Umniati Cooperative building was robbed some six times, and a great deal of property was lost.[109] The robberies were followed by the burning down of the building in the same year. The society was one of the most successful cooperatives in Gokwe, its leadership composed largely of immigrant master farmers. While many cooperatives faltered due to a lack of financial resources and poor mismanagement, the Umniati Cooperative stood out as a shining example of a successful enterprise led by farmers themselves.

The burning of the cooperative building is still shrouded in mystery, but some people believe that it was torched by guerrillas who regarded cooperatives as symbols of colonial exploitation. Others saw the burning as an attack on the arrogant Madheruka master farmers, who made up most of the management committee of the cooperative. However, the management strongly believed that Shangwe fired the building because they were jealous of the success of the cooperative. Furthermore, some Shangwe were heavily indebted to the cooperative, and may have believed that burning the building down would destroy the financial records so that their debts would be forgotten or written off. However, the financial records were not destroyed, because they had been transferred to Kwekwe town, where the manager worked during the duration of the war. After independence, the manager followed up on the debtors and recovered some of the money.[110]

It would be grossly incorrect to suggest that the Madheruka farmers were the only targets of guerrilla attacks. Chiefs in general were often targeted by guerrillas because of their association with the colonial government. Thus, some Shangwe chiefs were targeted for accepting checks for growing cotton or for enforcing conservation laws. Chief Goredema was shot by guerrilla forces in 1979, probably for enforcing conservation measures.[111] Shangwe chiefs and village heads were also targeted by guerrillas for selling *ivhu reZimbabwe* (the soil of Zimbabwe) to the immigrants who poured into Gokwe in search of land.[112]

Conclusion

In Gokwe, the rhetoric of "modernization" was often couched in ethnic terms by colonial officials. Colonial officials regarded immigrant master farmers as the embodiment of modernization because the latter had been exposed to the forces of modernization in their areas of origin. The immigrants themselves were very conscious of their modern status, and they perceived themselves as different from the people already settled in Gokwe. Colonial officials and Madheruka immigrants alike regarded the indigenous Shangwe stereotypically as backward and primitive in all aspects of their lives.

This chapter has argued that while the construction of a Shangwe ethnic identity dates back to the early colonial period, it was primarily during the early 1960s, with the coming of Madheruka immigrants and the introduction of cotton, that the Shangwe identity was consolidated. Shangwe, for their part, defined the immigrants as Madheruka, a term whose origins are recent and are to be found in the process of the eviction of the immigrants from crown land by colonial officials in the 1950s. However, each group perceived itself differently, Shangwe claiming that the term Shangwe referred to a place rather than to their identity, and Madheruka claiming to belong to authentic Shona groups. The guerrilla war of the 1970s witnessed an attack on Madheruka modernity as the guerrillas and their sympathizers became hostile to master farmers, whom they regarded as collaborators with the colonial modernization regime, and successful Madheruka farmers as well as agricultural demonstrators became targets of attacks by guerrillas and youths.

Notes

This chapter is a slightly adapted version of an article titled, "Madheruka and Shangwe: Ethnic Identities and the Culture of Modernity in Gokwe, Northwestern Zimbabwe, 1963–79," which was published in the *Journal of African History* 43, no. 2 (2002): 287–306. I wish to thank Cambridge University Press for allowing me to publish a version of this article.

1.   Madheruka is the name that was given by the indigenous people to the immigrants. The immigrants in turn called the indigenous people Shangwe.

2.   Rhodesdale was a vast ranch owned by Lonrho, a British multinational corporation. It was bounded by a line roughly connecting Gwelo, Que Que, Hartely, Enkeldorn, Umvuma, Lalapanzi, and Gutu. Between 10,000 and 12,000 "squatters" resided on this property before World War II. After the war, the property was bought by the state and divided into farms and ranches, which were allocated to European ex-servicemen. The state evicted the "squatters" who had been residing on the property and dumped them in Gokwe and the neighboring Sanyati Reserve. For a detailed study of "squatter" eviction from Rhodesdale, see Pius S. Nyambara, "'That Place was Wonderful!': African Tenants on Rhodesdale Estate, Colonial Zimbabwe, c. 1900-1952," *International Journal of African Historical Studies* 38, no. 2 (2005): 267–99.

3.   For a detailed study of the history of European immigration into Rhodesia, see Alois Mlambo, *The Dream and the Reality: White Immigration into Rhodesia* (Harare: University of Zimbabwe Publications, 2002).

4.   I constructed these categories from a random sample of 100 interviewees. Roughly four categories emerged: 40 percent were landless; 15 percent were former migrant workers; 15 percent were entrepreneurs who came to invest in small-scale business (or civil servants, who came to work in government departments); 30 percent were people evicted from crown land. For a detailed study of the history of immigration into Gokwe, see Pius S. Nyambara, "A History of Land Acquisition in Gokwe, Northwestern Zimbabwe, 1945–1997" (PhD diss., Northwestern University, 1999); and Pius S. Nyambara, "Immigrants, 'Traditional' Leaders and the Rhodesian State: The Power of

'Communal' Land Tenure and the Politics of Land Acquisition in Gokwe, Zimbabwe, 1963–1979," *Journal of Southern African Studies* 27, no. 4 (December 2001): 773–74.

5. Colonial agricultural officials defined master farmers as peasants who were trained on experimental farms and followed improved methods of farming prescribed by the Native Department. A fuller discussion of the origins of the master farmer concept is given later in this chapter. See also Montague Yudelman, *Africans on the Land: Economic Problems of African Agricultural Development of Southern, Central and East Africa, with Special Reference to Southern Rhodesia* (Cambridge, MA: Harvard University Press, 1964), 140.

6. Recent studies of ethnicity in northwestern Zimbabwe include the following: Eric Worby, "Remaking Labour, Reshaping Identity: Cotton, Commoditization and the Culture of Modernity in Northwestern Zimbabwe" (PhD diss., McGill University, 1992); Eric Worby, "Maps, Names and Ethnic Games: The Epistemology and Iconography of Colonial Power in Northwestern Zimbabwe," *Journal of Southern African Studies* 20, no. 3 (1994): 371–92; Jocelyn Alexander and JoAnn McGregor, "Modernity and Ethnicity in a Frontier Society: Understanding Difference in Northwestern Zimbabwe," *Journal of Southern African Studies* 23, no. 2 (1997): 187–201; Jocelyn Alexander, JoAnn McGregor, and Terence Ranger, *Violence and Memory: One Hundred Years in the "Dark Forests" of Matabeleland* (Oxford: James Currey, 2000).

7. The NLHA was one of the most ambitious rural "development" programs introduced by the Southern Rhodesian state, with the aim of abolishing the destructive "communal" land tenure system and replacing it with individual land holdings. The act was abandoned in 1962, largely as a result of African opposition to it. The literature on the NLHA is vast. An official interpretation of the NLHA is given in Southern Rhodesia, *What the Native Land Husbandry Act Means to the Rural African and to Southern Rhodesia* (Salisbury: Government Printers, 1955). Scholars have presented different interpretations of the act. See, for example, William Duggan, "The Native Land Husbandry Act of 1951 and the Rural African Middle Class of Southern Rhodesia," *African Affairs* 79, no. 315 (April 1980): 227–40; Ian Phimister, "Rethinking the Reserves: Southern Rhodesia's Land Husbandry Act Reviewed," *Journal of Southern African Studies* 19, no. 2 (1993): 225–39; Guy Thompson, "Cultivating Conflict: Agricultural 'Betterment,' the Native Land Husbandry Act (NLHA) and Ungovernability in Colonial Zimbabwe, 1951–1962," *Africa Development* 29, no. 3 (2004): 1–39.

8. For a detailed analysis of the impact of sanctions on the Rhodesian economy, see Harry R. Strack, *Sanctions: The Case of Rhodesia* (Syracuse, NY: Syracuse University Press, 1978). The most recent reassessment has been provided by William Minter and Elizabeth Schmidt, "When Sanctions Worked: The Case of Rhodesia Re-examined," *African Affairs* 87, no. 347 (April 1988): 207–37.

9. On cotton in Gokwe, see Melville Reid, "An Agricultural Programme at Gokwe," *Rhodesia Agricultural Journal* 71 (1977): 54–60; Derek Brian Bates, "Successful Agricultural Extension in a Rhodesian Tribal Trust Land: The Study and Identification of factors to the Success of an Extension Programme Based on Cotton Production in the Gokwe District" (BEd thesis, University of Rhodesia, 1977).

10. Worby, "Remaking Labour," 332.

11. For detailed studies of colonial centralization policies of the 1930s and 1940s, see, among others, Jocelyn Alexander, *The Unsettled Land: State-Making and the Politics of Land in Zimbabwe 1893–2003* (Oxford: James Currey, 2006); Michael

Drinkwater, *The State and Agrarian Change in Zimbabwe's Communal Areas* (London: McMillan Press, 1991); B. Davis and W. Dopcke, "Survival and Accumulation in Gutu: Class Formation and the Rise of the State in Colonial Zimbabwe, 1900–1939," *Journal of Southern African Studies* 14, no. 1 (1987): 75–80.

12.   E. Worby, "Discipline without Oppression: Sequence, Timing and Marginality in Southern Rhodesia's Post-war Development Regime," *Journal of African History* 41 (2000): 116.

13.   Alexander and McGregor, "Modernity and Ethnicity," 190–91. The Voice was one of the earliest and most active nationalist organizations in Zimbabwe. It was succeeded by the ANC in the early 1950s. Both organizations fought against racial discrimination and other colonial injustices. For further details of the activities of both nationalist organizations in urban and rural areas, see, among others, Ngwabi Bhebe, *Benjamin Burombo: African Politics in Zimbabwe, 1947–1958* (Harare, Zimbabwe: College Press, 1989); Terence Ranger, *The African Voice in Southern Rhodesia, 1898–1930* (Evanston, IL: Northwestern University Press, 1970); Terence Ranger, *Peasant Consciousness and Guerrilla War in Zimbabwe* (Harare: Zimbabwe Publishing House, 1985).

14.   Worby, "Remaking Labour," 324–25.

15.   S2929/7/3, Gokwe Delineation Reports, 1963–65: Reports by C. J. K. Latham, Delineation Officer, October 26, 1963, Zimbabwe National Archives (ZNA), Harare.

16.   On colonial "modernization" efforts in African colonies in general, see Frederick Cooper, *Decolonization and African Society: The Labor Question in French and British Africa* (Cambridge: Cambridge University Press, 1996), 177, 358–59; James Ferguson, *Expectations of Modernity: Myths and Meanings of Urban Life on the Zambian Copperbelt* (Berkeley: University of California Press, 1999).

17.   Worby, "Remaking Labour," 338.

18.   See Tim Burke, *Lifebuoy Men, Lux Women: Commodification, Consumption and Cleanliness in Modern Zimbabwe* (Durham, NC: Duke University Press, 1996), 35–62.

19.   See Worby, "Remaking Labour," 322; Alexander and McGregor, "Modernity and Ethnicity," 92.

20.   Worby, "Remaking Labour," 260.

21.   Ibid.

22.   . Ibid., 276

23.   Ibid.

24.   See Barry Kosmin, "The Inyoka Tobacco Industry of the Shangwe People: The Displacement of a Pre-colonial Economy in Southern Rhodesia, 1898–1938," in *Roots of Rural Poverty in Central and Southern Africa,* ed. Robin Palmer and Neil Parsons (Berkeley: University of California Press, 1977), 269.

25.   Makaza Tawonesi, Marungu, interview with the author, July 17, 1997. All interviews cited in this chapter were conducted by the author.

26.   F. Marr, "Some Notes on Chief Sileya (Chileya) Gokwe District, S. Rhodesia (As Told by the Chief and Recorded by F. Marr)," *Native Affairs Department Annual,* 39 (1962): 81–82.

27.   Worby, "Remaking Labour," 277.

28.   A3/18//28, Tribal Histories: Sebungwe District by W. E. Farrar, February 21, 1906 (ZNA), cited in Kosmin, "The Inyoka Tobacco Industry," 270.

29.   Much of Gokwe falls within regions III and IV of the country, where rainfall is very low (between 14 and 20 inches per year). Seasonal droughts and severe dry spells even during the rainy season are common. See George Kay, *Rhodesia: A Human Geography* (London: University of London Press, 1970), 20–21.

30.   Kosmin, "The Inyoka Tobacco Industry," 270.

31.   David Beach, "The Shona Economy: Branches of Production," in Palmer and Parsons, *Roots of Rural Poverty*, 43.

32.   Worby, "Remaking Labour," 322.

33.   Ibid., 263.

34.   For further details of the lives of immigrant communities in Rhodesdale and their forced removal, see Nyambara, "'That Place was Wonderful!" 267–99.

35.   Ibid.

36.   Worby, "Remaking Labour," 321.

37.   Musakari Musingadzani, Nyarupakwe, interview, April 23, 1997.

38.   Alexander and McGregor, "Modernity and Ethnicity," 194.

39.   Makaza Tawonesa, Marungu, interview, July 17, 1997; Maringisanwa Bhachi, Marungu, interview, July 19, 1997; Raymond Murandu, Marungu, interview, July 18, 1997.

40.   Alexander and McGregor, "Modernity and Ethnicity," 191–92.

41.   Nemadziwa Mupfugami, Nyarupakwe, interview, April 23, 1997.

42.   Patrick Dube, Nyarupakwe, interview, April 21, 1997.

43.   Personal correspondence with Terence Ranger.

44.   I am grateful to Vupenyu Dzingirayi for drawing my attention to this argument.

45.   Emory D. Alvord, "The Development of Native Agriculture and Land Tenure in Southern Rhodesia," unpublished manuscript, Harare, 1958, ZNA, 6; For a critical view of Alvord's work in the African areas, see Leslie Bessant, "Coercive Development: Land Shortage, Forced Labor and Colonial Development in Chiweshe Reserve, Colonial Zimbabwe, 1938–1946," *International Journal of African Historical Studies* 25, no, 1 (1992): 39–65; and Dickson Mungazi, *Colonial Agriculture for Africans: Emory Alvord's Policy in Zimbabwe* (New York: Peter Lang, 1998).

46.   Ranger, *Peasant Consciousness*, 62.

47.   R. H. W. Johnson gives the following definitions: "'Cooperator': any farmer who uses manure or fertilizer, carries out some crop rotation, and plants his crops in rows (other than broadcast); 'Plot-holder': a farmer who is under tuition by a demonstrator in order to become a master farmer, and whose cropping program is recorded; 'Master Farmer': a plot-holder who has reached certain minimum standards of crop and animal husbandry laid down by the Agricultural Department." Johnson, *African Agricultural Development in Southern Rhodesia: 1945–1960* (Stanford, CA: Stanford University Press, 1964), 181. "Ordinary Native Farmers" were peasants who were not influenced by extension services and farmed in the "traditional way."

48.   GOK/A/16, Umniati Area File: Annual Report of the Extension Supervisor, Munyati Area, for the Period Ending 31 July 1968, Agritex Office, Gokwe.

49.   GOK/A16, Umniati Area File, 1967, Agritex Office, Gokwe; Naome Marongwe, Nyarupakwe, interview, July 8, 1997.

50.   M. Reid, Gokwe Cotton: Major Events Sequence, File GOK C/14, Regional Office, Gokwe.

51. Justin Masewa, Nyarupakwe, interview, April 23, 1997.

52. F/91/2, CONEX: Development of the Gokwe District: 1963–65, P. A. Davies for Provincial Commissioner to Director, CONEX, June 15, 1965, ZNA; Joseph Dube, Nyarupakwe, interview, July 10, 1997; Peter Katanda, MaCongress village, interview, July 9, 1997.

53. F/91/2, Reid to Provincial Planning Officer, July 3, 1965, ZNA.

54. Since the establishment of this village, the village elders have never allowed any indigenous person to settle in the village, citing cultural differences as the main reason for this exclusiveness.

55. Joseph Dube, Nyarupakwe, interview, July 10, 1997.

56. Ibid.

57. Hlamba Moyo, MaCongress village, interview, June 19, 1997.

58. Joseph Dube, Nyarupakwe, interview, July 10, 1997.

59. GOK/A16, Umniati Area File, Report by D. A. Bokhorst, April 1963, Agritex Office, Gokwe. Umniati Cooperative was an agricultural marketing cooperative formed in 1962 by immigrants like Hlamba Moyo.

60. Ibid.

61. *African Times* (Harare) July 5, 1967. *Rapoko* is a variety of the drought-resistant millets common in much of sub-Saharan Africa.

62. *African Time* (Harare), December 6, 1967.

63. For details of farm sizes in purchase areas, see Angela Cheater, *Idioms of Accumulation: Rural Development and Class Formation among Freeholders in Zimbabwe* (Gweru, Zimbabwe: Mambo Press, 1984); Allison Shutt, "Purchase Area Farmers and the Middle Class of Southern Rhodesia, c. 1931–1952," *International Journal of African Historical Studies* 30, no. 3 (1997): 555–81.

64. GOK/A16, Report by D. Bates, Regional Agricultural Officer, June 17, 1980, Agritex Office, Gokwe.

65. GOK/A16, Report by D. Bates, Regional Agricultural Officer, June 11, 1980, Agritex Office, Gokwe.

66. Shimmer Chinodya, *Dew in the Morning* (Gweru, Zimbabwe: Mambo Press, 1982), 115–16.

67. Justin Masewa, Nyarupakwe, interview, April 23, 1997.

68. Makaza Tawonesa, Marungu, interview, July 17, 1997.

69. GOK/A16, Report by D. A. Bokhorst, April 1963, Agritex Office, Gokwe.

70. Annual Report of the Agricultural Officer, July 1967, Agritex Office, Gokwe.

71. GOK/A16, Report by D. A. Bokhorst, April 1963, Agritex Office, Gokwe.

72. Ibid.

73. Ibid.

74. E. Nyangani, "A Comparison of the Farming Practices of the Indigenous Shangwe Tribe and the More Recent 'Immigrants' in the Kana TTL of Gokwe District" (BA thesis, University of Rhodesia, Department of Geography, 1971).

75. Ibid.

76. Chinodya, *Dew in the Morning*, 50–51. *Sadza* is a thick porridge made from maize flour. It is the staple food of the majority of Africans in sub-Saharan Africa.

77. Kosmin, "The Inyoka Tobacco Industry," 268–88. See also H. Weinmann, *Agricultural Research and Development in Southern Rhodesia, 1890–1923,* University of

Rhodesia, Department of Agriculture Occasional Paper 4 (Salisbury, Southern Rhodesia: University of Rhodesia, 1972), 12.

78. For details of the indigenous cotton industry in precolonial Zimbabwe, particularly in the Zambezi Valley, of which Gokwe is a part, see, among others, Godfrey Ncube, "A History of Northwestern Zimbabwe, 1850–1950s: Comparative Change in Three Worlds" (MPhil thesis, University of Zimbabwe, 1993), 88–90; Thomas N. Huffman, "Cloth from the Iron Age in Rhodesia," *Arnoldia* 5, no. 14 (1971): 1–7; Weinmann, *Agricultural Research and Development in Southern Rhodesia*, 13, 68.

79. Beach, "The Shona Economy," 47.

80. Ncube, "A History of Northwestern Zimbabwe," chapter 7; Worby, "Remaking Labour," 75–76.

81. For a detailed study of the *citemene* system, see M. Vaughan and H. Moore, *Cutting Down Trees: Gender, Nutrition, and Agricultural Change in the Northern Province of Zambia, 1890–1990* (Portsmouth, NH: Heinemann, 1994).

82. Paul Richards, "Ecological Change and the Politics of African Land Use," *African Studies Review* 26, 2 (1983): 56.

83. Quoted in Worby, "Remaking Labour," 163–64.

84. Worby, "Remaking Labour," 164.

85. Frank Nyathi, Mazalahedwa, interview, July 5, 1997.

86. See, for instance, essays in *Cotton, Colonialism, and Social History in Sub-Saharan Africa,* ed. Allen Isaacman and Richard Roberts (Portsmouth, NH: Heinemann, 1995). For a general account of the effects of migrant labor on families, see Colin Murry, *Families Divided: The Impact of Migrant Labor in Lesotho* (Johannesburg: Raven Press, 1981).

87. GOK/A16, Report by Bokhorst, 1967, Agritex Office, Gokwe.

88. Alexander and McGregor, "Modernity and Ethnicity," 199.

89. Terence Ranger, "Violence and Identity in Northern Matabeleland," unpublished manuscript, St. Antony's College, Oxford, 1950, 6, cited in Alexander and McGregor, "Modernity and Ethnicity," 197.

90. Alexander and McGregor, "Modernity and Ethnicity," 198.

91. . Kuwana Matingisanwa, Mudzongwe, interview, July 19, 1997.

92. Alexander and McGregor, "Modernity and Ethnicity," 200.

93. Musakari Musingadzani, Nyarupakwe, interview, April 23, 1997.

94. Derek Bates, "Successful Agricultural Extension in a Rhodesian Tribal Trust Land: The Study and Identification of Factors Contributing to the Success of an Extension Programme Based on Cotton Production in the Gokwe District" (BEd thesis, University of Rhodesia, 1977), 76.

95. Agricultural Report on Nemangwe, Gokwe, October 18, 1968, Agritex Office, Gokwe.

96. Ibid.

97. See, for instance, official correspondence in AGR/3/6, Cotton, 1971–1973, ZNA; M. G. Reid to DC Que Que, "The Gokwe Cotton Crop: Marketing and Loan Repayment," August 5, 1972, ZNA.

98. Worby, "Remaking Labour," 333.

99. S. Maguranye, Gwehawa, interview, May 31, 1997.

100. Justin Masewa, Nyarupakwe, interview, April 23, 1997. For a fuller discussion of the effects of the war on the work of extension workers, see David Mutambara, "The

Effects of the Guerilla Warfare on the Agricultural Social and Economic Aspects of Madziwa" (BA thesis, Geography Department, University of Rhodesia, 1977).

101. "Cotton Hit by War and Drought," *Rhodesia Herald* (Salisbury), August 10, 1979.

102. Norma Kriger, *Zimbabwe's Guerrilla War: Peasant Voices* (Cambridge: Cambridge University Press, 1992).

103. Ibid., 185–91; See also Ranger, *Peasant Consciousness*, 269–75.

104. Kriger, *Zimbabwe's Guerrilla War*, 106.

105. Ian Phimister, "The Combined and Contradictory Inheritance of the Struggle against colonialism," in *Zimbabwe's Prospects*, ed. Colin Stoneman, 8–15 (London: McMillan, 1988).

106. Personal communication from Peter Katanda, June 30, 1998.

107. Peter Katanda, Ganyungu, interview, July 9, 1997.

108. J. M. Sithole, Nyarupakwe, interview, July 10, 1997.

109. Minutes of a Meeting of the Management Committee of the Umniati Cooperative Society for the Year Ending 31st December 1979, Umniati Co-operative Office, Nyarupakwe.

110. Hlamba Moyo, MaCongress Village, interview, July 7, 1997; and Joseph Dube, Nyarupakwe, interview, July 10, 1977.

111. Worby, "Remaking Labour," 333.

112. John Chifamba, Nyarupakwe, interview, April 24, 1997.

10

Displacement, Migration, and the Curse of Borders in Francophone West Africa

GHISLAINE GÉLOIN

The issues of displacement, migration, and borders in Francophone West Africa will be addressed here by studying *The Suns of Independence,* the famous novel by Ahmadou Kourouma, from the Ivory Coast, first published in 1968.[1] I will focus almost exclusively on the main character, Fama, a proud and "crazy Malinke," as people around him perceive him. The issues of displacement, migration, and borders, brought about by colonialism and the first years of independence, are still pertinent today. Borders are part of all kinds of "curses brought by the suns of Independence" (35) and "invented by the devil" (91),[2] along with colonization and district commissioners. Colonialism and the first years of independence have brought along with them a series of evils for African rural society, including the movement and displacement of populations. Fama, our Malinke, sees colonialism and independence as the same thing: independence has brought him only one thing, ruin, or worse, the "national identity card and the party membership card" (14). The politics of independence have made matters even worse. Borders were reshuffled and consolidated, according to the new ideology of nation-statehood, by African leaders. Whole segments of populations, such as the Malinke, were deprived of all political and economic power by the forces of independence. These populations fell back on a life of degradation, humiliation, and sterility, three words that the novel constantly hammers home. For example, the character Fama Doumbouya, the last legitimate descendant of the prince of Horodugu, is reduced almost to begging to survive, his cultural, political, and personal situation turned upside down, first by colonialism and then by independence. He is bitter and constantly expresses his frustrations, cursing those who are now in power, the illegitimate sons of Independence. "The sons of slaves" are ruling, and "the one party-system . . .

is like a society of witches" (14). He rails against "the bastard unlawful rule of presidents of the republic and single parties" (69). In brief, "the bastard politicians" (65) are "shameless people . . . liars and thieves" (66).

Even though Ahmadou Kourouma has created a work of fiction, an alert reader can identify names, places, and postcolonial political events. However, I must stress that Kourouma has insisted that these resemblances are fortuitous and the places described are symbolic of all Africa. The description of colonialism and independence in *The Suns of Independence* applies to all of Africa. But for the purpose of my analysis, I will identify the hidden references.

For example, the fictitious Ebony Coast is the Ivory Coast; its capital, Abidjan, never named, is recognizable from the description of its lagoon and its single bridge connecting the European quarter, where the rich Europeans, the Syrians, and the new political elite live, with the squalid African quarters of Treichville, where a crowd of wretched beggars and pitiful workers roam the streets and markets in search of food (40).

The present-day Malinke live in the Worodugu or Korodugu country (Horodugu in the text) that Guinea and the Ivory Coast share. The village of Togobala (a real village), where the protagonist was born and raised, is a village now located across the border in the territory of the Socialist Republic of Guinea (the Socialist Republic of Nikinai in the text). The River Boudomo mentioned in the text is the River Bandama, which runs partly through the country of Horodogu, as does the River Bafing.

The Malinke are a nation of about one million people, scattered today through six West African states: Gambia, Guinea, Guinea-Bissau, Mali, Mauritania, and the Ivory Coast. In Fama's Malinke homeland, the Horodugu country, the new borders cut the nation in two, one part being in the Socialist Republic of Guinea and the other in the Republic of Côte d'Ivoire. It is no wonder that for the Malinke these artificial borders, now enforced, are curses. It is also worth mentioning that Horodugu means the country (*dogu*) of the free, honest man (*horo*). We at once recall Fama's denunciations of the men of independence, "the bastard politicians."

The Malinke, from the Mande group, are descendants of the people of what was once a great Malinke empire that existed for over thirteen centuries (present-day Mali is what remains of it). Farmers migrated in small groups to the west and southwest in search of better farmland, while professional merchants (the Dyula) spread for trade purposes, bringing with them Islam. Socially, the Malinke consist of noble rulers, powerful merchants, farmers, former slaves, and *griots* (since their culture is essentially oral). They are mainly Muslim but practice traditional animistic beliefs like divination and the casting of spells. They live in clans divided up into villages whose houses are made of sun-dried mud brick and grass thatch roofs. Each village is headed by a chief (*fama*), assisted by a council of elders, and the chief also performs important religious functions.

When Fama, in the novel, returns to his homeland to perform the funeral rituals for his cousin, the chief of Togobala village, twenty years after he migrated to the capital, he is confronted by a decrepit village with houses in ruin. Emaciated people are surviving there; they are "as gaunt and parched as catfish," "their skin rough and dusty as a lizard's, their eyes red and rheumy with conjunctivitis" (71). Even the baobab in the marketplace is a ghost tree. In one word, in the colorful language that Fama always uses, what remains of the village is the "whiff of a fart" (70). But the cultural values have survived, and funerals, especially, continue to be lavishly conducted.

In an interview he gave to Badday,[3] in 1970, Kourouma stated that his characters were inseparable from his own people, the Malinke. Kourouma's avowed intentions were to provide a critical description not only of the Malinke world but above all of the entire African world. The prominent use of free indirect discourse represents Fama's stream of consciousness, which is the center of the novel's consciousness, but the character also speaks on behalf of all the Malinke. Fama's free indirect discourse is often interrupted by a narrator directly addressing the reader. The narrator identifies himself as a Malinke, using the collective "us Malinke," while the readership is split between the Malinke reader and the "non-Malinke" reader.[4] The complexity of the polyphonic voices in the novel may seem like a distancing device, but paradoxically the author's presence is all the more strongly felt. Kourouma presents himself as a Malinke, and collective consciousness is paramount to a Malinke.

However, it would be naïve to think that this "crazy Malinke" functions as the author's spokesman. The extremely ironic tone of the narrator and the actions of the grotesque, irascible character, always ready to pull out a knife to defend his honor, discredit every voice that is heard. Kourouma's position is furtive. The author plays hide and seek with his reader, but above all with censorship. What we can conclude is that the novel depicts the disillusionment and eventual tragedy that the politics of independence brought to the Malinke of the Ivory Coast and Guinea. On a broader scale, it illustrates the catastrophic impact that colonization and independence have had on African rural society, regardless of ethnicity.

Author and protagonist share common points but also reveal differences. These need to be highlighted.[5]

Kourouma's life is an exemplar of the lives of many intellectual blacks who were displaced because of political events. Born in the Ivory Coast in the village of Boundiali in 1927, Kourouma was a member of a royal Muslim family of the Malinke and spent his youth in Togobala (in Guinea), like his character.

The character Fama is believed to be a faithful portrait of Kourouma's marabout grandfather or at least a portrait of a member of his family. In the nineteenth century, Kourouma's grandfather may have had a conflict with Samory Touré, who refused to recognize him as a religious leader, an *almamy*.[6] Samory Touré, the great Mande leader and warrior, ruled a large territory stretching beyond the borders of the Ivory Coast and resisted colonialism for many years. Only after his defeat in 1898 was France able to gain control of Guinea and the Ivory Coast. The conquest of the Ivory Coast was completed only in 1912. Our character in the novel bears the title assumed by Samory Touré, *fama,* meaning "lord," coming from *fanga,* "strength." This is ironic, because if there is one thing that the gaunt and sterile Fama does not possess, it is strength. His sterility is symbolic of his powerlessness. If the word *fama,* in current usage, means "rich people," again it is ironic, since Fama is reduced to living off the charity of other Malinke.

Kourouma's father was at times a trader, a farmer, and a hunter. Trading is an important profession for the Malinke, as we shall see in the case of Fama. Kourouma's father would have been endowed with supernatural powers. The Malinke practice divination and believe in the *koma* fetish, as mentioned in the novel (107).

Kourouma as a child was educated in the rural primary school of Boundiali, then in Korhogo and Bingerville in the northern Ivory Coast. In 1946 he returned to Togobala. In 1947, as a student in Bamako (in present-day Mali), he took part in anticolonial movements, under the umbrella of the African Democratic Rally (Rassemblement démocratique africain; RDA), a party with members from several neighboring French colonies led at first by Félix Houphouët-Boigny. He was arrested as a leader of student demonstrations and sent back to the Ivory Coast. He experienced a series of dramatic displacements when he was enrolled as a Senegalese *tirailleur* (soldier) and sent to Indochina (1951–54) for refusing to participate in a crackdown on RDA agitators. When he was discharged from the military, he returned to his village of Togobala. In 1955, he went to Paris and Lyon to further his education at his own expense.

Fama, like Kourouma, is an anticolonialist. As "a legitimate son of chiefs," he considers it manly to take revenge for "fifty years of occupation by the infidels" (36). But, more precisely, his anticolonial stand is a form of vindication, since he lost the position of chief, first to a French administrator and then to a distant cousin, Lasina, who intrigued, cast spells, and performed sacrifices to cheat Fama out of his birthright. Consequently, he migrates to the capital but prospers during the colonial period. This is because the Malinke and the French at least had common interests. The French favored free trade, and "what matters most to a Malinke is freedom of trade" (13). Fama is a *dyula,* that is, a large-scale trader, who deals with all the "great African markets in Dakar, Bamako, Bobo, Bouake" (12) until he throws himself into the fight against French colonialism and neglects his business.

In 1961, on the arrival of independence, Kourouma returned to the Republic of Côte d'Ivoire as an assistant to the director of a bank in Abidjan. It was then that he gave a voice, from his privileged position, to the displaced Malinke and started writing *The Suns of Independence.*

In contrast, Fama's situation worsens with independence. A whole class of traders is ruined. What is implied is the politics of Houphouët-Boigny, who exclusively promoted a class of landowners that he considered had been exploited. The Malinke cultural values, summed up in the following quotation from the novel, indicate that the Malinke have no place in the new politics and have been short-changed:

> The colonial period outlawed and killed war, but favored trade; Independence ruined trade, and there was no sign of war. So the Malinke species, tribes, land and civilization, was dying: crippled, deaf, blind . . . and sterile. (13)

Fama is so disappointed that if he had a choice between the two poisons—colonialism and independence—he would prefer a return to colonial times (13). He had fancied that the end of colonization would mean a return to the precolonial time, to the grandeur of the Malinke nobility, the only authenticity. The old Malinke traders (the exact number of whom cannot even be specified), ruined by independence, have migrated to the capital and now perform Muslim funeral rites for the Malinke, as Fama himself does; people have nicknamed them "vultures." Fama's deplorable situation as a "scavenger" is summed up as that of "a panther totem in a hyena pack" (4). When there is no money, he relies on the solidarity of the Malinke community.

The year 1963 marks the beginning of the third wave of conspiracies fabricated by President Houphouët-Boigny to quell dissent and political competition from the intelligentsia and middle-class business people. In order to consolidate his political power with the landowners who had become exclusively his henchmen, he continued to favor close economic cooperation with the French, who still controlled the economy and were mainly responsible for what has been called the Ivoirian miracle. Houphouët-Boigny refused to Africanize the economic sector.

Kourouma was falsely accused of participating in the 1963 conspiracy, and he was jailed, but he was released because Houphouët-Boigny, a great advocate of *francophonie*, feared severe diplomatic tensions with France since Kourouma was married to a Frenchwoman. Jobless for seven months, Kourouma went into exile first in France and then in Algeria, where he worked for an insurance company. He continued to write his novel in the heat of these political events, as a way to support those still detained.

His novel's protagonist will have worse luck. The protagonist is implicated in an alleged conspiracy to assassinate the president for having had a dream that foresaw a plot and the downfall of the minister of state, Naku, a young Malinke intellectual of his acquaintance. His crime is that he failed to report his dream to the authorities. Fama is sent to a "camp without name" (for what does not have a name does not exist) for twenty years of solitary confinement and hard labor. It is well known that Houphouët-Boigny accused his enemies of using fetishist practices against him, in order to justify his enemies' elimination.[7] The Malinke, believing in divination and being fetish-worshippers, were easy prey for Houphouët Boigny's politics. Ministers, members of the assembly, and their close allies not belonging to the planters' class "disappeared," having been accused of using fetishist practices. In the novel, Naku's alleged suicide in prison mirrors the fate of a real individual, the freemason Ernest Boka, who "committed suicide" in his cell.

In 1966, the political prisoners were set free and granted a magnanimous presidential pardon. Finally, in 1980, Houphouët-Boigny admitted that the series of plots against him were baseless yet he held his security chief responsible for the machinations. In the novel, the president, in a big turnabout, declares a general amnesty, looking for reconciliation among his people to suit his political ends, and looking to restore his reputation in neighboring countries and his international prestige (121). After giving a speech about the brotherhood that "binds all black men together" and the importance of "humanism in Africa" (120), the president gives every one of the prisoners a kiss of reconciliation and a "thick wad of banknotes." Then they are taken to the capital and invited to a festival of reconciliation with parades, fireworks, and dancing. This cynical presidential mise-en-scène does not seem far-fetched if we consider the 1969 *dialogue fraternel permanent,* concocted by Houphouët-Boigny, in which group meetings of all sectors of Ivoirian society took place face-to-face with the president in a manner that mocked the traditional-style "palavers."[8] Kourouma seems to have anticipated the *Rendez-vous de la Réconciliation* (Meeting of Reconciliation) that crowned these group meetings in 1971. Houphouët-Boigny was ready to share limited power with social classes other than his henchmen the landowners.

But Fama won't have anything to do with this *Grand Rendez-vous,* which for him is just a farce. He could seize the opportunity to become the director of a cooperative, as he had longed so much to be at the arrival of independence, or invest in the new economy. Instead, without a word, he boards a bus to go back to his Malinke Horodugu homeland, the country of free, honest men.

In 1971, the year of the Reconciliation, Kourouma was invited to return to the Ivory Coast to take up an important position at the Société Générale Ivory Coast Bank (SGBCI). However, his play, *Tougnatigui, le possesseur de la vérité* (The Truth Teller), which played in Abidjan and on the Ivory Coast TV channel, was judged subversive. He suffered another displacement and was sent to Yaoundé (in Cameroon) as the director of the insurance bureau of the International Institute for the Pan African Agency, and stayed there until 1984. Then he went to Togo, where he held the same position until 1994. Thus Kourouma experienced a series of displacements, banished from his own country as persona non grata, because he dared to disagree with the politics of Houphouët-Boigny.

One main point separates author and protagonist: one is an intellectual, the other a wretched man. However, this binds them together in the strategy of the novel. The "crime" committed by Fama, which excludes him irrevocably from the politics of independence, is that he is an illiterate, "as illiterate as a donkey's tail" (14). He will be reminded of his crime in a perfunctory mass sentencing delivered by a Malinke guard in the Malinke language. The guard is asked to interpret "an endless statement full of dialogue and subordinate clauses. Fama and many others could make nothing of it." Quickly translated, this long statement becomes, "You're all jackals. You can't speak French and you tried to kill the president. That's what the judge said. He said the trial's over" (116).

The reader understands immediately that "being illiterate" is a matter of not speaking French. Houphouët-Boigny (a former medical student in France and a doctor in his own country, turned planter on his rich Baoule family plantations) enthusiastically embraced *francophonie*. The French colonizers had favored some ethnic groups over others, empowering some, disenfranchising others. The novel reminds the reader that Dahomeyans and Senegalese were brought into the Ebony Coast (the Ivory Coast) and given the jobs and money; consequently they took the women. These migrants "knew how to write and read and were French citizens or else Catholics; smarter, more civilized, harder-working Africans than the native inhabitants of the country" (59), complains someone from another group. The Dahomeyans were kicked out of the country in 1958 under the pretext that they held the best teaching positions. Interethnic conflicts continued after independence; for instance there were attacks on Mossi workers by the xenophobic Houphouët-Boigny's henchmen in 1969. Other large-scale movements of population occurred. The Ivoirian miracle needed a huge supply of cheap migrant workers to replace forced laborers. For this purpose, the Mossi came from the north, the Hausa from the east, the Nago[9] from the south, as one remarks in the novel. As for Fama, once independence is won, he cannot be co-opted. He is dismissed "like a leaf that's just been used to wipe somebody's arse," "thrown to the flies and forgotten" (14).

Francophone literacy has created linguistic boundaries between people. It is at this point that Ahmadou Kourouma becomes Fama's *griot*, offering his literacy so that those who have no voice can be given a voice and a space. *Griots* are the famous *maîtres de la parole* (masters of the spoken word) of the oral culture of the Malinke and of West Africa as a whole, and they are responsible for passing down the cultural heritage; they are essentially praise-song singers. Out of respect for his oral Manding language, Kourouma said that he "thought the book in Malinke and wrote it in French, taking liberties that seemed natural with the classical language."[10] What we read is often a literal translation from Manding to French, the text flowing with exuberant African narrative rhythms. The book was rejected by publishers in France.

Québécois publishers seized the opportunity of Kourouma's strategy of writing to define a new project for a new conception of *francophonie*, an era in which there would be reciprocity between French and the many languages of the Francophone world. As Senghor put it in his University of Laval speech in Québec in 1966, the "Francophonie will no longer be contained by the borders of France."[11] The *francophonie* will create pluralistic linguistic spaces, since Francophone writers are by definition part of two linguistic worlds that constantly interact. Texts *métissés* will break linguistic boundaries. It will be now the French reader's turn to be the one displaced and enter these new Francophone spaces reading cross-cultural texts, criss-crossing fluid linguistic boundaries. *The Suns of Independence* was hailed as redefining the *francophonie*, and it received Francité's literary prize.

The artificial political borders in Africa were mainly created at the Berlin Conference in 1884–85, when the imperial European powers met to carve up African territories into colonies. The French colonial empire was, from 1895 to 1958, a federation of eight colonies. These made up French West Africa (AOF), which was created in 1904 with Dakar as its capital. The borders of the colonies within the federation were specified. However the borders within the AOF were very porous, with rural people continuing to move freely and trade, with little awareness that they were moving into different colonies. Only the borders between the colonial powers were well defined, especially in populated areas. In 1958, French President Charles de Gaulle organized a referendum in which French African countries could choose to become self-governing republics within a federation, the Franco-African Community, under the control of the French Republic. All the West African countries voted for an association of states within the federation, except for Guinea, which voted for autonomy and immediate independence. France responded immediately by severing its links with Guinea. Houphouët-Boigny was at first the staunchest advocate of de Gaulle's vision of a French Community (Communauté française, 1958–62), in which African countries would continue to move toward a concept of supranational identity. However, once in power, the African presidents began to support the idea of their countries becoming strong nation-states. Attempts at federation between African states failed (the federation between Mali and Senegal in 1959 was short lived). We can say that the postcolonial African states furthered the balkanization of the AOF states, sanctioning the partition of Africa into nation-states out of a desire for total sovereignty, a new nationalism, patriotism, and security, and also for selfish reasons. For instance, the Republic of Côte d'Ivoire, the most prosperous former colony, refused to be the milch cow for the others. After some restructuring of its artificial borders, it enforced tight border-crossing control by creating border posts. These barriers restricted the freedom of circulation in West Africa. Border controls especially affected ethnic groups, such as the Malinke, that straddled borders.

This is the situation when Fama crosses the border between the Ebony Coast (Ivory Coast) and the Republic of Nikinai (Guinea) for the second time, to go back and finally accept his Togobala chiefdom. He is stopped at a rigorously guarded border post. The first time he had benefited from the tolerance of an intelligent Malinke guard, who had recognized him and let him pass without his papers. This time the travelers are told that the frontier is closed indefinitely for diplomatic reasons. But it is easy to conjecture the true reason. The novel mentions elsewhere that the Bambara and the Malinke of Nikinai have fled across the border, running away from state torture. They have settled in the Ebony Coast and have become involved in the black market in currency and in smuggling. Also the rural population has been required to engage in "self-help" (57), a euphemism for forced labor to build the country's infrastructure. The president of the Socialist Republic of Guinea, Sekou Touré, who relied on his Malinke ethnic group to rule, also followed paranoid politics, like Houphouët–Boigny, except that Touré engaged in a *complot permanent* (permanent plot) that would last until 1984. These alleged conspiracies were mainly directed against ministers, civil servants, high-ranking officers, farmers, traders, and village chiefdoms. Kéita Fodéba, from the Mande ethnic group, poet, dancer, and former director of Les Ballets Africains turned minister of the interior and of national defense, "disappeared" in prison in 1965 as did Diallo Telli, the secretary-general of the Supreme Council of the Organization of African Unity (OAU), and his companions in 1976.[12]

Unable to understand the new laws, the new geography, and a concept of borders that demands a national identity card making him an Ivoirian rather than a Malinke, Fama does not feel he needs authorization from those he calls "the bastard sons of dogs and slaves" to enter his Horodugu chiefdom where everything belongs to him. As an act of defiance, he proceeds calmly to cross the bridge between the two countries, shouting: "Look at Dumbuya, Prince of Horodugu! Admire me, sons of dogs, sons of Independence!" (132) Unable to find a hole in the barbed-wire barrier through which to enter the Republic of Nikinai, he walks down into a crocodile-infested river, sure that the crocodiles sacred to his lineage will not attack a legitimate heir to the chiefdom. But one does.[13]

Fama's death, though tragic, makes a mockery of a conception of identity based on nationality and national borders. Crossing borders in Africa is a matter of luck or bribery. Should we listen to a reactionary voice in the novel commenting that the problem with Africans is that they don't stay at home (59) and it is this that causes wars and misery? Migrations have always taken place across West Africa along trade route corridors. West African borders between nations are pointless and impede Africa's general development, regional economic development, and local integration. These borders are now perceived as causing "the bondage of boundaries." Organizations have been created to strive for African unity in the wake of Nkrumah's defunct ideal of Pan-Africanism. The Organization of African Unity (OAU) was founded in 1963 and was replaced by the current African Union (AU) in 2002. The Economic Community of West African States (ECOWAS), created in 1975, consists of fifteen member states. Since 2005, this organization has been striving to implement a West Africa without borders, with free circulation of people, goods, and services, in which Africans will be transnational citizens carrying a community passport. Achieving this will be a long process, due to the resistance of nation-states whose support of artificial colonial borders is deeply ingrained out of protectionist concerns, a fear of immigration, and the lack of a democratic culture. Kourouma stood up publicly against the policies of President Gbagbo, who espoused the concept of pure Ivoirian parentage.[14] Kourouma called this nationalistic stance an absurdity; indeed, it has led the country into chaos. A civil war flared up in 2002[15] because of this very issue of citizenship, which spilled over Côte d'Ivoire's borders. With this law, the government's xenophobic attitude had excluded, as nationals, one-third of the immigrants from neighboring countries who had settled in Côte d'Ivoire for two generations and some of whom were of Mande heritage.

To use a Malinke expression, the "harsh suns of Independence" (15) are just seasons, only transitory times. They won't last.

Fama is doomed for being "as intractable as a newly circumcised donkey" (88). Things have irrevocably fallen apart for him; a world falls apart for those who are incapable of the transnational negotiation of identity, for the aristocracy, for the ones who cling to their ancestral past, which, however glorious, in the postcolonial era exists only in fantasy, as Fama's last delirious words ironically stress: "Fama the One and only! The great! The strong! The virile! Sole possessor of strength and stiffness between the thighs!" (135). These strings of words do not apply to the living, impotent Fama. The text alludes to a supernatural intervention by the shades of the ancestors, because of some kind of transgression. Indeed, Fama is not killed by a bullet from the border guards but by a sacred crocodile that attacks "only if sent by the shades to kill a transgressor of law or custom, or a great sorcerer, or a great chief" (134). As if to confirm this, Fama's agony is accompanied by nature's supernatural manifestations mourning his death.

The future now belongs to the politics of independence and *francophonie*, and to those who learn how to compromise and negotiate. This ability is at the heart of the long traditional African palavers. A political maneuver by the Togobala council of elders in the novel points in the right direction. The elders resolve the governance conflict between the traditional and independence administrations, even before the palaver takes place, by deciding to keep both structures. Fama will be the chief according to custom, and the party delegate will remain the official president of the Horodugu country.

Their decision is met with Fama's usual "noble silence" (94), a euphemism used to hide his impotence. Their attitude might be considered duplicitous, but who said that politics are not duplicitous? Africa has entered the politics of independence and it is said that "in politics, true and false wear the same cloth, just and unjust go hand in hand, good and evil are bought and sold at the same price" (109). The text stresses that the Malinke are also capable of duplicity. "The Malinke are full of duplicity because deep down inside they are blacker than their skin, while the words they speak are whiter than their teeth. Are they fetish-worshippers? Are they Muslims?" (72). In the last resort, "Nothing is good and evil in itself. It is speech that transforms a thing into good or turns it into evil" (72). Political speech and palavers are one and the same and deemed unworthy. Other "suns of politics" (14) are in the making. There are no doomed ethnic groups as long as each group plays its political cards right. Prince Fama was incapable of playing the game right.

Notes

1.   The novel was first published in 1968 in Canada by Montreal University Press and won Francité's literary prize. However it was written between 1961 and 1966, at the time of the events to which it alludes and on which this chapter focuses.

2.   Ahmadou Kourouma, *Les Soleils des Indépendances* (Paris: Seuil, 1970). The English translation is by Adrian Adams and is titled *The Suns of Independence* (New York: Africana Publishing Company, 1981). All quotations in the present chapter are taken from the English translation, and all page references given in parenthetical citations refer to this translation.

3.   Moncef Badday, "Ahmadou Kourouma, écrivain africain," *L'Afrique littéraire et artistique*, no. 10 (April 1970).

4.   Christopher L. Miller, *Theories of Africans: Francophone Literature and Anthropology in Africa* (Chicago: University of Chicago Press, 1990).

5.   The following information is taken mainly from Jean-Claude Nicolas, *Comprendre Les Soleils des Indépendances d'Ahmadou Kourouma* (Issy-les-Moulineaux, France: Les Classiques africains, no. 858, 1985).

6.   Ibid., 3.

7.   For further reference, see Jacques Baulin, *La Politique intérieure d'Houphouët-Boigny* (Paris: Éditions Eurafor-Press, 1982).

8.   Miller, *Theories*, 241.

9.   The Nago (or Anago), a Yoruba subset, are found, today, in Benin, Nigeria, and Togo.

10.   Badday, "Ahmadou Kourouma, écrivain africain," 7.

11.   Miller, *Theories*, 185.

12.   It is worth noting that these two African countries used conspiracy theories and strategies that were inspired by Cold War politics in the USA and the Soviet Union in order to silence their intellectuals.

13. Many devout animists revere the crocodile as a sacred animal. Houphouët-Boigny, a Roman Catholic, who had the tallest Christian basilica, a replica of Saint Peter's in Rome, built in his new capital, Yamoussoukro, exploited this devotion. There is a widespread belief that prisoners were fed to the sacred caimans that he kept in the ponds around his palace. In 1993, at his death, young men threw themselves into these lakes.

14. Any candidate for the presidency must be born within Côte d'Ivoire and born of two Ivoirian parents. But, as Kourouma put it, this law defied all common sense and cannot possibly be implemented, since no birth records were maintained until 1960. What is at stake is a definition of national identity, eligibility for citizenship and land holding. The law was perceived as a new type of apartheid and an attempt at creating a pure race. Ivoirian identity and national preference are poisoned legacies of Houphouët-Boigny.

15. The Linas-Marcoussis Peace Accords were signed in January 2003; they established a government of national reconciliation. Other challenges had yet to be met. There were other violent flare-ups and political deadlock. The accords were followed by other agreements. Peace is still fragile in 2007.

11

Shifting Identities among Nigerian Yoruba in Dahomey and the Republic of Benin (1940s–2004)

Jean-Luc Martineau

Introduction: The Invented Origins of Foreign-Based Yoruba Associations

In many African cities, immigrants join associations that aim to recreate a social structure reminiscent of their native land or hometown. The size and recruiting areas of these associations depend mostly on the size of the immigrant communities and on the immigration policy, with regard to foreigners, of the country in which they are resident. Cross-border migrations are not necessary for the foundation of such groups, but their usefulness is more apparent when foreign immigrants are concerned. Shifting identities among Nigerian Yoruba in the Republic of Benin (ca. 1940–ca. 2005) raise two questions: To what extent can we identify the conceptual origins of these structures that attract migrants? And how did these associations cope with their political and social environments in the second half of the twentieth century, when they were confronted with radical challenges to their structures of self-integration or self-organization? This chapter aims to show that Yoruba identities have been subject to permanent changes and adaptations during the last fifty or sixty years.[1] Because well-known, familiar structures are imitated and copied in a different context from the original, these structures, half invented and half duplicated, contribute to the invention or the enhancement of identities.[2]

The Historical and Conceptual Origins of Migrant Groups

In the case of Nigerian Yoruba in the Republic of Benin,[3] the last sixty years clearly illustrate the necessity for migrants to cope with local conditions—not always in conformity with their own beliefs. Most of the Yoruba I interviewed from 1999 to 2005 said they preferred coming together in associations with people from their native city, but this is quite a recent preference. It is true, however, that hometown-based associations appear to be the "natural" way for people to organize themselves abroad. Some groups may even bring together individuals from a particular neighborhood or from a single extended family.[4] Listening to their members, we might deem this kind of practice as having existed from time "immemorial," but it is, in fact, a recent form of self-organization.

According to interviews I conducted,[5] local identity is now considered a guarantee against social insecurity. It is seen as the most efficient form of protection in an unknown environment and the best way to integrate into a foreign society. Cities, it would appear, provide a familiar reference point to individuals because Yoruba migrants are in the majority already urbanites. However, this idea is in fact a twentieth-century conception if not a postindependence development. In the past, migrants used to find other ways to deal with feelings of loneliness.[6] The novelty of the ethno-urban-based identity was first underlined by Akintoye, writing on the aftermath of the Yoruba civil wars: "Fragments of the various Yoruba sub-groups were thrown all over the Yoruba homeland, most getting absorbed into their new homes. It is surprising how little it is usually realised that each of the Oyo, Ekiti, Ijebu or any other Yoruba sub-group of today is really a synthesis of fragments from almost all parts of Yorubaland."[7]

It is quite difficult to identify the historical and ideological origins of modern-day associations. The invented yet useful origins bolster the process of identity building itself. The feeling of ethnic/identity insecurity among migrants has always led to the creation of solidarity groups and networks, but the forms taken by these protection groups varied considerably during the nineteenth and twentieth centuries. The hometown- or region-based structures are not as old as my informants believe when they describe them as "traditional" or existing from time "immemorial." The most we can say is that they are based on the geographical divisions of the southwestern part of what is now Nigeria after the Yoruba wars.

Forced migrations in the Yoruba area in the nineteenth century generated other nonethnic answers to insecurity, threats to identity, and the destruction of the Oyo Empire. The region-wide troubles required more than simple hometown solidarity. If the appeal of the ancestors' city was deeply rooted in the population, the new geopolitical organization of postwar Yoruba city-states, as well as the new worldwide religions, offered more radical solutions to individual insecurity than the perpetuation of the former political and subethnic framework. One does not find in the early nineteenth century the roots of the late-twentieth-century migrant associations. They are definitely an invention of the late twentieth century based on concepts dating back no further than the 1930s.

Nowadays, migrants' groups point to the progressive unions of the 1930s–40s in the Yoruba provinces. This comparison, however, has its limits. The aims of these Progressive Unions were completely different from those promoted by contemporary organizations: "... Descendants' Unions," "Egbe Omo ..." ("Association of the Sons of ..."), or "... Parapo" ("... Together"). Of course, when a Yoruba leaves his or her hometown nowadays for another Yoruba or non-Yoruba city in Nigeria, or when he or she crosses Nigeria's borders, the ancestral city[8] remains the main reference point.

This is the result of an identity-building process that started in the 1930s within the Yoruba area of Nigeria.[9] The British colonizers bound the inhabitants of southwestern Nigeria in a framework of local, urban identities whose limits vaguely recalled the limits of ancient "ancestral cities." These cities thus appeared as the cradle of families where members controlled the family properties and where one was recognized as a "son" or a "daughter" of the city. This process of identification deepened when the nationalist leader Obafemi Awolowo rooted his pan-Yoruba regional nationalism in a federation of all Yoruba cities. Individual adhesion to Awolowo's pan-Yoruba project started with homage to one's *oba* and to one's ancestral city. Awolowo had conceived this indirect individual membership of the "Yoruba nation" as the basis of the pyramidal political organization of the southwest. Not only was each citizen connected to the nation via his hometown identity and citizenship, but each individual *oba* was also federated with his peers in the Egbe Omo Oduduwa, to embody the Yoruba nation. At the top, Aderemi, the *Ooni* of Ife, and Awolowo himself embodied the nation.

But recent migrant and self-help groups are not following in the footsteps of the political and development-oriented progressive unions of the 1930s–40s, even though both the previous and the present groups refer to ancestral roots. Members of the progressive unions were privileged immigrants, mostly educated and politically conscious. They came together in the cities in which they lived and worked in order to contribute to the economic and political promotion of their home city-state. With transborder migrants, we are not dealing with the same issues. The confusion may come from the fact that ancient hometown associations and recent migrants' solidarity groups recently merged, following strong political input along the local-identities line now promoted in southwestern Nigeria in relation to demands for the creation of local governments and federated states. This recent and ongoing amalgamation of all hometown associations all over the world must not be allowed to hide the differences between associations at home and abroad.

The Migrants

Who Are These Migrants?

In early colonial times, circulation across the French-British colonial border was interrupted. The east-west roads crossing the Yoruba area were virtually closed by the British and French colonizers. Already disorganized by the Yoruba civil wars and the end of the slave trade, all of the intra-Yoruba east-west traffic was diverted to Lagos instead of going to Porto Novo or Ouidah. The east, which was to be part of Dahomey, and the areas that are in modern-day Nigeria developed separately. However, the precolonial (now international) movements did not stop. They have often been mentioned by scholars, even though transborder migrations of peasants crossing the new border to reach their fields, antitax migrations in rural areas, and the local impact of traders moving between Nigeria and Dahomey have not been extensively studied.

Moreover, demographers are reluctant to consider daily or weekly cross-border movements that involve groups of people who live on both sides of the boundaries as international migrations.[10] Finally, British and French colonial sources do not focus on these migrants. Many factors explain this gap in research. Sources are not available to assess the volume of these movements. The colonial archives in Ibadan, Porto Novo, Paris, and London do not focus on these groups. Border problems may occur from time to time (especially during tax season), but the colonial administrations were not particularly interested in border areas.[11] The difficulties experienced by both the French and British in finalizing the border line shows how neglected these questions were. The French and British discussed the issue several times up to the 1950s but always postponed the realization of the project, mostly for financial reasons.[12]

The cultural homogeneity of the border region also discouraged the study of Yoruba migrations as an international phenomenon. The political, cultural, and economic similarity between the populations on both sides of the border led administrators as well as scholars to consider the continuing movements as "natural" or "historical." The interruption of trade and political disruption between the Oyo and Ketu were studied more seriously because of their novelty. The twentieth century (up to independence) does not provide much material on the volume or the consequences of Nigerian Yoruba migrations between Nigeria and Dahomey. The French administration never wrote a single specific report on the issue, as if these migrants did not exist. When dealing with migration, the French emphasized internal migrations, rural-urban movements, the movement of educated administrative officers or unqualified laborers around the AOF (Afrique occidentale française), and north-south movements related to the labor market. Yet scholars and administrative reports[13] underscore the fact that the early twentieth century and the period leading up to the colonial conquest were periods of important migration.

In terms of identity, the historical links between the Yoruba from Ketu, Save, or Porto Novo and those living on the other side of the new border contributed to the fusion between settled groups and newcomers. Prior to 1960, these migrants were not so numerous and were not indefinitely perceived as foreigners. Some of them use this to explain their ease in obtaining Benin citizenship in 1960. However, French officials did start to identify Nigerian Yoruba as foreigners during the 1930s and 1940s in an attempt to introduce special identity cards; yet their registration revealed only a small community made up of traders and Muslim herbalists.[14] For all these reasons, it is difficult to grasp the impact of the migrations on the social environment and on identity-building processes among Nigerian Yoruba in border areas.

There are good reasons, however, to focus our attention on recent Nigerian Yoruba migrants and new forms of urban immigration in the two main southern towns of the Republic of Benin. This contemporary movement of people involves impoverished immigrants who are looking for an improvement in their employment and income and whose conditions of integration in Benin have had a real impact on the way they organize themselves and construct their identities.

How Many Nigerian Yoruba Are There in the Benin Republic?

The latest census does not provide an accurate description of Nigerian immigration in Benin. It is always difficult to count foreigners, who are mainly illegal in status. The Economic Community of West African States (ECOWAS) allows free movement across borders, but one needs to register when settling somewhere. An analysis of the demographics of the Nigerian Yoruba population in Cotonou and Porto Novo is impossible. According to informants, the biggest Yoruba community in the 1950s and 1960s was found in Porto Novo. Cotonou appeared to be a secondary destination. In those days, initially all Yoruba came together, regardless of their hometown origins, probably because they mostly came from Oyo Province or the former Oyo and Ibadan empires. But the initiative of one Nigerian known as "Ikorodu Photo," leader of the Nigerian Yoruba in Porto Novo, to connect his association with Ife in the mid-6os led to a split that provoked the setting up of hometown subgroups (for Ilorin, Ede, Ibadan, and so on). In the 1992 census, foreign groups were studied by nationality, and Nigerian Yoruba were classified simply as Nigerians. We can only try to evaluate the global immigration figures by using qualitative observations. Only 4,752 Nigerian citizens[15] were registered as immigrants in Benin (they made up 16 percent of foreigners and formed the third largest group among the foreigners) between 1987 and 1991. Only a few of them, however, seem to have been Yoruba. The fact that some of these Nigerian Yoruba migrants are now citizens of Benin does not simplify the process of qualitative analysis.

Prior to independence (1955–61), Cotonou received a great deal of public investment, which encouraged the migration of Dahomeyan northerners and natives of Porto Novo (8 percent of the demographic growth rate between 1961 and 1979). The town grew dramatically between 1940 and 1960. This growth continued thereafter, and the size of the town was 950 hectares in 1960 and 8,250 hectares in 1974.[16] The situation in Dahomey after independence (1960–72) was not favorable to cross-border migration. The period of dictatorship under the Marxist-Leninist Kérékou regime was a period of trouble for the Nigerian migrants who were already there.[17] Because of this situation, probably few new Yoruba came from Nigeria during this period, but some did come from the Ivory Coast or Ghana after massive expulsions from those countries.

The 1992 census[18] tried to determine how many foreign nationals were in Dahomey (the Republic of Benin). For political reasons, however, Kérékou-era census officials chose to disregard the geo-ethnic origins of migrants. Nationality was the only information provided. In 1992, despite the explicit return to geo-ethnic origins as a matter to be recorded in the census, it was still difficult to identify the Nigerian Yoruba. This is because the census mentioned 594,776 Yoruba among a total population of 4,915,555, but we also have to consider 24,315 foreigners, that is, people who were not living "naturally in Benin," as they were confusingly described in the census. Nigerian Yoruba could have been placed in either group. The interpretation of the census was complicated by something else: Benin citizens who return to their country and foreigners who come to Benin are counted together under the heading of "international immigration." Despite the difficulties in counting them, international migrants, more specifically Nigerian Yoruba, have played a significant part in leading to the creation of self-help organizations to welcome newcomers (see table 11.1).

The slowdown in international migration to Cotonou in the last ten years[19] was revealed by the disorganization and obvious weakness of the association called the Nigerian Yoruba Community in 2005. Although it was not the only reason for the disorganization and weakness, the demographic decline of the community weakens the influence of long-established groups on newcomers because solidarity is shared between fewer and fewer people, and weekly or monthly meetings do not provide answers to people's needs. In Porto Novo, economic stagnation and the weakness of pull factors[20] for Nigerian Yoruba were already obvious in 1995 and 1999. The Nigerian Yoruba Association of Porto Novo is virtually nonexistent today. As far as migrations are concerned, the town stopped being attractive between the two censuses (1979 and 1992): the migration balance was negative for "internal

Table 11.1. Comparison between internal immigration and immigration from abroad in two cities of the Benin Republic

	1975–79		1987–91[a]	
	External immigrants	Total immigrants	External immigrants	Total immigrants
Cotonou	10,510	56,399[b]	14,860	68,356[d]
Porto Novo	5,345	14,698[c]	3,679	20,225[e]

Source: Recensement général de la population et de l'habitation, mars 1979 (Cotonou: Bureau Central du Recensement, INSAE, République Populaire du Bénin, tome 1 [*juillet 1986*] and tome 2 [*décembre 1987*]); *Deuxième recensement général de la population et de l'habitation, février 1992* (Cotonou: Bureau Central du Recensement, INSAE, République Populaire du Bénin, vol. 1 [*décembre 1993*] and vol. 2 [*mars 1994*].

[a] 23,087 immigrants from Nigeria (Benin citizens and Nigerians) came to the Benin Republic between 1987 and 1991; most of them settled in Cotonou and Porto-Novo.

[b] With 22,076 people leaving Cotonou in the same period, the foreigners represent one-quarter of newcomers and one-third of the migration balance (+34,323).

[c] At 14,668, natives leaving the town are almost as numerous as the immigrants (positive net migration is +79 persons).

[d] With 61,171 people leaving Cotonou in the same period, the positive migration balance is only +7,185 people; although the foreigners are 4.6 times less numerous than Benin migrants, they are responsible for two-thirds of the increase in the total population (14,860/21,865).

[e] With 22,364 people leaving, the town would have lost inhabitants (-2,139) without the foreign immigration.

migrants" (-2,139). Even the slightly positive results for "external migrants" (+3679 persons between 1979 and 1992) are tricky, for, according to the censuses, most of these migrants were not foreigners but Benin citizens coming back from abroad. Obviously, immigrants have neglected Porto-Novo in favor of Cotonou, although the latter is not as popular as in the past: "internal migrants" at +7,185 (1979–92) instead of +34,323 (1961–79); "external migrants" at +14,860 (1979–92). Between 1979 and 1989, the Kérékou military regime favored Cotonou as a means of weakening Porto Novo, former political headquarters of the Legislative Assembly. The core of the power shifted to Cotonou, which received most of the state and private investments while rural population from the hinterland settled there.[21]

Policy and Group Attitudes toward Hometowns

In this chapter, instead of focusing on the motivation of migrants and the theories explaining their movements,[22] I propose to focus attention on Nigerian Yoruba communities in Dahomey/Benin and their shifting identities.

Having underlined the insufficiency of a strictly demographic approach, my aim is now to understand how these immigrants settled and organized themselves in Cotonou and Porto Novo, that is, the two major Benin towns where they are identified as foreigners or as of "Nigerian origin" by Benin citizens.

Cotonou has a fast-growing, cosmopolitan population—78,000 in 1961, 330,000 in 1979, and 536,827 in 1992—and it is a town in which foreign migrants seek security. This quest leads them to adapt their social needs to the environment. In recent decades, they wavered between a regional pan-Yoruba structure and hometown associations. Both existed at the time but they did not help in the same ways, nor did they have the same vitality. Despite their visibility, the pan-Yoruba groups and hometown subgroups should not overshadow the existence of other, smaller organizations. In addition, the discourse of community leaders about their own influence must be balanced by the point of view of informants of the same origin who are not necessarily registered with the hometown group or are not even interested in it.

This lack of interest in large hometown groups is obvious, to a lesser degree, in Porto Novo (64 000 inhabitants in 1961, 133,168 in 1979 and 179,138 in 1992). The sharp population increase has hidden the share of foreigners among migrants overall. Moreover, the usual rate in Africa of 60 percent growth in urban populations coming from rural-urban migration, which can explain the visibility of rural newcomers in towns, is not relevant with regard to most of the Nigerian Yoruba, who are already city dwellers and see themselves, according to interviews, as having been therefore rapidly integrated into Cotonou or Porto Novo.

Since the mid-twentieth century, Nigerian migrants who have settled in Cotonou and Porto Novo have been organized locally by a few immigrant leaders who retain links to their own Nigerian hometowns but whose influence may go beyond their hometown compatriots. Most of the newcomers have thus had to redefine their identities in Benin. One striking thing is the diversity of their shifting identity processes. On the one hand, the moment of migration, the policy of the Benin state toward Nigerians, the policy of the Nigerian embassy in Cotonou, the length of stay, and the cultural environment determine the forms and degree of integration into urban Benin society as well as the strengthening—or weakening—of individuals' ties with their hometowns. On the other hand, what is happening in Nigeria also shapes identity-building processes in Dahomey. The failure of the pan-Yoruba agenda of the Action Group (AG), the strengthening of urban-ethnic opposition to Awolowo from Ogbomoso, Modakeke, and Oyo in the 1950s and 1960s, and the split within the Oyo zone of influence with the demands for "independence" in Ibadan (late 1930s), in Osogbo (1980s–1990s), and in Ogbomoso (nowadays) in the context of state creation and the ethnicization of local politics in Nigeria appear to have had many consequences for the way in which emigrants have conceived their new identity.

First Attempts to Bring Together Yoruba Migrants

The Nigerian Yoruba Community and the
Nigerian Community Association in Cotonou

In the 1940s–60s, few Nigerian Yoruba were members of migrant groups or associations. Some Offa or Oyo individuals, for instance, met with others from their hometown, but there were no official city-based Yoruba organizations. The only official organization to unite migrants was the Nigerian Association of Cotonou (Association des Nigérians de Cotonou), whose president, a Hausa, was Alhadji Mudji Yawa.[23] This organization had neither monthly meetings nor even scheduled meetings. The president was responsible for the registration of migrants' names, which was required for obtaining "travel passes" from the British consulate. (No passport was then issued to British subjects of the colonial empire.)

In 1964, the Nigerian Community Association was officially created but it was not relevant in terms of self-identification for immigrants. The march to independence in Nigeria and independence itself influenced the way in which migrants organized themselves. The rivalry between the *Alàáfin* and the *Ooni* and between Akintola and Awolowo was also played out on the Benin scene. A more lively Nigerian Yoruba Community–Cotonou was thus created by Baba Oyo in Cotonou in 1964 as a substructure of the newly created Nigeria Community Association. The members of the Nigeria Community Association were then mostly Yoruba (40 people), Hausa (20 people), and Igbo (10/15 people), and the Yoruba individual, Baba Oyo, who had been a Yoruba community leader throughout the 1950s, was chosen as its leader of both associations.

When living in Savalou, Baba Oyo started out in 1932 as a petty trader in manufactured goods imported from Nigeria. He moved to Cotonou in 1940[24] and became a herbalist and "traditional doctor." When he settled in Cotonou, the individual migrants were isolated. In 1940, he bought a compound in Cotonou in the Gbebo-SCOA neighborhood. His house became an eight-room guesthouse where newcomers could obtain free accommodation for some months before being able to find their own way in Cotonou. Other people made it a habit of eating their daily meal there. Thus Baba Oyo's house became a well-known rallying point in Cotonou for Yoruba immigrants, mostly coming from Oyo Province.

Baba Oyo started to organize meetings in 1953–54, but people did not really start to attend until 1964. His Apapo Omo Yoruba (Gathering of Yoruba Sons) was still informal. The newly created regionally and nationally based organizations attracted newcomers. At that point, Baba Oyo appeared as a "natural" leader. Between 1965 and 1967, the *Alàáfin* three times sent Ali Kudefu, his *iledu,* the chief of his servants, to Baba Oyo in Cotonou. The aim was to bring together all the *Alàáfin*'s people to counterbalance the supposed influence of the *Ooni,* and Baba Oyo was asked to report his difficulties with the Dahomeyan authorities directly to Oyo.[25] Nevertheless, the Nigerian Yoruba Community–Cotonou created in 1964 by Baba Oyo was not strictly related to the *Alàáfin.* The community leadership was also based on family relations. Subordinated to Baba Oyo, the elected president of the Nigerian Yoruba Community in charge of administrative duties, Imam Gazali, had no personal ties with Oyo, but he married Alhadja Awao, Baba Oyo's sister. The aims of the Nigerian Yoruba Community–Cotonou in 1964 were not very different from what they are today: to help newly arrived Yoruba migrants, to encourage cooperation between Yoruba, to settle conflicts peacefully, and to ensure smooth relations with the Nigerian consulate in Cotonou and with the Benin police. By 1970, most of the one hundred Nigerian Yoruba living in Cotonou had joined the Nigerian Yoruba Community–Cotonou. This small group was overwhelmed because of the Biafran war (1967–70), during which Igbo fled in enormous numbers to Benin. The Nigeria Community Association, however, remained under the control of the Yoruba for a while.

The Porto Novo–Based Union of Nigerian Community in Dahomey

Before 1963, there existed a "Union of Nigerian Community in Dahomey" based in Porto Novo and headed by a Yoruba photographer from Ikorodu called "Ikorodu Photo." He is said to have registered the union around 1950. This pan-Yoruba structure did not survive its president's political involvement. Ikorodu Photo considered that his own origins linked him and his people to Ife and to the *Ooni.* This was unacceptable to the Oyo and the Ijebu of Porto Novo. In 1963, this disagreement led to the creation of the Osi Tiama (Ijebu Together). People from Saki, Abeokuta, Ilorin, and Ibadan eventually imitated the Ijebu and went their own way. All of them had to disband their organizations in 1972 during the Kérékou Revolution, when the new regime proscribed the expression of ethnicity. The early favor given in Porto Novo to strictly native, home-based organizations was later echoed in Cotonou. There, nonetheless, the home-based organizations coexisted with the pan-Yoruba group founded by Baba Oyo.

Well-Structured Groups in Cotonou: The Offa (Kwara State); Benin Citizenship Balanced by Fidelity to Hometowns

Among the Yoruba groups in Cotonou, the strongest organizations are the ones that are made up of immigrants who arrived in the 1960–80s and that are sometimes influenced by older, inherited associations. Most of their members are now Benin citizens, although the first immigrant generation retains a link with Nigeria. If they are now focused on the organization of a social life for members in their 60s or 70s, they still try to help newcomers despite the economic crisis. The Offa community as well as the Ede, Ogbomoso, and Ibadan, all being Oyo-related, are representative of these groups founded in the 1960s, victimized to some extent during the Kérékou regime and now imploding because of the deaths of their elders.[26] But something new keeps these associations alive: the process of ethnicization of local politics nourishes the renewed agenda of migrants' associations.

When the Offa immigrants choose to integrate fully into mainstream Benin society, it does not mean that references to their origins disappear. The strategy of the Offa people (Offa is now in Nigeria's Kwara State) is thus a synthesis of true integration into Benin society, notwithstanding their strong and permanently revitalized celebration of their ancestral city. While the Offa people in Cotonou chose overwhelmingly to become Benin citizens in the 1960s, Benin citizens of Offa origin as well as newcomers were invited to join the local Offa association.

The Iyeru Okin (The One Who Knows How to Fight) was the first Offa group. It was founded in the 1940s by M. Aladja.[27] His initial aim was to create in Cotonou a self-help network for poor Offa immigrants in order to help them find jobs. The association broadened its objectives in the 1950s and 1960s, welcoming any Offa descendants born in Benin in order to keep alive the links with their ancestral hometown. M. Aladja's son created and, until 1976, organized the Offa Progressive Union–Cotonou (OPU-C). Another community leader, Imam Lawani Yayi Bello, also became influential among the Offa during the 1960s, and his personal involvement in the Offa community as well as in Benin society is, when it comes to Offa integration, a case in point.

Imam Lawani Yayi Bello arrived in Dahomey in 1950. After a few years in Porto Novo, he settled in Cotonou. In 1960, he took Dahomeyan citizenship. He started to contribute to the organization of the Offa people in Dahomey by joining the OPU-C in 1962. He became the imam of the Central Mosque in Cotonou in 1968. As the son of a former *Olofa* of Offa, Oba Alebiosu, he was soon considered a "natural community leader." Lawani Yayi Bello, known in Offa as "Yayi Bello of Cotonou," spends several months in Offa every year and hopes he will one day be buried in Offa. His two eldest sons, both Benin citizens, have official positions in Benin, although they still attend Muslim ceremonies in Offa at least twice a year (during Ramadan and at New Year). Their life, however, is in Cotonou.

Because of strong links with their hometown, the Offa people who have become Benin nationals are reluctant to accept the control of the Egbe Omo Yoruba–Benin founded in 1972.[28] Although OPU-C has been a member of the Egbe Omo Yoruba–Benin (EOY-B) since its creation, the

OPU-C's president, Imam Lawani Yayi Bello, has always been anxious to remain independent. The last stage of the organization of the community was the creation of the Offa Descendants' Union (ODU), or Egbe Omo Offa, in Benin. Here again, the dual purpose of Offa community organizations—both integration into Benin society and fidelity to the hometown—was obvious, but a new international dimension was added. It started after a 1979 decision of the Offa Progressive Union in Offa to gather all its "sons and daughters" into a single association. The Offa Descendants' Union was founded in Nigeria, and foreign branches were asked to use the same name. The goal was to create an international network of Offa citizens in order to strengthen the Nigerian hometown in a context of ethnicization of local politics during the Nigerian Second Republic. In Benin, the move was opposed by the Kérékou regime.

The OPU in Benin was able to adopt the name Offa Descendants' Union only in 1989 with the collapse of the Marxist-Leninist regime. At the same time, a general meeting of the worldwide network of Egbe Omo Offa was held in Offa. Since then, a meeting has taken place every year between Christmas and New Year's Day. This meeting, which brings together the *Olofa* of Offa and Chief Emmanuel Adesoje, the president of ODU-Nigeria, is symptomatic of the growing ethnicization of Nigerian politics, including Yoruba politics, both at home and abroad. The former pan-Yoruba agenda is strongly challenged by parochial hometown identities. In 1999, to implement the Nigerian policy, the Offa Descendants' Union (ODU) or Egbe Omo Offa was re-founded in Djijé, a Cotonou neighborhood, and a huge meeting was held, with delegations of Offa people from across Benin. Nevertheless, local factors sometimes thwart policies that have been drawn up in Nigeria. The enhancement of a hometown identity is only possible when there are enough Yoruba from the same town. It is difficult to get precise figures from the books of the ODU in Cotonou because many members do not pay their fees regularly (there were 78 paid-up members in 1998–99 but only 26 in 2003). The association in Cotonou still registers new immigrants (88 between 1999 and 2005), which is a way of keeping alive its original purpose. But the Offa people in Cotonou are mainly Benin citizens now, despite a sincere commitment to maintaining their historical affiliation with their Nigerian hometown.

Local political factors can thus be obstacles to any worldwide pan-Offa movement. For more than ten years now, the five Benin branches of ODU have failed to agree on a common federal structure, because ODU-Cotonou and ODU-Porto Novo both want the central office to be located in their town. Regarding this resistance to ODU-Offa wishes, the balance between Offa people's local interests in Benin and the process of identity building in Nigeria may explain ODU's chief difficulties in formulating a clear policy. In Cotonou, ODU is now considered a social club of Benin citizens linked together by their Offa origin, rather than as an immigrant group. In a way, this affects the will to follow Nigerian policies. In Cotonou and Porto Novo, none of the leaders show any enthusiasm for giving up a leadership position that carries social weight among the Offa people in Benin and in Nigeria. Imam Yayi Bello has thus been able to impose his leadership regardless of official structures.

While unable to create a federated ODU for Benin, Imam Yayi Bello did oversee the creation of strong Offa community groups in five towns, all of which renamed themselves as ODU branches. Annual meetings are being organized in each of them: Cotonou (2001), Porto Novo (2002), Bantè (2003), Savé (2004), and Porto Novo (2005).[29] ODU leaders claimed about 1,000 members in Cotonou in 2005 despite the small number of paid-up members because of the economic crisis. ODU membership remains a significant building block when it comes to Offa identity, even though the weekly or monthly contribution (1,000 CFA francs per month per member in Cotonou) is often a matter of theory rather than practice (see table 11.2). The use of ODU-Cotonou's money and the speeches about the financial aims of ODU also betray the hesitations of its most important members. Paradoxically, although more integrated than ever into Benin, their main demand is to contribute to development in Offa. The speeches contrast with the modest amounts (ODU-Benin, 15,000 CFA francs; ODU-Cotonou, 60,000 CFA francs) given in 1999 to the Nigerian Offa Descendants' Union, which is nonetheless regarded as a strong symbolic link, by Offa descendants in Cotonou. In 1999, a special contribution of 8,000 CFA francs from ODU-Cotonou was sent to Offa for a football pitch. At the same time, gifts for marriages or baptisms, payments for the expenses of administrative correspondence with the Nigerian embassy, and transport fees for delegates to Offa, Porto Novo, and Savé remain important.

There is one way in particular in which the aims of ODU-Cotonou are clearly different from those of the initial self-help association. The community is no longer in charge of emergencies. Age groups or neighborhood groups made up of Offa workers or traders have taken over "solidarity": one of them brings together twenty-five traders who contribute 2,500 CFA francs every two weeks for use in an *esusu* arrangement; the total amount is then handed over to one of the members. Participants take turns in collecting the money.

With a growing and permanent Offa community in Cotonou, the welcoming of immigrants is now a matter for their own families. The Offa are probably the best-organized community of Nigerian Yoruba origin in Cotonou. They are not living in specific neighborhoods. But one can find them mostly around Djijé, the Misebo market, and the Zongo Mosque. The community is still made up of immigrants—about twenty newcomers every year, according to community leaders—but most are now Benin-born "Offa sons and daughters." Offa women constitute almost half of the community. Street vendors for decades, Offa people sell a wide variety of items in Cotonou markets, including spare parts for cars, secondhand clothing, and food.

Table 11.2. Income and expenditures of the Offa Descendants' Union in Cotonou

Year	Income[a]	Expenditures[a]
1997	28,250	11,000
1998	33,750	35,200[b]
1999	87,700	32,150
2000	7,500	—[c]
2003	19,500	—

Source: ODU-Cotonou, "Cahier de comptes" for 1997, 1998, 1999, 2000, 2003, and 2005.
[a] In CFA francs.
[b] The difference is accounted for by a private gift of 28,500 CFA francs.
[c] There were no expenditures between 2000 and 2005, according to the vice president.

Regarding its integration into Benin, the community is very proud of some of its members. Some Offa people fought for the independence of Dahomey: Mouibi Adeoti, Adeati Ibrahim (in Cotonou), and Mustapha Babata (in Porto Novo). The successful integration of Offa people into Benin is personified by a former justice minister, Tidjani Serpos, who has been justice minister, attorney general, and Wassi Mouftaou, a former vice president then president of Benin's Chamber of Commerce and Industry from 1993 to 2002. At the same time, 2005 was a year of consecration. Cotonou welcomed a worldwide meeting of Offa descendants' unions under the chairmanship of Emmanuel O. Adesoje, the president of ODU's worldwide network. The *Olofa* of Offa, Oba Mustapha Olawore Olanipekun II (who has reigned since 1970), came with followers, among them local government chairmen and Dr. Bukola Saraki, the Peoples Democratic Party (PDP) governor of Kwara State, in a convoy of twenty-four cars. Nonetheless, not all Yoruba migrants' associations in Benin have managed to shift through the decades in such a way as to achieve a balance between local and Nigerian allegiances. In many other cases, the shifts in identity-building processes have led to deep conflicts.

A Period of Trouble and Insecurity, 1972 to the Present

Geo-Ethnic Organizations Banned

The Kérékou regime discouraged the expression of geo-ethnic claims among the inhabitants of Benin. Its policy toward migrant associations followed the same lines without, however, any strict or permanent ban on regional or local gatherings. In those arbitrary and unpredictable times, Baba Oyo sought the support of the *Alàáfin,* who sent his chief messenger, Ali Kudefu, to advise Baba Oyo not to call for any formal Yoruba meetings. During the dictatorship, the interference of Kérékou in Nigerian Yoruba Community affairs was important. Either to play the peacemaker or to set the rules, Kérékou was kept informed of the daily life of the Nigerian community. When Iman Gazali was chief of the Cotonou imams as well as the president of the Nigerian Yoruba Community, his authority, backed by Baba Oyo, was clearly established among the Oyo Yoruba, who always asked him to settle internal disputes. A succession crisis arose when Imam Gazali died in June 1977. Alhadji Mouïbi Bello from Ogbomoso, Alhadji Yayi Bello from Offa, and Alhadji Baba Oyo were all strong candidates. Kérékou was thus given the opportunity to choose the leader of the Nigerian Yoruba Community in Cotonou. After three meetings with Baba Oyo, he called Baba Oyo's elder son, Alhadji Aziz Lassisi Rufaï Ogbalajobi, Ibrahim Adewumi and M. Aminu, youth representatives, the three candidates, and some Igbo and Hausa leaders to a meeting at the Presidential Palace. The meeting was attended by four ministers (the ministers of home affairs, foreign affairs, and defense, and the vice president).

Kérékou let them know his wish to see Baba Oyo appointed as the Yoruba leader as well as the leader of all Nigerians in Cotonou, that is, of the Nigerian Community Association (NCA). The "choice" was validated by Yoruba and Nigerians. The subgroups of the NCA had to merge. In other words, no specific public meeting of a Yoruba subgroup was supposed to be held after 1977, and no ethno-regional association was allowed to exist. Yoruba migrants in Dahomey were to meet only privately, dealing with their embassy in Cotonou through unofficial leaders.

The Kérékou Regime and Reorganization in the 1980s

Although no change was made in the law under Kérékou, his position regarding foreign ethnic movements changed slightly in the 1980s. Some groups did not even complain of his regime. The Ede, for instance, were always able to organize their own meetings; they note only that their travels to Nigeria were limited (this was due to the visa system). Initial attempts to set up their own organizations were not discouraged after the Hausa and Igbo became free of Baba Oyo's authority. In the beginning of the 1980s both groups named their own community leaders. They remained members of the Nigerian Community Association (NCA), whose presidency rotated every five years among the three subgroups (Hausa, Yoruba, Igbo). The arrangement was still the same in 2005, but the relevance of the NCA had been greatly weakened. Baba Oyo occupied the position of NCA president from 1980 to 1985. He was succeeded by the chief imam of the Zongo Mosque, Mama Yàro from Kano (from 1985 to 1990), and then by an Igbo trader, M. Okafo-Okere (from 1990 to 1995).[30]

The Yoruba were able to reorganize themselves despite official policy. The tougher government policy, however, sometimes led to crises. The late 1970s constituted a turning point in the history of the Nigerian Yoruba in Cotonou. The Ede people decided to split off from the EOY-Benin. With internal rivalries among the Ede, Alhadji Aburamane then created a sub-group of Ede sons with headquarters in his own Jericho house. A majority of the Ede followed another leader, Ogodi, who had settled in Cotonou in 1987. Other groups also challenged Baba Oyo's authority. The 1980s paved the way for hometown-based meetings as well as a monthly pan-Yoruba meeting headed by an ever weaker Baba Oyo.

Nevertheless, Nigerian associations were viewed with suspicion. During the Kérékou dictatorship, unofficial Offa meetings were organized by Ibrahim Adeoti, then president of OPU-C, in Zongo, a Cotonou neighborhood. But community life along ethno-regional lines was still officially proscribed, and it was thus difficult for Offa people as Benin citizens to maintain a link with their hometowns. Travelers to Nigeria needed visas from the police. The Kérékou police arrested five Offa elders in a private meeting (although they were released the same evening). On the evening of August 16, 1987, Kérékou sent four policemen to arrest some Yoruba leaders who were holding a meeting (without authorization) in Baba Oyo's house. Baba Oyo himself, Alabi Olubi from Ilorin, Alhadji Bello, Baba Banku from Ogbomoso, and Baba Lassisi from Saki were detained. It quickly became clear that the regime had nothing to fear from this meeting of elders, but everybody understood that the community was under surveillance. The 1988 visit of the *Alàáfín* to Cotonou improved the relations between the Yoruba communities and the regime, but the decisions of the regime were still arbitrary.

Democratization in Benin Boosts Ethnicity among the Yoruba

After political arbitrariness had enhanced their authority, when democracy was established in Benin, Baba Oyo and the Egbe Omo Yoruba–Cotonou (EOY-C) were even more challenged.[31] The end of the antiethnic policy gave the different subgroups (Ilorin, Ede, Ijebu-Epe, Ogbomoso, Osogbo, and even Oyo) the opportunity to organize and to revert to their hometown identities, which had never really been forgotten. Although many had been living in Cotonou or Porto Novo for decades, they still considered themselves Nigerian Yoruba. They continued to come together along hometown-based but also generational lines. The democratization process that began in 1989 allowed references to the ancestral city, and such references have since then been clearly promoted.

The collapse of the Egbe Omo Yoruba–Benin (EOY-B) reveals the impact of internal Nigerian expectations and the ethnicization of politics on emigrant communities. Even the Oyo were reluctant to merge with other groups, asking for their own specific meetings. Instead of poorly attended general assemblies of the Yoruba community, Baba Oyo preferred to convene meetings with delegations of two representatives of each of the different subgroups. This strategy revealed widespread dissatisfaction with the federal Yoruba organization but allowed Baba Oyo to appear as the Yoruba leader in Cotonou until his death—especially when Nigerian presidents Murtala Muhammed, Obasanjo, Buhari, Shagari, and Babangida visited Benin.

In Porto Novo, the small Yoruba community never recovered from the 1970s ban on hometown groups, and the economic crisis in the 1980s discouraged further immigration. Since the 1970s, all the Nigerian groups in Porto Novo have been headed by Hausa traders. With the growth of their community in the 1990s, the Yoruba were able to regain a specific organization regardless of hometown origins. In 1996, the Nigerian Association of Porto Novo split into three, and between ten and twenty Yoruba elected Kasumu Gafari as their president. In 1999, an unusual experience was initiated when an attempt was made to strengthen Yoruba transborder relations as well as relations between the large number of precolonial Yoruba migrants and the small number of recently arrived migrants. It was the second attempt to do this, after the 1964 failure of a similar policy. The association of Nigerian Yoruba migrants in Porto Novo promoted the coronation of an Oyo-born *oba* in Porto Novo. He was crowned but never received any formal recognition. Obviously, this attempt, which had its origins in Oyo, was seen as a foreign initiative and was not welcomed by the Benin Yoruba *collectivités* of Porto Novo. It was, however, at least a sign of the ability of Yoruba migrants to adapt their integration strategies according to their needs.

Among the migrant groups that have strengthened their identity recently, in contradiction to the tradition suggested by their Oyo historical background, the Ogbomoso proceeded in almost the same manner as the Offa. They mainly became Benin citizens. But their need to achieve visibility as Ogbomoso natives in Benin has grown recently and is strongly related to Nigerian political events. The former almost invisible Omo Ogbomoso became the Ogbomoso Parapo in the 1970s despite Kérékou's ban on geo-ethnic associations. Its leader, Alpha Yessufu Mouibi, who died in November 1998, had been in Cotonou since 1957. He was a Muslim preacher, the first teacher of Arabic language in Cotonou, and headmaster of a *mahad*, the Institut d'enseignement arabique islamique, in Aidjedo, a ward of Cotonou. His school was financially supported by the *Soun* of Ogbomoso as well as the Ogbomoso Parapo (at 20,000/25,000 CFA francs per year). Nevertheless there was a difference between the agendas of the Offa and Ogbomoso people. For years, the latter hesitated to insist on their foreign origins because they were afraid of the xenophobia some of them had experienced in the Ivory Coast in the 1950s. The feeling of belonging to the hometown community did exist, but most of the oldest men (80–90 years old) of the Ogbomoso Parapo were reluctant to oppose Baba Oyo, whose seniority could not be challenged according to this generation due to his historical role in Cotonou and his relation to Oyo kings. Moreover, almost 100 percent of them were Benin citizens and saw no need to claim a foreign origin, such as Ogbomoso. As former Oyo Empire subjects, they have been living for decades under the protection of Baba Oyo. The Ogbomoso recognized the authority of Baba Oyo who, at the same time, gave them a sign of respect through the following agreement: Alhadji Latifou Bello-Isola, one of the closest friends of Alpha Yessufu, became the treasurer of the EOY-Benin and its vice president in 1989.[32]

At the beginning of the 1990s, a move began that led to a strong demand for recognition by the Ogbomoso people in Benin. Several factors pushed in that direction, factors both of Benin and Nigerian origin. First, the democratization in Benin allowed the creation of movements and associations without restriction. Due to his age, Alpha Yessufu Mouibi had not been able to impose his influence on the young newcomers, and the Ogbomoso identity successfully challenged Oyo control. The political crisis in Nigeria after June 12, 1993, as a result of the nullification of the results of the general election by the military, and its economic aftermath led to an increase in Nigerian immigration in all the studied communities. Newcomers aware of the identity struggle in the western Yoruba states were eager to be recognized as Ogbomoso people, and the middle-aged generation, even those who held Benin citizenship, shared these views.

In 1999, the Ogbomoso Parapo treasurer, M. Bakany,[33] could thus declare that he was "an Ogbomoso from Sakété" with no need to be affiliated with the EOY-B and the Nigerian embassy. Yessufu Abdul Jalili, thirty-five years old in 1999, who succeeded his father as headmaster of the *mahad*, proudly asserts his Ogbomoso origins although he has been to his ancestors' town only three times. He does not deny being a Yoruba but does not see any *raison d'être* for the Egbe Omo Yoruba–Benin (EOY-B) of Ibrahim Adewumi, who became president of the EOY-Benin in 1999 with the support of the Nigerian embassy when Baba Oyo died. The illness and death of Baba Oyo weakened the domination of the Oyo over the Yoruba community in Cotonou. Ibrahim Adewumi, despite his royal origin in Iree, was not able to inherit Baba Oyo's prestige and was unable to keep everybody together. Many young community leaders, regardless of their local identities, criticized his personal ambitions.

The strengthening of Ogbomoso identity among the Nigerian Yoruba of Cotonou was also related to Nigerian political events for another reason:

with the demands for a new state with its headquarters in Ogbomoso, all "sons and daughters" were mobilized to finance the lobbying. The *Alàáfin* of Oyo understood the danger. He used an unofficial representative in Cotonou to bring the Ogbomoso people back into the EOY-B. This representative, Chief Majeobaje Olofindji Akande, "vizir" of the Cotonou-based and UNDP-financed NGO called Africa Culture, tried to avoid a split in 1998 after the death of the old leader. The *Soun* of Ogbomoso, himself in conflict with the *Alàáfin* because of his demands for a new state, encouraged his people to achieve their independence. Following Adewumi's semi-failure to keep the Cotonou Ogbomoso people under Oyo control, the embassy in Cotonou officially recognized the Ogbomoso Parapo, which was already registered by the Benin Home Affairs Ministry. In the case of the Ogbomoso, in less than ten years we have seen a real invention of an expatriated identity disconnected from the Oyo.

Immigration in the 1990s Does Not Rely on the Old Groups

The invention of an identity and the rejection of a former one have not always been the result of a political agenda. Economic crisis and local issues in the 1990s led some of the Yoruba immigrants to cease relying on old groups. Among the very young newcomers, precariousness was greater than in the past. Finding places to live and looking for food proved hard, and working conditions were poor. Instead of relying on big institutionalized groups, immigrants preferred age groups or professional groups of smaller size, informally organized but of course still based on friendship among people of same-town origin, sometimes with family connections. In these immigrants' case, relations with the hometowns are stronger, because their migration is still considered temporary. Although they are too poor to go back often to Nigeria, they nourish a strong consciousness of being, say, Ogbomoso or Ibadan or Ede people. The age of the migrants and their poverty keep them away from groups where monthly or weekly contributions (even if these are only symbolic) are collected. The young migrants rely on small groups (of four or eight members) in which membership is initially limited to self-help and socialization. They are still anxious to get recognition from their *oba* and their hometown and therefore participate in festivals such as Ede Day or Ogbomoso Day, which are recently invented celebrations.

This independence from old structured groups is nourished by skepticism with regard to personal rivalries between the new leaders who try to succeed people like Baba Oyo. The generation gap is the main reason why newcomers forge their own path. In such a situation, the Nigerian Yoruba Association, providing consular assistance and official protection, is the only organization they deal with. The newcomers' behavior also reflect, in Cotonou, the increasing ethnicization of politics at a parochial level in Nigeria. Nevertheless there is no open opposition to the bigger organizations. Simply, the small groups now provide solidarity, job opportunities, and accommodation. The others maintain memories of the hometown. The former groups complement the latter and the remaining gap between them is mainly due to age differences and years of residence.

Conclusion

Obviously, for the oldest migrants, the proximity of Nigeria does not lead Nigerian Yoruba people in Cotonou or Porto Novo to favor the idea of a definitive return to their hometown, but their Benin citizenship is still most of the time counterbalanced by a strong feeling of belonging to their hometown. Speeches clearly betray this ambivalence. The degree of integration of a community into Benin society has depended on a variety of factors. Some personalities played a major role in the shaping of the collective behavior of their countrymen. They were looked on as "elders"; for years, partly because of the dictatorship in Benin, their authority was not challenged and their personal houses were community meeting points.

Length of stay in Benin has also shaped the structure of the different groups. The elders have mostly been Benin citizens while the younger migrants are not, but the death of the elders in recent years has disorganized the communities and changed the landmarks for all individuals. Most of the young migrants, as well as some elders' descendants who may be Benin citizens, are anxious to enhance their hometown identities and to contribute to the development of the hometowns. Although confronted by economic difficulties, from these lively identities they achieve solidarity with their countrymen. Apart from local factors and personal strategies, this enhancement of native hometown identities is definitely a consequence of the ever-stronger hometown-based identity in Nigeria during the last thirty years. During the second half of the twentieth century, from the Nigeria-based progressive unions to the "Association des ressortissants de . . ." in French or the "Egbe Omo . . ." in Yoruba, several generations of associations have taken charge, at different levels, of these processes of identity building. Despite apparent commonalities, these processes have been of varied nature, even though they have all contributed to the ever-more parochial agenda of emigrants today.

Notes

1.   See Jean-Luc Martineau, *Oba et constructions identitaires dans l'espace yoruba nigérian (début XXe–1966)* (thesis, Université Paris 7–Denis Diderot, 2004).

2.   Southeastern Dahomey (now the Republic of Benin) has a substantial Yoruba population, but it has no consequences on the subject of that paper. The Yoruba Benin citizens are mainly rural people. In Porto Novo, where some of them settled during the nineteenth century, the Yoruba *collectivités* (extended families) come from the Oyo and Ibadan empires; their Dahomeyan citizenship is old enough not to be questionable and the question of their Nigerian origins does not have the same implications in terms of identity as for the Nigerian newcomers. According to all the interviews, their relations with the Nigerian Yoruba migrants have therefore been very limited. These migrants have always been considered as foreigners. They behaved as the Hausa or the Igbo did, sometime together in the same associations. The 1999 Oyo initiative aiming at installing a Nigerian *oba* in Porto Novo failed in the first decade of the twenty-first century due to indifference and lack of support on the part of the Porto Novo Yoruba.

3.   The country was named Dahomey (before independence, which was achieved on August 1, 1960, and up to 1975), the Popular Republic of Benin (November 30, 1975, to 1990), and the Republic of Benin (after March 1, 1990). In this chapter, the country will be called Benin after 1960.

4.   The Okoro family from Ejigbo in Abidjan provide a dynamic example of such a group from the 1950s onward.

5.   The fieldwork took place in 1995, 1999, and 2005.

6.   Jean-Luc Martineau, "Communautés yoruba et réseaux de solidarité et d'entraide face aux incertitudes des grandes agglomérations du sud béninois et du sud-ouest nigérian aux XIXe et XXe siècles: L'identité locale comme garantie de sécurité en ville, une idée récente," in *Sécurité, crime et ségrégation dans les villes d'Afrique de l'Ouest du XXe siècle à nos jours,* ed. Laurent Fourchard and I. Olawale Alberts, 395–415 (Paris and Ibadan: Karthala-IFRA, 2003).

7.   S. A. Akintoye, *Revolution and Power Politics in Yorubaland, 1840–1893: Ibadan Expansion and the Rise of Ekitiparapo* (Ibadan: Longman, 1971), xviii–xix.

8.   David D. Laitin, *Hegemony and Culture: Politics and Religious Change among the Yoruba* (Chicago: University of Chicago Press, 1986).

9.   I will not use the term "Yorubaland," in order not to appear to approve the idea of an old, preexisting Yoruba political entity as referred to by nationalists in the 1940s–60s. I prefer to use neutral geographical terminology that dissociates the vocabulary of politicians from that of academics. This allows me to speak of an attempt to create a "Yorubaland" in the 1930s–60s, making clear that the geographical entity was not automatically predestined to become a pan-Yoruba political unit.

10.   Aderanti Adepoju, "Migration and Socio-economic Links between Urban Migrants and Their Home Communities in Nigeria," *Africa* (London) 44, no. 4 (1974): 383–96; *Deuxième recensement général de la population et de l'habitation, février 1992,* vol. 2, tome 1, *Répartition spatiale, migration et structure par âge, mars 1994* (Cotonou, Republic of Benin: Bureau Central du Recensement, Institut National de la Statistique et de l'Analyse Economique (INSAE), Ministère du Plan et de la Restructuration Économique, 1994), 91.

11.   The materials held in the Archives nationales in Porto Novo and the National Archives in Ibadan do not allow us to arrive at any interpretation. This may be due to the marginal position of border areas, which were percieved to be of negligible economic and political value. Only one point is clear: whenever the question

of the border arose, administrative officers quickly went back to what they obviously thought were more important affairs.

12.   Archives nationales, Porto Novo, Série E: Affaires politiques (5 E: Relations extérieures).

13.   *Deuxième recensement général de la population et de l'habitation, février 1992*, vol. 2, tome 1, *Répartition spatiale, migration et structure par âge, mars 1994*, 84.

14.   Archives nationales, Porto Novo, Série E: Affaires politiques (1 E: Politique générale, rapports politiques, 2 E: Politique indigène, commendement indigene, 3 E: Cultes, 4 E: Politique musulmane, 5 E: Relations extérieures); Série F: Police et prisons (1 F: Etrangers et Police des frontières) ; Sous-série 5 D: Recensements 1914, 1949, 1952, 1957 ; Série S: Travail, main d'oeuvre. It is difficult to appreciate the volume of the migrations and transborder movements to Dahomeyan towns that started again after World War II. Files on legal and illegal trade movements, market women, and criminal cases are the only ones to mention Nigerians migrating to Dahomey. Regional origins, however, are not mentioned. Private archives and interviews are the main sources of information. The information I have used in this chapter was collected in 1995 and 1999 and completed during a two-month visit in July–August 2005. The French colonial archives (in Porto Novo and Aix-en-Provence) as well as the British ones (the Nigerian National Archives, Ibadan [NNAI], and the Public Record Office [PRO], Kew, London) are quite disappointing on the subject of Nigerians migrating to Dahomey. *Deuxième recensement général de la population et de l'habitation, février 1992*, vol. 2, tome 1, *Répartition spatiale, migration et structure par âge, mars 1994*, 120-21.

15.   A total of 29,525 non-Benin citizens were officially registered as immigrants (1987–91) in the Census of February 1992. The census registered returning Benin citizens as "external immigrants" (62.1 percent). As far as settlement strategies are concerned, the census does not distinguish between Benin citizens and foreigners. Even though we can presume that the Nigerian Yoruba mainly settled in Cotonou, this cannot be verified.

16.   K. Julien Guingnido Gaye, *Croissance urbaine, migrations et population au Bénin* (Paris: Les études du CEREP no. 5—UEPA, December 1992).

17.   Interviews with Iman Yayi (Offa), Cotonou, 1999, and Lawani Yayi Bello (Offa), Cotonou, 2005.

18.   *Deuxième recensement général de la population et de l'habitation, février 1992*, vol. 1, *Résultats définitifs, Principaux tableaux, décembre 1993*, and vol. 2, tome 1, *Répartition spatiale, migration et structure par âge, mars 1994* (Cotonou: Bureau Central du Recensement, INSAE, Ministère du Plan et de la Restructuration Économique, 1993 and 1994).

19.   *Deuxième recensement général de la population et de l habitation, février 1992*, vol. 2, tome 1, *Répartition spatiale, migration et structure par âge, mars 1994*, 132-33.

20.   There was nothing in particular to attract newcomers to Benin, owing to the economic situation.

21.   Kolawolé Sikirou Adam and Michel Boko, *Le Benin* (Paris-Cotonou: Edicef-Sodimas, 1983).

22.   See M. P. Toraro, *Internal Migration in Developing Countries, A Review of Theory, Evidence, Methodology and Research Priorities* (Geneva: ILO, 1976) or the works of Victor Piché.

23.   Interview with Alhadji Aziz Lalemi from Otta (Ogun State), Porto Novo, 1999. Alhadji Lalemi left Nigeria when he was sixteen years old, and lived in Cotonou (1952–66), Kumasi (1966–69), Otta (1969–73), Cotonou (1973–83), and Porto Novo (1983–99). In Kumasi, he was an active member of the Western State Yoruba Association, whose president was also president of the local Egba Descendants Union, which had 200 members. Alhadji Aziz Lalemi was general secretary of the Yoruba Association of Kumasi.

24.   According to a nonfamily informant (1999), Baba Oyo spent eleven years in Kumasi (1933–44) before settling in Savalou in 1944 and settling in Cotonou only in 1958. Various family sources seem more reliable.

25.   Interview with Alhadji Aziz Lassisi Rufaï Ogbalajobi, elder son of Baba Oyo, Cotonou, 2005.

26.   From interviews, it seems that the individualism of newcomers and the economic weakness of the descendants of the first migrants are probably the reasons why nobody is able or willing to assume the leadership of migrant communities. The respect due to former leaders among the migrants did not survive the emergence of ambitious individuals who do not have the same prestige. Former community associations can be seen to have outlived their usefulness when young migrants seek support from various other institutions or groups (mosques, youth groups, families, or illegal organizations).

27.   Alhadja Mrs. Elelubo, born in Offa, seems to have had great influence in the community too. She is said to have been the first Offa citizen to move into Misebo, a ward of Cotonou. She married an Ilorin man and all her children were born in Dahomey. She is said to have died at 143 in 2002 and her funerals in Offa are still remembered.

28.   The EOY-B was created in 1972. It is the new name of the Nigerian Yoruba Community in Cotonou, although its name could let the people believe that it is a Benin-wide organization. When it was created in 1972, it was indeed intended to gather all the Nigerian Yoruba living in different towns of Benin. But because of individual rivalries and difficulties to meet it remained mainly a group of Yorubas living in Cotonou. Despite these difficulties there has been since then permanent attempts to create this unique structure.

29.   Although these meetings were organized, no permanent common body with one president and one chairman was created gathering all ODU of Benin. Each local group being connected to the central ODU in Nigeria, local ODU in Porto Novo or Savé does not see the need of a Benin-wide structure.

30.   In 1985, the easterners seem to have had difficulties in appointing one of their members as president when they were supposed to take over. Alabi Olibi, a Yoruba from Ilorin, was president from 1995 to 2000; he was succeeded by a Hausa, Ousmane Balla (2000–2005). In May 2005, with Anambra, Imo, and Edo candidates, the easterners could not agree on a name and the Nigerian embassy in Cotonou asked the Yoruba to propose a candidate.

31.   EOY-C, formerly Akpapo Omo Yoruba, then Nigerian Yoruba Community Cotonou, formed in 1964 by Baba Oyo, was renamed EOY-C in 1972 as a section of the EOY-Benin.

32.   Interview with Alhadji Latifou Bello-Isola, Cotonou, 1999.

33.   Interview with M. Bakany, Cotonou, 1999.

12

Identity, "Foreign-ness," and the Dilemma of Immigrants at the Coast of Kenya

Interrogating the Myth of "Black Arabs" among Kenyan Africans

Maurice N. Amutabi

Introduction

The aim of this study is threefold. First, it is a reevaluation of ethnicity and identity at the coast of Kenya, focusing on the false identity of "Black Arabs" that has been invented among the Swahili people of the coast of Kenya.[1] The study reveals that while there is a copious collection of cultural and social histories with strong indications of ethnic tensions in Kenya, the coast of Kenya has often been seen as homogenous and cohesive. Studies have privileged the records of descendants of Arabs and Muslim archival and written sources, while ignoring the everyday experiences of descendants of Africans and their role in defining their identity and historical processes. My contention is that the ordinary voices of African folk have not found their way into historical studies at the coast of Kenya.

Second, through a discussion of the way people define themselves, the study seeks to throw light on how identity has increasingly become fluid and flexible, creating new multicultural and hybrid threads that are highly visible in the urban areas at the coast of Kenya. I believe that addressing these critical issues of cultural identity is pivotal at a time when we can see deepening patterns of cultural balkanization and all kinds of violence—a product of the uncertainty precipitated by the proliferation of difference as a consequence of globalization. The objective is to affirm that contrary to previous studies, which have embellished, valorized, and sanitized the dominant Swahili coastal culture as fixed, static, and unchanging, there has been a great deal of hybridity and multiculturalism that has been added to the Swahili culture through the diffusion of mainly African ideas and that has not been interrogated.

Third, the study problematizes Arabism, Islam, and "foreign-ness" at the coast of Kenya and their role in defining Swahili identity, using a historical trajectory. A commonly held view is that the ethnic identity of the Swahili and the majority of the people of the coast of Kenya is unproblematic and that the Swahili culture has been a harmonious endeavor benefiting from the activities of a nonracial or nonhegemonic society over many years. I contend that the African element in Swahili culture has often been downplayed. I argue that even the Swahili culture's greatest legacy to the region, the Kiswahili language, is not without hegemonic and patronizing tendencies attendant on the tensions between its speakers and the various dialects that they speak. Using historical trajectories, I affirm that the traumatic memories of slavery have largely mediated the social, cultural, and political processes of the coast of Kenya. The trauma has worked to divest former slaves and the less dominant groups of their identities and redeployed these within the societal institutions under the social control of the dominant groups—Arabs and Africans claiming Arab descent. There is also ample evidence to suggest that foreign scholars, perhaps unknowingly, have aided Arabs in furthering their schema of isolating and denying the legacy of Africans in the identity of the Swahili.

Thus, many studies have examined the Kiswahili language and "Swahiliness" as an identity without paying due attention to its highly politicized origins. This is simply erroneous, because the Kiswahili language was spread with a certain agenda, mainly for Arab traders and Muslim proselytizers in the region. It is only in the recent past that scholars have started to purge Swahili culture of its exaggeratedly Arab and Muslim origins. I believe that the very broad territorial domain of Swahili people and the Kiswahili language and its increasing vocabulary constantly calls for new questions concerning possession and appropriation. The fact that Kiswahili has expanded beyond its native speakers (the coastal belt of eastern Africa) means that being Swahili is not necessarily a fixed attribute.

My discussion is based on postcolonial and postmodern theoretical frameworks in which heterogeneity, multiculturalism, and hybridity are increasingly emerging as acceptable forms of identity.[2] I believe that addressing these critical issues of identity in the migration history of Kenya is pivotal at a time when there are deepening patterns of cultural balkanization, race, and ethnicity and what Friedrich Nietzsche called "ressentiment" (resentment) or the practice in which one defines one's identity through the negation of the other—a product of the uncertainty precipitated by the proliferation of difference as a consequence of scarce resources and globalization. Thus, it is clear that people have manipulated their racial and ethnic identity at the coast of Kenya for political and economic survival. So the idea of "Black Arabs" among the people of the coast of Kenya should be seen as a way of negotiating social change and a form of hybridity. Arabism and Islam are useful sites for recovering past hegemonic relationships, and for understanding the nature of the oppositional binary of "us" and "them" between those of Arab ancestry and those of African ancestry. In other words, Arabism and Islam have been used in constructing "otherness" and entrenching a process of segregation.

Thus, this chapter faults the ways in which ethnic identity has been studied in Kenya, using the Swahili as a case study. It carefully interrogates this phenomenon at the coast of Kenya, using experiential views, songs and poetry, works of art, interviews, and textual historical materials. Interviews are particularly important, as they have not previously been subjected to scholarly interpretation and interlocutory discourse. Thus, through interviews, I deploy memory through believable remembering, for memory is not just a passive repository of facts about the past but also an active process of accurately reciting and rescripting the past. I use memory to create meanings and deploy them in the rewriting of the past of the coast of Kenya. I debunk old ideas and rewrite the history of the people based on interviews, in a way rescripting the subscript. Rescripting, as the oral interviews reveal, seeks to make life stories coherent and believable, as against previous notions, which have tended to ignore such alternative sources of information on the history of the coast, preferring instead to focus on the majority and mainstream sources that are dominated by Muslim and Arab agency. In what follows, I problematize the ways in which ethnicity, cultural identity, cultural difference, and cultural community have been addressed at the coast of Kenya in these times of rapid globalizing change, where hybridity and multiculturalism are becoming critical.

Locating Self in the Discourse on Identity

I first lived at the coast of Kenya as a child in the 1970s, at Mombasa, when my father, a civil servant, worked there. At that time, as at present, civil servants were often moved to different parts of the country from time to time. As a family, we always accompanied my father wherever he went on his tours of duty throughout Kenya. Before arriving in Mombasa, I had already traveled to many other parts of Kenya. The frequent transfers were quite traumatic to us as children. I did not like the frequent movements because they meant leaving many friends behind. When I was a child, the movements troubled me, in fact distressed me, as each time we moved I had to go to a new school and make new relationships all over again. Being new was not easy, especially in dealing with bullies and establishing a rapport with people.

I was quick at making friends, but it bothered me to realize that I would be leaving them not long afterward. I had left friends in Nairobi, Kisumu, Kakamega, Eldoret, and every other place my father had worked, but Mombasa was different. This was the first place where I was treated as an alien in my own country, and it bothered me. Everyone that was not from the coast was referred to as *mwanabara* (up-country person; plural, *wanabara*) and it was repeated to us everywhere, all the time. The Kiswahili spoken at the coast is different from the Kiswahili spoken by "up-country" (inland or interior) Africans (mainly Bantu groups such as Mijikenda). I wondered why we were "othered" or segregated on account of our dialect or accent when speaking Kiswahili (Kenya's national language) that was slightly different from that of the people in Mombasa. There was also the common connection between speaking "good Kiswahili" and being Arab or *chotara* (people of mixed race, usually as a result of intermarriage). Some of the people who segregated us were not even Kenyans but Arab immigrants to Mombasa and their descendants. I knew that some of my classmates claimed to have Arab blood in order to belong. Invoking Arab ancestry automatically earned you immunity from isolation, and indeed many of my classmates did make such claims in order to belong. Some of our tormentors were not even Arab themselves, but their skins appeared lighter. These were the so-called "Black Arabs" or "Black Persians" who are an expanding group at the coast of Kenya. Whereas this is quite normal in contemporary multicultural discourses on identity and the new forms of identity such as hybridity, what bothered me was that the movers of the ideas that led to these identities at the coast of Kenya were Arabs who positioned themselves as high priests and gatekeepers to "Swahili-ness" and a proper Kiswahili accent. They appropriated the agency and terms of belonging. It was claimed that people of African descent did not speak proper Kiswahili. At the market, at school, in the residential areas, on the beaches, this was repeated as soon as you opened your mouth to speak Kiswahili. The emphasis was that you did not belong. To speak English was even worse, for you were called *kibaraka* (colonial agent).

There was solidarity among coastal people of Arab descent and their "Arabized clique" around their appropriation of *Kiswahili sanifu* (correct Kiswahili) against the "up-country" folk like us. This bothered a lot of people from up-country, and many started to mimic the local accent, in order to be accepted as *wamwambao* (coastal folk) and escape the *wanabara* label. After a year, my siblings and I had started to speak Kiswahili with a coastal accent, and in fact started to belong. I have often wondered whether we changed our accents in order to belong, or if the effort was unconscious, although forced on us. Our parents never even made an effort to speak with the coastal accent. I later realized why they were reluctant to pick up the local accent; it was because we were soon headed back up-country. *Bara* (up-country) provided a surprise for us when we arrived at Eldoret, my father's new station. It was our turn to be segregated by the up-country folk as *wam-wambao*. We were now regarded as hybrids. Even though the label was a privileging one, as everyone thought my siblings and I spoke Kiswahili better for having lived at the coast and constantly consulted us, it was a devastating indictment of the cultural harmony and national identity that Kenya had been constructing since independence in 1963. We were slow to transition to up-country Kiswahili again, and this created anxiety and tensions concerning identity. But, however much we tried to speak Kiswahili like the Swahili people, we always fell short due to the constant introduction of Arabic words and pronunciation.

The Arab hegemony was apparent in the fact that many Arabic words continued to be stealthily introduced into Kiswahili vocabulary, a practice that goes on to this day. While the Arabic words were often similar to their Kiswahili counterparts, many had no cognates in Kiswahili, making it difficult to learn them. We were forced to mimic speakers of Arabic. Common Arabic words and phrases that were used included *shukran* (thank you), *naam* (yes), *la* (no), and *salaam aleikum* (peace be upon you). These words have now been accepted as Kiswahili words. Today, *salaam aleikum* has become the principal greeting among coastal speakers, whereas *habari* (hello) and *jambo* (hi) remain the principal greetings in the rest of Kenya. At school, I was concerned by the fact that words such as *alamsiki* (good night), *insha'Allah* (if Allah wills), *bismillah* (in the name of Allah), and *al-hamdu-lilah* (praise be to Allah) became part of our common and ordinary vocabulary. The Islamic influence is very clear in the last two words.

For Bantu children like me, it was hard if not impossible to blend into the Arab and Islamic-dominated coastal society. Our isolation came from the religious and linguistic differences between coastal Muslim and Swahili speakers on the one hand and ourselves (inland Bantu and Christians) on the other. This created tensions and frustrations. But some coastal people and Muslims were friendly. We were often invited into Swahili and Muslim homes. We often participated in celebrating Muslim holidays and rituals such as *idd-el-fitir* (the end of fasting at the sighting of the moon at the end of the holy month of Ramadan). But we were still regarded as outsiders. Even though Muslims and Swahili admit others into their community, especially those that will totally accept their way of life, including language, dress, and Islam, this takes time. For a transient family like mine, the possibility of "acceptance" and incorporation was remote.

The suspended animation in which my identity and that of my siblings was held due to the way we spoke Kiswahili and the way we unknowingly imbibed Islamic terminology would only begin to unfold and make meaning to me many years later, when I was a university student. When I became a student at the University of Nairobi, I wanted answers to all my historical questions, fears, and suspicions. I was curious to know why the coast and up-country binaries, especially the politicization of Kiswahili dialects at the coast, had taken so long to be studied. This was not normal. It was a vexing question and yet no one had bothered to examine the subject. I wanted to know why certain dialects of Kiswahili were privileged over others. I wanted to know why people at the coast wanted to be associated with Arabs and Islam rather than with Bantu such as the Mijikenda and with up-country people and dialects such as mine. Unfortunately for me, the professor who specialized in coastal history did not seem to answer these questions as directly as I might have wanted. Obviously, as I later realized, I was asking the impossible, for the professor did not have the answers. He failed to unravel these mysteries and tensions for me. I was not able to find answers in the many history texts that I read. No textbook explained the differences based on *lahaja* (dialect) in discussing the peoples of Kenya, and this bothered me.

The most authoritative work on the history of the coastal peoples in Kenya remained my teacher Ahmed Idha Salim's work (1973), *The Swahili-Speaking Peoples of Kenya's Coast, 1895–1965*. I had asked him many questions in class, only some of which he had answered satisfactorily. If he could not answer some of these questions in class, I doubted that he could answer them in his book, which seemed to privilege Arab agency in what purported to be a history of the Swahili speakers. His first chapter on the Swahili dwelled mainly on the activities of the sultans of Zanzibar and other Arab actors. I knew that the history of the Swahili certainly included other actors apart from Arabs; and in fact Arabs were not the primary group in the history of the Swahili. Salim wrote that the transfer of the capital of the Oman sultan from Muscat to Zanzibar "was to prove to be a choice of great significance not only for Zanzibar but also for the rest of the mainland dominions. Zanzibar soon outstripped the other coastal towns in economic and political development."[3] He went on to praise the sultan's genius in coming to East Africa and exploiting the region. He wrote, "Within a short period, Seyyid Said's business acumen and his liberal and *far-sighted* [my emphasis] policies made Zanzibar the greatest single emporium on the western shore of the Indian Ocean. It became the most important market on the east coast for ivory, slaves, cloves, gum copal, cowries and agricultural products."[4] I still hold that the sultan was certainly not a genius. I wondered why Salim did not state that Sultan Seyyid Said benefited from enslaving Africans. He looted the coast of East Africa of its resources, and there was no genius in looting and robbing.

I was bothered that Ahmed Idha Salim did not point out that ethnic and linguistic differences have sometimes been constructed at the coast of Kenya as elsewhere, through identity. It is possible that he did not know that identity had been defined and redefined by Arabism and Islam, to suit certain entrenched social interests. I knew that since Salim had Arab ancestry himself, there were some tensions that he could not adequately address without causing friction in the society in which he grew up and in which he came to believe. I knew that, although he researched his project at a time when many historians still held to the principle of objectivity in the historical enterprise, there were many gaps in his narrative. I knew that he tried very hard to remain neutral and uninvolved. I knew that this was the dilemma that faced many Kenyan historians studying local phenomena in the 1960s and 1970s. They researched innocent subjects; and asked harmless and innocent questions that would not disturb the peace and the status quo. I thought there was a need to understand the tensions surrounding identity and "otherness" if these tensions were to be accounted for historically.

Whenever I inquired about these tensions, many of which I had encountered as a child in Mombasa, the answer I got was always the same: that the research on the coastal history of Kenya was not complete. Hence, armed with a questionnaire on issues of ethnicity and identity, I set about interviewing people at the coast of Kenya, in 1999 and again in 2003, about their history. I wanted to unravel the mystery of the memories of trauma and identity in my life at the coast of Kenya as a child. I was surprised, in fact shocked, by what I found. No amount of academic training could have prepared me for it. The fact that identity was constructed was well known to me, but to find that it could be fabricated so bizarrely and legitimatized by scholarship, reinvented, and disseminated as truth was shocking. I came face to face with people who had two or even three versions of family histories. I wondered why this had not been written about. This made me imagine that perhaps there was collusion among scholars in perpetuating the fabrications. However, I encountered bold voices that were ready to spill the beans and stop the lies. I liked the experiential views of the people I encountered, as they were able to share with me the ways in which they had experienced segregation, and how they had witnessed their neighbors shifting identities in order to belong to the dominant group. It is against this background that one should understand my contribution in this chapter. It seems to me that identity is something people manipulate in their attempts at defining or redefining their relationship with others. In this case, the Arab factor is used as a hegemonic tenet, for the purpose of subordinating the African factor, and this has implications for the history of the coast of Kenya.

The Impact of Slavery on Identity at the Coast of Kenya

Scholars have tended to ignore the legacy and impact of the Arab slave trade and slavery on identity at the coast of Kenya. My argument is that the legacy of slavery, the slave trade, and Islam at the coast of Kenya has been the production of oppositional identities of "African-ness" and "Arab-ness," which many studies have tended to sweep under the carpet. In the era of the slave trade, slave traders and masters, who were mainly Arabs, and those that converted to Islam were privileged, while Africans, who constituted the underclass, servants, and *kefirs* (non-Muslims), were underprivileged. When the Kiswahili language and the Swahili culture developed, the slave image and any knowledge of slave origins were regarded as taboo subjects. Because of the status associated with being Arab, many of those born as a result of intermarriage between Africans and Arabs held to the identity of the latter while rejecting that of the former.

Following this line, many coastal people, who are Bantu in outlook and appearance, deny their "African-ness," which is regarded as an indicator of slave descent, while they remain fixated on the Arab "ancestry" that connects them to former masters.[5] Kiswahili was embraced as a neutral language, and the Mvita dialect (Kimvita) became the preferred one in the coastal region of Kenya. How it became privileged and regarded as the model type of Kiswahili has not been thoroughly investigated, but at the heart of it are power and race and religious dynamics.[6] The Bajuni (local coastal Creoles or colored people who claim Arab rather than African descent although they are of mixed blood) regarded themselves as true descendants of the masters and seem to have led the initiative that started the "othering" process upon which my essay is predicated. The Mijikenda were ignored in the construction of this identity. Scholars have also often ignored and marginalized Mijikenda voices in the narratives on identity at the coast of Kenya.[7]

During the course of my research, the answers of my research opportunities on what they defined themselves to be and on other aspects of identity in Kenya revealed that the ways in which we personally acquire our own group identities are often complex. Similarly, the way we assign group identities to others is not always straightforward. Racial and ethnic labels at the coast of Kenya are not clearly based on criteria that everyone understands, agrees with, and can easily use. That is why, in the use of any criteria to describe race and ethnicity, there is always misunderstanding, meaning that the method is possibly not rational or based on any logical criteria that would be easily discernible to anyone. Many respondents noted that if others labeled them, the labels were inaccurate and very offensive. This instantly created a barrier to open communication, even if the slight was unintended. Khadija Maulid noted: "Many tell me that I look like a Taita, but I am actually an Arab."[8] Another respondent, Abdullah Msanifu, pointed out that "It is not easy to tell whether a person is an Arab or African just by looking at them. You must ask them."[9] To comprehend the ethnic diversity of the coast of Kenya, it is important to first understand the criteria commonly used for making distinctions between groups. These are generally based on cultural and/or biological factors. Kenyans tend to see each other in terms of age, economic class, religion, gender, ethnicity, and race. Kenyans usually identify a member of a particular group according to one or several of these criteria. Which of our group identities is most important varies with the social situation. Today, religion, gender, ethnicity, and race often have the most far-ranging impact on Kenyans as individuals.

For many people in Kenya, ethnic categorization implies a connection between biological inheritance and culture. People believe that biological inheritance determines much of cultural identity. If this were true, for instance, Mijikenda traits, such as speaking the Mwambao (coastal) dialect of Kiswahili, would stem from genetic inheritance. But it is not true. The pioneering nineteenth-century English anthropologist E. B. Tylor was able to demonstrate conclusively that biological race and culture are not the same thing.[10] Any person can be placed in another culture shortly after birth and become thoroughly acculturated to that culture, regardless of skin color, body shape, and other presumed racial features.

The "Black Arab" phenomenon in Kenya may be taken as exemplary of the problematic nature of the plural society as historically constituted. While the antagonism between Arabs and Africans dates back to the arrival of Arabs at the coast of Kenya around 800 CE, the present tension is not racial but fundamentally economic and political. The Arabs tried to establish theocratic rule over the coastal strip and islands but failed to subdue the Bantu and other communities. When we examine the existing conflicts between Muslims and non-Muslims and Arabs and Africans over identity at the coast of Kenya, we find these dualisms inadequate as other identities begin to emerge. For instance, when we talk of the ideals of Islam and Arabism and "proper" Kiswahili in enabling social change, the question of hegemony as a directive force uniting individuals as groups or collectivities cannot be avoided, particularly if we assume that Islam, Arabism, and "proper" Kiswahili are the sites where the power of social capital is allocated and articulated, where cultural action or the production of meanings and affects takes place. In this context, Islam and Arab culture act as the controllers of "consensus" and also serve as the sites where hegemonic struggles occur and African voices are purged.

The direct association of traditional Swahili dress (a slightly modified version of Arab dress) with the religion of Islam at the coast demonstrates the amalgamation of religious and secular life in Swahili culture. It also demonstrates the hegemony of Arab influence and Islam in the life of the Swahili. To the Swahili, Islam is a profound source of identity and pride, and it is here that the Arab influence is so pronounced. Being Swahili is almost synonymous with being a Muslim, so that Islam is perhaps the most significant element of the Swahili way of life. I believe that it is only when we factor in the historical process of the struggle between Arabs and Africans (and, by extension, between Arabs and Bantu or Mijikenda) at the coast that we can really begin a substantive discussion of identity and Arab-Muslim hegemony.[11]

Arab and Muslim hegemony might explain why Kiswahili words coined by people like Ahmed Sheikh Nabhani have been privileged and readily incorporated into the Kiswahili vocabulary, rather than those coined by non-Arabs and non-Muslims in Kenya. Although he did not receive formal education, Sheikh Nabhani is acknowledged as having coined the word *runinga* (television), whereas claims by non-Arabs and non-Muslims such as Jay Kitsao, Rocha Chimera, John H. Habwe, and Kazungu Kadenge to have coined the word have been disregarded.[12] This is also relevant to other coastal versus interior, Arab versus African, Muslim versus non-Muslim discourses, just as it is relevant to discourses involving coastal and interior Tanzania, where coastal peoples of Arab descent always try to establish the proper accent and how Kiswahili should be spoken.

This is clearly demonstrated by Susan Geiger's claims in her book *TANU Women*, in which she says that Bibi Titi Mohammed, a semi-literate female politician from coastal Tanzania, taught Julius Nyerere (Tanzania's first president) how to speak Kiswahili.[13] Although the proposition is preposterous, it should be realized that Bibi Titi Mohammed was from the coast of Tanzania; she was Muslim and had "Arab" blood running in her veins. Therefore, the assumption would be that since she was from the coast she spoke better Kiswahili than Nyerere. Of course, such a claim is ridiculous, and essentializing at best, making Kiswahili intrinsic to coastal people.

Postcolonial writers such as Homi Bhabha, Stuart Hall, Octavio Paz, and Gayatri Spivak have pointed to the limitations of monological and homogenizing approaches to culture, identity, and social institutions. They argue that culture and identity are the products of human encounters, the inventories of cross-cultural appropriation and hybridity of dominant groups such as Arabs and Muslims at the coast of Kenya. They maintain that race and ethnic identity are usually contextual and situational. From my research, it seems one's ethnic declaration is often open to the scrutiny of others who may either corroborate or invalidate the declaration. In the course of constructing and maintaining ethnic identity, common historical symbols are identified, shared, and passed along to future generations. The symbols—clothing, decals, adornments, food, language, religion and rituals—may also serve as public affirmations of one's ethnic claim. Although dominant cultures seem to dictate in defining what is acceptable, there are some people from the minority cultures (I call them cultural nationalists) who are never intimidated by the mainstream culture. Most of my informants were drawn from this group.

Based on extensive interviews with people of mixed ethnic backgrounds, I identified three basic ways in which people choose identity at the coast of Kenya. From my interviews, first, wealthier families seemed not to care what type of ethnic identity was assigned to them. It was poor families that sought to be seen to belong to the dominant identity, even if this required them to fabricate their past and their family tree. Second, parental and grandparental influences seemed to promote the choice of identity, through the provision of genealogical information. Third, the racism and prejudice associated with certain groups and the location of a family determined what identity it would affirm. Recent demographic figures for the coastal region reveal a faster population increase for Arabs, which I think might be an indication not of natural increase but of a shifting of identity to Arab-ness.

Islam and the Promotion of Arab Identity at the Coast of Kenya

Islam has contributed to the development of Arab hegemony at the coast of Kenya. During the time when it was necessary for imams, sheikhs, *malims*, and other Muslim clergy members to be related to the Prophet Mohammed (especially under Shia Islam), people of Arab descent had privilege, prestige, and power. Some of my informants revealed that during this period, African converts seeking entry to the inner circle of the Islamic *ulama* (Islamic leaders) often falsified their lineage in order to be incorporated into that inner circle. To achieve wider local appeal, Islam began to be spread using Kiswahili, the local language. Thus, Islam has also contributed to the Kiswahili language and its literature. Kiswahili has also contributed to the creation of separate identities at the coast. Local chronicles speak of Arabs having arrived on the East African coast as early as the days of the Islamic caliphate, in the eighth century CE.[14] The pre-Islamic contacts between the coast and the Arab world were reinforced and developed during the Islamic era, when many Muslim city-states arose on the coast.[15] It is reasonably certain that many Africans had converted to Islam between 1000 and 1600 but had remained African in most ways. The point I want to emphasize is that notably non-Islamic religious and other social practices persisted into the modern era, with Kiswahili remaining the language of choice as against Arabic.[16]

The arrival of Islam on the east coast of Africa seems to have led to many changes in identity in Kenya. The *ulama* doubled as rulers, and the *umma* (the public) often consisted of both free people and slaves. There emerged a small coterie of Islamic scholars who slowly spread their influence along the coast, with a focus on the knowledge of Arabic and Islam as markers of civilization and social hierarchy. As a result of this emphasis, literacy in Arabic was introduced and blossomed, and became a marker of class and identity. Influential traders and clan leaders were glad to patronize the *ulama* because their people looked on the literary culture of Islam as conferring prestige. An indigenous literature in classical Arabic began to develop. The Arabic script was used in the introduction of Kiswahili literacy, and Arabic models of composition were propagated by the literati.[17] This situation prevailed till the period of European colonialism, when the Roman script was introduced and slowly replaced the Arabic script in public communications, although the Arabic script continued to thrive in private homes and other spaces in the region. Imbued with the ideology of Islam, poets wrote about moral, social, and political life. Thus, written Swahili verse at the time was wholly Islamic in content, purpose, and form. Later on, when secular verse was introduced, Islamic mores and attitudes controlled it, and so the dominance of Islamic ideas and the Islamic identity was retained.[18]

Islam spread in the interior of Kenya through trade. For many years before the arrival of Islam, Arab mariners had journeyed to the region for trade. Persians and Arabs established trading posts that later became permanent homes. They spread to offshore islands, especially Mombasa, Pemba, and Zanzibar islands, in the ninth and tenth centuries and developed friendships with local people. Starting from these trading settlements, Arab trade routes into the interior of Africa assisted the slow acceptance of Islam and helped to lead to the development of the Swahili culture and language. Trading posts became Muslim nuclei, as Arabs and Swahili traders settled in them, married local women, and gave birth to children whose language of communication was Kiswahili. Islam was implanted and Kiswahili spread. Places such as Mumias, Kendu Bay, Managua, Nyeri, and Sultan Hamud owe their growth to the events described here.

In many cases after the fifteenth century, conversion to Islam for Kenyan ethnic groups was probably a means of protection against being sold into slavery, as the slave trade was flourishing between the coast and the interior. For the rulers of the interior peoples, such as the *nabongo* of Wanga, who were not active proselytizers, conversion remained somewhat formal, a gesture perhaps aimed at gaining political support from the Arabs and facilitating commercial relationships. For example, conversion probably helped the Wanga to obtain guns, which they used to keep their competitors, such as the Maasai, in check. The Arab dominance led to more Arab immigration and settlement in the region. This increased presence connected the region to the Arab and Persian cultures, linking the East African religious intelligentsia with the main centers of Islam in the Middle East. This interaction accounted for the privileging of Arabs, and for Arab dominance in the shaping of Kiswahili and Swahili at the coast of Kenya.[19]

Historicizing Identity and Arab Hegemony at the Coast of Kenya

In the historical discourse of the Swahili culture and the Kiswahili language, there seems to be a great deal of privileging of Muslim and Arab agency, usually at the expense of the agency of Africans or Bantu.[20] Some have suggested that Arabs have defined Swahili identity in such a way as to place themselves at the top of the hierarchy and to place Africans in a subordinate position.[21] For example, in his discussions of the Swahili speakers, Salim seems to privilege the Bajuni (his own ethnic group). "Ethnically," he writes, "the Bajunis are an amalgam of Bantu, Hamitic [*sic*] and Arab groups . . . . However, Bajunis also claim Arab ancestry from places as varied as Egypt, Syria, the Hijaz, South Arabia and the Persian Gulf,"[22] almost making the Bajuni supplant the Swahili at the coast of Kenya, without considering other groups of people who were not Arabs or Persians, and who had contributed a great deal in the development of Kiswahili.

Apart from privileging the Arab side, the dominant approach to the contemporary challenges of multiplicity and difference in social and cultural aspects at the coast of Kenya, an approach increasingly associated with non-Arabs and non-Muslims as well as with Arabs and Muslims, is to think of "identity" and "culture" within the crisis language of imaginary unity, of singular origins, singular ancestry, bounded nationality, and so forth, where Arabism dominates. For this reason, it is the Arab factor and Islam that receive a great deal of attention in Salim's discussion of the Swahili. On the encounter between Europeans and the Swahili, Salim suggests that it is the Arabs and Swahili who have been affected more than the Bantu. According to Salim, "All that the Arab and Swahili communities had cherished and jealously guarded was being threatened: the system of slavery and hereditary titles to land were being undermined, traditional government was being weakened, and a representative voice or effective leadership was absent."[23] In this interpretation, Arabs are portrayed as contributing more to the Swahili than the Bantu did, with the Bantu factor depicted as inconsequential. Salim made the same argument in 1985, seeing the Swahili identity as emanating from an Arab root, and omitting the Bantu presence.[24]

Some scholars of the history of the coast of Kenya have grappled with the identity of the Swahili, which still remains unresolved.[25] That Africans (mainly Bantu), Arabs, Persians, and the Islamic religion have all contributed to transformation at the coast is not in doubt, given the continued revelations from research based on material culture.[26] However, even though the Arab presence has been regarded as significant due to a plethora of sources and the legacy of Arabic, I want to suggest that the majority of people at the coast of Kenya do not have Arab blood running in their veins. This runs against the grain and does not represent popular opinion on the history of the coast. This is because African and Bantu "blood" and identity are silenced and increasingly regarded as unimportant.

The Bantu underpinnings of coastal civilization were laid down during the first millennium CE, when the earliest village-based culture appeared with the spread of Sabaki Bantu speakers into the coastal areas of Kenya from the African interior, probably the Great Lakes region.[27] A pre-Islamic phase of cultural and linguistic differentiation lasted from about 700 to 1000 CE. This was followed by a "golden age," lasting from about 1000 to

1500, which saw the emergence of the characteristic features of coastal African civilization, namely, a city-state form of organization, an economy that featured cultivation and maritime activities, Islamization, and both local and international trade.[28]

To understand the history of the coast of Kenya, one needs to pay careful attention to the history of the Mijikenda people (a cluster of nine closely related Bantu groups who share a common linguistic and cultural heritage, but who have become differentiated through separate settlement during the last five hundred years). The nine groups are the Kauma, Rabai, Duruma, Chonyi, Jibana, Giriama, Kambe, Ribe, and Digo. They adopted the name Mijikenda (the nine villages) early in the nineteenth century in place of the pejorative term "Nyika," meaning "bush," which had been applied to all the African groups. The rich Swahili culture has emerged from the Mijikenda and their interaction with neighboring ethnic groups and newcomers from outside.[29] The origin narratives of the Mijikenda posit their arrival in Kenya through migration from Shungwaya, a place possibly in southern Somalia, where they lived with the Taita, Pokomo, Segeju, and Galla.[30] Many of the narratives are based on the interpretation of oral sources, corroborated by Arabic and European sources.

I suggest that the tendency among many non-African scholars has been to privilege written works more than oral sources, and as a result to privilege Arab agency at the coast of Kenya. The tendency to distrust oral sources and rely on written Arab sources came from various assumptions. One was that Africans were incapable of innovation or memory. At the coast of Kenya, the literate Muslim culture of the Swahili towns with their hereditary rulers offered a seemingly obvious source of innovations and consistency in memory. A second assumption was that Arab scripts could be believed without any interrogation as to whether they were authentic or fabricated. Consciously aware that they were foreigners and that their "foreign-ness" would later be a disadvantage, many Arab families seem to have fabricated lineages, as some of my informants revealed. In addition, many researchers failed to realize that as scribes the Arabs were historians in their own right, marshaling the facts in support of their arguments, and revealing only those details that they deemed pertinent to their cause.

Based on Arab sources, many scholars have placed the Bantu at the coast of Kenya around 800 CE.[31] Some scholars have refuted this date, comparing it with the apartheid theories on the Bantu arrival in South Africa,[32] which apartheid historians placed after 1652 when Jan van Reebeck set foot at the Cape.[33] Many Arab narratives tended to privilege stories that placed them at the coast even before the Bantu, but this has been proved wrong by recent archaeological discoveries that have unearthed Bantu settlements going as back as far as 400 CE.[34] Archaeologists such as Henry Mutoro have used ceramics to study the spread and movement of the Bantu. Sites with the same type of pottery reflect a similar origin and a shared culture. The start-ing point is those communities that have a clearly excavated sequence. Study of their ceramics shows that there is a logical progression of types spanning hundreds of years.

Just like Mutoro, Mark Horton and John Middleton have provided addi-tional information that is helpful in understanding Bantu origins at the coast of East Africa. They have revealed that sequences dating to the eighth to tenth centuries are found at coastal sites such as Shanga, Manda, Kilwa, Kisimani Mafia, and Ungwana, and in the Comoros. These have revealed close similarities with pottery found in the coastal hinterland. Materials collected "from Wenje a village on the middle of Tana River [have been] compared to ssherds that [have been] found on the beach at Kiunga" and the two have been found to be similar.[35] Through the research of Mutoro, Horton, and Middleton, among others, it became clear by 1987 that the "pottery of the coast and hinterland belonged to the same ceramic tradition, a simple observation that proved beyond doubt the African nature of early Swahili society."[36] Horton and Middleton have also pointed out that "the spatial distribution of this ceramic tradition corresponded closely with that of the North-East coastal Bantu speakers—that is the Swahili, Mijikenda and Pokomo—and perhaps most convincingly its presence at Kaya Shungwaya, one of the early 'traditional' sites of the Mijikenda, [has] further demon-strated this link."[37] Thus, the claims that the Arab presence on the coast pre-dates that of the Bantu are unfounded. Archaeological, linguistic, and oral sources seem to confirm that the Mijikenda together with the Pokomo and Wazimba were the first arrivals at the coast of Kenya.[38] . The *kaya* (fortified village) became the central institution of Mijikenda life on the coast. By the seventeenth and eighteenth centuries, due to population increase and pres-sure from Arab and European slave raiders, the Mijikenda began to move out of their original *kayas*.[39] The Arabs had the advantage of guns, and they continually harassed the Mijikenda people and made them gradually with-draw from the coast, making way for Arab elements to gradually replace them. The geographic and economic expansion of the Arabs undermined the communal life that had existed in the *kayas,* because slave raids intensi-fied and many Mijikenda people were captured and taken into slavery. The history of the Mijikenda people in relation to the coast is therefore one of unequal power relations, one being the master and the other the servant, one expanding and the other in retreat.

When in 1840 the sultan of Oman, Seyyid Said, moved his headquar-ters to Zanzibar from Muscat, this privileged people of Arab descent even more. The relationship that developed between the Arabs and the Bantu (Mijikenda), produced the Swahili. Thus, Kiswahili is an African Bantu lan-guage fused with Arabic languages. Many Swahili favored the Arab identity due to the Arabs' power. Although an interdependence existed between the Swahili and the Mijikenda, as is revealed by a strong Mijikenda influence on the culture, politics, and economy of the Swahili, the Arab factor has been privileged.[40] This was the source of the Arab hegemony, which was continued under the British colonial system and still resonates in the local politics of identity today.

When the British took over the coastal area from Arab control in 1895, the Arab hegemony did not wane. Besides English, Kiswahili was given prominence as an important language for administrators in communicating with Africans. The use of Kiswahili by the British privileged the Swahili people in the colonial administration. As a result many of them were given senior positions in the colonial bureaucracy. This had many consequences. First, it isolated the native speakers of Swahili from their fellow Africans who saw them as representatives of foreign domination. Second, it gave the Swahili the monopoly of developing Kiswahili, coining and defining what was regarded as proper Kiswahili. Third, native speakers of Kiswahili became the teachers of the language, a dominance that is still visible in Kenyan schools and universities. Native speakers of Kiswahili also dominated the courts as translators and the media (print and electronic), especially broadcasting—both radio and television. These gave the Swahili a lot of power and influence among fellow Africans.

The British favored Arabs and Swahili under "indirect rule," privileging their political, social, and cultural institutions. The Swahili and Arabs were placed together and regarded as self-governing (rulers) whereas others were regarded as subordinate. The British allowed various Muslim chiefdoms to retain administrative control of their areas of jurisdiction, whereas African chiefdoms in the interior were brought under the direct control of colonial officials. It was the Mijikenda who were the first to experience the impact of this privileging of Arabs and Swahili at the coast when the first colonial administrator Hardinge established his office. On this, Salim says, "Several factors . . . assured the Arabs and Swahili of a special position in the new administration which Hardinge established. First, there was Hardinge's own personal attitude towards them. Service in Muslim capitals, like Istanbul and Cairo, had implanted in him a sympathetic understanding of Islam and Muslims."[41] Salim believes that this appreciably softened Hardinge's policy toward Muslims at the coast, hence privileging them against non-Muslims. Many Arabs and Swahili were conscripted into the pacification campaigns of the British, in the conquest of inland African ethnic groups.

Deconstruction of Identity through Songs and Art

Songs, poetry, and works of art have greatly problematized identity at the coast of Kenya, although no single historical work has addressed this. Some artists, however, have been bold in addressing the disjuncture. They have told it like it is, deconstructing the text and subtext of identity in the region. These were the voices that I had been looking for, and I liked them. A Mijikenda woman, Bibi Wanduka, has composed many songs, in the "Taarab" genre, which has a uniquely Swahili flavor that incorporates Bantu and Arab lyrical arrangements. Her two most popular songs are "Wote ni Sawa" (literally, "We are all the same") and "Wape Vidonge Vyao" (literally, "Give them their medicine or pills"), which question some of the tensions that attend African and Arab relations at the coast of Kenya.

In "Wote ni Sawa," Bibi Wanduka asks why differences between Arabs and Africans are stressed, although they are brothers and sisters. She says that she knows of a family where the son says he is an Arab and the daughter says she is a Mijikenda. She sings, "Huu ni upuzi jamani" (literally, "Honestly my people, this is ridiculous"). She says this is because, if the man said he was Mijikenda, he would not get a bride; on the other hand, if the woman said she was an Arab, she would not attract any potential husband in her Mijikenda community. If a man says he is an Arab, many opportunities are opened to him, since the identity of the father determines the identity of the children in a marriage. It is apparent that identity is not a permanent marker, since people seem to have the freedom to choose an identity. The only problem is that one's identity can be doubted and even repudiated by society, which highlights the problem of hegemony and dominant agency. Wanduka's sarcastic use of this hypothetical case is interesting, as it places identity at the center of societal lies and manipulation at the coast of Kenya. From the song, it is clear that Wanduka believes identity is not something real but something constructed to serve mostly selfish and banal purposes. The same theme is pursued in Bibi Malika's "Wape Vidonge Vyao."

In "Wape Vidonge Vyao," Bibi Malika says, "I know you are my aunt's son and I am your uncle's daughter and wonder why we are different." Bibi Malika asks why there are differences in society, with some people preferring to be called Arabs, although she does not see any difference between them and Mijikenda. Bibi Wanduka's songs became very popular in the 1990s and enjoyed enormous amounts of airtime on local radio stations and television. Bibi Malika rearranged "Wape Vidonge Vyao" and enabled it to reach global audiences before it was taken and re-arranged yet again by many bands such as the Orchestra Virunga of Samba Mapangala. Bibi Malika's song is a project in deconstruction. She is questioning the societal arrangements and is aware that this is a grave matter and likely to raise tensions between Africans and Arabs at the coast.

The message of "Wape Vidonge Vyao" is metaphorical and political at the same time. It questions why only certain sections of society have been given power to define who is Arab and who is African. Bibi Malika says, "Wape wape vidonge vyao, wakimeza wakitema ni shauri yao" (literally, "Give them the pills to take; whether they swallow them or not is up to them"). Her song is an indictment of artificial and meaningless politics of identity. To her, the definitions of identity are unnecessary, and she disagrees with them "whether they like it or not"; and accepting the sharing of the platform of identity-creation is one of the pills she is giving them to swallow, whether they like it or not. In the song, she seems to be aware that the dominant group causes the separation between "Arabs" and "Africans" and other identity forms in the region. There is always the desire of the dominant culture or the majority to force nonconformists and eccentrics to conform to the conventional worldview.

Other good examples of the problematization of identity are the paintings of a Mijikenda artist, Kajembe Mpindi. In his art, Mpindi, the son of a "Chonyi" father and an "Arab" mother, documents his struggle with the profound personal and political issues historically surrounding identity formation at the coast of Kenya. Mpindi's parents' marriage is itself almost unique, because it is almost always African women who marry Arab men and not African men who marry Arab women. Mpindi came to be an artist relatively late in life. He taught himself painting and drawing in the 1980s but brought his work into public displays in Mombasa from 1995, the year Kenya celebrated the centenary of the European colonial arrival in Kenya. His art works represent important historical trajectories. His work registers a rejection of the hegemonic strands of the dominant culture and the attendant tensions and concerns of this historical moment in Kenya. I would like to foreground here two of his pivotal paintings, *Mtoro* (1996) and *Shujaa* (1998). These bright paintings combine Mijikenda culture and uniquely coastal perspective painting to dazzling effect. The paintings show vast waters, dhows, seagulls, marine life, and the coastal mangrove and *nyika* plateau landscape in the background, with people engaged in what looks like different activities in an open area, probably a market. The figure at the center of *Mtoro* is vague, almost in transition, looking semi-African, semi-Arab, semi-female, and semi-male. In short, one cannot tell the race or the gender of image at the center of *Mtoro*. It is only those images in the background that give us vague clues as to the race of the people portrayed, the environment and occupations of the characters. It depicts what must be a real cultural mosaic. Does this vivid but vague picture reflect Mpindi's own anxieties and ambivalence about his identity, in having mixed parentage? This question is answered in *Shujaa*, a later piece that points to Mpindi's resolve and clearly indicates his preferred identity.

In *Shujaa*, Mpindi clearly characterizes exploitation and neocolonialism. The image deconstructs the work of familiar Arab painters, such as Abdullah Ratib's *Muscat* and *The Sultan's Harem*, which place *kanzu*-wearing males and *hijab*-wearing female Arabs at the center, thereby privileging Muslim symbols, motifs, and backgrounds. For instance, *Muscat* has an obvious

Muslim and Arab audience listening to a speaker (either a member of the ulama, a sultan, or someone else in authority) with the sun, shrubs and sand dunes, camels, and other features that one would find in a Middle Eastern environment, in the background. Mpindi's *Shujaa* depicts African motifs, images, and symbols, in the intensified and heightened atmosphere of the brisk, vigorous, startling coast in more details than one sees in *Mtoro* or in Abdullah Ratib's paintings. From both *Mtoro* and *Shujaa*, one notices that Mpindi's paintings are overloaded with African agency and details. They are concerned with specific African ("Black") details, such as shapes of noses, skin color, hair, height, and various activities in which people are engaged. These paintings are an engagement in a deconstructive discourse. In *Shujaa*, one notices the foregrounding of Mijikenda traditions at the coast and the locking out of Arab motifs. *Shujaa* reveals a desire to set the record straight, showing an activist artist engaged in a crusade to shift the identity paradigm at the coast.

Shujaa is presented against an unsettling cultural mosaic and what looks like a rejection of Arab and Muslim hegemony in Swahili culture, as for instance, a Mijikenda *makuti* hut replaces the mosque, and the Mijikenda *msuli* (traditional robe) replaces the Muslim *kanzu* (the Islamic/Arab robe). Most importantly, Mpindi interposes a unique scenario into the settings in *Shujaa*, revealing the double exploitation of Africans, by Arabs and Europeans, showing a decapitated native body stumbling toward a basin full of blood while two people (Arab and European) are sucking the blood that has been extracted from the African. I believe Mpindi is returning the colonial and oppressive gaze, casting the Arabs and Europeans as cannibals, exactly as Africans, the Wazimba[42] were portrayed in Portuguese literature for much of the period before the eighteenth century. Against this backdrop of the African as victim, Mpindi casts the Swahili as truly having an African rather than Arab identity, having suffered many years of marginalization and oppression, first at the hands of Arabs and later at the hands of the British. In this way, I believe, the essential ground of Mijikenda authenticity is celebrated and valorized by Mpindi in clearer terms even than in written works. Here, the hegemonic Persian-Arab identities are rejected or disavowed, leading to the acceptance of alternative paradigms such as hybridity, which Mpindi finds attractive better than Arab hegemony. At the same time, through this new paradigm, Mpindi highlights the incompleteness of the modern Mijikenda and Swahili search for identity, for hybridity creates a new identity that is, in my opinion, perhaps more confusing.

However, I believe that Mpindi's paintings (both *Mtoro* and *Shujaa*) are empowering for the African-related identity of the Swahili, as they seem to disavow the centrality of the Arab factor at the coast. This is sharply underscored in Mpindi's use of space in both paintings. Avoiding the linear display of space of the Arab oil painting in which the African is clinically separated from the foreign and dominating Arab and Muslim influence, Mpindi deliberately yokes the dominator and dominated into the same space, often pushing Arabs and their artifacts indistinctly into the background. He even replaces mosques with *makuti* huts and changes bodies, neutralizing them. Putting the African component of the Swahili at the center means that the boundaries between the Arab and the African, between Muslim and non-Muslim, are collapsed, and the antagonistic spaces of the dominator (Arab) and dominated (African) identities are folded into each other in a violent, eruptive, but peaceful manner that advantages the African identity.

Conclusion

This chapter has highlighted significant historical trajectories in the politics of identity at the coast of Kenya through commonly taken for granted social constructs such as "ethnicity," "culture," "color," and so forth. I have shown that there is a need to rethink the identity politics of "African-ness" and "Arab-ness" and Muslim homogeny and hegemony among the Swahili at the coast of Kenya. I have shown how Arab hegemony is responsible for the artificial identity of "Black Arabs" among the Swahili. I have also shown that the phenomenon of "Black Arabs" is deeply influenced by the long history of social and cultural domination by the Arab-Muslim axis at the coast of Kenya. I have highlighted how Arabs have defined the cultural parameters, such as the Kiswahili accent, and how other groups serve as the objects of such parameters. Within this discourse, I have shown how ethnic identity has worked to divest young Swahili people and speakers of Kiswahili of their identities. I have shown how "Arabism" and "Islam" have impeded the prospects for a fully invested Swahili multiculturalism free from Arab-Muslim hegemony at the coast. I have also demonstrated that this hegemonic structure attempts to hold the Arab and Muslim cultural core among the Swahili in place, by simply adding on selective, nonconflictual items from the cultures and experiences of African groups such as the Mijikenda. Using interviews, songs, and art, I have shown that scholars have marginalized the expression of the alternative discourses on Swahili identity (mainly the African connection) in the past, by privileging the Arab discourse.

Through this analysis of the evolution of the identity of the Swahili, it has emerged that politics, religion, social expediency, and culture create new identities, so that "Swahili-ness" and proper Kiswahili are largely fashioned by cultural and historical constructs. There is no doubt that Swahili identity is primarily a social rather than a biological phenomenon. Black Africans at the coast of Kenya may gain acceptance by playing according to the dictates of the dominant culture. Discrimination, segregation, and ethnic distancing, such as those I encountered at the coast as a child and an adult, is part of the larger societal schema. Such socialization, which is organized informally in ways that fracture people's cultural and ethnic identities, creating social, linguistic, and cultural divisions among them, is hard to unravel, for it is often located in ordinary, mundane places, so that religious sites such as mosques, marketplaces, beaches, and other public places become the instruments of maintenance of hegemonic relationships, in that they constitute arms of the society through which belief systems and cultural associations are taught and reinforced.

The chapter has shown that Arabs have appropriated the legitimacy of defining Swahili-ness and what constitutes proper Kiswahili. In 2003, during my research, people of Arab descent and some "Black Arabs" reminded me on several occasions that I spoke a Kiswahili dialect that was neither coastal nor up-country. It looked as if I was required to make a choice, for there was no middle ground in the social politics of identity. Given a choice, many up-country folk obviously end up choosing the coastal dialect. One sees all of these dynamics at work, especially now in the fratricidal wars still going on in music, art, and politics, and the new vocabulary that is added to Kiswahili.

These vastly transformed circumstances consequent upon the movement and collision of people impose new imperatives on up-country folk coming to the coast of Kenya. Increasingly, people seem to lack the empathy, the desire for collaboration, cooperation, and negotiation, or the magnanimity of spirit to engage with the other as a member of the human community or even species. The Mijikenda world integrates the ancient and the modern, as Khadija Maulid and Abdullah Msanifu, among other non-Arabs, revealed in their testimonies. Just as Mpindi's art reveals, these Mijikenda, historically displaced by the dominance of Arabism and Islam, create in their daily lives a re-memory of their past and the ways they have dealt with Arab and British dominance.[43] In so doing, they add an extraordinary ritual and artistic nuance to the folk culture of the Mijikenda as a whole. In the art of everyday life, such as the life represented by Mpindi, we can deduce that the Mijikenda and Swahili peasants triumph over the imposed history of marginalization and the history of slavery.

Notes

1.   Scholars agree that Kiswahili is a Bantu language that originated at the coast of East Africa many centuries before the coming of the Arabs and Persians, and certainly before Islam. Proto-Swahili, known as Kingozi, hardly intelligible now but traceable in the pre-twentieth-century historical records of northern Swahili dialects, was an elegant language used for social discourse. The present form of Kiswahili is very largely a twentieth-century construct. The language extends northward into southern Somalia, southward into northern Mozambique, eastward to the major Indian Ocean islands of Pemba, Zanzibar, the Comoros, and Madagascar (the northern tip),

and westward into Uganda, Rwanda, Burundi, and the eastern Democratic Republic of Congo. It is believed that Kiswahili, which is also spoken in some urban centers of Malawi, Zambia, South Africa, and southern Sudan and has a growing number of speakers in the African diasporas in the Eastern and Western Hemispheres, is the most widespread African language. Its speech community is estimated at about one hundred million people.

2.   Maurice Amutabi, *The NGO Factor in Africa: The Case of Arrested Development in Kenya* (New York: Routledge, 2006).

3.   Ahmed Idha Salim, *The Swahili-Speaking Peoples of Kenya's Coast, 1895–1965* (Nairobi, Kenya: East African Publishing House, 1973).

4.   Ibid., 15–16.

5.   Maurice Amutabi, "Sheikh Khalid Balala, IPK and Islamic Extremism in Kenya," Occasional Paper no. 34, Association for World Education, Nairobi, Kenya, 1996.

6.   Maurice Amutabi, "Islam and Urban Violence in Kenya: Revisiting the Mombasa and Malindi Riots." Occasional Paper no. 12, Association for World Education, Nairobi, Kenya, 2000; see also M. Amutabi. "Globalization and the Mainstreaming of Kiswahili Research in the Twenty-First Century," in *Utafiti wa Kiswahili*, ed. Kenneth Simala, 176–83 (Eldoret, Kenya: Moi University Press, 2004); Thomas Spear and Derek Nurse, *The Swahili: Reconstructing the History and Language of an African Society, 800–1500* (Philadelphia: University of Pennsylvania Press, 1985).

7.   For more on this, see C. Brantley, "Gerontocratic Government: Age Sets in Pre-colonial Giriama," *Africa* 48, no. 3 (1978): 248–64; C. Brantley, "Historical Perspective of the Giriama and Witchcraft Control," *Africa* 49, no. 2 (1979): 112–33; C. Brantley, "Giriama Rising, 1914: Focus for Political Development in the Kenya Hinterland 1850–1963" (PhD diss., University of California, Los Angeles, 1973); C. Brantley, *The Giriama and Colonial Resistance in Kenya 1800–1920* (Los Angeles: University of California Press, 1981); J. Willis, *Mombasa, the Swahili, and the Making of Mijikenda* (Oxford: Clarendon Press, 1993); and Henry Mutoro, "Tana Ware and the Kaya Settlements of the Coastal Hinterland of Kenya," *AZANIA, Journal of the British Institute in Eastern Africa* 29– 30 (1996): 257–60.

8.   Khadija Maulid, Tudor, Mombasa, interview with the author, November 17, 2003.

9.   Abdullah Msanifu, Changamwe, Mombasa, interview with the author, November 18, 2003.

10.   J. Leopold, *Culture in Evolutionary and Comparative Perspective: E. B. Tylor and the Making of "Primitive Culture"* (Berlin: Dietrich Reimer Verlag, 1980).

11.   Amutabi, "Globalization.".

12.   Kenneth Simala, "Religion and the Development of Kiswahili Political Poetry," *Journal of Islamic Studies* 22 (2002): 96–125.

13.   Susan Geiger, *TANU Women: Gender and Culture in the Making of Tanganyikan Nationalism, 1955–1965* (Portsmouth, NJ: Heinemann, 1997).

14.   Henry Mutoro, "Precolonial Trading Systems of the East African Interior," in *Transformations in Africa: Essays on Africa's Later Past,* ed. Graham Connah, 186–203 (London: Leicester University Press, 1998).

15.   Ahmed Idha Salim, "The Impact of Colonialism upon Muslim Life in Kenya," *Journal of the Institute of Muslim Minority Affairs* 4, nos. 1 and 2 (1992): 76–84.

16. D. Parkin, "Swahili Mijikenda: Facing Both Ways in Kenya," *Africa* 59, no. 2 (1989): 161–75; and Simala, "Religion and the Development of Kiswahili Political Poetry.".

17. Abdallah Khalid, *Liberation of Kiswahili* (Nairobi, Kenya: East Africa Literature Bureau, 1977).

18. See Simala, "Religion and the Development of Kiswahili Political Poetry."

19. Brantley, "Historical Perspective of the Giriama," and *The Giriama and Colonial Resistance.*

20. Johnson Mwangudza, *Kenya's People: Mijikenda* (Nairobi, Kenya: Evans Brothers, 1983); Salim, *The Swahili-Speaking Peoples*; and Thomas Spear, *Traditions of Origin and Their Interpretation: The Mijikenda of Kenya* (Athens: Ohio University Press, 1982).

21. F. Constantine, "Social Stratification on the Swahili Coast: From Race to Class," *Africa* 59 (1989): 145–61.

22. Salim, *The Swahili-Speaking Peoples*, 19.

23. Ibid., 98.

24. Ahmed Idha Salim, "The Elusive Mswahili: Some Reflections on His Culture and Identity," in *Swahili Language and Society: Papers from the Workshop held at the University of London, School of Oriental and African Studies, April 1982*, ed. J. Maw and D. Perkin, 215–27 (Vienna, Wien: Afro-Pub, 1985).

25. W. Arens, "The Waswahili: The Social History of an Ethnic Group," *Africa* 45 (1975): 426–38; H. N. Chittick, "The Book of Zenj and the Mijikenda," *International Journal of African Historical Studies* 9 (1976): 68–73; Frederick Cooper, *From Slaves to Squatters: Plantation Labor and Agriculture in Zanzibar and Coastal Kenya, 1890–1925* (Nairobi, Kenya: Kenya Literature Bureau, 1980); C. Eastman, "Who Are the Waswahili?" *Africa* 41 (1971): 228–36; and Willis, *Mombasa, the Swahili, and the Making of Mijikenda.*

26. Spear, *Traditions of Origin and Their Interpretation*; and Willis, *Mombasa, the Swahili, and the Making of Mijikenda.*

27. W. E. H. Barrett, "Notes on the Customs and Beliefs of the Wagiriama," *Journal of the Royal Anthropological Institute* 41 (1911): 23–27; P. L. Gerlach, "The Social Organization of the Digo of Kenya" (PhD diss., University of London, 1961); B. A. Ogot and J. A. Kieran, *Zamani: A Survey of East African History* (Nairobi, Kenya: East African Publishing House and Longmans, 1968); and Spear, *Traditions of Origin and Their Interpretation.*

28. R. Pouwels, "Swahili Literature and History in the Post-Structuralist Era," *International Journal of African Historical Studies* 35 (1992): 214–22.

29. Maurice Amutabi, "Globalization"; and Thomas Spear, *Kaya Complex: A History of The Mijikenda Peoples of the Kenya Coast to 1900* (Nairobi, Kenya: Kenya Literature Bureau, 1978); and Spear, *Traditions of Origin and Their Interpretation.*

30. J. de V. Allen, "Shungwaya, the Mijikenda, and Their Traditions," *International Journal of African Historical Studies* 16, no. 3 (1983): 455–84; B. A. Ogot, ed., *Kenya before 1900: Eight Regional Studies* (Nairobi, Kenya: East African Publishing House, 1978); Willis, *Mombasa, the Swahili, and the Making of Mijikenda*; and Paul Tiyambe Zeleza, *Mijikenda* (New York: Rosen Publication Group, 1995).

31. See, for example, D. Nurse and T. Spear, *The Swahili: Reconstructing the History and Language of an African Society, 800–1500* (Philadelphia: University of Pennsylvania Press, 1984); J. Middleton, *The World of the Swahili: An African Mercantile Civilization*

(New Haven: Yale University Press, 1992); and James de Vere Allen, *Swahili Origins: Swahili Culture and the Shungwaya Phenomenon* (Athens: Ohio University Press, 1993).

32.   See, for example, Alamin M Mazrui and Ibrahim N Shariff, *The Swahili: Idiom and Identity of an African People* (Trenton, NJ: Africa World Press, 1994).

33.   Henry Mutoro, "The Mijikenda Kaya as a Sacred Site," in *Sacred Sites, Sacred Places*, ed. D. Carmichael, J. Hubert, B. Reeves, and A. Schanche, 56–65 (New York: Routledge, 1994).

34.   See Henry Mutoro, "Settlement Origins and Development on the Kenya Coastal Hinterland," in *Urban Origins in East Africa*, ed. P. Sinclair, 73-75 (Stockholm, 1988).

35.   H. Horton and J. Middleton, *The Swahili* (Boston: Blackwell Publishers, 2001), 39. See also Mutoro, «Precolonial Trading Systems of the East African Interior," 186–203; Mutoro, "Settlement Origins and Development," 73–75; Mutoro, "Tana Ware"; Henry Mutoro, 'Techniques of Pottery Manufacture Among the Mijikenda: Use and Discard, Implications for Archaeological Interpretation," paper presented at the Anthropology of Urban Origins in Eastern Africa Workshop, Maputo, Mozambique, 1990; Henry Mutoro, "The Development of Settlement Pattern Studies on the Kenya Coast," paper presented at the Panafrican Association of Anthropologists' congress, Nairobi, 1990; Henry Mutoro, "Singwaya Myth and the Settlement History of the Kenya Coast," paper presented at World Archaeological Congress 2, Baraquismento, Venezuela, 1990; Henry Mutoro, "Theory and Practice: A Case of Coastal Hinterland Settlements on Kenya Coastal Hinterland," paper presented at the Urban Origins Workshop, Antananarivo, Madagascar, 1989; Henry Mutoro, "A Nearest Neighbour Analysis of the Mijikenda Kaya Settlements on the Hinterland Kenya Coast," *Kenya Journal of Sciences*, Series C., Social Sciences of the Kenya National Academy of Sciences, 1, 2 (1988): 5–17.

36.   Horton and Middleton, *The Swahili*, 42.

37.   Ibid.

38.   Mutoro, "Theory and Practice"; and Mutoro, "A Nearest Neighbour Analysis," 5–17.

39.   Allen, "Shungwaya, the Mijikenda, and Their Traditions"; Ogot, *Kenya before 1900*; Spear, *Kaya Complex* and *Traditions of Origin and Their Interpretation*; Willis, *Mombasa, the Swahili, and the Making of Mijikenda*.

40.   See Brantley, "Giriama Rising, 1914," "Gerontocratic Government," "Historical Perspective of the Giriama," and *The Giriama and Colonial Resistance*.

41.   Salim, *The Swahili-Speaking Peoples*, 75.

42.   Zimba is an ethnic group of people in Southern Africa who have been depicted by colonialists as practicing cannibalism, but scholars have come to refute this as fabrications invented by Europeans to conceal their oppression. See, for example, William Ariens, *The Man-Eating Myth* (Oxford: Oxford University Press, 1980).

43.   See Spear and Nurse, *The Swahili*.

13

Labor Market Constraints and Competition in Colonial Africa

Migrant Workers, Population, and Agricultural Production in Upper Volta, 1920–32

ISSIAKA MANDE

People from the French colony of Upper Volta were the major contributors to efforts of the federal government of French West Africa (Afrique occidentale française, or AOF) to develop other colonies in the federation. In a word, the colonial government put them to work. The decision to carve the colony of Upper Volta out of AOF territory coincided with another decision, to extend existing railroads and also build another that crossed the federation.[1] On railway construction sites, Voltaic workers replaced forced labor mobilized from the other colonies that were, in fact, slated to benefit from the projects. Voltaic railroad workers were indeed so important that the federal government appointed a special delegate to work with the administrations of the colonies to help coordinate their deployment. Prior to this time, businessmen in the AOF had been interested primarily in the quick profits derived from commercial exchange and the export of forest products. However, sharp rises in the prices of agricultural products led them to turn their attention to export agriculture. By the mid-1920s, for example, the government of the colony of Côte d'Ivoire received a flood of requests for concessions for commercial agriculture. As the need for labor became increasingly acute, French planters asked colonial officials in the neighboring colony of Upper Volta to help by recruiting labor for their needs. But was Upper Volta really in a situation to provide the migrant labor needed elsewhere in French West Africa?

Population Data for Upper Volta: An "Uneven Reservoir"

The lands along the upper reaches of the Volta River, which came to be called Upper Volta, attracted the attention of the European colonial powers in the late nineteenth century. In addition to their strategic location in the heart of West Africa, these lands were coveted for their alleged economic potential and high population density. The Mossi peoples constituted the largest population in the area. The French "explorer" Binger offered an ambivalent characterization of the Mossi, noting that, if well managed, the Mossi country and its people could well become quite productive:

> Mossiland is now a country that has become lethargic, allowing the peoples around it to outstrip it in civilization . . . . Favored by nature, farming is possible everywhere. But the Mossi people are inclined to sit back, growing only what is necessary for them to survive and no more; so that while there are no poor people, neither are there rich. A common saying fits the situation very well, "everyone just gets by." To sum up, then, Mossi country is not prosperous, although with wise administration and an energetic leader it could become so.[2]

After serving five years in Mossi country with the colonial infantry, and then returning to France for graduate study, Lucien Marc focused on ecological issues in his doctoral thesis, asserting that the grain yield in the region came to 1,200 kilograms per hectare.[3] Based on more systematic data, however, Jean-Yves Marchal wrote in 1986 that even in the year 2000 this level of production would have been an agronomist's dream.[4] Marc's optimistic estimates about the economic vitality of Mossi country undoubtedly stemmed from a different fact altogether: high population densities. For many authors of Marc's era, large, dense populations were equated with wealth. Marc asserted that the lands along the Volta were home to three million people, making them a major labor reservoir. However, given Marc's incomplete and approximate data, how far can we trust such judgments?[5]

Historian and demographer Raymond Gervais devoted substantial effort to analyzing the way in which the colonial administration generated population figures, as well as to the evolution of Upper Volta's population over time.[6] His work sheds light on an entire chapter of colonial history in Upper Volta and provides the basis of the following analysis. Gervais' major premise is that population figures were produced for two principal reasons: to control the population more effectively and to impose new demands on people. Hence, the generation of data was probably more about producing numbers that supported the political and economic agendas of the administration than about accuracy. Local agents, whose role was to reinforce colonial authority, played complex roles in this process. Taken together, these factors lead us to call into question the validity of the figures that created the illusion that Upper

Volta colony was densely populated. Specific "accounting" practices also raise doubts. These included a procedure called "the rule of three," which took the growth estimates from the smallest territorial units, called *cantons,* and extended them to much larger administrative districts called *cercles.* Lieutenant Governor Hesling described the arbitrary manner whereby administrators derived population figures:

> It is important to say it: figures on Mossi population are unreliable, being [based]only on the number of taxpayers who live in each village according to the word of the chief. This number is [then] raised by a fourth to arrive at alleged population estimates.[7]

Such an admission calls into question the credibility of some censuses that claimed to record the names of individual inhabitants as recommended by the administration. Even these "good" counts paid little attention to a "sacred" census rule in demography: enumerations should be exhaustive and simultaneous across a district. Gervais delves further into these issues—describing the "methodologies" used to arrive at population figures, and analyzing the data in exhaustive and elaborate ways. His research demonstrates that "the Upper Volta drama" was presented on a stage supported by unreliable and exaggerated numbers. These overestimates of the size of the population gave rise to the belief that Upper Volta was a "manpower reservoir":

> At the level of the colony, which should not be confused with the dynamics at play in separate colonial districts which varied according to their own histories, demographic estimates . . . wavered between the fantasies of administrators anxious to justify and make profits in this peripheral area, and [those with] good intentions, whose ability to evaluate the negative impacts of migration, minor or major, was limited by the absence of adequate infrastructure. As a result, the numbers become indicators of symptoms [of a disease endemic] within the administration and the larger population as well—the never-ending tension between colonizer and colonized.[8]

Gervais' analysis goes to the heart of the debate about the advisability of creating a separate colony of Upper Volta in the first place. In part, the justification for founding the colony stemmed from challenges in administering the much larger territorial unit that preceded it, the colony of Haut-Sénégal-Niger. The authorities had found it difficult to control several hotbeds of revolt in the area of the Niger bend. In addition, many regions were very far away from the colony's capital.[9] This said, however, economic motives appear to have been the most important reason for the decision to create Upper Volta. Partisans in the AOF administration claimed that putting the Mossi together with similar neighboring peoples would produce a homogeneous (and hence manageable) colony. It would also give the French a way to thank the Mossi rulers for actively repressing secessionist movements during World War I. In economic terms, the proposition linked together prevalent clichés about the Upper Volta region: first, that population densities were high; and second, that creating a colony would allow the French to undermine existing flows of migrants to the British colony of the Gold Coast by integrating the area into a larger, French-dominated zone focused on the forests of southern Côte d'Ivoire. AOF Governor-General Angoulvant succinctly summarized this line of thinking:

> Mossi country is densely populated when compared with surrounding regions. Natural resources are minimal. Since its inhabitants are understandably inclined to offer their services in the Gold Coast to make a little money, it is important to do whatever is possible to ensure that this labor brings profit to French colonies rather than to a foreign colony. We have the right to rely on manpower from Mossi lands to develop regions that are more sparsely populated, but richer in natural resources. This is the problem.[10]

The French began to exploit their empire intensively after World War I, a drive led by Albert Sarraut, whose mantra was "development," which meant supporting private economic initiatives in the colonies and building basic infrastructure.[11] In the ensuing debate about creating a colony anchored by Mossi populations, the "manpower reservoir" argument prevailed. But opponents of the decision missed no chance to criticize. To respond to detractors and counter insinuations that the colony was not viable, the Upper Volta administration pushed the people who lived there to accept requests to work on public works projects, plantations, and forestry enterprises all over the AOF. In addition, the administration mobilized many people to build the capital at Ouagadougou and to "develop" the colony itself. These policies simply confirmed the by-now accepted conventional wisdom spread by journalists and publicists such as Albert Londres of the *Petit Parisien*:

> And so we arrived in Upper Volta, in Mossi country. It is known in Africa as a reservoir of manpower—three million blacks. Everyone comes looking for them, like going to a well for water. The Mossi were called upon to build the Thiès-Kayes and Kayes-Niger railroads. The Mossi were also called to build the railroad in Côte-d'Ivoire. Timber operators came from the lagoon [on the Atlantic in the far south] to tap Mossi manpower.[12]

In fact, the renewed efforts to build railroads in the AOF after World War I encountered enormous obstacles in finding labor. Beyond the fact that the colonial government in Senegal did not requisition labor from its own people,[13] the federal government sent workers from colonial Soudan (today's

Table 13.1. Total numbers of Upper Volta workers recruited for railroad construction in AOF between 1920 and 1931, according to different sources

Year	Chemin de fer de la Côte d'Ivoire				Thiès-Kayes-Niger		
	Source 1	Source 2	Source 3	Source 4	Source 1	Source 2	Source 3
1920	1,924	1,921	1,922	3,002	3,002	3,002	
1921	3,510	3,510	3,510	7,724	7,724	7,724	
1922	4,900	4,900	4,900	9,550	9,550	9,550	
1923	6,800	6,800	6,800	4,500	4,500	4,500	
1924	2,150	2,150	2,150	500	500	500	
1925	3,700	3,700	3,700	2,342	500	500	
1926	4,885	4,885	4,885	2,876	500	500	
1927	5,060	5,060	5,060	2,400	500	500	
1928	5,967	5,967	5,957	3,000	500	500	
1929	5,095	5,095	4,515	3,000	65	65	65
1930	6,600	6,600	903	6,000			
1931	6,500						

Sources:
1. ANS, Dakar, 2G (1920–31), Données revues et corrigées (data reviewed and corrected).
2. ANS, Dakar, K121 (26).
3. Gouvernement Général de l'A.O.F., *Exposition coloniale, Haute-Volta* (Paris: Société d'éditions géographiques, maritimes et coloniales, 1931).
4. CAOM, Aix-en-Provence, Travaux Publics, 1è série, carton 13, dossier 10.

Mali) and other hinterland colonies to work on other projects. As a result, the federal government found itself forced to commit all workers from Upper Volta to work on the Thiès-Kayes-Niger railroad (TKN).[14] The situation repeated itself in 1925 in Côte d'Ivoire, despite the polite protests of the lieutenant governor of Upper Volta, who suggested that it would be better to recruit more workers from colonial Soudan.

Table 13.1 presents several series of data that purport to trace the recruiting of Voltaic labor between 1920 and 1931 for work on the two railroad construction projects mentioned above. The rather large differences between the numbers in each series do not stem solely from distortions in statistics; different administrators also evaluated the flows of workers differently. In some cases the totals from different sources are the same; in others they vary by as much as a factor of two if the totals recruited over an entire year and the totals reported from the worksites of the two railroads are compared.

In contrast to workers from Senegal and colonial Soudan (on the TKN railroad), Voltaic administrative recruits, employed as "specialists and hired laborers," had no rights. This situation well served worksite managers, who wanted more than anything else a pliable workforce that they could work to the limit. Such treatment of Voltaic workers reflected convictions at the highest levels of the AOF federal government that Upper Volta was a "labor reservoir." In addition to being segregated from other workers, Voltaics also suffered wage discrimination. On TKN worksites, they received daily wages of 1.25 francs, in contrast to contract workers from elsewhere who made between 2 and 2.5 francs per day. They were also assigned the most arduous tasks. For example, the large majority worked on the construction of the roadbed—ten hours a day, including a half-day on Sunday, which was necessary to meet their production targets. Elsewhere in the AOF, such work was done by laborers pressed into service in the districts crossed by the railroad. By this time, the offices and departments of the TKN had some motor vehicles. Nonetheless, Voltaic porters were used to deliver food to the work camps; they also carried water and dirt used to construct the embankments for the railroad. Such company practices not only brought the reprobation of colonial administrators but also set the tone for ongoing ill-conceived and thoughtless waste of labor in the colonies. In addition, they led to dramatic denunciations by humanitarians such as Albert Londres. However, there was little concern to evaluate labor productivity in a systematic way, so that the workers themselves were often targets of accusations when the real fault lay with poorly adapted tools or badly maintained equipment,[15]

Pushed pitilessly, Voltaic workers were also assigned to erect structures that were works of art, build railroad stations, and lay track. But this list of horrors is still incomplete. Railroad management seized any pretext (illness, stealing food, taking empty bags, lying, laziness . . .) to withhold part of their wages. Finally, by multiplying verification requirements and putting off the deployment of newly arrived labor contingents (for reasons usually justified as delays for adaptation or delousing), the railroad companies found still other ways to tax Voltaic workers less.

The limited ability of the Upper Volta colony to protect its interests in the face of AOF demands raises questions about its administrators. A fundamental issue that bothered scholars at the time was whether or not the Upper Volta administration received sufficient funds to promote growth and development, or whether those in charge had to settle for expediency—leading to the extroversion of the colony, and thus reinforcing the flows of migrants who left to find work elsewhere. Research on these questions is extensive and offers possible explanations. Some are included in reports of the missions from the Inspection des Colonies, the investigative branch of the ministry. Without a doubt, migration was a crucial factor. More than anything else, the growth of migration seems to have been dictated by general policies that were poorly conceived.[16]

As for agricultural policy in Upper Volta, the decision to concentrate on cotton and peanuts, both of which were commercial crops, raises suspicions of collusion between trading houses and colonial administrators. Lieutenant Governor Hesling, for example, embarked on intensive cotton production, despite warnings from his own technical services that it would endanger the local economy.[17] Such zeal led Inspector Bernard Sol to conclude that "the cotton 'bluff' was Lieutenant Governor Hesling's personal crusade."[18] Hesling's enthusiasm was rewarded with a position with the Association Cotonnière Coloniale after he retired from colonial service. William B. Cohen has observed that such ties between colonial administrations and private enterprises with colonial interests were not at all limited to the French empire.[19] New in Upper Volta, however, was the ease with which administrators could commit workers to large-scale agricultural projects with little regard for the best interests of the people of the colony. Hesling's successor, Lieutenant Governor Fousset, for example, set his sights on western Upper Volta. This region had been more or less spared the ill-effects of Hesling's craze for cotton. However, Fousset launched peanut production in the west under the pressure of another colonial lobby, the Compagnie Française de Côte d'Ivoire. Robert Delavignette, the local administrator at that time, analyzed the negative impact of peanut production in Banfora.[20] Because the colonial government in Upper Volta feared that private companies would move their operations to other, potentially richer colonies, it accorded these companies major privileges. Local French settlers also pushed for more favorable terms of business.[21] In a large part of the colony, then, the administration pressured people to produce commercial crops to the detriment of the production of food for themselves, which led to subsistence crises and more migration.[22]

An "Under-Administered" Colony

The list of colonial exactions (forced labor, head taxes, forced recruitment, and so on) reveals just how much the government of Upper Volta relied on its own resources. By such self-reliance, the administration hoped to avoid criticism and, at the same time, promote the notion that the colony was indeed economically viable. For want of sufficient French administrators, the administration fell back on the chiefs in Mossi lands and "created" chiefs in the west and southwest, where such hierarchical social relationships were unknown prior to colonial rule.

Table 13.1 shows that the colonial administration was very stretched in Upper Volta. Administrators managed twice the population in districts twice as large as their counterparts in other colonies of the AOF. Yet these figures fail to reveal other ways in which the colony made do in a difficult situation. Upper Volta was launched with too few government officials. Departments lacked adequate personnel. To deal with the shortfall, the governor turned to nepotism, appointing members of administrators' families to technical positions:[23] "Wherever possible, wives of officials are provisionally hired as 'wife-employees' to fill in—to some extent—for the lack of personnel."[24]

Given the colony's poor reputation among administrators, virtually no one requested appointment to Upper Volta after their first assigned postings in the colonies, over which they had no choice. This lack of personnel undermined enthusiasm among those already in place, making it difficult to sustain government programs. An interim lieutenant governor echoed comments made five years earlier by Inspector Picanon,[25] who feared the political consequences of such a situation:

> A good number of administrators have devolved into pen-pushers, diligently writing their newsletters, reports, and minutes for superiors with the sole objective of camouflaging with highfaluting language their utter ignorance of reality . . . . As for us, we find it excessive that the upper administration tolerates such rubbish. What we've seen in Upper Volta leads us to declare—at least as far as this colony is concerned—that such reports are *exercises in style*[26] and nothing more. The department ends up with very general reports that have no relationship—even distant—to the truth.[27]

The shortage of administrators contrasts markedly with the many workers they mobilized. However, the importance of the infrastructural projects identified by the administration—many of which required large numbers of workers—is highly questionable. The massive mobilization of laborers allowed the colony to build and maintain 6,000 kilometers of roads, one-eighth of the total in all of the AOF, but the usefulness of such a network was never apparent.[28] The "pharonic" project to construct the colonial capital at Ouagadougou, carried out without machines, produced only "adobe palaces" according to Albert Londres—in a city tagged "Bankoville" or "Adobe City."[29] In defense of the administrators, they had no choice with regard to building materials—adobe was also used in Niamey and Bamako. However, the Ouagadougou project was unusual. It transformed the city from the capital of a kingdom into an administrative capital. The "built environment" became much denser between 1920 and 1923, with the addition of buildings for administrative services attached to the governor's palace and others for social and economic services and public health operations. In order to sustain these efforts, authorities mobilized a permanent contingent of 3,000 from throughout Mossi country and settled them outside Ouagadougou.[30]

Another paradox in the Upper Volta saga is the mobilization of financial resources for the administration's economic objectives. Lacking a budget that included external revenue, the administration relied entirely on taxes. Moreover, an analysis of expenditures and receipts from 1920 to 1932 shows that three-quarters of government revenue came from head taxes:

> [T]his source of revenue is the major financial pillar supporting the colonial government—in the absence of any other financial policy. Human capital in Upper Volta has been considered to be taxable property, taking the form of a head tax . . . . In the frenetic search for sources of revenue, new taxes are invented. For example, taxes in kind may be bought back, for a daily fee of 1.75 or 2.50 francs depending on the region. The decree of September 25 introduced a tax known as *zekkat* for the Touareg and Bella in the *cercle* of Dori. They are compelled to pay both the head tax and the zekkat, set at 1/40 of the value of all categories of livestock . . . . We also take note of taxes on trade, which came to one million in 1929—basically made up of fees (1 franc per kilogram) levied on products such as kola nuts and strips of cotton cloth. Finally, rental fees [for space] in the market are set at 5 francs daily for cattle and 50 *centimes* for food products. All these receipts will fall noticeably in 1932, creating a dilemma for Upper Volta.[31]

Tax pressures impoverished farmers and forced them to sell their labor outside the colony. Upper Volta's small wage labor market and limited circulation of currency led Voltaics to head across the border to the British colony of the Gold Coast to work in the mines or industry, or on plantations. Remittances from migrants served in most cases to pay the head taxes for family members still at home.

It is appropriate to analyze where these excessive taxes ended up. A review of the budget of Upper Volta and the final account statements of 1919–32[32] reveals two significant developments: first, the atrophy of productive investment in the colony, even though there was a marked upswing in overall expenditures after 1924;[33] and second, a constant level of expenditure for personnel. This situation led Gervais to note that "by allotting the major portion of its resources to its own administrative and economic 'reproduction,' the government signaled its priorities. These priorities may well have [indeed] shifted from political and administrative, in the phase of consolidation of colonial rule . . . to economic development . . . but they did not stem from any greater attention to the needs of the population."[34]

The 1929 crash laid bare these distortions, and led to the decision of the minister for the colonies to dissolve Upper Volta, with important consequences for migration. Charged with "auditing" the colony, Inspector Bernard Sol concluded that "the crisis had not ruined Upper Volta; it was [already] an empty cipher." He went on to criticize the initial decision to create the colony, a decision, according to him, made without serious consideration of the financial preconditions for survival:

A pipe dream at the outset, and an illusion along the way, when it came to considering the conditions for its creation, its entire existence has been but pretence. It's no longer [an issue of] fragility, it is rather [a question of] paradox. Because it pushes the limits of artifice and underscores the price paid for illusion, the current crisis without doubt forces us to put our cards on the table without delay; [before this] it wasn't possible to play the game fairly. There was never a balance between usual resources and usual needs.[35]

It is important to acknowledge Inspector Sol's dedicated work, even though he came to be accused of being responsible for the dismemberment of Upper Volta by zealous supporters of the colony who were either motivated by ideology or ignored the complexity of the situation and the way the colonial ministry worked. Most of Sol's documents on management and socioeconomic trends in the colony are now invaluable historical sources. Sol did indeed conclude that the colony was not financially viable, but he was not part of the decision-making process that led to its dismemberment:

The project to suppress the colony was drafted in Dakar, and the report to the *département* was not sent to me. Therefore, I did not know, and still do not know, the grounds for it. However, you don't have to be a genius to figure it out. The crux of the matter was undoubtedly that the global [economic] crisis—while for now shutting Upper Volta out of the potential market for cattle and seasonal workers in the Gold Coast—came on top of deeper fiscal troubles that other funds—and especially the overall budget—were unable to fix. It was also time to cut expenses, and it was urgently necessary to do it wherever possible. Being a borrower, AOF had to present evidence of sound economic management and a restrained consumption.[36]

Sol's reservations[37] are even more salient in light of later comments by Bargues, another inspector of colonies,[38] charged with the reconstitution of the colony in 1947. Indeed, in light of Bargue's conclusions, it seems that lack of economic viability was not the crucial reason behind the dismembering of Upper Volta—particularly in light of the fact that other colonies in the AOF, such as Niger and Mauritania, faced similarly disastrous financial situations. From what he wrote, it seems more accurate to conclude that, pressured by private interests in the federation, Upper Volta was sacrificed to boost the economic revival in France.[39]

The Roles of Labor and Migration in the Dissolution of the Colony

With all due respect to the scholars and interest groups that pushed for the reconstitution of Upper Volta, the labor issue, although very important, was not the principal factor in its dismemberment. Rather, the continuing global economic crisis forced France to "fall back on the empire" and inten-sify the exploitation of natural resources in the colonies. These efforts led to economic plans to foster "poles of development" and, in turn, to ambi-tious projects,[40] such as the those sponsored by the Office du Niger, where hundreds of thousands of Mossi were put to work.[41] In Côte d'Ivoire, the production of commercial crops destined for metropolitan France boomed with the granting of economic concessions to European entrepreneurs.[42]

The belief that Ivoirian enterprises were the principal beneficiaries of the dismemberment of Upper Volta stems from a presumption that the eco-nomic dynamism of Côte d'Ivoire was made possible by immigrant workers and that Voltaic migrants only went to this one colony. This "analysis," how-ever, does not take into consideration two other major factors. First, through the middle 1920s, private companies in several other colonies recruited many Voltaic workers—for sisal farms in colonial Soudan (owned by the lim-ited liability company of Diakadapé), in Senegal (owned by La Compagnie des cultures tropicales en Afrique at Tambakounda) and in Côte d'Ivoire (owned by the Société des Scieries de Grand Bassam). Second, many work-ers destined for commercial plantations and the forestry industry in south-ern Côte d'Ivoire came, in fact, from northern (Kong and Korogho) and western (Man) regions of Côte d'Ivoire itself. Despite recruiting workers from within the colony, however, the forestry industry, handicapped by dif-ficult working conditions, found it difficult to recruit all the manpower it needed. Indeed, the forestry industry was the major recruiter of labor from outside Côte d'Ivoire through the early 1930s.

Entrepreneurs, who had earlier been interested in short-term profits from trade and forestry products, shifted their investment to commercial agriculture with the takeoff in agricultural prices. By the middle 1920s, the government of Côte d'Ivoire began receiving increased numbers of requests for agricultural concessions. Limited liability companies set up to manage these concessions played a pivotal role in the changing Ivoirian economy. Besides offering concessions of "unoccupied lands without owners," the administration helped recruit labor from northern Côte d'Ivoire. With the economic crisis of 1929, forest managers caught with young trees were help-less; production dropped and the economic sector was reshaped. Demands for Voltaic labor decreased. The data on labor recruiting reflect the decline in demand for labor from outside the colony (see table 13.2).

For most companies, Upper Volta labor was an unexpected windfall but not essential to their success—hence the variation from year to year recorded in the table. The year 1927, characterized by intense economic activity, was an exception. This year also marked the end of the careers of Lieutenant Governor Hesling of Upper Volta and Lieutenant Governor Lapland of Côte d'Ivoire. Reports from inspection missions sent to both colonies and internal documents of the federal government of the AOF and the French colonial

Table 13.2. Upper Volta workers recruited for external private enterprises, 1920 to 1930

Year	Source 1	Source 2
1920	2,172	
1921	1,287	
1922	307	
1923	154	
1924	2,516	
1925	1,060	
1926	1,792	
1927	3,365	
1928	932	777
1929	1,360	1,458
1930	1,506	1,018

Source 1: Exposition coloniale internationale de 1931. La Haute-Volta (Paris: Société d'éditions géographiques, maritimes et coloniales, 1931). The figures up to 1925 are the same as those found in documents from the Mission d'inspection Picanon, CAOM, Aix-en-Provence, Affaires politiques, carton 3057.
Source 2: Archives Nationales du Sénégal (ANS), Dakar, K126 (26), document: "Lettre du Lieutenant-gouverneur de la Haute-Volta au Gouverneur général de l'A.O.F.," September 28, 1931. The data in source 1 through 1927 and in source 2 from 1928 to 1930 agree with those in the annual reports. See the recapitulation in Centre d'accueil et de recherche des Archives nationales (CARAN), Paris, 200Mi 1737 (2G31–10), document: Rapport de 1931.

ministry in Paris raised questions about how these lieutenant governors had managed their colonies—how they had managed labor in particular.

In contrast to Hesling and Lapland, the interim lieutenant governor of Côte d'Ivoire, Brunot, adopted a courageous position in 1924, when he forcefully objected to the poor treatment of unskilled workers from the northern part of the colony. He imposed stringent conditions on the recruiting practices of forestry companies. In the ensuing controversy, which set him against his own bureaucracy, as well as against the managers of commercial agriculture and forestry enterprises, the inspection mission led by Kair sided with Brunot, and recommended measures favoring conservation.[43] In the face of all this, French settlers hoped to meet their labor needs by recruiting in Upper Volta—as an alternative to recruiting in Côte d'Ivoire, where Londres had called the recruiters "slave traders." Londres was a witness to these events:

France is rich. The colonies are rich, but we don't have the mindset that the era requires. Capital interests distrust colonial policy, and the Frenchman, despite being [on top of] a goldmine, works a short week, nonetheless. The English have it all, the Belgians have it all. We only have the black, fueled by *foutou,* the local dish . . . . And so, what do we see? We see the demand for men in Bouaké. It's pretty picturesque. Knowing the difficulties confronting timber operators, the crafty ones [recruiters] head to Upper Volta to recruit from "the reservoir" any way they can. Aware of the going rate, they go back with their "goods" in trucks and pass them off to perplexed entrepreneurs at two hundred francs per head. But, there are no more slave traders![44]

To solve the labor crisis, the consular chamber of Côte d'Ivoire proposed diverting migration flows from the Gold Coast to Côte d'Ivoire without any compensation other than increased pay. This proposal irritated the government of Upper Volta, which in its correspondence reviewed the socioeconomic context of migration (to the Gold Coast) and urged entrepreneurs in Côte d'Ivoire to create the same socioeconomic conditions that their competitors in Gold Coast had created, which would spontaneously attract the workers they needed.[45]

This response illustrates the Upper Volta government's dilemma. "Regulation" did not provide it with the authority needed to supervise labor contracts; at the most, it afforded the right to oversight—which is to say, to collaborate—during recruitment campaigns. Pressured by his *commandants de cercles,* Lieutenant Governor Fousset signed an order in 1928 requiring companies that hired labor in the colony to send regular reports on morbidity and mortality rates on their worksites. In the face of the irregular practices and abuses highlighted in these documents, the Upper Volta governor subsequently claimed that his government should have the right to regulate the employment of its subjects on private worksites beyond the colony's borders:

> It is doubtful that administrative authorities at their worksites give these workers the desired consideration. It is [therefore] indispensable that the government of Upper Volta—which can intervene to defend some of the workers' interests—be informed about the condition of manpower contingents recruited in its territory and employed outside the colony that are removed from its immediate jurisdiction.[46]

This demand is relevant because it highlights the ups and downs in the way colonial authorities in both colonies—and subsequent government agencies after independence—reacted to the ill-treatment encountered by emigrants and immigrants. In this particular case, neither the other colonies nor the AOF authorities acceded to Upper Volta's demands, which would implicitly have recognized the legitimacy of legal borders (or frontiers) between the individual colonies of the federation.

The Upper Volta administration's campaign to alter the administrative status quo regarding labor aimed at staving off plans for major labor recruitment drives for worksites in Côte d'Ivoire. Given the combined effects of the crisis in subsistence agriculture in Upper Volta and famine in some regions, business declined for many trading companies in the colony. Using the influence that grew out of broader economic and political commitments across the AOF, and in alliance with European commercial agriculture interests, the trading companies then pushed for the dissolution of Upper Volta for two reasons: to obtain "compensation" for investments lost when Upper Volta went "bankrupt," and to make it easier to send Upper Volta labor to other colonies where it was in short supply.

Some administrators and politicians—the colonial lobby—fell into step with the trading companies. Yet, the inspection mission led by Sol expressed reservations and issued recommendations with regard to the way the dissolution of the colony would impact Voltaic labor.[47] In November 1933, the interim lieutenant governor of Côte d'Ivoire reassured Mossi traditional chiefs, who had sent letters protesting the elimination of the colony. They were particularly apprehensive about the prospect of their lands being reduced to little more than labor reservoirs. The lieutenant governor expressed doubts about this eventuality, given the prevailing economic crisis.[48]

This position supporting the position of the minister for the colonies, who also doubted that the lands of former Upper Volta would become labor reservoirs for Southern Côte d'Ivoire,[49] was affirmed by the new lieutenant governor of Côte d'Ivoire, Jean François Reste. The same factor led him to this conclusion—the economic crisis. The mechanization of the forestry industry confirmed his conclusion:

> As far as the recruitment of labor in particular—needed by European settlers, on one hand, and forestry entrepreneurs in lower Côte d'Ivoire, on the other—[is concerned] I haven't the slightest intention of extending it to Mossi country . . . . The issue is not even up for discussion; most of the timber sites have closed down due to a downturn in sales . . . . I doubt that this business will ever enjoy its earlier success. Among other things, the forestry industry is more tightly organized, and now [that it is] equipped with tractors and Decauville tracks, it does not require the considerable numbers of workers that it did earlier . . . . The really hard work has never been cutting down the trees, but rather getting the timber out of the forest, usually on tracks in poor condition. These days, the trees are squared on the spot and the blocks of wood are towed away by tractor . . . . On the other hand, agricultural enterprises still do need a lot of labor. In the years ahead, harvesting of coffee and cocoa in particular will require many seasonal workers . . . . When that happens, Côte d'Ivoire will be as attractive to people in the north as the Gold Coast is today.[50]

The predictions of Lieutenant Governor Reste proved true with the revival of economic activity in Côte d'Ivoire in the middle 1930s. Ironically, increased recruitment of workers this time around was propelled by the "humanistic colonial policy" of the left-wing Front Populaire, a paradox that speaks volumes about the ambiguities of colonial policy in Côte d'Ivoire.

Notes

1.   A. Voir Sarraut, *La Mise en valeur des colonies françaises, 1923* (Paris: Payot, 1923), 372–88.

2.   Le Capitaine Binger, *Du Niger au Golfe de Guinée par le pays de Kong et le Mossi (1887–1889)* (Paris: Hachette, 1892).

3.   L. Marc, *Le pays Mossi* (Paris: Éditions Larose, 1909), 94–95.

4.   J.-Y. Marchal, "Prémisses d'un État moderne? Les projets coloniaux dans le bassin des Volta, 1897–1960," *Cahiers d'études africaines,* no. 103 (1986): 404.

5.   Marc, *Le pays Mossi,* 112.

6.   Raymond Gervais, "Population et politiques agricoles coloniales dans le Mosi, 1919–1940" (thèse de doctorat, Université Paris 7, 1990), 3 vols; Louis Lohlé-Tart and Michel François, *État civil et recensements en Afrique francophone. Pour une collecte administrative de données administratives* (Paris: CEPED, 1999) (Les Documents et Manuels du CEPED 10); Raymond R. Gervais and Issiaka Mande, "Comment compter les sujets de l'Empire? Les étapes d'une démographie impériale en AOF avant 1946," *Vingtième siècle,* no 95 (2007), 63–74.

7.   Archives Nationales du Sénégal (ANS), Dakar, 10G 7 (107), document: "Lettre du Lieutenant Gouverneur de la Haute-Volta au Gouverneur Général de l'A. O.F.," January 23, 1920.

8.   On this debate, see Gervais, "Contrôler, compter, comparer. La production et la gestion de l'information démographique en Haute-Volta avant 1960," paper presented at the Séminaire-atelier sur l'histoire démographique du Burkina Faso, Ouagadougou, May 1993. Also see Dennis D. Cordell and Joel W. Gregory, "Labor Reservoirs and Population: French Colonial Strategies in Koudougou," *Journal of African History* 23, no. 22 (1982): 205–24; Raymond Gervais, "Vérités et mensonges. Les statistiques coloniales de population," *Canadian Journal of African Studies/Revue Canadienne des Etudes Africaines* 17, no. 1 (1983), 101–3; Dennis D. Cordell and Joel W. Gregory, "A Response to Raymond Gervais's Research Note, 'Vérités et mensonges. Les statistiques coloniales de population,'" *Canadian Journal of African Studies/Revue Canadienne des Etudes Africaines* 17, no. 1 (1983): 105–6.

9.   G. Madiéga, "Esquisse de la conquête et de la formation territoriale de la colonie de Haute-Volta," *Bulletin de l'IFAN* 43 (série B), nos. 3–4 (1981): 217–77.

10.   Centre des archives d'outre-mer (CAOM), Aix-en-Provence, France, Affaires politiques, carton 3048, document: Mission Demaret, report 17, 1919.

11.   Albert Sarraut, *La mise en valeur des colonies françaises* (Paris: Payot, 1923).

12.   Albert Londres, *Terre d'ébène, la traite des noirs* (Paris: A. Michel, 1929), 126.

13.   ANS, Dakar, 10G 11, document: "Lettre du Directeur du Chemin de fer du Thiès-Kayes au Lieutenant-gouverneur de la Haute-Volta," Thiès, September 6, 1922.

14. ANS, Dakar, 10G 11, document: "Lettre du Lieutenant-gouverneur de la Haute-Volta au Gouverneur général de l'A.O.F.," October 7, 1922. The lieutenant governor of Soudan Français condemned these efforts to send migrant workers from his colony to work in other French colonies.

15. We cannot resist giving an example of Taillebourg's beautiful prose, with its ironic tone describing Voltaic workers on the Thiès-Kayes railroad:

Those who put down rails, push the rail cars, carry the stones and gravel, go get wood, water, and straw, clear the land and so on are more easily able to put up with the fatigue that comes with their tasks.

However, those that carry in the dirt, lost in the midst of a group of workers who repeat their movements for a machine for hours on end—this guy, although the most primitive, the most savage, the most free of all thought, the most oppressed that can be imagined, he tries to work as little as possible.

And this is the guy who has been compared to a machine. . . . However, one maintains a machine, and when it does not work like it is supposed to, it's not the machine that gets the blame, but rather he who doesn't know how to use it.

See ANS, Dakar, 10G11 (107), document: "Rapport de Taillebourg."

16. See Dennis D. Cordell, Joel W. Gregory, and Victor Piché, *Hoe and Wage: A Social History of a Circular Migration System in West Africa* (Boulder, CO: Westview, 1996), 45–124.

17. Dieudonné Ouédraogo, "Les causes de la suppression de la colonie de la Haute-Volta en 1932" (mémoire de maîtrise, Université Paris 7, 1985), 25–31. A detailed and systematic analysis of agricultural policy may be found in Gervais, "Population et politiques," 82–128, and in W. M. Batenga, "La politiques coloniale de la production du coton en Haute-Volta (1919–1932)," *Cahiers du CERLESHS* (Université de Ouagadougou, Burkina Faso) 10: 36-55.

18. CAOM, Aix-en-Provence, Inspection du Contrôle, cartons 948–50, document: Mission Sol, Report 36.

19. William B. Cohen, "The French Governors," in *African Proconsuls: European Governors in Africa*, ed., L. H. Gann and Peter Duignan, 19–50 (New York: Free Press, 1978).

20. R. Delavignette, *Les paysans noirs* (Paris: Stock, 1931), 221.

21. See Laurent Fourchard, *De la ville coloniale à la cour africaine. Espaces, pouvoirs et sociétés à Ouagadougou et à Bobo-Dioulasso (Haute-Volta), fin 19ème siècle 1960* (Paris: L'Harmattan, 2002).

22. Alfred Schwartz disagrees with this conclusion. See his paper, "La culture du coton et le démembrement de la Haute-Volta en 1932," presented at the colloquium "Cent ans d'histoire du Burkina Faso," Ouagadougou, December 12–17, 1996. However, the thesis of A. G. Boureima supports the conclusion. See his "Crises alimentaires et stratégies de subsistance en Afrique sahélienne (Burkina-Faso, Mali, Niger" (thèse de doctorat, Université Paris 7, 1988), 3 vols.

23. L. Hesling, *Une vie comme un jour en Afrique, 1917–1957* (Paris: Le Cannet, 1988).

24. CAOM, Aix-en-Provence, Affaires politiques, carton 3057, document: Mission Picanon, report 124, "Observations du Lieutenant-gouverneur Hesling au constat de Picanon," 1924–25, 21a and 22a. As Inspector Bernard Sol wrote in 1932,

"[w]hen the inspection mission arrived, the personnel were insufficient in number, poorly distributed, and overall of a mediocre quality. I did not come across a single official who spoke the local language. This situation stems in large measure from the policy of a revolving door, according to which administrators are in principle never sent back to the colony where they just served. This policy should be absolutely forbidden. It is responsible, for the most part, for the obvious gap between the administration and the locals." See CAOM, Aix-en-Provence, Affaires économiques, carton 105, dossier 2, document: "Lettre de l'inspecteur Bernard Sol au Ministre des colonies," November 10, 1932.

25. CAOM, Aix-en-Provence, Affaires politiques, carton 3057, document: Mission Picanon, report 124, "Situation politique et administrative de la Haute-Volta," 1924–25, 20–21.

26. This phrase is underlined in the original report.

27. Centre d'accueil et de recherche des Archives nationales (CARAN), Paris, 200Mi 1744 (2G32-16), document: "Rapport politique annuel de la Haute-Volta," 1932, 3.

28. Delavignette wrote as follows: "[o]ne built, for a territory of 300,000 square kilometers, 6,000 kilometers of roads, 2,192 of which were very permanent (the much richer Côte d'Ivoire only had 468 kilometers of permanent routes). It was the eighth largest road system in AOF." See R. Delavignette, "Le dynamisme de l'A.O.F., une nouvelle colonie: D'Abidjan à Ouagadougou," *Bulletin du comité de l'Afrique française*, no. 9 (September 1932): 529.

29. Marc Julienne, *Bankoville* (Paris: R. Debresse, 1938).

30. See Fourchard Laurent, *De la ville coloniale à la cour africaine. Espaces, pouvoirs et sociétés à Ouagadougou et à Bobo-Dioulasso (Haute-Volta), fin 19ème siècle 1960* (Paris: L'Harmattan, 2002), and Claude Sissao, "Urbanisation et rythme d'évolution des équipements à Ouagadougou et dans l'ensemble du Burkina Faso (1947–1985)" (thèse de doctorat, Université Paris 7, 1992).

31. Naye Pierre Bicaba, "La crise économique de 1929 en Haute-Volta" (thèse de 3è cycle, Université de Nice, France, 1988), 97–103.

32. Apart from offering a quantitative analysis of the budget of Upper Volta, Gervais situates the decisions made by the government in their historical context ("Population et politiques," 1990, vol. 2, sec. 4).

33. These choices were, all in all, counterproductive, and reveal better than any declaration the absence of clarity in the economic direction of the local government. Marc Julienne, an eyewitness, noted that "this colony is completely isolated, but that does not matter. They buy cars left and right. Administrative transportation is an exceptional undertaking. They waste 500,000 francs for the famous Renard train, a lamentable wreck. But not to worry about [creating] a work of art. No bridges, no smooth grades, no really well done workshop, garage, or storage facility. But there is no time to think about that. It is temporary. They live from one day to the next: provisional, provisional. How ill-fated for the budget of Upper Volta." See Julienne, *Bankoville*, 158–61, cited by Désiré Ouédraogo, "Les causes de la suppression de la Haute-Volta" (mémoire de maîtrise, Université Paris 7, 1985), 47.

34. Gervais, "Population et politiques," 276.

35. CAOM, Aix-en-Provence, Affaires politiques, carton 3068, document: Mission Sol, report 76, October 13, 1932.

36.   CAOM, Aix-en-Provence, Affaires politiques, carton 3068, document: Mission Sol, report 76, correspondence with the minister for the colonies, October 13, 1932.

37.   CAOM, Aix-en-Provence, Affaires politiques, cartons 3068 and 3069, document: AOF, Haute Volta, Mission d'Inspection, Sol, 1931–32.

38.   CAOM, Aix-en-Provence, Affaires politiques, carton 2186, dossier 9, "Dossiers relatifs au rapport de l'inspecteur général des colonies, Bargues, sur la reconstitution de la Haute-Volta," 1947.

39.   Naye Pierre Bicaba writes that "the dissolution of Upper Volta also appeared as a symbol of the failure of the colonial system in the colony, and a condemnation of this form of exploitation. It also made apparent the malleable character of capitalism, which adapts to failure. Dismantled in one way, it reproduces itself in another in order to become more productive. The dismantling of the colony was not an isolated act, but an action inscribed within an international and global political and economic context." "La crise économique de 1929 en Haute-Volta," 109.

40.   Please see the analyses of G. Meynier, "La France coloniale de 1914 à 1931," and Catherine Coquery-Vidrovitch, "La colonisation française, 1931–1939," both in *Histoire de la France coloniale*, vol. 2, ed. J. Thobie et al. (Paris: Albin Michel), 69–209 and 227–57 respectively.

41.   CAOM, Aix-en-Provence, Affaires politiques, cartons 1003 (1947) and 2186 (1947). Jean Suret-Canale maintained that the colonial authorities planned to settle a million and a half Mossi in the Niger valley as part of this project. See Suret-Canale, *Afrique Noire, l'ère coloniale (1900 à 1945)* (Paris: Editions sociales, 1982), 636. However, these figures appear too large when compared with the demographic data on Upper Volta and French Soudan (today's Mali). Nor are they corroborated by other authors who have systematically studied this issue.

42.   For further details on development in Côte d'Ivoire, see P. Braibant, "La crise économique de 1929 en Côte d'Ivoire et ses conséquences sociales et politiques" (mémoire de maîtrise, Université Paris 7, n.d.); Alain Tirefort, "Approche de la société coloniale: La communauté française en basse Côte d'Ivoire, pendant l'entre deux guerres (1920–1940)" (thèse de 3è cycle, Université Paris 7, 1979), 2 vols.; Alain Tirefort, "Européens et assimilés en basse Côte d'Ivoire, 1893–1960, Mythes et réalités d'une société coloniale" (thèse d'état en histoire, Université Bordeaux 3, 1989), 3 vols.

43.   CAOM, Aix-en-Provence, Affaires politiques, carton 3066, document: Mission d'inspection Kair, "Rapport de l'inspecteur Maret concernant la question de la main-d'œuvre et le régime du travail en Côte d'Ivoire," 1931. On the "affaire Brunot," see CAOM, Aix-en-Provence, Papiers Moutet, PA 28, carton 4, dossier 127. The report by Kair sheds light on the labor practices of European enterprises and their lobbying. Pressured by these same interests, Governor-General Card took administrative measures against Brunot, and in 1929 pronounced him "undesirable" in the AOF. Also see Archives nationales de la Côte d'Ivoire (ANCI), Abidjan, XV-18-29/5500 and XV-18-31/5500, files that bring together the correspondence between Brunot and the colony's European entrepreneurs.

44.   Londres, *Terre d'ébène*, 165.

45.   CARAN, Paris, 200Mi 1729 (2G30-10), document: "Rapport annuel d'ensemble," 1930, 31–33.

46. Ibid., 30.

47. Sol wrote the following: "It is entirely natural that those associated with 'the inexhaustible labor reservoir' feel a certain apprehension about seeing themselves attached to Côte d'Ivoire. The colony to the south is an insatiable devourer of men, and personifies in Mossi eyes the pain and suffering of reparations and poorly paid forced labor. The contemporary administrative border between the two limits to some degree the pretensions of southern planters. Admittedly a fragile barrier, it does offer real protection in that the . . . employer interests on the coast—chambers of commerce and others—must accept that they are dealing with a foreign territory. That, it seems to me, is the heart of the matter. The giving over of Mossi land to Côte d'Ivoire must be matched by increased employment regulation, which, along with employer interests, must take into account the legitimate aspirations of workers, the first of which is to receive appropriate wages and sustenance, and the second of which is to enjoy working conditions that are very different from those that have prevailed up to now." See CAOM, Aix-en-Provence, Affaires politiques, carton 3068, document: Mission d'inspection Sol, report 76, October 13, 1932.

48. The lieutenant governor wrote that the "apprehensions of the chiefs in Upper Volta about the use of Mossi labor on forest worksites may now be dismissed. Well before the economic crisis hit Côte d'Ivoire, commerce in African wood was affected. This development was due to an increased taste for marble and worked iron created by the decorative arts exposition of 1925, the poorly organized tropical woods market in metropolitan France (forestry interests complain that they are at the mercy of wholesalers), and competition from foreign wood, favored by lower prices and excellent marketing. As a result, most worksites are closed, and it may be feared that the forestry industry may never again find markets that will allow it to resume business. Labor recruiting in Upper Volta should only be authorized with prudence and in the context of guarantees to assure the success of the undertaking." See ANS, Dakar, K130 (26), document: "Lettre du Lieutenant-Gouverneur par *intérim* de la Côte d'Ivoire au Gouverneur Général de l'AOF," November 7, 1932.

49. ANS, Dakar, K130 (26), document: "Lettre du Ministre des colonies, Sarraut, au Gouverneur-Général de l'AOF, a/s de la nécessité d'intensifier les cultures vivrières dans l'ex-Haute-Volta," January 20, 1933.

50. ANCI (bidjan, V20-88/5086; and ANS, Dakar, K130 (26), document: "Lettre du Lieutenant-Gouverneur de la Côte d'Ivoire au Gouverneur-Général de l'AOF a/s de l'emploi de la main d'œuvre voltaïque," April 22, 1933.

Contributors

EDMUND ABAKA, PhD, is associate professor of history and director of Africana studies at the University of Miami. He has published a number of articles and he is the author of *Kola is God's Gift: Agricultural Production, Export Initiatives and the Kola Industry of Asante and the Gold Coast, c. 1820–1950* (James Currey, 2005). He is currently working on two monographs—"The Gold Coast/Ghana Slave Forts and Castles and the Atlantic Slave Trade," and "The Hausa Diaspora in Asante and the Gold Coast."

MAURICE AMUTABI received his PhD in history (Africa) from the University of Illinois at Urbana–Champaign, and is an assistant professor of history at Central Washington University. Amutabi is the author of *The NGO Factor in Africa: The Case of Arrested Development in Kenya* (Routledge, 2006) and coauthor of *Nationalism and Democracy for People-Centered Development in Africa* (Moi University Press, 2000) and *Foundations of Adult Education in Africa* (Pearson/UNESCO, 2005). His articles have appeared in journals such as the *African Studies Review, Africa Today, Change and Development,* the *Canadian Journal of African Studies,* and the *International Journal of Educational Development.* He has contributed chapters to numerous edited volumes and made various presentations at conferences.

TOYIN FALOLA, PhD, is the Frances Higginbotham Nalle Centennial Professor in History at the University of Texas at Austin. He is the editor of a five-volume series on Africa and the author of numerous books, including *Key Events in African History: A Reference Guide* (Greenwood Press, 2002), *Nationalism and African Intellectuals* (University of Rochester Press, 2001). He has edited many books, including *Tradition and Change in Africa* (Africa World Press, 1999) and *African Writers and Their Readers* (Africa World Press, 2003). He has received various awards and honors, including the Jean Holloway Award for Teaching Excellence and the Ibn Khaldun Distinguished Award for Research Excellence.

GHISLAINE GELOIN, PhD, is an associate professor at Rhode Island College teaching French studies in the Department of Modern languages. Her research interests and publications are in modern French culture, literature, and film with a concentration on Francophone Africa. In 2003 she edited for L'Harmattan Publishing House in Paris a new French edition of *Anténor Firmin De L'Égalité des Races Humaines* (first published in 1885), a seminal work in the theory of race relations in Haitian intellectual thought and in the struggle for the recognition of a black civilization that was not properly acknowledged by intellectual and scientific circles at the time. She has also been working on Benito Sylvain and Jean Louis Janvier, two other Haitian champions of the advancement of the black race.

Issiaka Mande teaches African history and history and computing in the Department of History, University of Paris 7–Denis Diderot. He is working on West African contemporary history, specializing in African historical demography, migration, and immigration. He has published a number of articles in journals and books.

Jean-Luc Martineau, PhD, is a senior lecturer at INALCO (the Institut National des Langues et Civilisations Orientales) in Paris, where he teaches African history. He is responsible for the "Afrique Océan Indien" group of the CNRS research team, SEDET–Paris 7. In connection with the building of identities in southwest Nigeria, he is now working on the impact of home-town identities in the processes of state creation and on Yoruba citizenship in relation to education since the 1950s. He has published several articles, in French and English, on Nigeria in journals and edited books. His publications include "Yoruba Nationalism and the Reshaping of Obaship," in Toyin Falola and Ann Genova, eds., *Yoruba Identity and Power Politics* (University of Rochester Press, 2006).

Pius S. Nyambara holds a PhD in African history with a minor in Latin American history from Northwestern University, Evanston, IL. He is currently an assistant professor at Jackson State University, Mississippi, where he teaches African history, Latin American history, and world history. He has previously taught in the Department of Economic History at the University of Zimbabwe. He has published several articles and book chapters on aspects of the economic history of Zimbabwe, including articles in the *Journal of African History*, the *International Journal of African Historical Studies*, *Africa*, the *Journal of Agrarian Change*, and the *Journal of Southern African Studies*.

Akinwumi Ogundiran, PhD, is the chair of Africana Studies at the University of North Carolina, Charlotte. His research interests cover the cultural history, material culture, and historical archaeology of the Bight of Benin hinterlands of West Africa. He is the author of *Archaeology and History in Ilare District, Central Yorubaland (1200–1900)* in the Cambridge Monographs in African Archaeology series (Archaeopress, 2002), the editor of *Precolonial Nigeria: Essays in Honor of Toyin Falola* (Africa World Press, 2005), and the co-editor of *Archaeology of Atlantic Africa and the African Diaspora* (Indiana University Press, 2007). His articles have appeared in journals such as the *African Archaeological Review*, the *Journal of Field Archaeology*, and *the International Journal of African Historical Studies*, as well as in edited books.

ADISA OGUNFOLAKAN attended Moscow State University, Russia, and the University of Ibadan, Nigeria. He is a lecturer in archaeology at Obafemi Awolowo University in Nigeria. His research focuses on the history of settlements and the related material culture of the Yoruba in the Osun area of southwestern Nigeria. He was a research fellow of Du Bois Institute, Harvard University, as well as Copeland Fellow at Amherst College in 2005–6. He has published articles in journals such as *ODU: A Journal of West African Studies,* and the *West African Journal of Archaeology.*

OLATUNJU OJO, PhD, teaches history at Brock University, St Catharines, Ontario, Canada. He has taught African history in universities in Nigeria and the United States. His research is centered on nineteenth-century West African social and economic history, women, slavery, and the African diaspora, and he has published on Yoruba religious rituals, credit and the slave trade, and Yoruba identity consciousness.

BRIGITTE KOWALSKI OSHINEYE lectures at the Ecole du Louvre, Paris, France. After earning degrees in archaeology, she turned to studies in African arts and civilization. She pursues research on African architecture as a witness to African history and migrations inside and outside western Africa. Her purposes are to determine the effects of the slave trade on cultures and movements of population between Hausaland and the Gulf of Guinea and between the Gulf of Guinea and the mainland of America and the Caribbean islands. She is also preparing projects for the rehabilitation of historical sites in Nigeria in collaboration with Craterre, a member of the UNESCO project, Africa 2009, and Legacy, a Nigerian association in Lagos. She has written articles for edited volumes in Europe on African history and patrimony. Her researches on Afro-Brazilian architecture on the Slave Coast are to be published by the French Institute of Research in Africa, Ibadan, Nigeria.

MESHACK OWINO is an assistant professor of history at Cleveland State University, Cleveland, Ohio. He earned a BEd and MA at Kenyatta University, Kenya, and an MA and PhD at Rice University, Houston, Texas. He specializes in the social history of African soldiers in Kenya during the precolonial and colonial periods. He has taught African history at several universities, including Egerton University, Kenya, and Bloomsburg University, Pennsylvania. He has been a visiting professor of African history at Stanford University, Palo Alto, California, and an adjunct professor at Texas Southern University, Houston, Texas.

GERALD STEYN holds a PhD from the University of Pretoria, South Africa, and BArch and MArch degrees from the University of the Free State, South Africa. His academic and research interests include settlement dynamics, affordable housing, and vernacular African architecture and urbanism. After his graduation in 1976, he did research under Frei Otto in Germany and for the Council for Scientific and Industrial Research (CSIR) in Pretoria before going into private practice as an architect in 1980, specializing in low-cost housing and medium-density residential projects. He joined the Tshwane University of Technology in 1999, where he is responsible for postgraduate program development and is currently a research professor.

ARIBIDESI USMAN, PhD, is associate professor of African and African American studies and anthropology at Arizona State University. His research and publications focus on African history and archaeology, especially in the pre-colonial and contact period, African urbanism, regional political and economic interaction, social transformation, frontier dynamics, Africans and transatlantic contacts, and cultural resource management. His publications include *State-Periphery Relations and Sociopolitical Development in Igbominaland, Northcentral Yoruba, Nigeria,* a BAR monograph (Archaeopress, 2001), and several articles in anthologies and journals. He is currently working on a book—"The Yoruba Frontier: A Regional History of Community Formation, Experience, and Changes in West Africa (ca. 1200–1900 AD)."

Index

An italicized page number indicates a figure or table.

Rochester Studies in
African History and the Diaspora

Migration, whether forced or voluntary, continues to be an issue vital to Africa, arguably the continent most affected by internal displacement. Over centuries, in groups or as individuals, Africans have been forced to leave their homes to escape unfavorable natural, social, or political circumstances, or simply to seek better lives elsewhere. This essential volume establishes the centrality of human migration and movement to the evolution of African societies.

Using oral, archaeological, and written sources, and focusing on various geographical areas, the contributors show that migration is a multifaceted phenomenon, historically varied in nature and character. *Movements, Borders, and Identities in Africa* incorporates carefully selected case studies drawn from across the continent, and provides a broad but insightful overview of migration and its complex relationships to slavery, commerce, religion, architecture, material culture, poverty, diaspora life and identity formation, and the development of states and societies on the continent. Chapters examine subjects as varied as the Atlantic slave trade, rural outmigration and metropolitan resettlement, compulsory labor and forced displacement in the nineteenth century, ethnicity's role in establishing coastal communities, and the long legacy of European colonialism. Taken as a whole, this collection offers a groundbreaking interrogation of the myriad causes and effects of African migration, from the pre-colonial to the modern era.

Contributors: Edmund Abaka, Maurice Amutabi, Toyin Falola, Ghislaine Geloin, Issiaka Mande, Jean-Luc Martineau, Pius S. Nyambara, Akinwumi Ogundiran, Adisa Ogunfolakan, Olatunji Ojo, Brigitte Kowalski Oshineye, Meshack Owino, Gerald Steyn, and Aribidesi Usman.

TOYIN FALOLA is a Fellow of the Nigerian Academy of Letters and Fellow of the Historical Society of Nigeria. He is the recipient of the 2006 Cheikh Anta Diop Award for Exemplary Scholarship in African Studies, and the 2008 Quintessence Award by the Africa Writers Endowment. He holds an honorary doctorate from Monmouth University and he is University Distinguished Teaching Professor at the University of Texas at Austin where he is also the Frances Higginbotham Nalle Centennial Professor in History. His books include *Nationalism and African Intellectuals* and *The Power of African Cultures,* both from the University of Rochester Press.

ARIBIDESI USMAN is associate professor of African and African American studies and anthropology at Arizona State University. He is the author of *State-Periphery Relations and Sociopolitical Development in Igbominaland, North-Central Yoruba, Nigeria* (Archeopress, London, 2001), and several articles in anthologies and journals.

"*Movements, Borders, and Identities in Africa* is an excellent multidisciplinary contribution to African Studies, emphasizing the migratory experiences of Africans across the continent and globally, from the crucible of humanity in east Africa to transregional movements across Africa and internationally."

—Gloria Emeagwali, professor of history and
African studies, Central Connecticut State University

"Falola and Usman have set the standard by bringing together in one volume some of the best studies on migration, border crossings, population movement, and shifting identities within the African continent. A remarkable contribution to the understanding of the dynamics and forms of such understudied areas within African history. The volume comes in handy as a textbook on the history and ethnography of migration and population displacement in the precolonial, colonial, and postcolonial Africa."

—Salah M. Hassan, Goldwin Smith Professor and director of
Africana Studies and Research Center and
History of Art, Cornell University